2011 SUPPLEMENT TO
AMERICAN CRIMINAL PROCEDURE
CASES AND COMMENTARY

Ninth Edition

■ ■ ■

By

Stephen A. Saltzburg
Wallace and Beverley Woodbury University Professor,
George Washington University Law School

Daniel J. Capra
Philip D. Reed Professor of Law
Fordham University School of Law

AMERICAN CASEBOOK SERIES®

WEST®

A Thomson Reuters business

Mat #41123787

American Casebook Series is a trademark registered in the U.S. Patent and Trademark Office.

COPYRIGHT © 1996 WEST PUBLISHING CO.
© West, a Thomson business, 1997-2001, 2003-2008
© 2009, 2010 Thomson Reuters
© 2011 Thomson Reuters
    610 Opperman Drive
    St. Paul, MN 55123
    1–800–313–9378
Printed in the United States of America

ISBN: 978–0–314–27462–5

TABLE OF CONTENTS

	Page
TABLE OF CASES	vii

Chapter One. Basic Principles **1**

I. A Criminal Case 1

Criminal Contempt Proceedings Brought in the Name of an Individual: Robertson v. United States ex rel. Watson 1

Right to Counsel in Civil Contempt Proceedings: Turner v. Rogers 3

II. Two Special Aspects of Constitutional Law: The Incorporation Doctrine and Retroactive Application of Constitutional Decisions 3

A. Incorporation 3

Incorporation of the Second Amendment Right to Bear Arms: 3

Chapter Two. Searches and Seizures of Persons and Things **5**

V. To Apply or Not Apply the Warrant Clause 5

A. Arrests in Public and in the Home 5

6. Material Witness 5

Allegations of Pretextual Use of the Material Witness Statute: Ashcroft v. al-Kidd 5

Ashcroft v. Al–Kidd 5

G. Exigent Circumstances 13

3. Police and Public Safety 13

Application of Brigham City v. Stuart: Michigan v. Fisher 13

Michigan v. Fisher 13

5. Impermissibly Created Exigency 16

Bad Faith Creation of Exigent Circumstances and Prior Opportunity to Get a Warrant: Kentucky v. King 16

Kentucky v. King 16

6. Prior Opportunity to Obtain a Warrant 25

H. Administrative Searches and Other Searches and Seizures Based on "Special Needs" 25

3. Searches and Seizures of Individuals Pursuant to "Special Needs" 25

City of Ontario v. Quon 25

VII. Remedies for Fourth Amendment Violations 34

E. Limitations on Exclusion 34

2. The Good Faith Exception and Warrantless Searches 34

Good Faith—New Rules Protecting Fourth Amendment Rights Cannot Be Applied Retroactively to Exclude Evidence: Davis v. United States 34

Davis v. United States 34

Page

Chapter Three. Self–Incrimination and Confessions ---------------- **48**

III. Fifth Amendment Limitations on Confessions -------------------------- 48

  D. Open Questions After *Miranda* ------------------------------------- 48

    1. What Is Custody? -- 48

    Relevance of the Age of a Child in the Custody Enquiry: J.D.B. v. North Carolina --- 48

    J.D.B. v. North Carolina --- 48

    5. How Complete and Accurate Must the Warnings Be? --------- 61

    Ambiguity About the Right to Have an Attorney Present Throughout the Questioning: Florida v. Powell --------------- 61

    Florida v. Powell --- 61

  E. Waiver of *Miranda* Rights -- 66

    2. Waiver After Invocation of Miranda *Rights* --------------------- 66

    Right to Silence Must Be Clearly Invoked; Waiver Can Be Implied From the Confession Itself; and Interrogation After Warnings Is Permissible So Long As Waiver Is Ultimately Found: Berghuis v. Thompkins --- 66

    Berghuis v. Thompkins --- 67

    The Requirement of Continuous Custody for Edwards Protection: Maryland v. Shatzer --- 78

    Maryland v. Shatzer -- 78

Chapter Five. The Right to Counsel ---------------------------------- **87**

IV. The Scope of the Right -- 87

  D. Civil Contempt Proceedings -------------------------------------- 87

    Turner v. Rogers --- 87

Chapter Ten. Trial and Trial–Related Rights ------------------------- **95**

III. Constitutionally Based Proof Requirements --------------------------- 95

  C. The Scope of the Reasonable Doubt Requirement: What Is an Element of the Crime? --- 95

    Construing Criminal Statutes to Distinguish a Sentencing Factor from an Element of the Crime: United States v. O'Brien ------------- 95

    United States v. O'Brien -- 95

IV. Trial by Jury --- 103

  D. Jury Selection and Composition ---------------------------------- 103

    5. The Use of Peremptory Challenges ---------------------------- 103

    b. Constitutional Limits on Peremptory Challenges ---------- 103

    Review of Demeanor–Based Grounds of Exclusion When the Court Did Not Personally Observe the Voir Dire: Thaler v. Haynes -- 103

    Thaler v. Haynes --- 103

V. The Impartiality of the Tribunal and the Influence of the Press ----- 106

  B. Controlling the Media's Impact ---------------------------------- 106

    1. Controlling Access to Courts; Public Trials ------------------ 106

    Sixth Amendment Limitation on Excluding Public From Juror Voir Dire: Presley v. Georgia ------------------------------------- 106

    Presley v. Georgia -- 106

VII. The Right to Effective Assistance of Counsel ------------------------ 111

  A. Ineffectiveness and Prejudice ------------------------------------- 111

    3. Assessing Counsel's Effectiveness ---------------------------- 111

    The Duty to Investigate Mitigating Evidence in a Capital Case— the Relevance of ABA Standards: Bobby v. Van Hook. ------------- 111

    Bobby v. Van Hook --- 111

Page

VII. The Right to Effective Assistance of Counsel—Continued
  Detailed and Fact–Intensive Review Under AEDPA of Claim of
    Ineffectiveness for Failure to Investigated and Present Mitigat-
    ing Evidence at the Penalty Phase: Cullen v. Pinholster............ 115
  Cullen v. Pinholster... 115
  The Duty to Inform the Defendant About Immigration Conse-
    quences of a Conviction: Padilla v. Kentucky 132
  Padilla v. Kentucky 132
  Application of Strickland—and AEDPA Standards of Deference—
    To Trial Counsel's Failure To Present a Forensic Expert: Har-
    rington v. Richter 141
  Harrington v. Richter 141
  Application of Strickland and AEDPA Review Standards to Coun-
    sel's Conduct When a Guilty Plea Is Entered Early in the
    Proceedings: Premo v. Moore 151
  Premo v. Moore.. 151
  4. Assessing Prejudice... 159
  Failure to Present Mitigating Evidence of Combat Trauma at the
    Sentencing Phase of a Capital Trial: Analysis of Ineffectiveness
    and Prejudice: Porter v. McCollum...................................... 159
  Porter v. McCollum 159
  Prejudice Must Be Assessed By What Evidence—Including Dam-
    aging Evidence—Would Have Been Admitted Had Defense
    Counsel Acted Effectively: Wong v. Belmontes 165
  Wong v. Belmontes 165
  Defense Counsel's Argument at the Penalty Phase of a Capital
    Trial, Stressing the Severity of the Crimes, Was Not Prejudicial:
    Smith v. Spisak 170
  Smith v. Spisak 170

Chapter Eleven. Sentencing 175
  I. Introduction 175
    D. Constitutional Limitations on Punishment 175
      2. Eighth Amendment Limitations on Sentencing..................... 175
      Categorical Constitutional Limitation on Sentencing in a Non–
        Capital Case: Graham v. Florida..................................... 175
      Graham v. Florida 175
  II. Guidelines Sntencing 196
    D. Supreme Court Construction of the Sentencing Guidelines 196
      2. Application of Advisory Guidelines After Booker 196
      Rehabilitation and Guidelines Sentencing: United States v. Tapia 196
      Considering Post–Sentence Rehabilitation When a Sentence Is
        Vacated on Appeal: Pepper v. United States. 196

Chapter Twelve. Double Jeopardy 202
  III. Aborted Proceedings 202
    B. Mistrial Declared Over Defendant's Objection 202
      2. Manifest Necessity as a Flexible Test 202
      Trial Court's Declaring Mistrial Was Not an Unreasonable Appli-
        cation of Manifest Necessity Standard: Renico v. Lett 202
      Renico v. Lett 202

Page

Chapter Thirteen. Post–Conviction Challenges ---------------------- **212**

  II. Grounds for Direct Attacks on a Conviction -------------------------- 212

    A. Insufficient Evidence --- 212

      2. The Standard of Appellate Review of Sufficiency of the Evidence --- 212

        Court Reviewing Sufficiency of the Evidence Must Consider All Evidence Admitted at Trial, Even If Erroneously: McDaniel v. Brown --- 212

        McDaniel v. Brown -- 212

    D. The Effect of an Error on the Verdict ------------------------- 218

      2. Plain Error -- 218

        "Any Possibility" Test Is Too Permissive For Plain Error Review: United States v. Marcus ----------------------------------- 218

        United States v. Marcus ---------------------------------- 218

  III. Collateral Attack --- 223

    B. Federal Habeas Corpus: The Procedural Framework ------------- 223

      2. General Principles Concerning Habeas Relief After AEDPA 223

        Equitable Tolling: Holland v. Florida ------------------------ 223

        Holland v. Florida -------------------------------------- 223

      3. Factual Findings and Mixed Questions of Law and Fact. ----- 233

        Recent Applications of Section 2254(d) ------------------------ 233

    D. Limitations on Obtaining Habeas Relief ----------------------- 234

      4. Adequate and Independent State Grounds ---------------------- 234

        Discretionary Rules as Adequate State Grounds: Beard v. Kindler 234

        Flexible Rules as Adequate State Grounds: Walker v. Martin -------- 235

      5. Abuse of the Writ --- 237

        Is a Claim "Successive" When Brought In a Challenge to a Resentencing, When It Could Have Been Brought to Challenge the Initial Sentencing? Magwood v. Patterson --------------------- 237

THE FEDERAL RULES OF CRIMINAL PROCEDURE

    I. Applicability --- 241

    II. Preliminary Proceedings --------------------------------------- 243

  III. The Grand Jury, the Indictment, and the Information ---------------- 248

  IV. Arraignment and Preparation for Trial ------------------------- 254

    V. Venue --- 271

  VI. Trial --- 273

  VII. Post–Conviction Procedures ----------------------------------- 279

 VIII. Supplementary and Special Proceedings ------------------------- 292

  IX. General Provisions -- 298

TABLE OF CASES

The principal cases are in bold type. Cases cited or discussed in the text
are in roman type. References are to pages. Cases cited in principal
cases and within other quoted materials are not included.

Ashcroft v. al–Kidd, ___ U.S. ___, 131 S.Ct.
2074 (2011), **5**

Beard v. Kindler, ___ U.S. ___, 130 S.Ct. 612,
175 L.Ed.2d 417 (2009), 234

Berghuis v. Thompkins, ___ U.S. ___, 130
S.Ct. 2250, 176 L.Ed.2d 1098 (2010), **66**

Bobby v. Van Hook, ___ U.S. ___, 130 S.Ct.
13, 175 L.Ed.2d 255 (2009), **111**

City of (see name of city)

Cullen v. Pinholster, ___ U.S. ___, 131 S.Ct.
1388, 179 L.Ed.2d 557 (2011), **115**

Davis v. United States, ___ U.S. ___, 131
S.Ct. 2419 (2011), **34**

Dixon, United States v., 509 U.S. 688, 113
S.Ct. 2849, 125 L.Ed.2d 556 (1993), 2

Florida v. Powell, ___ U.S. ___, 130 S.Ct.
1195, 175 L.Ed.2d 1009 (2010), **61**

Graham v. Florida, ___ U.S. ___, 130 S.Ct.
2011, 176 L.Ed.2d 825 (2010), **175**

Harrington v. Richter, ___ U.S. ___, 131
S.Ct. 770, 178 L.Ed.2d 624 (2011), **141**

Holland v. Florida, ___ U.S. ___, 130 S.Ct.
2549, 177 L.Ed.2d 130 (2010), **223**

J.D.B. v. North Carolina, ___ U.S. ___, 131
S.Ct. 2394 (2011), **48**

Kentucky v. King, ___ U.S. ___, 131 S.Ct.
1849, 179 L.Ed.2d 865 (2011), **16**, 25

Magwood v. Patterson, ___ U.S. ___, 130 S.Ct.
2788, 177 L.Ed.2d 592 (2010), 237

Marcus, United States v., ___ U.S. ___, 130
S.Ct. 2159, 176 L.Ed.2d 1012 (2010), **218**

Maryland v. Shatzer, ___ U.S. ___, 130 S.Ct.
1213, 175 L.Ed.2d 1045 (2010), **78**

McDaniel v. Brown, ___ U.S. ___, 130 S.Ct.
665, 175 L.Ed.2d 582 (2010), **212**

McDonald v. City of Chicago, Ill., ___ U.S. ___,
130 S.Ct. 3020, 177 L.Ed.2d 894 (2010), 3

Michigan v. Fisher, ___ U.S. ___, 130 S.Ct.
546, 175 L.Ed.2d 410 (2009), **13**

O'Brien, United States v., ___ U.S. ___, 130
S.Ct. 2169, 176 L.Ed.2d 979 (2010), **95**

Ontario, Cal., City of v. Quon, ___ U.S. ___,
130 S.Ct. 2619, 177 L.Ed.2d 216 (2010), **25**

Padilla v. Kentucky, ___ U.S. ___, 130 S.Ct.
1473, 176 L.Ed.2d 284 (2010), **132**

Pepper v. United States, ___ U.S. ___, 131
S.Ct. 1229, 179 L.Ed.2d 196 (2011), 196

Porter v. McCollum, ___ U.S. ___, 130 S.Ct.
447, 175 L.Ed.2d 398 (2009), **159**

Premo v. Moore, ___ U.S. ___, 131 S.Ct. 733,
178 L.Ed.2d 649 (2011), **151**

Presley v. Georgia, ___ U.S. ___, 130 S.Ct.
721, 175 L.Ed.2d 675 (2010), **106**

Renico v. Lett, ___ U.S. ___, 130 S.Ct. 1855,
176 L.Ed.2d 678 (2010), **202**

Robertson v. United States ex rel. Watson, ___
U.S. ___, 130 S.Ct. 2184, 176 L.Ed.2d 1024
(2010), 1

Smith v. Spisak, ___ U.S. ___, 130 S.Ct. 676,
175 L.Ed.2d 595 (2010), **170**

Tapia v. United States, ___ U.S. ___, 131 S.Ct.
2382 (2011), 196

Thaler v. Haynes, ___ U.S. ___, 130 S.Ct.
1171, 175 L.Ed.2d 1003 (2010), **103**

Turner v. Rogers, 2011 WL 2437010, ___
U.S. ___ (2011), **87**

**United States v. _____ (see opposing par-
ty)**

Walker v. Martin, ___ U.S. ___, 131 S.Ct. 1120,
179 L.Ed.2d 62 (2011), 235

Wong v. Belmontes, ___ U.S. ___, 130 S.Ct.
383, 175 L.Ed.2d 328 (2009), **165**

2011 SUPPLEMENT TO

AMERICAN CRIMINAL PROCEDURE

CASES AND COMMENTARY

Ninth Edition

CHAPTER ONE

BASIC PRINCIPLES

■ ■ ■

I. A CRIMINAL CASE

Page 6. Add after the section on *UMWA v. Bagwell*

Criminal Contempt Proceedings Brought in the Name of an Individual: Robertson v. United States ex rel. Watson

The question of what qualifies as a criminal case arose in an unusual way in Robertson v. United States ex rel. Watson, 130 S.Ct. 2184 (2010). Wykenna Watson was violently assaulted by her then-boyfriend, John Robertson in March 1999. Watson obtained a civil protective order prohibiting Robertson from approaching within 100 feet of her and from assaulting, threatening, harassing, physically abusing or contacting her. On June 26, 1999, Robertson violated the protective order by again violently assaulting Watson. A grand jury indicted Robertson for the March assault on July 8, 1999. The prosecutor agreed to a plea deal in which Robertson would plead guilty to attempted aggravated assault in exchange for the government dismissing remaining charges and not pursuing any charges arising from the June 26 assault. A few months later, Watson filed a motion to initiate criminal contempt charges against Robertson for violating the protective order. After a two-day bench trial, the judge found Robertson guilty of three counts of contempt and sentenced him to three consecutive 180–day terms of imprisonment, suspended execution of the last 180–day sentence in favor of five years' probation, and ordered Robertson to pay $10,000 in restitution. Robertson appealed to the District of Columbia Court of Appeals and argued that the criminal contempt proceedings were barred by the earlier plea agreement. The court of appeals disagreed and concluded that the contempt proceedings were brought in Watson's name and did not constitute a public action brought in the name and interest of the United States, and therefore the proceedings were not barred by the plea agreement between Robertson and the government.

The Supreme Court granted certiorari to review whether the criminal contempt proceeding could be brought in the name and interest of Watson but ultimately dismissed the writ as improvidently granted. Chief Justice

1

Roberts, joined by Justices Scalia, Kennedy and Sotomayor, dissented and argued that the Court's prior decision in United States v. Dixon, 509 U.S. 688 (1993), [Casebook Page 1531] holding that a private party's prosecution for criminal contempt barred—under the Double Jeopardy Clause—the government's second prosecution if it was for the same criminal offense, clearly demonstrated that the court of appeals was wrong. The Chief Justice noted that the court of appeals did not follow the majority's holding in *Dixon* and instead quoted four times from a separate opinion by Justice Blackmun in which he dissented from the majority's view but commanded only his own vote. The Chief Justice wrote as follows:

> That we treated the criminal contempt prosecution in *Dixon* as an exercise of government power should not be surprising. More than two centuries ago, Blackstone wrote that the king is "the proper person to prosecute for all public offenses and breaches of the peace, being the person injured in the eye of the law." 1 W. Blackstone, Commentaries *268. Blackstone repeated that principle throughout his fourth book. See, *e.g.,* 4 *id.,* at *2, *8, *177. Not long after Blackstone, then-Representative John Marshall agreed, stating on the House floor that "administer[ing] criminal judgment . . . is a duty to be performed at the demand of the nation, and with which the nation has a right to dispense. If judgment . . . is to be pronounced, it must be at the prosecution of the nation." 10 Annals of Cong. 615 (1800).

* * *

> Our entire criminal justice system is premised on the notion that a criminal prosecution pits the government against the governed, not one private citizen against another. The ruling below is a startling repudiation of that basic understanding.

* * *

> Watson's arguments based on American precedent fail largely for the same reason: To say that private parties could (and still can, in some places) exercise some control over criminal prosecutions says nothing to rebut the widely accepted principle that those private parties necessarily acted (and now act) on behalf of the sovereign.
> * * *

* * *

> Allegorical depictions of the law frequently show a figure wielding a sword—the sword of justice, to be used to smite those who violate the criminal laws. Indeed, outside our own courthouse you will find a statue of more than 30 tons, Authority of Law, which portrays a male figure with such a sword. According to the sculptor, James Earle Fraser (who also designed the buffalo nickel), the figure sits "wait[ing] with concentrated attention, holding in his left hand the tablet of laws, backed by the sheathed sword, symbolic of enforcement through law." Supreme Court of the United States, Office of the

Curator, Contemplation of Justice and Authority of Law Information Sheet 2 (2009) (available in Clerk of Court's case file). A basic step in organizing a civilized society is to take that sword out of private hands and turn it over to an organized government, acting on behalf of all the people. Indeed, "[t]he ... power a man has in the state of nature is the power to punish the crimes committed against that law. [But this] he gives up when he joins [a] ... political society, and incorporates into [a] commonwealth." Locke, Second Treatise, § 128, at 64.

* * *

Right to Counsel in Civil Contempt Proceedings: Turner v. Rogers

In Turner v. Rogers, 131 S.Ct. ___ (2011), the Court held that a defendant who was imprisoned for civil contempt for failure to pay child support orders did not have an absolute right to counsel at the contempt proceedings. The Court noted that the proceeding was civil in nature because the defendant could not have been incarcerated if he had an inability to pay the child support. On the facts, the Court held that the defendant's due process rights were violated because he was not given a fair opportunity, with the assistance of counsel or alternative safeguards, to establish an inability to pay. The opinion in *Turner* is set forth in Chapter Five of this Supplement, infra.

II.   TWO SPECIAL ASPECTS OF CONSTITUTIONAL LAW: THE INCORPORATION DOCTRINE AND RETROACTIVE APPLICATION OF CONSTITUTIONAL DECISIONS

A.   INCORPORATION

Page 15. Add at the end of the section.

Incorporation of the Second Amendment Right to Bear Arms:

The Court had occasion to revisit its history with respect to incorporation in *McDonald v. City of Chicago*, 130 S.Ct. 3020 (2010), in which Justice Alito summarized the holding for a 5–4 Court:

Two years ago, in District of Columbia v. Heller, 554 U.S. 570 (2008), we held that the Second Amendment protects the right to keep and bear arms for the purpose of self-defense, and we struck down a District of Columbia law that banned the possession of handguns in the home. The City of Chicago (City) and the village of Oak Park, a Chicago suburb, have laws that are similar to the District of Columbia's, but Chicago and Oak Park argue that their laws are constitutional because the Second Amendment has no application to the States. We have previously held that most of the provisions of the Bill of Rights apply with full force to both the Federal Government and the States. Applying the standard that is well established in our case law, we hold that the Second Amendment right is fully applicable to the States.

Four Justices agreed that the Due Process Clause required incorporation while Justice Thomas relied upon the privileges and immunities clause of the Fourteenth Amendment. In a plurality portion of his opinion, Justice Alito noted that Justice Black's "total incorporation" theory was never adopted by the Court, and that "the Court eventually moved in that direction by initiating what has been called a process of 'selective incorporation' ".... He quoted from *Duncan* and explained that the Court no longer asks whether *any* "civilized system [can] be imagined that would not accord the particular protection" and instead asks "whether a particular Bill of Rights guarantee is fundamental to *our* scheme of ordered liberty and system of justice."

Justice Stevens's dissenting opinion also examined the Court's approach to due process and incorporation and wrote: "In my judgment, this line of cases is best understood as having concluded that, to ensure a criminal trial satisfies essential standards of fairness, some procedures should be the same in state and federal courts: The need for certainty and uniformity is more pressing, and the margin for error slimmer, when criminal justice is at issue."

CHAPTER TWO

SEARCHES AND SEIZURES OF PERSONS AND THINGS

∎ ∎ ∎

V. TO APPLY OR NOT APPLY THE WARRANT CLAUSE

A. ARRESTS IN PUBLIC AND IN THE HOME

6. Material Witness

Page 193. Add at the end of the section.

Allegations of Pretextual Use of the Material Witness Statute: Ashcroft v. al-Kidd

The following case reviews allegations of pretextual use of the Material Witness Statute—as a means of detaining suspects rather than preserving witness testimony. The majority relies on a number of cases that are set forth later in the Casebook. As such it is a good introduction to the Court's benchmark principle of Fourth Amendment analysis—the validity of any suspicion-based search or seizure is determined objectively, without regard to any bad faith on the officer's part.

ASHCROFT v. AL–KIDD

Supreme Court of the United States, 2011.
131 S.Ct. 2074

JUSTICE SCALIA delivered the opinion of the Court.

We decide whether a former Attorney General enjoys immunity from suit for allegedly authorizing federal prosecutors to obtain valid material-witness warrants for detention of terrorism suspects whom they would otherwise lack probable cause to arrest.

I

The federal material-witness statute authorizes judges to "order the arrest of [a] person" whose testimony "is material in a criminal proceeding . . . if it is shown that it may become impracticable to secure the presence of the person by subpoena." 18 U.S.C. § 3144. Material witnesses enjoy the same constitutional right to pretrial release as other federal detainees, and federal law requires release if their testimony "can adequately be secured by deposition, and if further detention is not necessary to prevent a failure of justice."

Because this case arises from a motion to dismiss, we accept as true the factual allegations in Abdullah al-Kidd's complaint. The complaint alleges that, in the aftermath of the September 11th terrorist attacks, then-Attorney General John Ashcroft authorized federal prosecutors and law enforcement officials to use the material-witness statute to detain individuals with suspected ties to terrorist organizations. It is alleged that federal officials had no intention of calling most of these individuals as witnesses, and that they were detained, at Ashcroft's direction, because federal officials suspected them of supporting terrorism but lacked sufficient evidence to charge them with a crime.

It is alleged that this pretextual detention policy led to the material-witness arrest of al-Kidd, a native-born United States citizen. FBI agents apprehended him in March 2003 as he checked in for a flight to Saudi Arabia. Two days earlier, federal officials had informed a Magistrate Judge that, if al-Kidd boarded his flight, they believed information "crucial" to the prosecution of Sami Omar al-Hussayen would be lost. Al–Kidd remained in federal custody for 16 days and on supervised release until al-Hussayen's trial concluded 14 months later. Prosecutors never called him as a witness.

In March 2005, al-Kidd filed this *Bivens* action, see Bivens v. Six Unknown Fed. Narcotics Agents, 403 U.S. 388 (1971) to challenge the constitutionality of Ashcroft's alleged policy; he also asserted several other claims not relevant here against Ashcroft and others. Ashcroft filed a motion to dismiss based on absolute and qualified immunity, which the District Court denied. A divided panel of the United States Court of Appeals for the Ninth Circuit affirmed, holding that the Fourth Amendment prohibits pretextual arrests absent probable cause of criminal wrongdoing, and that Ashcroft could not claim qualified or absolute immunity.

Judge Bea dissented, and eight judges dissented from the denial of rehearing en banc. We granted certiorari.

II

Qualified immunity shields federal and state officials from money damages unless a plaintiff pleads facts showing (1) that the official violated a statutory or constitutional right, and (2) that the right was "clearly established" at the time of the challenged conduct. Harlow v. Fitzgerald, 457 U.S. 800, 818 (1982). We recently reaffirmed that lower courts have discretion to decide which of the two prongs of qualified-immunity analysis to tackle first. See Pearson v. Callahan, 555 U.S. 223, 236 (2009).

Courts should think carefully before expending scarce judicial resources to resolve difficult and novel questions of constitutional or statutory interpretation that will have no effect on the outcome of the case. When, however, a Court of Appeals does address both prongs of qualified-immunity analysis, we have discretion to correct its errors at each step. Although not necessary to reverse an erroneous judgment, doing so ensures that courts do not insulate constitutional decisions at the frontiers of the law from our review or inadvertently undermine the values qualified immunity seeks to promote. The former occurs when the constitutional-law question is wrongly decided; the latter when what is not clearly established is held to be so. In this case, the Court of Appeals' analysis at both steps of the qualified-immunity inquiry needs correction.

A

The Fourth Amendment protects "[t]he right of the people to be secure in their persons, houses, papers, and effects, against unreasonable searches and seizures." An arrest, of course, qualifies as a "seizure" of a "person" under this provision, *Dunaway v. New York*, 442 U.S. 200, 207–208 (1979), and so must be reasonable under the circumstances. Al–Kidd does not assert that Government officials would have acted unreasonably if they had used a material-witness warrant to arrest him for the purpose of securing his testimony for trial. He contests, however (and the Court of Appeals here rejected), the reasonableness of using the warrant to detain him as a suspected criminal.

Fourth Amendment reasonableness "is predominantly an objective inquiry." *City of Indianapolis v. Edmond*, 531 U.S. 32, 47 (2000). We ask whether "the circumstances, viewed objectively, justify [the challenged] action." Scott v. United States, 436 U.S. 128, 138 (1978). If so, that action was reasonable "whatever the subjective intent" motivating the relevant officials. Whren v. United States, 517 U.S. 806, 814 (1996). This approach recognizes that the Fourth Amendment regulates conduct rather than thoughts; and it promotes evenhanded, uniform enforcement of the law, Devenpeck v. Alford, 543 U.S. 146, 153–154 (2004).

Two "limited exception[s]" to this rule are our special-needs and administrative-search cases, where "actual motivations" do matter. A judicial warrant and probable cause are not needed where the search or seizure is justified by "special needs, beyond the normal need for law enforcement," such as the need to deter drug use in public schools, Vernonia School Dist. 47J v. Acton, 515 U.S. 646, 653 (1995), or the need to assure that railroad employees engaged in train operations are not under the influence of drugs or alcohol, Skinner v. Railway Labor Executives' Assn., 489 U.S. 602 (1989); and where the search or seizure is in execution of an administrative warrant authorizing, for example, an inspection of fire-damaged premises to determine the cause, Michigan v. Clifford, 464 U.S. 287, 294 (1984) (plurality opinion), or an inspection of residential premises to assure compliance with a housing code, Camara v. Municipal Court of City and County of San Francisco, 387 U.S. 523, 535–538 (1967). But those exceptions do not apply where the officer's purpose is not to attend to the special needs or to the investigation for which the administrative inspection is justified. See *Whren, supra*, at 811–812. The Government seeks to justify the present arrest on the basis of a properly issued judicial warrant—so that the special-needs and administrative-inspection cases cannot be the basis for a purpose inquiry here.

Apart from those cases, we have almost uniformly rejected invitations to probe subjective intent. See Brigham City v. Stuart, 547 U.S. 398, 404 (2006). There is one category of exception, upon which the Court of Appeals principally relied. In *Edmond*, we held that the Fourth Amendment could not condone suspicionless vehicle checkpoints set up for the purpose of detecting illegal narcotics. Although we had previously approved vehicle checkpoints set up for the purpose of keeping off the road unlicensed drivers, Delaware v. Prouse, 440 U.S. 648, 663 (1979), or alcohol-impaired drivers, Michigan Dept. of State Police v. Sitz, 496 U.S. 444 (1990); and for the purpose of interdicting those who illegally cross the border, United States v. Martinez–Fuerte, 428 U.S. 543 (1976); we found the drug-detection purpose in *Edmond* invalidating because it was "ultimately indistinguishable from the general interest in crime control." In the Court of Appeals' view, *Edmond* established that " 'programmatic purpose' is relevant to Fourth Amendment analysis of programs of seizures without probable cause."

That was mistaken. It was not the absence of probable cause that triggered the invalidating-purpose inquiry in *Edmond*. To the contrary, *Edmond* explicitly said that it would approve checkpoint stops for "general crime control purposes" that were based upon merely "some quantum of individualized suspicion." Purpose was relevant in Edmond because "programmatic purposes may be relevant to the validity of Fourth Amendment intrusions undertaken pursuant to a general scheme *without individualized suspicion*," id., at 45–46 (emphasis added).

Needless to say, warrantless, suspicionless intrusions pursuant to a general scheme are far removed from the facts of this case. A warrant issued by a neutral Magistrate Judge authorized al-Kidd's arrest. The affidavit accompanying the warrant application (as al-Kidd concedes) gave individualized reasons to believe that he was a material witness and that he would soon

disappear. The existence of a judicial warrant based on individualized suspicion takes this case outside the domain of not only our special-needs and administrative-search cases, but of *Edmond* as well.

A warrant based on individualized suspicion in fact grants more protection against the malevolent and the incompetent than existed in most of our cases eschewing inquiries into intent. In *Whren* and *Devenpeck* we declined to probe the motives behind seizures supported by probable cause but lacking a warrant approved by a detached magistrate. Terry v. Ohio, 392 U.S. 1, 21–22 (1968) * * * applied an objective standard to warrantless searches justified by a lesser showing of reasonable suspicion. We review even some suspicionless searches for objective reasonableness. See Bond v. United States, 529 U.S. 334, 335–336, 338, n. 2 (2000). If concerns about improper motives and pretext do not justify subjective inquiries in those less protective contexts, we see no reason to adopt that inquiry here.

Al–Kidd would read our cases more narrowly. He asserts that *Whren* establishes that we ignore subjective intent only when there exists "probable cause to believe that a violation of law has occurred"— which was not the case here. That is a distortion of *Whren*. Our unanimous opinion held that we would not look behind an objectively reasonable traffic stop to determine whether racial profiling or a desire to investigate other potential crimes was the real motive. In the course of our analysis, we dismissed Whren's reliance on our inventory-search and administrative-inspection cases by explaining that those cases do not "endors[e] the principle that ulterior motives can invalidate police conduct that is justifiable on the basis of probable cause to believe that a violation of law has occurred," id., at 811. But to say that ulterior motives do not invalidate a search that is legitimate because of probable cause to believe a crime has occurred is not to say that it does invalidate all searches that are legitimate for other reasons.

"[O]nly an undiscerning reader," ibid., would think otherwise. We referred to probable cause to believe that a violation of law had occurred because that was the legitimating factor in the case at hand. But the analysis of our opinion swept broadly to reject inquiries into motive generally. We remarked that our special-needs and administrative-inspection cases are unusual in their concern for pretext, and do nothing more than "explain that the exemption from the need for probable cause (and warrant), which is accorded to searches made for the purpose of inventory or administrative regulation, is not accorded to searches that are not made for those purposes," id., at 811–812. And our opinion emphasized that we had at that time (prior to *Edmond*) rejected every request to examine subjective intent outside the narrow context of special needs and administrative inspections. Thus, al-Kidd's approach adds an "only" to a sentence plucked from the *Whren* opinion, and then elevates that sentence (as so revised) over the remainder of the opinion, and over the consistent holdings of our other cases.

Because al-Kidd concedes that individualized suspicion supported the issuance of the material-witness arrest warrant; and does not assert that his arrest would have been unconstitutional absent the alleged pretextual use of the warrant; we find no Fourth Amendment violation. Efficient and evenhanded application of the law demands that we look to whether the arrest is objectively justified, rather than to the motive of the arresting officer.

B

A Government official's conduct violates clearly established law when, at the time of the challenged conduct, "[t]he contours of [a] right [are] sufficiently clear" that every "reasonable official would have understood that what he is doing violates that right." *Anderson v. Creighton*, 483 U.S. 635, 640 (1987). We do not require a case directly on point, but existing precedent must have placed the statutory or constitutional question beyond debate. The constitutional question in this case falls far short of that threshold.

At the time of al-Kidd's arrest, not a single judicial opinion had held that pretext could render an objectively reasonable arrest pursuant to a material-witness warrant unconstitutional. A district-court opinion had suggested, in a footnoted dictum devoid of supporting citation, that using such a warrant for preventive detention of suspects "is an illegitimate use of the statute"—implying (we accept for the sake of argument) that the detention would therefore be unconstitutional. United States v. Awadallah, 202 F.Supp.2d 55, 77, n. 28 (S.D.N.Y.2002). The Court of Appeals thought nothing could "have given John Ashcroft fair[er] warning" that his conduct violated the Fourth Amendment, because the footnoted dictum "call[ed] out Ashcroft by name"! We will indulge the assumption (though it does not seem to us realistic) that Justice Department lawyers bring to the Attorney General's personal attention all district judges' footnoted speculations that boldly "call him out by name." On that assumption, would it prove that for him (and for him only?) it became clearly established that pretextual use of the material-witness statute rendered the arrest unconstitutional? An extraordinary proposition. Even a district judge's ipse dixit of a holding is not "controlling authority" in any jurisdiction, much less in the entire United States; and his ipse dixit of a footnoted dictum falls far short of what is necessary absent controlling authority: a robust consensus of cases of persuasive authority.

The Court of Appeals' other cases "clearly establishing" the constitutional violation are, of course, those we rejected as irrelevant in our discussion of whether there was any constitutional violation at all. And the Court of Appeals' reference to those cases here makes the same error of assuming that purpose is only disregarded when there is probable cause to suspect a violation of law.

The Court of Appeals also found clearly established law lurking in the broad "history and purposes of the Fourth Amendment." We have repeatedly told courts * * * not to define clearly established law at a high level of generality. The general proposition, for example, that an unreasonable search or seizure violates the Fourth Amendment is of little help in determining whether the violative nature of particular conduct is clearly established.

The same is true of the Court of Appeals' broad historical assertions. The Fourth Amendment was a response to the English Crown's use of general warrants, which often allowed royal officials to search and seize whatever and whomever they pleased while investigating crimes or affronts to the Crown. According to

the Court of Appeals, Ashcroft should have seen that a pretextual warrant similarly "gut[s] the substantive protections of the Fourth Amendmen[t]" and allows the State "to arrest upon the executive's mere suspicion."

Ashcroft must be forgiven for missing the parallel, which escapes us as well. The principal evil of the general warrant was addressed by the Fourth Amendment's particularity requirement, which Ashcroft's alleged policy made no effort to evade. The warrant authorizing al-Kidd's arrest named al-Kidd and only al-Kidd. It might be argued, perhaps, that when, in response to the English abuses, the Fourth Amendment said that warrants could only issue "on probable cause" it meant only probable cause to suspect a violation of law, and not probable cause to believe that the individual named in the warrant was a material witness. But that would make all arrests pursuant to material-witness warrants unconstitutional, whether pretextual or not—and that is not the position taken by al-Kidd in this case.

While featuring a District Court's footnoted dictum, the Court of Appeals made no mention of this Court's affirmation in *Edmond* of the "predominan[t]" rule that reasonableness is an objective inquiry. Nor did it mention *Whren's* * * * statements that subjective intent mattered in a very limited subset of our Fourth Amendment cases; or *Terry's* objective evaluation of investigatory searches premised on reasonable suspicion rather than probable cause; or *Bond 's* objective evaluation of a suspicionless investigatory search. The Court of Appeals seems to have cherry-picked the aspects of our opinions that gave colorable support to the proposition that the unconstitutionality of the action here was clearly established.

Qualified immunity gives government officials breathing room to make reasonable but mistaken judgments about open legal questions. When properly applied, it protects all but the plainly incompetent or those who knowingly violate the law. Ashcroft deserves neither label, not least because eight Court of Appeals judges agreed with his judgment in a case of first impression. He deserves qualified immunity even assuming—contrafactually—that his alleged detention policy violated the Fourth Amendment.

———

We hold that an objectively reasonable arrest and detention of a material witness pursuant to a validly obtained warrant cannot be challenged as unconstitutional on the basis of allegations that the arresting authority had an improper motive. Because Ashcroft did not violate clearly established law, we need not address the more difficult question whether he enjoys absolute immunity. The judgment of the Court of Appeals is reversed, and the case is remanded for further proceedings consistent with this opinion.

It is so ordered.

Justice KAGAN took no part in the consideration or decision of this case.

JUSTICE KENNEDY, with whom JUSTICE GINSBURG, JUSTICE BREYER, and JUSTICE SOTOMAYOR join as to Part I, concurring.

* * *

I

The Court's holding is limited to the arguments presented by the parties and leaves unresolved whether the Government's use of the Material Witness Statute in this case was lawful. Under the statute, a Magistrate Judge may issue a warrant to arrest someone as a material witness upon a showing by affidavit that "the testimony of a person is material in a criminal proceeding" and "that it may become impracticable to secure the presence of the person by subpoena." 18 U.S.C. § 3144. The scope of the statute's lawful authorization is uncertain. For example, a law-abiding citizen might observe a crime during the days or weeks before a scheduled flight abroad. It is unclear whether those facts alone might allow police to obtain a material witness warrant on the ground that it "may become impracticable" to secure the person's presence by subpoena. The question becomes more difficult if one further assumes the traveler would be willing to testify if asked; and more difficult still if one supposes that authorities delay obtaining or executing the warrant until the traveler has arrived at the airport. These possibilities resemble the facts in this case.

In considering these issues, it is important to bear in mind that the Material Witness Statute might not provide for the issuance of warrants within the meaning of the Fourth Amendment's Warrant Clause. The typical arrest warrant is based on probable cause that the arrestee has committed a crime; but that is not the standard for the issuance of warrants under the Material Witness Statute. If material witness warrants do not qualify as "Warrants" under the Fourth Amendment, then material witness arrests might still be governed by the Fourth Amendment's separate reasonableness requirement for seizures of the person. See United States v. Watson, 423 U.S. 411 (1976). Given the difficulty of these issues, the Court is correct to address only the legal theory put before it, without further exploring when material witness arrests might be consistent with statutory and constitutional requirements.

II

* * *

JUSTICE GINSBURG, with whom JUSTICE BREYER and JUSTICE SOTOMAYOR join, concurring in the judgment.

* * * Given Whren v. United States, I agree with the Court that no "clearly established law" renders Ashcroft answerable in damages for the abuse of authority al-Kidd charged. But I join Justice SOTOMA-YOR in objecting to the Court's disposition of al-Kidd's Fourth Amendment claim on the merits; as she observes, that claim involves novel and trying questions that will have no effect on the outcome of this case.

In addressing al-Kidd's Fourth Amendment claim against Ashcroft, the Court assumes at the outset the existence of a validly obtained material witness warrant. Is a warrant "validly obtained" when the affidavit on which it is based fails to inform the issuing Magistrate Judge that "the Government has no intention of using [al-Kidd as a witness] at [another's] trial," and does not disclose that al-Kidd had cooperated with FBI agents each of the several times they had asked to interview him?

Casting further doubt on the assumption that the warrant was validly obtained, the Magistrate Judge was not told that al-Kidd's parents, wife, and children were all citizens and residents of the United States. In addition, the affidavit misrepresented that al-Kidd was about to take a one-way flight to Saudi Arabia, with a first-class ticket costing approximately $5,000; in fact, al-Kidd had a round-trip, coach-class ticket that cost $1,700. Given these omissions and misrepresentations, there is strong cause to question the Court's opening assumption—a valid material-witness warrant—and equally strong reason to conclude that a merits determination was neither necessary nor proper.

I also agree with Justice KENNEDY that al-Kidd's treatment presents serious questions, unaddressed by the Court, concerning "the [legality of] the Government's use of the Material Witness Statute in this case." In addition to the questions Justice KENNE-DY poses, and even if the initial material witness classification had been proper, what even arguably legitimate basis could there be for the harsh custodial conditions to which al-Kidd was subjected: Ostensibly held only to secure his testimony, al-Kidd was confined in three different detention centers during his 16 days' incarceration, kept in high-security cells lit 24 hours a day, strip-searched and subjected to body-cavity inspections on more than one occasion, and handcuffed and shackled about his wrists, legs, and waist.

However circumscribed al-Kidd's *Bivens* claim against Ashcroft may have been, his remaining claims against the FBI agents who apprehended him invite consideration of the issues Justice KENNEDY identified. His challenges to the brutal conditions of his confinement have been settled. But his ordeal is a grim reminder of the need to install safeguards against disrespect for human dignity, constraints that will control officialdom even in perilous times.

JUSTICE SOTOMAYOR, with whom JUSTICE GINSBURG and JUSTICE BREYER join, concurring in the judgment.

I concur in the Court's judgment reversing the Court of Appeals because I agree with the majority's conclusion that Ashcroft did not violate clearly established law. I cannot join the majority's opinion, however, because it unnecessarily resolves a difficult and novel question of constitutional interpretation that will have no effect on the outcome of the case.

Whether the Fourth Amendment permits the pretextual use of a material witness warrant for preventive detention of an individual whom the Government has no intention of using at trial is, in my view, a closer question than the majority's opinion suggests. Although the majority is correct that a government official's subjective intent is generally irrelevant in determining whether that officer's actions violate the Fourth Amendment, none of our prior cases recognizing that principle involved prolonged detention of an individual without probable cause to believe he had committed any criminal offense. We have never considered whether an official's subjective intent matters for purposes of the Fourth Amendment in that novel context, and we need not and should not resolve that question in this case. All Members of the Court agree that, whatever the merits of the underlying Fourth Amendment question, Ashcroft did not violate clearly established law.

The majority's constitutional ruling is a narrow one premised on the existence of a valid material-witness warrant, a premise that, at the very least, is questionable in light of the allegations set forth in al-Kidd's complaint. Based on those allegations, it is not at all clear that it would have been "impracticable to secure [al-Kidd's] presence . . . by subpoena" or that his testimony could not "adequately be secured by deposition." 18 U.S.C. § 3144. Nor is it clear that the affidavit supporting the warrant was sufficient; its failure to disclose that the Government had no intention of using al-Kidd as a witness at trial may very well have rendered the affidavit deliberately false and misleading. The majority assumes away these factual difficulties, but in my view, they point to the artificiality of the way the Fourth Amendment question has been presented to this Court and provide further reason to avoid rendering an unnecessary holding on the constitutional question.

* * *

G.   EXIGENT CIRCUMSTANCES

3.   Police and Public Safety

Page 366. Add after *Brigham City v. Stuart*.

Application of Brigham City v. Stuart: Michigan v. Fisher

MICHIGAN v. FISHER

Supreme Court of the United States, 2009
130 S.Ct. 546

Per Curiam

Police officers responded to a complaint of a disturbance near Allen Road in Brownstown, Michigan. Officer Christopher Goolsby later testified that, as he and his partner approached the area, a couple directed them to a residence where a man was "going crazy." Upon their arrival, the officers found a household in considerable chaos: a pickup truck in the driveway with its front smashed, damaged fenceposts along the side of the property, and three broken house windows, the glass still on the ground outside. The officers also noticed blood on the hood of the pickup and on clothes inside of it, as well as on one of the doors to the house. * * * Through a window, the officers could see respondent, Jeremy Fisher, inside the house, screaming and throwing things. The back door was locked, and a couch had been placed to block the front door.

The officers knocked, but Fisher refused to answer. They saw that Fisher had a cut on his hand, and they asked him whether he needed medical attention. Fisher ignored these questions and demanded, with accompanying profanity, that the officers go to get a search warrant. Officer Goolsby then pushed the front door partway open and ventured into the house. Through the window of the open door he saw Fisher pointing a long gun at him. Officer Goolsby withdrew.

Fisher was charged under Michigan law with assault with a dangerous weapon and possession of a firearm during the commission of a felony. The trial court concluded that Officer Goolsby violated the Fourth Amendment when he entered Fisher's house, and granted Fisher's motion to suppress the evidence obtained as a result—that is, Officer Goolsby's statement that Fisher pointed a rifle at him. [The Michigan Court of Appeals affirmed.] Because the decision of the Michigan Court of Appeals is indeed contrary to our Fourth Amendment case law, particularly

Brigham City v. Stuart, we grant the State's petition for certiorari and reverse.

* * * [A]lthough searches and seizures inside a home without a warrant are presumptively unreasonable, that presumption can be overcome. For example, the exigencies of the situation may make the needs of law enforcement so compelling that the warrantless search is objectively reasonable.

Brigham City identified one such exigency: "the need to assist persons who are seriously injured or threatened with such injury." Thus, law enforcement officers "may enter a home without a warrant to render emergency assistance to an injured occupant or to protect an occupant from imminent injury." This "emergency aid exception" does not depend on the officers' subjective intent or the seriousness of any crime they are investigating when the emergency arises. It requires only an objectively reasonable basis for believing, that a person within the house is in need of immediate aid.

[The Court reviews the facts and holding of Brigham City, page 364 of the Casebook.]

A straightforward application of the emergency aid exception, as in Brigham City, dictates that the officer's entry was reasonable. Just as in Brigham City, the police officers here were responding to a report of a disturbance. Just as in Brigham City, when they arrived on the scene they encountered a tumultuous situation in the house—and here they also found signs of a recent injury, perhaps from a car accident, outside. And just as in Brigham City, the officers could see violent behavior inside. Although Officer Goolsby and his partner did not see punches thrown, as did the officers in *Brigham City*, they did see Fisher screaming and throwing things. It would be objectively reasonable to believe that Fisher's projectiles might have a human target (perhaps a spouse or a child), or that Fisher would hurt himself in the course of his rage. In short, we find it as plain here as we did in *Brigham City* that the officer's entry was reasonable under the Fourth Amendment.

The Michigan Court of Appeals, however, thought the situation "did not rise to a level of emergency justifying the warrantless intrusion into a residence." Although the Court of Appeals conceded that "there was evidence an injured person was on the premises," it found it significant that "the mere drops of blood did not signal a likely serious, life-threatening injury." The court added that the cut Officer Goolsby observed on Fisher's hand "likely explained the trail of blood" and that Fisher "was very much on his feet and apparently able to see to his own needs."

Even a casual review of *Brigham City* reveals the flaw in this reasoning. Officers do not need ironclad proof of "a likely serious, life-threatening" injury to invoke the emergency aid exception. The only injury police could confirm in *Brigham City* was the bloody lip they saw the juvenile inflict upon the adult. Fisher argues that the officers here could not have been motivated by a perceived need to provide medical assistance, since they never summoned emergency medical personnel. This would have no bearing, of course, upon their need to assure that Fisher was not endangering someone else in the house. Moreover, even if the failure to summon medical personnel conclusively established that Goolsby did not subjectively believe, when he en-

tered the house, that Fisher or someone else was seriously injured (which is doubtful), the test, as we have said, is not what Goolsby believed, but whether there was an objectively reasonable basis for believing that medical assistance was needed, or persons were in danger.

It was error for the Michigan Court of Appeals to replace that objective inquiry into appearances with its hindsight determination that there was in fact no emergency. It does not meet the needs of law enforcement or the demands of public safety to require officers to walk away from a situation like the one they encountered here. Only when an apparent threat has become an actual harm can officers rule out innocuous explanations for ominous circumstances. But "[t]he role of a peace officer includes preventing violence and restoring order, not simply rendering first aid to casualties." *Brigham City*. It sufficed to invoke the emergency aid exception that it was reasonable to believe that Fisher had hurt himself (albeit nonfatally) and needed treatment that in his rage he was unable to provide, or that Fisher was about to hurt, or had already hurt, someone else. The Michigan Court of Appeals required more than what the Fourth Amendment demands.

* * * The judgment of the Michigan Court of Appeals is reversed, and the case is remanded for further proceedings not inconsistent with this opinion.

JUSTICE STEVENS, with whom JUSTICE SOTMAYOR joins, dissenting.

* * * We have * * * explained that a warrantless entry is justified by the need to protect or preserve life or avoid serious injury. The State bears the burden of proof on that factual issue and relied entirely on the testimony of Officer Goolsby in its attempt to carry that burden. Since three years had passed, Goolsby was not sure about certain facts—such as whether Fisher had a cut on his hand—but he did remember that Fisher repeatedly swore at the officers and told them to get a warrant, and that Fisher was screaming and throwing things. Goolsby also testified that he saw "mere drops" of blood outside Fisher's home, and that he did not ask whether anyone else was inside. Goolsby did not testify that he had any reason to believe that anyone else was in the house. Thus, the factual question was whether Goolsby had "an objectively reasonable basis for believing that [Fisher was] seriously injured or imminently threatened with such injury." Brigham City v. Stuart.

After hearing the testimony, the trial judge was "even more convinced" that the entry was unlawful.* * * He found the police decision to leave the scene and not return for several hours—without resolving any potentially dangerous situation and without calling for medical assistance—inconsistent with a reasonable belief that Fisher was in need of immediate aid. In sum, the one judge who heard Officer Goolsby's testimony was not persuaded that Goolsby had an objectively reasonable basis for believing that entering Fisher's home was necessary to avoid serious injury.

* * *

Today, without having heard Officer Goolsby's testimony, this Court decides that the trial judge got it wrong. I am not persuaded that he did, but even if we make that assumption, it is hard to see how the Court is justified in micromanaging the day-to-day business of state tribunals making fact-intensive decisions of this kind. We ought not usurp the role of the factfinder when faced with a close question of the reasonableness of an officer's actions, particularly in a case tried in a state court. I therefore respectfully dissent.

5. Impermissibly Created Exigency

Page 375. Add the following case at the end of the section.

Bad Faith Creation of Exigent Circumstances and Prior Opportunity to Get a Warrant: Kentucky v. King.

KENTUCKY v. KING

Supreme Court of the United States, 2011.
131 S.Ct. 1849

JUSTICE ALITO **delivered the opinion of the Court.**

It is well established that exigent circumstances, including the need to prevent the destruction of evidence, permit police officers to conduct an otherwise permissible search without first obtaining a warrant. In this case, we consider whether this rule applies when police, by knocking on the door of a residence and announcing their presence, cause the occupants to attempt to destroy evidence. The Kentucky Supreme Court held that the exigent circumstances rule does not apply in the case at hand because the police should have foreseen that their conduct would prompt the occupants to attempt to destroy evidence. We reject this interpretation of the exigent circumstances rule. The conduct of the police prior to their entry into the apartment was entirely lawful. They did not violate the Fourth Amendment or threaten to do so. In such a situation, the exigent circumstances rule applies. I

This case concerns the search of an apartment in Lexington, Kentucky. Police officers set up a controlled buy of crack cocaine outside an apartment complex. Undercover Officer Gibbons watched the deal take place from an unmarked car in a nearby parking lot. After the deal occurred, Gibbons radioed uniformed officers to move in on the suspect. He told the officers that the suspect was moving quickly toward the breezeway of an apartment building, and he urged them to hurry up and get there before the suspect entered an apartment.

In response to the radio alert, the uniformed officers drove into the nearby parking lot, left their vehicles, and ran to the breezeway. Just as they entered the breezeway, they heard a door shut and detected a very strong odor of burnt marijuana. At the end of the breezeway, the officers saw two apartments, one on the left and one on the right, and they did not know which apartment the suspect had entered. Gibbons had radioed that the suspect was running into the apartment on the right, but the officers did not hear this statement because they had already left their vehicles. Because they smelled marijuana smoke emanating from the apartment on the left, they approached the door of that apartment.

Officer Steven Cobb, one of the uniformed officers who approached the door, testified that the officers banged on the left apartment door as loud as [they] could and announced, This is the police or Police, police, police. Cobb said that [a]s soon as [the officers] started banging on the door, they could hear people inside moving, and [i]t sounded as [though] things were being moved inside the apartment. These noises, Cobb testified, led the officers to believe that drug-related evidence was about to be destroyed.

At that point, the officers announced that they were going to make entry inside the apartment. Cobb then kicked in the door, the officers entered the apartment, and they found three people in the front room: respondent Hollis King, respondent's girlfriend, and a guest who was smoking marijuana.[1] The officers performed a protective sweep of the apartment during which they saw marijuana and powder cocaine in plain view. In a subsequent search, they also discovered crack cocaine, cash, and drug paraphernalia.

Police eventually entered the apartment on the right. Inside, they found the suspected drug dealer who was the initial target of their investigation.

B

[The lower state courts rejected the defendant's argument that the evidence should be suppressed for lack of exigent circumstances.]

The Supreme Court of Kentucky reversed. As a preliminary matter, the court observed that there was certainly some question as to whether

---

1. Respondent's girlfriend leased the apartment, but respondent stayed there part of the time, and his child lived there. Based on these facts, Kentucky conceded in state court that respondent has Fourth Amendment standing to challenge the search.

the sound of persons moving [inside the apartment] was sufficient to establish that evidence was being destroyed. But the court did not answer that question. Instead, it assume[d] for the purpose of argument that exigent circumstances existed.

To determine whether police impermissibly created the exigency, the Supreme Court of Kentucky announced a two-part test. First, the court held, police cannot deliberately creat[e] the exigent circumstances with the bad faith intent to avoid the warrant requirement. Second, even absent bad faith, the court concluded, police may not rely on exigent circumstances if it was reasonably foreseeable that the investigative tactics employed by the police would create the exigent circumstances. Although the court found no evidence of bad faith, it held that exigent circumstances could not justify the search because it was reasonably foreseeable that the occupants would destroy evidence when the police knocked on the door and announced their presence. We granted certiorari.

II

A

* * *

One well-recognized exception [to the warrant requirement] applies when the exigencies of the situation make the needs of law enforcement so compelling that [a] warrantless search is objectively reasonable under the Fourth Amendment. Mincey v. Arizona, 437 U.S. 385, 394 (1978).

This Court has identified several exigencies that may justify a warrantless search of a home. Under the emergency aid exception, for example, officers may enter a home without a warrant to render emergency assistance to an injured occupant or to protect an occupant from immi-

nent injury. Police officers may enter premises without a warrant when they are in hot pursuit of a fleeing suspect. See United States v. Santana, 427 U.S. 38, 4243 (1976). And what is relevant here the need to prevent the imminent destruction of evidence has long been recognized as a sufficient justification for a warrantless search.

B

Over the years, lower courts have developed an exception to the exigent circumstances rule, the so-called police-created exigency doctrine. Under this doctrine, police may not rely on the need to prevent destruction of evidence when that exigency was created or manufactured by the conduct of the police. In applying this exception for the creation or manufacturing of an exigency by the police, courts require something more than mere proof that fear of detection by the police caused the destruction of evidence. An additional showing is obviously needed because, as the Eighth Circuit has recognized, in some sense the police always create the exigent circumstances. United States v. Duchi, 906 F.2d 1278, 1284 (C.A.8 1990). That is to say, in the vast majority of cases in which evidence is destroyed by persons who are engaged in illegal conduct, the reason for the destruction is fear that the evidence will fall into the hands of law enforcement. Destruction of evidence issues probably occur most frequently in drug cases because drugs may be easily destroyed by flushing them down a toilet or rinsing them down a drain. Persons in possession of valuable drugs are unlikely to destroy them unless they fear discovery by the police. Consequently, a rule that precludes the police from making a warrantless entry to prevent the destruction of evidence whenever their conduct causes the exigency would unreasonably shrink the reach of this well-established exception to the warrant requirement.

Presumably for the purpose of avoiding such a result, the lower courts have held that the police-created exigency doctrine requires more than simple causation, but the lower courts have not agreed on the test to be applied. Indeed, the petition in this case maintains that [t]here are currently five different tests being used by the United States Courts of Appeals, and that some state courts have crafted additional tests.

III

A

Despite the welter of tests devised by the lower courts, the answer to the question presented in this case follows directly and clearly from the principle that permits warrantless searches in the first place. As previously noted, warrantless searches are allowed when the circumstances make it reasonable, within the meaning of the Fourth Amendment, to dispense with the warrant requirement. Therefore, the answer to the question before us is that the exigent circumstances rule justifies a warrantless search when the conduct of the police preceding the exigency is reasonable in the same sense. Where, as here, the police did not create the exigency by engaging or threatening to engage in conduct that violates the Fourth Amendment, warrantless entry to prevent the destruction of evidence is reasonable and thus allowed.[4]

We have taken a similar approach in other cases involving warrantless searches. For example, we have held that law enforcement officers may seize evidence in plain view, provided that they have not violated the Fourth Amendment in arriving at the spot from which the observation of the evidence is made. See *Horton v. California,* 496 U.S. 128, 136140 (1990). As we put it in *Horton,* [i]t is . . . an essential predicate to any valid warrantless seizure of incriminating evidence that the officer did not violate the Fourth Amendment in arriving at the place from which the evidence could be plainly viewed. So long as this prerequisite is satisfied, however, it does not matter that the officer who makes the observation may have gone to the spot from which the evidence was seen with the hope of being able to view and seize the evidence. See *id.,* at 138 (The fact that an officer is interested in an item of evidence and fully expects to find it in the course of a search should not invalidate its seizure). Instead, the Fourth Amendment requires only that the steps preceding the seizure be lawful.

Similarly, officers may seek consent-based encounters if they are lawfully present in the place where the consensual encounter occurs. See INS v. Delgado, 466 U.S. 210, 217, n. 5 (1984) (noting that officers who entered into consent-based encounters with employees in a factory building were lawfully present [in the factory] pursuant to consent or a warrant). If consent is freely given, it makes no difference that an officer

---

4. There is a strong argument to be made that, at least in most circumstances, the exigent circumstances rule should not apply where the police, without a warrant or any legally sound basis for a warrantless entry, threaten that they will enter without permission unless admitted. In this case, however, no such actual threat was made, and therefore we have no need to reach that question.

may have approached the person with the hope or expectation of obtaining consent.

B

Some lower courts have adopted a rule that is similar to the one that we recognize today. See United States v. MacDonald, 916 F.2d 766, 772 (C.A.2 1990) (en banc) (law enforcement officers do not impermissibly create exigent circumstances when they act in an entirely lawful manner). But others, including the Kentucky Supreme Court, have imposed additional requirements that are unsound and that we now reject.

Bad faith. Some courts, including the Kentucky Supreme Court, ask whether law enforcement officers deliberately created the exigent circumstances with the bad faith intent to avoid the warrant requirement. This approach is fundamentally inconsistent with our Fourth Amendment jurisprudence. Our cases have repeatedly rejected a subjective approach, asking only whether the circumstances, viewed *objectively,* justify the action. Indeed, we have never held, outside limited contexts such as an inventory search or administrative inspection . . . , that an officer's motive invalidates objectively justifiable behavior under the Fourth Amendment. Whren v. United States, 517 U.S. 806, 812 (1996).

The reasons for looking to objective factors, rather than subjective intent, are clear. Legal tests based on reasonableness are generally objective, and this Court has long taken the view that evenhanded law enforcement is best achieved by the application of objective standards of conduct, rather than standards that depend upon the subjective state of mind of the officer. *Horton, supra,* at 138.

Reasonable foreseeability. Some courts, again including the Kentucky Supreme Court, hold that police may not rely on an exigency if it was reasonably foreseeable that the investigative tactics employed by the police would create the exigent circumstances. Courts applying this test have invalidated warrantless home searches on the ground that it was reasonably foreseeable that police officers, by knocking on the door and announcing their presence, would lead a drug suspect to destroy evidence.

Contrary to this reasoning, however, we have rejected the notion that police may seize evidence without a warrant only when they come across the evidence by happenstance. In *Horton,* as noted, we held that the police may seize evidence in plain view even though the officers may be interested in an item of evidence and fully expec[t] to find it in the course of a search. 496 U.S., at 138.

Adoption of a reasonable foreseeability test would also introduce an unacceptable degree of unpredictability. For example, whenever law enforcement officers knock on the door of premises occupied by a person who may be involved in the drug trade, there is *some* possibility that the occupants may possess drugs and may seek to destroy them. Under a reasonable foreseeability test, it would be necessary to quantify the degree of predictability that must be reached before the police-created exigency doctrine comes into play.

A simple example illustrates the difficulties that such an approach would produce. Suppose that the officers in the present case did not smell marijuana smoke and thus knew only that there was a 50% chance that the fleeing suspect had entered the apartment on the left rather than the apartment on the right. Under those circumstances, would it have been reasonably foreseeable that the occupants of the apartment on the left would seek to destroy evidence upon learning that the police were at the door? Or suppose that the officers knew only that the suspect had disappeared into one of the apartments on a floor with 3, 5, 10, or even 20 units? If the police chose a door at random and knocked for the purpose of asking the occupants if they knew a person who fit the description of the suspect, would it have been reasonably foreseeable that the occupants would seek to destroy evidence?

We have noted that [t]he calculus of reasonableness must embody allowance for the fact that police officers are often forced to make split-second judgments in circumstances that are tense, uncertain, and rapidly evolving. Graham v. Connor, 490 U.S. 386, 396–397 (1989). The reasonable foreseeability test would create unacceptable and unwarranted difficulties for law enforcement officers who must make quick decisions in the field, as well as for judges who would be required to determine after the fact whether the destruction of evidence in response to a knock on the door was reasonably foreseeable based on what the officers knew at the time.

Probable cause and time to secure a warrant. Some courts, in applying the police-created exigency doctrine, fault law enforcement officers if, after acquiring evidence that is sufficient to establish probable cause to search particular premises, the officers do not seek a warrant but instead knock on the door and seek either to speak with an occupant or to obtain consent to search. This approach unjusti-

fiably interferes with legitimate law enforcement strategies. There are many entirely proper reasons why police may not want to seek a search warrant as soon as the bare minimum of evidence needed to establish probable cause is acquired. Without attempting to provide a comprehensive list of these reasons, we note a few.

First, the police may wish to speak with the occupants of a dwelling before deciding whether it is worthwhile to seek authorization for a search. They may think that a short and simple conversation may obviate the need to apply for and execute a warrant. Second, the police may want to ask an occupant of the premises for consent to search because doing so is simpler, faster, and less burdensome than applying for a warrant. A consensual search also may result in considerably less inconvenience and embarrassment to the occupants than a search conducted pursuant to a warrant. Third, law enforcement officers may wish to obtain more evidence before submitting what might otherwise be considered a marginal warrant application. Fourth, prosecutors may wish to wait until they acquire evidence that can justify a search that is broader in scope than the search that a judicial officer is likely to authorize based on the evidence then available. And finally, in many cases, law enforcement may not want to execute a search that will disclose the existence of an investigation because doing so may interfere with the acquisition of additional evidence against those already under suspicion or evidence about additional but as yet unknown participants in a criminal scheme.

We have said that [l]aw enforcement officers are under no constitutional duty to call a halt to criminal investigation the moment they have the minimum evidence to establish probable cause. Hoffa v. United States, 385 U.S. 293, 310 (1966). Faulting the police for failing to apply for a search warrant at the earliest possible time after obtaining probable cause imposes a duty that is nowhere to be found in the Constitution.

Standard or good investigative tactics. Finally, some lower court cases suggest that law enforcement officers may be found to have created or manufactured an exigency if the court concludes that the course of their investigation was contrary to standard or good law enforcement practices (or to the policies or practices of their jurisdictions). This approach fails to provide clear guidance for law enforcement officers and authorizes courts to make judgments on matters that are the province of those who are responsible for federal and state law enforcement agencies.

C

Respondent argues for a rule that differs from those discussed above, but his rule is also flawed. Respondent contends that law enforcement officers impermissibly create an exigency when they engage in conduct that would cause a reasonable person to believe that entry is imminent and inevitable. In respondent's view, relevant factors include the officers' tone of voice in announcing their presence and the forcefulness of their knocks. But the ability of law enforcement officers to respond to an exigency cannot turn on such subtleties.

Police officers may have a very good reason to announce their presence loudly and to knock on the door with some force. A forceful knock may be necessary to alert the occupants that someone is at the door. Furthermore, unless police officers identify themselves loudly enough, occupants may not know who is at their doorstep. Officers are permitted indeed, encouraged to identify themselves to citizens, and in many circumstances this is cause for assurance, not discomfort. United States v. Drayton, 536 U.S. 194, 204 (2002). Citizens who are startled by an unexpected knock on the door or by the sight of unknown persons in plain clothes on their doorstep may be relieved to learn that these persons are police officers. Others may appreciate the opportunity to make an informed decision about whether to answer the door to the police.

If respondent's test were adopted, it would be extremely difficult for police officers to know how loudly they may announce their presence or how forcefully they may knock on a door without running afoul of the police-created exigency rule. And in most cases, it would be nearly impossible for a court to determine whether that threshold had been passed. The Fourth Amendment does not require the nebulous and impractical test that respondent proposes.[5]

---

5. Contrary to respondent's argument, Johnson v. United States, 333 U.S. 10 (1948), does not require affirmance in this case. In *Johnson,* officers noticed the smell of burning opium emanating from a hotel room. They then knocked on the door and demanded entry. Upon seeing that Johnson was the only occupant of the room, they placed her under arrest, searched the room, and discovered opium and drug paraphernalia. Defending the legality of the search, the Government attempted to justify the warrantless search of the room as a valid search incident to a lawful arrest. The Government did not contend that the officers entered the room in order to prevent the destruction of evidence. Although the officers said that they heard a shuffling noise inside the room after they knocked on the door, the Government did

D

For these reasons, we conclude that the exigent circumstances rule applies when the police do not gain entry to premises by means of an actual or threatened violation of the Fourth Amendment. This holding provides ample protection for the privacy rights that the Amendment protects. When law enforcement officers who are not armed with a warrant knock on a door, they do no more than any private citizen might do. And whether the person who knocks on the door and requests the opportunity to speak is a police officer or a private citizen, the occupant has no obligation to open the door or to speak. When the police knock on a door but the occupants choose not to respond or to speak, the investigation will have reached a conspicuously low point, and the occupants will have the kind of warning that even the most elaborate security system cannot provide. And even if an occupant chooses to open the door and speak with the officers, the occupant need not allow the officers to enter the premises and may refuse to answer any questions at any time.

Occupants who choose not to stand on their constitutional rights but instead elect to attempt to destroy evidence have only themselves to blame for the warrantless exigent-circumstances search that may ensue.

IV

We now apply our interpretation of the police-created exigency doctrine to the facts of this case.

A

We need not decide whether exigent circumstances existed in this case. Any warrantless entry based on exigent circumstances must, of course, be supported by a genuine exigency. * * * We, too, assume for purposes of argument that an exigency existed. We decide only the question on which the Kentucky Supreme Court ruled and on which we granted certiorari: Under what circumstances do police impermissibly create an exigency? Any question about whether an exigency actually existed is better addressed by the Kentucky Supreme Court on remand.

B

In this case, we see no evidence that the officers either violated the Fourth Amendment or threatened to do so prior to the point when they entered the apartment. Officer Cobb testified without contradiction that the officers banged on the door as loud as [they] could and announced either Police, police, police or This is the police. This conduct was entirely consistent with the Fourth Amendment, and we are aware of no other evidence that might show that the officers either violated the Fourth Amendment or threatened to do so (for example, by announcing that they would break down the door if the occupants did not open the door voluntarily).

Respondent argues that the officers demanded entry to the apartment, but he has not pointed to any evidence in the record that supports this assertion. * * * There is no evidence of a demand of any sort, much less a demand that amounts to a threat to violate the Fourth Amendment. * * *

Finally, respondent claims that the officers explained to [the occupants

---

not claim that this particular noise was a noise that would have led a reasonable officer to think that evidence was about to be destroyed.

Thus, *Johnson* is simply not a case about exigent circumstances.

that the officers] were going to make entry inside the apartment, but the record is clear that the officers did not make this statement until after the exigency arose. As Officer Cobb testified, the officers knew that there was possibly something that was going to be destroyed inside the apartment, and *[a]t that point,* . . . [they] explained . . . [that they] were going to make entry. Given that this announcement was made *after* the exigency arose, it could not have created the exigency.

* * *

Like the court below, we assume for purposes of argument that an exigency existed. Because the officers in this case did not violate or threaten to violate the Fourth Amendment prior to the exigency, we hold that the exigency justified the warrantless search of the apartment.

The judgment of the Kentucky Supreme Court is reversed, and the case is remanded for further proceedings not inconsistent with this opinion.

It is so ordered.

JUSTICE GINSBURG, **dissenting.**

The Court today arms the police with a way routinely to dishonor the Fourth Amendment's warrant requirement in drug cases. In lieu of presenting their evidence to a neutral magistrate, police officers may now knock, listen, then break the door down, never mind that they had ample time to obtain a warrant. I dissent from the Court's reduction of the Fourth Amendment's force.

* * *

I

* * * There was little risk that drug-related evidence would have been destroyed had the police delayed the search pending a magis-

trate's authorization. As the Court recognizes, [p]ersons in possession of valuable drugs are unlikely to destroy them unless they fear discovery by the police. Nothing in the record shows that, prior to the knock at the apartment door, the occupants were apprehensive about police proximity. * * * How secure do our homes remain if police, armed with no warrant, can pound on doors at will and, on hearing sounds indicative of things moving, forcibly enter and search for evidence of unlawful activity?

II

* * *

The existence of a genuine emergency depends not only on the state of necessity at the time of the warrantless search; it depends, first and foremost, on actions taken by the police *preceding* the warrantless search. [W]asting a clear opportunity to obtain a warrant, therefore, disentitles the officer from relying on subsequent exigent circumstances. S. Saltzburg & D. Capra, American Criminal Procedure 376 (8th ed.2007).

Under an appropriately reined-in emergency or exigent circumstances exception, the result in this case should not be in doubt. The target of the investigation's entry into the building, and the smell of marijuana seeping under the apartment door into the hallway, the Kentucky Supreme Court rightly determined, gave the police probable cause . . . sufficient . . . to obtain a warrant to search the . . . apartment .. As that court observed, nothing made it impracticable for the police to post officers on the premises while proceeding to obtain a warrant authorizing their entry. * * *

I * * * would not allow an expedient knock to override the warrant requirement. Instead, I would accord that core requirement of the Fourth Amendment full respect. When possible, a warrant must generally be se-cured, the Court acknowledges. There is every reason to conclude that securing a warrant was entirely feasible in this case, and no reason to contract the Fourth Amendment's dominion.

6. Prior Opportunity to Obtain a Warrant

Add at the end of the section:

In Kentucky v. King, 131 S.Ct. 1849 (2011), the Court in an 8–1 decision cast doubt on whether a warrantless search based on exigent circumstances could ever be found illegal on the ground that officers had an opportunity to obtain a warrant before the exigency arose. The decision in *King*—including the discussion about prior opportunity to obtain a warrant—is set forth immediately above in this Supplement.

H.   ADMINISTRATIVE SEARCHES AND OTHER SEARCHES AND SEIZURES BASED ON "SPECIAL NEEDS"

3.   Searches and Seizures of Individuals Pursuant to "Special Needs"

Page 406. Add after the Section on *National Treasury Employees v. Von Raab*

CITY OF ONTARIO v. QUON

Supreme Court of the United States, 2010
130 S.Ct. 2619

JUSTICE KENNEDY **delivered the opinion of the Court.**

This case involves the assertion by a government employer of the right, in circumstances to be described, to read text messages sent and received on a pager the employer owned and issued to an employee. The employee contends that the privacy of the messages is protected by the ban on "unreasonable searches and seizures" found in the Fourth Amendment to the United States Constitution, made applicable to the States by the Due Process Clause of the Fourteenth Amendment. Though the case touches issues of far-reaching signifi-cance, the Court concludes it can be resolved by settled principles determining when a search is reasonable.

I

The City of Ontario (City) is a political subdivision of the State of California. The case arose out of incidents in 2001 and 2002 when respondent Jeff Quon was employed by the Ontario Police Department (OPD). He was a police sergeant and member of OPD's Special Weapons and Tactics (SWAT) Team. The City, OPD, and OPD's Chief, Lloyd Scharf, are petitioners here. As will be discussed, two respondents share the last name Quon. In this opinion "Quon" refers to Jeff Quon, for the relevant events mostly revolve around him.

In October 2001, the City acquired 20 alphanumeric pagers capable of sending and receiving text messages. Arch Wireless Operating Company provided wireless service for the pagers. Under the City's service contract with Arch Wireless, each pager was allotted a limited number of characters sent or received each month. Usage in excess of that amount would result in an additional fee. The City issued pagers to Quon and other SWAT Team members in order to help the SWAT Team mobilize and respond to emergency situations.

Before acquiring the pagers, the City announced a "Computer Usage, Internet and E–Mail Policy" (Computer Policy) that applied to all employees. Among other provisions, it specified that the City "reserves the right to monitor and log all network activity including e-mail and Internet use, with or without notice. Users should have no expectation of privacy or confidentiality when using these resources." In March 2000, Quon signed a statement acknowledging that he had read and understood the Computer Policy.

The Computer Policy did not apply, on its face, to text messaging. Text messages share similarities with e-mails, but the two differ in an important way. In this case, for instance, an e-mail sent on a City computer was transmitted through the City's own data servers, but a text message sent on one of the City's pagers was transmitted using wireless radio frequencies from an individual pager to a receiving station owned by Arch Wireless. It was routed through Arch Wireless' computer network, where it remained until the recipi-

ent's pager or cellular telephone was ready to receive the message, at which point Arch Wireless transmitted the message from the transmitting station nearest to the recipient. After delivery, Arch Wireless retained a copy on its computer servers. * * *

Although the Computer Policy did not cover text messages by its explicit terms, the City made clear to employees, including Quon, that the City would treat text messages the same way as it treated e-mails. At an April 18, 2002, staff meeting at which Quon was present, Lieutenant Steven Duke, the OPD officer responsible for the City's contract with Arch Wireless, told officers that messages sent on the pagers "are considered e-mail messages. This means that [text] messages would fall under the City's policy as public information and [would be] eligible for auditing." Duke's comments were put in writing in a memorandum sent on April 29, 2002, by Chief Scharf to Quon and other City personnel.

Within the first or second billing cycle after the pagers were distributed, Quon exceeded his monthly text message character allotment. Duke told Quon about the overage, and reminded him that messages sent on the pagers were "considered e-mail and could be audited." Duke said, however, that "it was not his intent to audit [an] employee's text messages to see if the overage [was] due to work related transmissions." Duke suggested that Quon could reimburse the City for the overage fee rather than have Duke audit the messages. Quon wrote a check to the City for the overage. Duke offered the same arrangement to other employees who incurred overage fees.

Over the next few months, Quon exceeded his character limit three or four times. Each time he reimbursed the City. Quon and another officer again incurred overage fees for their pager usage in August 2002. At a meeting in October, Duke told Scharf that he had become " 'tired of being a bill collector.' " Scharf decided to determine whether the existing character limit was too low—that is, whether officers such as Quon were having to pay fees for sending work-related messages—or if the overages were for personal messages. Scharf told Duke to request transcripts of text messages sent in August and September by Quon and the other employee who had exceeded the character allowance.

At Duke's request, an administrative assistant employed by OPD contacted Arch Wireless. After verifying that the City was the subscriber on the accounts, Arch Wireless provided the desired transcripts. Duke reviewed the transcripts and discovered that many of the messages sent and received on Quon's pager were not work related, and some were sexually explicit. Duke reported his findings to Scharf, who, along with Quon's immediate supervisor, reviewed the transcripts himself. After his review, Scharf referred the matter to OPD's internal affairs division for an investigation into whether Quon was violating OPD rules by pursuing personal matters while on duty.

The officer in charge of the internal affairs review was Sergeant Patrick McMahon. Before conducting a review, McMahon used Quon's work schedule to redact the transcripts in order to eliminate any messages Quon sent while off duty. He then reviewed the content of the messages Quon sent during work hours. McMahon's report noted that Quon sent or received 456 messages during work hours in the month of August

2002, of which no more than 57 were work related; he sent as many as 80 messages during a single day at work; and on an average workday, Quon sent or received 28 messages, of which only 3 were related to police business. The report concluded that Quon had violated OPD rules. Quon was allegedly disciplined.

B

* * * Quon filed suit against petitioners in the United States District Court for the Central District of California. Arch Wireless and an individual not relevant here were also named as defendants. Quon was joined in his suit by * * * the other respondents, each of whom exchanged text messages with Quon during August and September 2002: Jerilyn Quon, Jeff Quon's then-wife, from whom he was separated; April Florio, an OPD employee with whom Jeff Quon was romantically involved; and Steve Trujillo, another member of the OPD SWAT Team. Among the allegations in the complaint was that petitioners violated respondents' Fourth Amendment rights * * * by obtaining and reviewing the transcript of Jeff Quon's pager messages and that Arch Wireless had violated the SCA by turning over the transcript to the City. The parties filed cross-motions for summary judgment. The District Court * * * denied petitioners' motion for summary judgment on the Fourth Amendment claims. * * * Relying on the plurality opinion in O'Connor v. Ortega, 480 U.S. 709, 711 (1987) [Casebook pages 82 and 395], the District Court determined that Quon had a reasonable expectation of privacy in the content of his text messages. Whether the audit of the text messages was nonetheless reasonable, the District Court concluded, turned on Chief Scharf's intent: "[I]f the purpose for the audit was to determine if Quon was using his pager to 'play games' and 'waste time,' then the audit was not constitutionally reasonable"; but if the audit's purpose "was to determine the efficacy of the existing character limits to ensure that officers were not paying hidden work related costs, ... no constitutional violation occurred." The District Court held a jury trial to determine the purpose of the audit. The jury concluded that Scharf ordered the audit to determine the efficacy of the character limits. The District Court accordingly held that petitioners did not violate the Fourth Amendment. It entered judgment in their favor.

The United States Court of Appeals for the Ninth Circuit reversed in part. The panel agreed with the District Court that Jeff Quon had a reasonable expectation of privacy in his text messages but disagreed with the District Court about whether the search was reasonable. Even though the search was conducted for "a legitimate work-related rationale," the Court of Appeals concluded, it "was not reasonable in scope." * * * The opinion pointed to a "host of simple ways" that the chief could have used instead of the audit, such as warning Quon at the beginning of the month that his future messages would be audited, or asking Quon himself to redact the transcript of his messages. * * *

II

* * * It is well settled that the Fourth Amendment's protection extends beyond the sphere of criminal investigations. "The Amendment guarantees the privacy, dignity, and security of persons against certain arbitrary and invasive acts by officers of the Government," without regard to whether the government actor is investigating crime or performing another function. Skinner v. Railway Labor Executives' Assn. [Casebook Page 401]. The Fourth Amendment applies as well when the Government acts in its capacity as an employer. Treasury Employees v. Von Raab [Casebook Page 403]. The Court discussed this principle in *O'Connor.* There a physician employed by a state hospital alleged that hospital officials investigating workplace misconduct had violated his Fourth Amendment rights by searching his office and seizing personal items from his desk and filing cabinet. All Members of the Court agreed with the general principle that individuals do not lose Fourth Amendment rights merely because they work for the government instead of a private employer. A majority of the Court further agreed that " 'special needs, beyond the normal need for law enforcement,' " make the warrant and probable-cause requirement impracticable for government employers.

The *O'Connor* Court did disagree on the proper analytical framework for Fourth Amendment claims against government employers. A four-Justice plurality concluded that the correct analysis has two steps. First, because "some government offices may be so open to fellow employees or the public that no expectation of privacy is reasonable," a court must consider "[t]he operational realities of the workplace" in order to determine whether an employee's Fourth Amendment rights are implicated. On this view, "the question whether an employee has a reasonable expectation of privacy must be addressed on a case-by-case basis." Next, where an employee has a legitimate privacy expectation, an employer's intrusion on that expectation "for noninvestigatory, work-related purposes, as well as for investigations of work-related misconduct, should be judged by the standard of reasonableness under all the circumstances."

JUSTICE SCALIA, concurring in the judgment, outlined a different approach. His opinion would have dispensed with an inquiry into "operational realities" and would conclude "that the offices of government employees . . . are covered by Fourth Amendment protections as a general matter." But he would also have held "that government searches to retrieve work-related materials or to investigate violations of workplace rules—searches of the sort that are regarded as reasonable and normal in the private-employer context—do not violate the Fourth Amendment."

Later, in the *Von Raab* decision, the Court explained that "operational realities" could diminish an employee's privacy expectations, and that this diminution could be taken into consideration when assessing the reasonableness of a workplace search. In the two decades since *O'Connor,* however, the threshold test for determining the scope of an employee's Fourth Amendment rights has not been clarified further. Here, though they disagree on whether Quon had a reasonable expectation of privacy, both petitioners and respondents start from the premise that the *O'Connor* plurality controls. It is not necessary to resolve whether that premise is correct. The case can be decided by determining that the search was reasonable even assuming Quon had a reasonable expectation of privacy. The two *O'Connor* approaches—the plurality's and JUSTICE SCALIA's—therefore lead to the same result here.

III

A

Before turning to the reasonableness of the search, it is instructive to note the parties' disagreement over whether Quon had a reasonable expectation of privacy. The record does establish that OPD, at the outset, made it clear that pager messages were not considered private. The City's Computer Policy stated that "[u]sers should have no expectation of privacy or confidentiality when using" City computers. Chief Scharf's memo and Duke's statements made clear that this official policy extended to text messaging. The disagreement, at least as respondents see the case, is over whether Duke's later statements overrode the official policy. Respondents contend that because Duke told Quon that an audit would be unnecessary if Quon paid for the overage, Quon reasonably could expect that the contents of his messages would remain private.

At this point, were we to assume that inquiry into "operational realities" were called for, it would be necessary to ask whether Duke's statements could be taken as announcing a change in OPD policy, and if so, whether he had, in fact or appearance, the authority to make such a change and to guarantee the privacy of text messaging. It would also be necessary to consider whether a review of messages sent on police pagers, particularly those sent while officers are on duty, might be justified for other reasons, including performance evaluations, litigation concerning the lawfulness of police actions, and perhaps compliance with state open records laws. These matters would all bear on the legitimacy of an employee's privacy expectation.

The Court must proceed with care when considering the whole concept of privacy expectations in communications made on electronic equipment owned by a government employer. The judiciary risks error by elaborating too fully on the Fourth Amendment implications of emerging technology before its role in society has become clear. See, e.g., Olmstead v. United States, 277 U.S. 438 (1928), overruled by Katz v. United States, 389 U.S. 347, 353 (1967). In Katz, the Court relied on its own knowledge and experience to conclude that there is a reasonable expectation of privacy in a telephone booth. It is not so clear that courts at present are on so sure a ground. Prudence counsels caution before the facts in the instant case are used to establish far-reaching premises that define the existence, and extent, of privacy expectations enjoyed by employees when using employer-provided communication devices.

Rapid changes in the dynamics of communication and information transmission are evident not just in the technology itself but in what society accepts as proper behavior. As one amici brief notes, many employers expect or at least tolerate personal use of such equipment by employees because it often increases worker efficiency. Another amicus points out that the law is beginning to respond to these developments, as some States have recently passed statutes requiring employers to notify employees when monitoring their electronic communications. See Brief for New York Intellectual Property Law Association 22 (citing Del. Code Ann., Tit. 19, § 705 (2005); Conn. Gen. Stat. Ann. § 31–48d (West 2003)). At present, it is uncertain how workplace norms, and the law's treatment of them, will evolve.

Even if the Court were certain that the *O'Connor* plurality's approach were the right one, the Court would have difficulty predicting how employees' privacy expectations will be shaped by those changes or the degree to which society will be prepared to recognize those expectations as reasonable. Cell phone and text message communications are so pervasive that some persons may consider them to be essential means or necessary instruments for self-expression, even self-identification. That might strengthen the case for an expectation of privacy. On the other hand, the ubiquity of those devices has made them generally affordable, so one could counter that employees who need cell phones or similar devices for personal matters can purchase and pay for their own. And employer policies concerning communications will of course shape the reasonable expectations of their employees, especially to the extent that such policies are clearly communicated.

A broad holding concerning employees' privacy expectations vis-à-vis employer-provided technological equipment might have implications for future cases that cannot be predicted. It is preferable to dispose of this case on narrower grounds. For present purposes we assume several propositions arguendo: First, Quon had a reasonable expectation of privacy in the text messages sent on the pager provided to him by the City; second, petitioners' review of the transcript constituted a search within the meaning of the Fourth Amendment; and third, the principles applicable to a government employer's search of an employee's physical office apply with at least the same force when the employer intrudes on the employee's privacy in the electronic sphere.

B

Even if Quon had a reasonable expectation of privacy in his text messages, petitioners did not necessarily violate the Fourth Amendment by obtaining and reviewing the transcripts. Although as a general matter, "warrantless searches are per se unreasonable under the Fourth Amendment," there are "a few specifically established and well-delineated exceptions" to that general rule. The Court has held that the " 'special needs' " of the workplace justify one such exception. Under the approach of the *O'Connor* plurality, when conducted for a "noninvestigatory, work-related purpos[e]" or for the "investigatio[n] of work-related misconduct," a government employer's warrantless search is reasonable if it is " 'justified at its inception' " and if " 'the measures adopted are reasonably related to the objectives of the search and not excessively intrusive in light of' " the circumstances giving rise to the search.

The search here satisfied the standard of the *O'Connor* plurality and was reasonable under that approach. The search was justified at its inception because there were "reasonable grounds for suspecting that the search [was] necessary for a noninvestigatory work-related purpose." As a jury found, Chief Scharf ordered the search in order to determine whether the character limit on the City's contract with Arch Wireless was sufficient to meet the City's needs. This was, as the Ninth Circuit noted, a "legitimate work-related rationale." The City and OPD had a legitimate interest in ensuring that employees were not being forced to pay out of their own pockets for work-related expenses, or on the other hand that

the City was not paying for extensive personal communications.

As for the scope of the search, reviewing the transcripts was reasonable because it was an efficient and expedient way to determine whether Quon's overages were the result of work-related messaging or personal use. The review was also not " 'excessively intrusive.' " Although Quon had gone over his monthly allotment a number of times, OPD requested transcripts for only the months of August and September 2002. While it may have been reasonable as well for OPD to review transcripts of all the months in which Quon exceeded his allowance, it was certainly reasonable for OPD to review messages for just two months in order to obtain a large enough sample to decide whether the character limits were efficacious. And it is worth noting that during his internal affairs investigation, McMahon redacted all messages Quon sent while off duty, a measure which reduced the intrusiveness of any further review of the transcripts.

Furthermore, and again on the assumption that Quon had a reasonable expectation of privacy in the contents of his messages, the extent of an expectation is relevant to assessing whether the search was too intrusive. Even if he could assume some level of privacy would inhere in his messages, it would not have been reasonable for Quon to conclude that his messages were in all circumstances immune from scrutiny. Quon was told that his messages were subject to auditing. As a law enforcement officer, he would or should have known that his actions were likely to come under legal scrutiny, and that this might entail an analysis of his on-the-job communications. Under the circumstances, a reasonable employee would be aware that sound management principles might require the audit of messages to determine whether the pager was being appropriately used. Given that the City issued the pagers to Quon and other SWAT Team members in order to help them more quickly respond to crises—and given that Quon had received no assurances of privacy— Quon could have anticipated that it might be necessary for the City to audit pager messages to assess the SWAT Team's performance in particular emergency situations.

From OPD's perspective, the fact that Quon likely had only a limited privacy expectation, with boundaries that we need not here explore, lessened the risk that the review would intrude on highly private details of Quon's life. OPD's audit of messages on Quon's employer-provided pager was not nearly as intrusive as a search of his personal e-mail account or pager, or a wiretap on his home phone line, would have been. That the search did reveal intimate details of Quon's life does not make it unreasonable, for under the circumstances a reasonable employer would not expect that such a review would intrude on such matters. The search was permissible in its scope.

The Court of Appeals erred in finding the search unreasonable. * * * The panel suggested that Scharf "could have warned Quon that for the month of September he was forbidden from using his pager for personal communications, and that the contents of all his messages would be reviewed to ensure the pager was used only for work related purposes during that time frame. Alternatively, if [OPD] wanted to review past usage, it could have asked Quon to count the characters himself, or asked him to redact personal mes-

sages and grant permission to [OPD]to review the redacted transcript." Ibid.

This approach was inconsistent with controlling precedents. This Court has repeatedly refused to declare that only the "least intrusive" search practicable can be reasonable under the Fourth Amendment. That rationale could raise insuperable barriers to the exercise of virtually all search-and-seizure powers, because "judges engaged in post hoc evaluations of government conduct can almost always imagine some alternative means by which the objectives of the government might have been accomplished," *Skinner*. The analytic errors of the Court of Appeals in this case illustrate the necessity of this principle. Even assuming there were ways that OPD could have performed the search that would have been less intrusive, it does not follow that the search as conducted was unreasonable.

Respondents argue that the search was per se unreasonable in light of the Court of Appeals' conclusion that Arch Wireless violated the Stored Communications Act by giving the City the transcripts of Quon's text messages. The merits of the SCA claim are not before us. But even if the Court of Appeals was correct to conclude that the SCA forbade Arch Wireless from turning over the transcripts, it does not follow that petitioners' actions were unreasonable. Respondents point to no authority for the proposition that the existence of statutory protection renders a search per se unreasonable under the Fourth Amendment. And the precedents counsel otherwise. See Virginia v. Moore, 553 U.S. 164, 168 (2008) (search incident to an arrest that was illegal under state law was reasonable); California v. Greenwood, 486 U.S. 35, 43 (1988) (rejecting argument that if state law forbade police search of individual's garbage the search would violate the Fourth Amendment). * * *

Because the search was motivated by a legitimate work related purpose, and because it was not excessive in scope, the search was reasonable under the approach of the *O'Connor* plurality. For these same reasons—that the employer had a legitimate reason for the search, and that the search was not excessively intrusive in light of that justification—the Court also concludes that the search would be "regarded as reasonable and normal in the private-employer context" and would satisfy the approach of JUSTICE SCALIA's concurrence. The search was reasonable, and the Court of Appeals erred by holding to the contrary. Petitioners did not violate Quon's Fourth Amendment rights.

C

Finally, the Court must consider whether the search violated the Fourth Amendment rights of Jerilyn Quon, Florio, and Trujillo, the respondents who sent text messages to Jeff Quon. Petitioners and respondents disagree whether a sender of a text message can have a reasonable expectation of privacy in a message he knowingly sends to someone's employer-provided pager. It is not necessary to resolve this question in order to dispose of the case, however. Respondents argue that because "the search was unreasonable as to Sergeant Quon, it was also unreasonable as to his correspondents." They make no corollary argument that the search, if reasonable as to Quon, could nonetheless be unreasonable as to Quon's correspondents. In light of this litigating position and the

Court's conclusion that the search was reasonable as to Jeff Quon, it necessarily follows that these other respondents cannot prevail.

* * *

[The concurring opinion of Justice Stevens is omitted.]

JUSTICE SCALIA, **concurring in part and concurring in the judgment.**

I join the Court's opinion except for Part III–A. I continue to believe that the "operational realities" rubric for determining the Fourth Amendment's application to public employees invented by the plurality in O'Connor v. Ortega, is standardless and unsupported. In this case, the proper threshold inquiry should be not whether the Fourth Amendment applies to messages on public employees' employer-issued pagers, but whether it applies in general to such messages on employer-issued pagers.

Here, however, there is no need to answer that threshold question. Even accepting at face value Quon's and his co-plaintiffs' claims that the Fourth Amendment applies to their messages, the city's search was reasonable, and thus did not violate the Amendment. Since it is unnecessary to decide whether the Fourth Amendment applies, it is unnecessary to resolve which approach in *O'Connor* controls: the plurality's or mine. That should end the matter.

The Court concedes as much, yet it inexplicably interrupts its analysis with a recitation of the parties' arguments concerning, and an excursus on the complexity and consequences of answering, that admittedly irrelevant threshold question. That discussion is unnecessary. (To whom do we owe an additional explanation for declining to decide an issue, once we have explained that it makes no difference?) It also seems to me exaggerated. Applying the Fourth

Amendment to new technologies may sometimes be difficult, but when it is necessary to decide a case we have no choice. The Court's implication that where electronic privacy is concerned we should decide less than we otherwise would (that is, less than the principle of law necessary to resolve the case and guide private action)—or that we should hedge our bets by concocting case-specific standards or issuing opaque opinions—is in my view indefensible. The-times-they-are-a-changin' is a feeble excuse for disregard of duty.

Worse still, the digression is self-defeating. Despite the Court's insistence that it is agnostic about the proper test, lower courts will likely read the Court's self-described "instructive" expatiation on how the *O'Connor* plurality's approach would apply here (if it applied) as a heavy-handed hint about how they should proceed. Litigants will do likewise, using the threshold question whether the Fourth Amendment is even implicated as a basis for bombarding lower courts with arguments about employer policies, how they were communicated, and whether they were authorized, as well as the latest trends in employees' use of electronic media. In short, in saying why it is not saying more, the Court says much more than it should.

The Court's inadvertent boosting of the *O'Connor* plurality's standard is all the more ironic because, in fleshing out its fears that applying that test to new technologies will be too hard, the Court underscores the unworkability of that standard. Any rule that requires evaluating whether a given gadget is a "necessary instrumen[t] for self-expression, even self-identification," on top of assessing the degree to which "the law's treatment of [workplace norms has] evolve[d]," is (to put it mildly) unlikely to yield objective answers.

VII. REMEDIES FOR FOURTH AMENDMENT VIOLATIONS

E. LIMITATIONS ON EXCLUSION

2. The Good Faith Exception and Warrantless Searches

Page 540. Add after *Herring*

Good Faith—New Rules Protecting Fourth Amendment Rights Cannot Be Applied Retroactively to Exclude Evidence: *Davis v. United States*

DAVIS v. UNITED STATES

Supreme Court of the United States, 2011.
131 S.Ct. 2419

JUSTICE ALITO **delivered the opinion of the Court.**

The Fourth Amendment protects the right to be free from "unreasonable searches and seizures," but it is silent about how this right is to be enforced. To supplement the bare text, this Court created the exclusionary rule, a deterrent sanction that bars the prosecution from introducing evidence obtained by way of a Fourth Amendment violation. The question here is whether to apply this sanction when the police conduct a search in compliance with binding precedent that is later overruled. Because suppression would do nothing to deter police misconduct in these circumstances, and because it would come at a high cost to both the truth and the public safety, we hold that searches conducted in objectively reasonable reliance on binding appellate precedent are not subject to the exclusionary rule.

I

The question presented arises in this case as a result of a shift in our Fourth Amendment jurisprudence on searches of automobiles incident to arrests of recent occupants.

A

Under this Court's decision in Chimel v. California, 395 U.S. 752 (1969), a police officer who makes a lawful arrest may conduct a warrantless search of the arrestee's person and the area "within his immediate control." This rule "may be stated clearly enough," but in the early going after *Chimel* it proved difficult to apply, particularly in cases that involved searches inside of automobiles after the arrestees were no longer in them. See New York v. Belton, 453 U.S. 454, 458–459 (1981). A number of courts upheld the constitutionality of vehicle searches that were "substantially contemporaneous" with occupants' arrests. Other courts disapproved of automobile searches incident to arrests, at least absent some continuing threat that the arrestee might gain access to the vehicle and "destroy evidence or grab a weapon." In New York v. Belton, this Court granted certiorari to resolve the conflict.

In *Belton*, a police officer conducting a traffic stop lawfully arrested four occupants of a vehicle and ordered the arrestees to line up, unhandcuffed, along the side of the thruway. The officer then searched the vehicle's passenger compartment and found cocaine inside a jacket that lay on the backseat. This Court upheld the search as reasonable incident to the occupants' arrests. In an opinion that repeatedly stressed the need for a "straightforward," "workable rule" to guide police conduct, the Court announced "that when a policeman has made a lawful custodial arrest of the occupant of an automobile, he may, as a contemporaneous incident of that arrest, search the passenger compartment of that automobile."

For years, *Belton* was widely understood to have set down a simple, bright-line rule. Numerous courts read the decision to authorize automobile searches incident to arrests of recent occupants, regardless of whether the arrestee in any particular case was within reaching distance of the vehicle at the time of the search. See Thornton v. United States, 541 U.S. 615, 628 (2004) (Scalia, J., concurring in judgment) (collecting cases). Even after the arrestee had stepped out of the vehicle and had been subdued by police, the prevailing understanding was that *Belton* still authorized a substantially contemporaneous search of the automobile's passenger compartment.

Not every court, however, agreed with this reading of *Belton*. In State v. Gant, 216 Ariz. 1, 162 P.3d 640 (2007), the Arizona Supreme Court considered an automobile search conducted after the vehicle's occupant had been arrested, handcuffed, and locked in a patrol car. The court distinguished *Belton* as a case in which "four unsecured" arrestees "presented an immediate risk of loss of evidence and an obvious threat to [a] lone officer's safety." The court held that where no such "exigencies exis[t]"—where the arrestee has been subdued and the scene secured—the rule of *Belton* does not apply.

This Court granted certiorari in *Gant*, and affirmed in a 5–to–4 decision. Arizona v. Gant [Casebook page 312]. Four of the Justices in the majority agreed with the Arizona Supreme Court that Belton's holding applies only where "the arrestee is unsecured and within reaching distance of the passenger compartment at the time of the search." The four dissenting Justices, by contrast, understood *Belton* to have explicitly adopted the simple, bright-line rule stated in the *Belton* Court's opinion. (opinion of Alito, J.). To limit *Belton* to cases involving unsecured arrestees, the dissenters thought, was to overrule the decision's clear holding. Justice Scalia, who provided the fifth vote to affirm in *Gant*, agreed with the dissenters' understanding of *Belton's* holding. Justice Scalia favored a more explicit and complete overruling of *Belton*, but he joined what became the majority opinion to avoid "a 4–to–1–to–4" disposition .. As a result, the Court adopted a new, two-part rule under which an automobile search incident to a recent occupant's arrest is constitutional (1) if the arrestee is within reaching distance of the vehicle during the search, or (2) if the police have reason to believe that the vehicle contains "evidence relevant to the crime of arrest."

B

The search at issue in this case took place a full two years before this

Court announced its new rule in *Gant*. On an April evening in 2007, police officers in Greenville, Alabama, conducted a routine traffic stop that eventually resulted in the arrests of driver Stella Owens (for driving while intoxicated) and passenger Willie Davis (for giving a false name to police). The police handcuffed both Owens and Davis, and they placed the arrestees in the back of separate patrol cars. The police then searched the passenger compartment of Owens's vehicle and found a revolver inside Davis's jacket pocket.

Davis was indicted in the Middle District of Alabama on one count of possession of a firearm by a convicted felon. In his motion to suppress the revolver, Davis acknowledged that the officers' search fully complied with "existing Eleventh Circuit precedent." Like most courts, the Eleventh Circuit had long read *Belton* to establish a bright-line rule authorizing substantially contemporaneous vehicle searches incident to arrests of recent occupants. Davis recognized that the District Court was obligated to follow this precedent, but he raised a Fourth Amendment challenge to preserve "the issue for review" on appeal. The District Court denied the motion, and Davis was convicted on the firearms charge.

While Davis's appeal was pending, this Court decided *Gant*. The Eleventh Circuit, in the opinion below, applied *Gant's* new rule and held that the vehicle search incident to Davis's arrest "violated [his] Fourth Amendment rights." 598 F. 3d 1259, 1263 (CA11 2010). As for whether this constitutional violation warranted suppression, the Eleventh Circuit viewed that as a separate issue that turned on "the potential of exclusion to deter wrongful police conduct." (quoting Herring v. United States, 555 U.S. 135, 137 (2009); internal quotation marks omitted). The court concluded that "penalizing the [arresting] officer" for following binding appellate precedent would do nothing to "dete[r] ... Fourth Amendment violations." It therefore declined to apply the exclusionary rule and affirmed Davis's conviction. We granted certiorari.

II

The Fourth Amendment * * * says nothing about suppressing evidence obtained in violation of this command. That rule—the exclusionary rule—is a "prudential" doctrine, Pennsylvania Bd. of Probation and Parole v. Scott, 524 U.S. 357, 363 (1998), created by this Court to "compel respect for the constitutional guaranty." Elkins v. United States, 364 U.S. 206, 217 (1960); see Weeks v. United States, 232 U.S. 383 (1914); Mapp v. Ohio, 367 U.S. 643 (1961). Exclusion is "not a personal constitutional right," nor is it designed to "redress the injury" occasioned by an unconstitutional search. Stone v. Powell, 428 U.S. 465, 486 (1976); see United States v. Janis, 428 U.S. 433, 454, n. 29 (1976) (exclusionary rule "unsupportable as reparation or compensatory dispensation to the injured criminal" (internal quotation marks omitted)). The rule's sole purpose, we have repeatedly held, is to deter future Fourth Amendment violations. United States v. Leon, 468 U.S. 897, 909, 921, n. 22 (1984); *Elkins,* supra, at 217 ("calculated to prevent, not to repair"). Our cases have thus limited the rule's operation to situations in which this purpose is "thought most efficaciously served." United States v. Calandra, 414 U.S. 338, 348 (1974). Where suppression

fails to yield "appreciable deterrence," exclusion is "clearly ... unwarranted." *Janis,* supra, at 454.

Real deterrent value is a "necessary condition for exclusion," but it is not "a sufficient" one. Hudson v. Michigan, 547 U.S. 586, 596 (2006). The analysis must also account for the "substantial social costs" generated by the rule. Exclusion exacts a heavy toll on both the judicial system and society at large. It almost always requires courts to ignore reliable, trustworthy evidence bearing on guilt or innocence. And its bottom-line effect, in many cases, is to suppress the truth and set the criminal loose in the community without punishment. See *Herring,* supra, at 141. Our cases hold that society must swallow this bitter pill when necessary, but only as a "last resort." *Hudson,* supra, at 591. For exclusion to be appropriate, the deterrence benefits of suppression must outweigh its heavy costs.

Admittedly, there was a time when our exclusionary-rule cases were not nearly so discriminating in their approach to the doctrine. "Expansive dicta" in several decisions, see *Hudson,* supra, at 591, suggested that the rule was a self-executing mandate implicit in the Fourth Amendment itself. See Olmstead v. United States, 277 U.S. 438, 462 (1928) (remarking on the "striking outcome of the *Weeks* case" that "the Fourth Amendment, although not referring to or limiting the use of evidence in courts, really forbade its introduction"); *Mapp,* supra, at 655 ("[A]ll evidence obtained by searches and seizures in violation of the Constitution is, by that same authority, inadmissible in a state court"). As late as our 1971 decision in Whiteley v. Warden, Wyo. State Penitentiary, 401 U.S. 560, 568–569, the Court "treated identification of a Fourth Amendment violation as synonymous with application of the exclusionary rule." Arizona v. Evans, 514 U.S. 1, 13 (1995). In time, however, we came to acknowledge the exclusionary rule for what it undoubtedly is—a "judicially created remedy" of this Court's own making. *Calandra,* supra, at 348. We abandoned the old, "reflexive" application of the doctrine, and imposed a more rigorous weighing of its costs and deterrence benefits. Evans, supra, at 13; INS v. Lopez–Mendoza, 468 U.S. 1032 (1984); United States v. Havens, 446 U.S. 620 (1980). In a line of cases beginning with United States v. Leon, 468 U.S. 897, we also recalibrated our cost-benefit analysis in exclusion cases to focus the inquiry on the "flagrancy of the police misconduct" at issue.

The basic insight of the *Leon* line of cases is that the deterrence benefits of exclusion "var[y] with the culpability of the law enforcement conduct" at issue. *Herring,* 555 U.S., at 143. When the police exhibit "deliberate," "reckless," or "grossly negligent" disregard for Fourth Amendment rights, the deterrent value of exclusion is strong and tends to outweigh the resulting costs. But when the police act with an objectively "reasonable good-faith belief" that their conduct is lawful, *Leon,* supra, at 909, or when their conduct involves only simple, "isolated" negligence, *Herring,* supra, at 137, the "deterrence rationale loses much of its force, "and exclusion cannot "pay its way." See *Leon,* supra, at 919, 908, n. 6 (quoting United States v. Peltier, 422 U.S. 531, 539 (1975)).

The Court has over time applied this "good-faith" exception across a range of cases. *Leon* itself, for example, held that the exclusionary rule

does not apply when the police conduct a search in "objectively reasonable reliance" on a warrant later held invalid. The error in such a case rests with the issuing magistrate, not the police officer, and "punish[ing] the errors of judges" is not the office of the exclusionary rule. See also Massachusetts v. Sheppard, 468 U.S. 981, 990 (1984) (companion case declining to apply exclusionary rule where warrant held invalid as a result of judge's clerical error).

Other good-faith cases have sounded a similar theme. Illinois v. Krull, 480 U.S. 340 (1987), extended the good-faith exception to searches conducted in reasonable reliance on subsequently invalidated statutes. Id., at 349–350 ("legislators, like judicial officers, are not the focus of the rule"). In Arizona v. Evans, supra, the Court applied the good-faith exception in a case where the police reasonably relied on erroneous information concerning an arrest warrant in a database maintained by judicial employees. Most recently, in Herring v. United States, 555 U.S. 135, we extended *Evans* in a case where police employees erred in maintaining records in a warrant database. "[I]solated," "nonrecurring" police negligence, we determined, lacks the culpability required to justify the harsh sanction of exclusion.

III

The question in this case is whether to apply the exclusionary rule when the police conduct a search in objectively reasonable reliance on binding judicial precedent. At the time of the search at issue here, we had not yet decided Arizona v. Gant. * * * Although the search turned out to be unconstitutional under *Gant,* all agree that the officers' conduct was in strict compliance with then-binding Circuit law and was not culpable in any way.

Under our exclusionary-rule precedents, this acknowledged absence of police culpability dooms Davis's claim. Police practices trigger the harsh sanction of exclusion only when they are deliberate enough to yield meaningful deterrence, and culpable enough to be "worth the price paid by the justice system." *Herring*, 555 U.S., at 144. The conduct of the officers here was neither of these things. The officers who conducted the search did not violate Davis's Fourth Amendment rights deliberately, recklessly, or with gross negligence. Nor does this case involve any "recurring or systemic negligence" on the part of law enforcement. The police acted in strict compliance with binding precedent, and their behavior was not wrongful. Unless the exclusionary rule is to become a strict-liability regime, it can have no application in this case.

Indeed, in 27 years of practice under *Leon's* good-faith exception, we have never applied the exclusionary rule to suppress evidence obtained as a result of nonculpable, innocent police conduct. If the police in this case had reasonably relied on a warrant in conducting their search, see *Leon*, supra, or on an erroneous warrant record in a government database, *Herring*, supra, the exclusionary rule would not apply. And if Congress or the Alabama Legislature had enacted a statute codifying the precise holding of [*Belton*] we would swiftly conclude that "[p]enalizing the officer for the legislature's error . . . cannot logically contribute to the deterrence of Fourth Amendment violations." See *Krull*, 480 U.S., at 350. The same should be true of Davis's attempt here to penalize the officer for the appellate judges' error.

About all that exclusion would deter in this case is conscientious police work. Responsible law-enforcement officers will take care to learn "what is required of them" under Fourth Amendment precedent and will conform their conduct to these rules. *Hudson*, 547 U.S., at 599. But by the same token, when binding appellate precedent specifically authorizes a particular police practice, well-trained officers will and should use that tool to fulfill their crime-detection and public-safety responsibilities. An officer who conducts a search in reliance on binding appellate precedent does no more than act as a reasonable officer would and should act under the circumstances. The deterrent effect of exclusion in such a case can only be to discourage the officer from doing his duty.

That is not the kind of deterrence the exclusionary rule seeks to foster. We have stated before, and we reaffirm today, that the harsh sanction of exclusion should not be applied to deter objectively reasonable law enforcement activity. Evidence obtained during a search conducted in reasonable reliance on binding precedent is not subject to the exclusionary rule.

IV

Justice Breyer's dissent and Davis argue that, although the police conduct in this case was in no way culpable, other considerations should prevent the good-faith exception from applying. We are not persuaded.

A

1

The principal argument of both the dissent and Davis is that the exclusionary rule's availability to enforce new Fourth Amendment precedent is a retroactivity issue, see Griffith v. Kentucky, 479 U.S. 314 (1987), not a good-faith issue. They contend that applying the good-faith exception where police have relied on overruled precedent effectively revives the discarded retroactivity regime of Linkletter v. Walker, 381 U.S. 618 (1965).

In *Linkletter*, we held that the retroactive effect of a new constitutional rule of criminal procedure should be determined on a case-by-case weighing of interests. For each new rule, *Linkletter* required courts to consider a three-factor balancing test that looked to the "purpose" of the new rule, "reliance" on the old rule by law enforcement and others, and the effect retroactivity would have "on the administration of justice." 381 U.S., at 636. After "weigh[ing] the merits and demerits in each case," courts decided whether and to what extent a new rule should be given retroactive effect. Id., at 629. In *Linkletter* itself, the balance of interests prompted this Court to conclude that Mapp v. Ohio, 367 U.S. 643—which incorporated the exclusionary rule against the States—should not apply retroactively to cases already final on direct review. The next year, we extended *Linkletter* to retroactivity determinations in cases on direct review. See Johnson v. New Jersey, 384 U.S. 719, 733 (1966) (holding that Miranda v. Arizona, 384 U.S. 436 (1966), and Escobedo v. Illinois, 378 U.S. 478 (1964), applied retroactively only to trials commenced after the decisions were released).

Over time, *Linkletter* proved difficult to apply in a consistent, coherent way. Individual applications of the standard "produced strikingly divergent results," see Danforth v. Minnesota, 552 U.S. 264, 273 (2008), that many saw as "incompatible" and

"inconsistent." Desist v. United States, 394 U.S. 244, 258 (1969) (Harlan, J., dissenting). Justice Harlan in particular, who had endorsed the *Linkletter* standard early on, offered a strong critique in which he argued that "basic judicial" norms required full retroactive application of new rules to all cases still subject to direct review. 394 U.S., at 258–259; see also Mackey v. United States, 401 U.S. 667, 675–702 (1971) (Harlan, J., concurring in part and dissenting in part). Eventually, and after more than 20 years of toil under *Linkletter*, the Court adopted Justice Harlan's view and held that newly announced rules of constitutional criminal procedure must apply "retroactively to all cases, state or federal, pending on direct review or not yet final, with no exception." *Griffith*, supra, at 328.

2

The dissent and Davis argue that applying the good-faith exception in this case is "incompatible" with our retroactivity precedent under *Griffith*. We think this argument conflates what are two distinct doctrines.

Our retroactivity jurisprudence is concerned with whether, as a categorical matter, a new rule is available on direct review as a *potential* ground for relief. Retroactive application under *Griffith* lifts what would otherwise be a categorical bar to obtaining redress for the government's violation of a newly announced constitutional rule. See *Danforth*, supra, at 271, n. 5 (noting that it may "make more sense to speak in terms of the 'redressability' of violations of new rules, rather than the 'retroactivity' of such new rules"). Retroactive application does not, however, determine what "appropriate remedy" (if any) the defendant should obtain.

See *Powell v. Nevada*, 511 U.S. 79, 84 (1994) (noting that it "does not necessarily follow" from retroactive application of a new rule that the defendant will "gain . . . relief"). Remedy is a separate, analytically distinct issue. As a result, the retroactive application of a new rule of substantive Fourth Amendment law raises the question whether a suppression remedy applies; it does not answer that question. See *Leon*, 468 U.S., at 906 ("Whether the exclusionary sanction is appropriately imposed in a particular case . . . is 'an issue separate from the question whether the Fourth Amendment rights of the party seeking to invoke the rule were violated by police conduct' ").

When this Court announced its decision in *Gant*, Davis's conviction had not yet become final on direct review. *Gant* therefore applies retroactively to this case. Davis may invoke its newly announced rule of substantive Fourth Amendment law as a basis for seeking relief. See *Griffith*, supra, at 326, 328. The question, then, becomes one of remedy, and on that issue Davis seeks application of the exclusionary rule. But exclusion of evidence does not automatically follow from the fact that a Fourth Amendment violation occurred. The remedy is subject to exceptions and applies only where its "purpose is effectively advanced." *Krull*, 480 U.S., at 347.

The dissent and Davis recognize that at least some of the established exceptions to the exclusionary rule limit its availability in cases involving new Fourth Amendment rules. Suppression would thus be inappropriate, the dissent and Davis acknowledge, if the inevitable-discovery exception were applicable in this case. The good-faith exception, however, is no less an established

limit on the remedy of exclusion than is inevitable discovery. Its application here neither contravenes *Griffith* nor denies retroactive effect to *Gant*.

It is true that, under the old retroactivity regime of *Linkletter*, the Court's decisions on the "retroactivity problem in the context of the exclusionary rule" did take into account whether "law enforcement officers reasonably believed in good faith" that their conduct was in compliance with governing law. As a matter of retroactivity analysis, that approach is no longer applicable. See *Griffith*, 479 U.S. 314. It does not follow, however, that reliance on binding precedent is irrelevant in applying the good-faith exception to the exclusionary rule. * * * That reasonable reliance by police was once a factor in our retroactivity cases does not make it any less relevant under our Leon line of cases.

B

Davis also contends that applying the good-faith exception to searches conducted in reliance on binding precedent will stunt the development of Fourth Amendment law. With no possibility of suppression, criminal defendants will have no incentive, Davis maintains, to request that courts overrule precedent.

1

This argument is difficult to reconcile with our modern understanding of the role of the exclusionary rule. We have never held that facilitating the overruling of precedent is a relevant consideration in an exclusionary-rule case. Rather, we have said time and again that the sole purpose of the exclusionary rule is to deter misconduct by law enforcement.

We have also repeatedly rejected efforts to expand the focus of the exclusionary rule beyond deterrence of culpable police conduct. In *Leon,* for example, we made clear that "the exclusionary rule is designed to deter police misconduct rather than to punish the errors of judges." 468 U.S., at 916; see id., at 918 ("If exclusion of evidence obtained pursuant to a subsequently invalidated warrant is to have any deterrent effect ... it must alter the behavior of individual law enforcement officers or the policies of their departments"). *Krull* too noted that "legislators, like judicial officers, are not the focus" of the exclusionary rule. 480 U.S., at 350. And in *Evans,* we said that the exclusionary rule was aimed at deterring "police misconduct, not mistakes by court employees." 514 U.S., at 14. These cases do not suggest that the exclusionary rule should be modified to serve a purpose other than deterrence of culpable law-enforcement conduct.

2

And in any event, applying the good-faith exception in this context will not prevent judicial reconsideration of prior Fourth Amendment precedents. In most instances, as in this case, the precedent sought to be challenged will be a decision of a Federal Court of Appeals or State Supreme Court. But a good-faith exception for objectively reasonable reliance on binding precedent will not prevent review and correction of such decisions. This Court reviews criminal convictions from 12 Federal Courts of Appeals, 50 state courts of last resort, and the District of Columbia Court of Appeals. If one or even many of these courts uphold a particular type of search or seizure, defendants in jurisdictions in which the question remains open will still have

an undiminished incentive to litigate the issue. This Court can then grant certiorari, and the development of Fourth Amendment law will in no way be stunted.

Davis argues that Fourth Amendment precedents of this Court will be effectively insulated from challenge under a good-faith exception for reliance on appellate precedent. But this argument is overblown. For one thing, it is important to keep in mind that this argument applies to an exceedingly small set of cases. Decisions overruling this Court's Fourth Amendment precedents are rare. Indeed, it has been more than 40 years since the Court last handed down a decision of the type to which Davis refers. Chimel v. California, 395 U.S. 752 (overruling United States v. Rabinowitz, 339 U.S. 56 (1950), and Harris v. United States, 331 U.S. 145 (1947)). And even in those cases, Davis points out that no fewer than eight separate doctrines may preclude a defendant who successfully challenges an existing precedent from getting any relief. Moreover, as a practical matter, defense counsel in many cases will test this Court's Fourth Amendment precedents in the same way that *Belton* was tested in *Gant*—by arguing that the precedent is distinguishable.

At most, Davis's argument might suggest that—to prevent Fourth Amendment law from becoming ossified—the petitioner in a case that results in the overruling of one of this Court's Fourth Amendment precedents should be given the benefit of the victory by permitting the suppression of evidence in that one case. Such a result would undoubtedly be a windfall to this one random litigant. But the exclusionary rule is "not a personal constitutional right."

Stone, 428 U.S., at 486. It is a "judicially created" sanction, *Calandra,* 414 U.S., at 348, specifically designed as a "windfall" remedy to deter future Fourth Amendment violations. See *Stone,* supra, at 490. The good-faith exception is a judicially created exception to this judicially created rule. Therefore, in a future case, we could, if necessary, recognize a limited exception to the good-faith exception for a defendant who obtains a judgment overruling one of our Fourth Amendment precedents. Cf. Friendly, The Bill of Rights as a Code of Criminal Procedure, 53 Cal. L. Rev. 929, 952–953 (1965) ("[T]he same authority that empowered the Court to supplement the amendment by the exclusionary rule a hundred and twenty-five years after its adoption, likewise allows it to modify that rule as the lessons of experience may teach.")

But this is not such a case. Davis did not secure a decision overturning a Supreme Court precedent; the police in his case reasonably relied on binding Circuit precedent. That sort of blameless police conduct, we hold, comes within the good-faith exception and is not properly subject to the exclusionary rule.

————

It is one thing for the criminal "to go free because the constable has blundered." People v. Defore, 242 N.Y. 13, 21, 150 N.E. 585, 587 (1926) (Cardozo, J.). It is quite another to set the criminal free because the constable has scrupulously adhered to governing law. Excluding evidence in such cases deters no police misconduct and imposes substantial social costs. We therefore hold that when the police conduct a search in objectively reasonable reliance on binding appellate precedent, the exclusionary rule does not apply. The judgment of the Court of Appeals for the Eleventh Circuit is

Affirmed.

JUSTICE SOTOMAYOR, concurring in the judgment.

* * *

This case does not present the * * * question whether the exclusionary rule applies when the law governing the constitutionality of a particular search is unsettled. As we previously recognized in deciding whether to apply a Fourth Amendment holding retroactively, when police decide to conduct a search or seizure in the absence of case law (or other authority) specifically sanctioning such action, exclusion of the evidence obtained may deter Fourth Amendment violations:

"If, as the Government argues, all rulings resolving unsettled Fourth Amendment questions should be nonretroactive, then, in close cases, law enforcement officials would have little incentive to err on the side of constitutional behavior. Official awareness of the dubious constitutionality of a practice would be counterbalanced by official certainty that, so long as the Fourth Amendment law in the area remained unsettled, evidence obtained through the questionable practice would be excluded only in the one case definitively resolving the unsettled question." United States v. Johnson, 457 U.S. 537, 561 (1982).

In my view, whether an officer's conduct can be characterized as "culpable" is not itself dispositive. We have never refused to apply the exclusionary rule where its application would appreciably deter Fourth Amendment violations on the mere ground that the officer's conduct could be characterized as nonculpable. Rather, an officer's culpability is relevant because it may inform the overarching inquiry whether exclusion would result in appreciable deterrence. * * * Whatever we have said about culpability, the ultimate questions have always been, one, whether exclusion would result in appreciable deterrence and, two, whether the benefits of exclusion outweigh its costs. See, e.g., *Herring,* 555 U.S., at 141; *Krull,* 480 U.S., at 347.

As stated, whether exclusion would result in appreciable deterrence in the circumstances of this case is a different question from whether exclusion would appreciably deter Fourth Amendment violations when the governing law is unsettled. The Court's answer to the former question in this case thus does not resolve the latter one.

JUSTICE BREYER, **with whom** JUSTICE GINSBURG **joins, dissenting.**

* * *

I

I agree with the Court about whether Gant's new rule applies. It does apply. * * * The Court today, following *Griffith,* concludes that Gant's new rule applies here. And to that extent I agree with its decision.

II

The Court goes on, however, to decide how *Gant's* new rule will apply. And here it adds a fatal twist. While conceding that, like the search in *Gant,* this search violated the Fourth Amendment, it holds that, unlike *Gant* , this defendant is not entitled to a remedy. That is because the Court finds a new "good faith" exception which prevents application of the normal remedy for a Fourth Amendment violation, namely, sup-

pression of the illegally seized evidence. Leaving Davis with a right but not a remedy, the Court "keep[s] the word of promise to our ear" but "break[s] it to our hope."

A

At this point I can no longer agree with the Court. A new "good faith" exception and this Court's retroactivity decisions are incompatible. For one thing, the Court's distinction between (1) retroactive application of a new rule and (2) availability of a remedy is highly artificial and runs counter to precedent. To determine that a new rule is retroactive is to determine that, at least in the normal case, there is a remedy. As we have previously said, the "source of a 'new rule' is the Constitution itself, not any judicial power to create new rules of law"; hence, "[w]hat we are actually determining when we assess the 'retroactivity' of a new rule is not the temporal scope of a newly announced right, but whether a violation of the right that occurred prior to the announcement of the new rule will entitle a criminal defendant to the relief sought." Danforth v. Minnesota, 552 U.S. 264, 271 (2008). The Court's "good faith" exception (unlike, say, inevitable discovery, a remedial doctrine that applies only upon occasion) creates a categorical bar to obtaining redress in every case pending when a precedent is overturned.

For another thing, the Court's holding recreates the very problems that led the Court to abandon *Linkletter's* approach to retroactivity in favor of Griffith's . One such problem concerns workability. The Court says that its exception applies where there is "objectively reasonable" police "reliance on binding appellate precedent." But to apply the term "binding appellate precedent" often requires resolution of complex questions of degree. Davis conceded that he faced binding anti-*Gant* precedent in the Eleventh Circuit. But future litigants will be less forthcoming. Indeed, those litigants will now have to create distinctions to show that previous Circuit precedent was not "binding" lest they find relief foreclosed even if they win their constitutional claim.

At the same time, Fourth Amendment precedents frequently require courts to "slosh" their "way through the fact bound morass of 'reasonableness.' "Scott v. Harris, 550 U.S. 372, 383 (2007). Suppose an officer's conduct is consistent with the language of a Fourth Amendment rule that a court of appeals announced in a case with clearly distinguishable facts? Suppose the case creating the relevant precedent did not directly announce any general rule but involved highly analogous facts? What about a rule that all other jurisdictions, but not the defendant's jurisdiction, had previously accepted? What rules can be developed for determining when, where, and how these different kinds of precedents do, or do not, count as relevant "binding precedent"? The *Linkletter*-like result is likely complex legal argument and police force confusion.

Another such problem concerns fairness. Today's holding, like that in *Linkletter,* "violates basic norms of constitutional adjudication." *Griffith*, supra, at 322. It treats the defendant in a case announcing a new rule one way while treating similarly situated defendants whose cases are pending on appeal in a different way. Justice Harlan explained why this approach is wrong when he said:

> "We cannot release criminals from jail merely because we think one

case is a particularly appropriate one [to announce a constitutional doctrine] . . . . Simply fishing one case from the stream of appellate review, using it as a vehicle for pronouncing new constitutional standards, and then permitting a stream of similar cases subsequently to flow by unaffected by that new rule constitute an indefensible departure from [our ordinary] model of judicial review."

And in *Griffith*, the Court "embraced to a significant extent the comprehensive analysis presented by Justice Harlan." 479 U.S., at 322.

Of course, the Court may, as it suggests, avoid this unfairness by refusing to apply the exclusionary rule even to the defendant in the very case in which it announces a "new rule." But that approach would make matters worse. What would then happen in the lower courts? How would courts of appeals, for example, come to reconsider their prior decisions when other circuits' cases lead them to believe those decisions may be wrong? Why would a defendant seek to overturn any such decision? After all, if the (incorrect) circuit precedent is clear, then even if the defendant wins (on the constitutional question), he loses (on relief). To what extent then could this Court rely upon lower courts to work out Fourth Amendment differences among themselves—through circuit reconsideration of a precedent that other circuits have criticized?

B

Perhaps more important, the Court's rationale for creating its new "good faith" exception threatens to undermine well-settled Fourth Amendment law. The Court correctly says that pre-*Gant* Eleventh Circuit precedent had held that a Gant-type search was constitutional; hence the police conduct in this case, consistent with that precedent, was "innocent." But the Court then finds this fact sufficient to create a new "good faith" exception to the exclusionary rule. It reasons that the "sole purpose" of the exclusionary rule "is to deter future Fourth Amendment violations." The "deterrence benefits of exclusion vary with the culpability of the law enforcement conduct at issue." Those benefits are sufficient to justify exclusion where "police exhibit deliberate, reckless, or grossly negligent disregard for Fourth Amendment rights." But those benefits do not justify exclusion where, as here, the police act with "simple, isolated negligence" or an "objectively reasonable good-faith belief that their conduct is lawful."

If the Court means what it says, what will happen to the exclusionary rule, a rule that the Court adopted nearly a century ago for federal courts, and made applicable to state courts a half century ago through the Fourteenth Amendment, Mapp v. Ohio, 367 U.S. 643? The Court has thought of that rule not as punishment for the individual officer or as reparation for the individual defendant but more generally as an effective way to secure enforcement of the Fourth Amendment's commands. This Court has deviated from the "suppression" norm in the name of "good faith" only a handful of times and in limited, atypical circumstances: where a magistrate has erroneously issued a warrant, United States v. Leon, 468 U.S. 897 (1984); where a database has erroneously informed police that they have a warrant, Arizona v. Evans, 514 U.S. 1 (1995), Herring v. United States, 555 U.S. 135 (2009); and where an un-

constitutional statute purported to authorize the search, Illinois v. Krull, 480 U.S. 340 (1987). See Herring, supra, at 142 ("good faith" exception inaptly named).

The fact that such exceptions are few and far between is understandable. Defendants frequently move to suppress evidence on Fourth Amendment grounds. In many, perhaps most, of these instances the police, uncertain of how the Fourth Amendment applied to the particular factual circumstances they faced, will have acted in objective good faith. Yet, in a significant percentage of these instances, courts will find that the police were wrong. And, unless the police conduct falls into one of the exceptions previously noted, courts have required the suppression of the evidence seized. 1 W. LaFave, Search and Seizure § 1.3, pp. 103–104 (4th ed. 2004) ("good faith" exception has not yet been applied to warrantless searches and seizures beyond the "rather special situations" of Evans, Herring, and Krull).

But an officer who conducts a search that he believes complies with the Constitution but which, it ultimately turns out, falls just outside the Fourth Amendment's bounds is no more culpable than an officer who follows erroneous "binding precedent." Nor is an officer more culpable where circuit precedent is simply suggestive rather than "binding," where it only describes how to treat roughly analogous instances, or where it just does not exist. Thus, if the Court means what it now says, if it would place determinative weight upon the culpability of an individual officer's conduct, and if it would apply the exclusionary rule only where a Fourth Amendment violation was "deliberate, reckless, or grossly negligent," then the "good faith" exception will swallow the exclusionary rule. Indeed, our broad dicta in *Herring*—dicta the Court repeats and expands upon today—may already be leading lower courts in this direction. See United States v. Julius, 610 F.3d 60, 66–67 (CA2 2010) (assuming warrantless search was unconstitutional and remanding for District Court to "perform the cost/benefit analysis required by Herring" and to consider "whether the degree of police culpability in this case rose beyond mere . . . negligence" before ordering suppression); United States v. Master, 614 F.3d 236, 243 (CA6 2010) ("[T]he *Herring* Court's emphasis seems weighed more toward preserving evidence for use in obtaining convictions, even if illegally seized unless the officers engage in deliberate, reckless, or grossly negligent conduct"). Today's decision will doubtless accelerate this trend.

Any such change (which may already be underway) would affect not an exceedingly small set of cases, but a very large number of cases, potentially many thousands each year. And since the exclusionary rule is often the only sanction available for a Fourth Amendment violation, the Fourth Amendment would no longer protect ordinary Americans from unreasonable searches and seizures. It would become a watered-down Fourth Amendment, offering its protection against only those searches and seizures that are egregiously unreasonable.

III

In sum, I fear that the Court's opinion will undermine the exclusionary rule. And I believe that the Court wrongly departs from *Griffith* regardless. Instead I would follow *Griffith*, apply *Gant's* rule retroactively to this case, and require suppression of the evidence. Such an approach is consistent with our precedent, and it would indeed affect no more than "an exceedingly small set of cases." Ante, at 18.

CHAPTER THREE

SELF-INCRIMINATION AND CONFESSIONS

■ ■ ■

III. FIFTH AMENDMENT LIMITATIONS ON CONFESSIONS

D. OPEN QUESTIONS AFTER *MIRANDA*

1. What Is Custody?

Page 725. Add after the headnote on *Alvarado*.

Relevance of the Age of a Child in the Custody Enquiry: J.D.B. v. North Carolina

J.D.B. v. NORTH CAROLINA

Supreme Court of the United States
131 S.Ct.2394

JUSTICE SOTOMAYOR **delivered the opinion of the Court.**

This case presents the question whether the age of a child subjected to police questioning is relevant to the custody analysis of Miranda v. Arizona, 384 U. S. 436 (1966). It is beyond dispute that children will often feel bound to submit to police questioning when an adult in the same circumstanccs would feel free to leave. Seeing no reason for police officers or courts to blind themselves to that commonsense reality, we hold that a child's age properly informs the *Miranda* custody analysis.

I

A

Petitioner J. D. B. was a 13–year-old, seventh-grade student attending class at Smith Middle School in Chapel Hill, North Carolina when he was removed from his classroom by a uniformed police officer, escorted to a closed-door conference room, and questioned by police for at least half an hour.

This was the second time that police questioned J. D. B. in the span of a week. Five days earlier, two home break-ins occurred, and various items were stolen. Police stopped and questioned J. D. B. after he was seen behind a residence in the neighborhood where the crimes occurred. That same day, police also spoke to J.

48

D. B.'s grandmother—his legal guardian—as well as his aunt.

Police later learned that a digital camera matching the description of one of the stolen items had been found at J. D. B.'s middle school and seen in J. D. B.'s possession. Investigator DiCostanzo, the juvenile investigator with the local police force who had been assigned to the case, went to the school to question J. D. B. Upon arrival, DiCostanzo informed the uniformed police officer on detail to the school (a so-called school resource officer), the assistant principal, and an administrative intern that he was there to question J. D. B. about the break-ins. Although DiCostanzo asked the school administrators to verify J. D. B.'s date of birth, address, and parent contact information from school records, neither the police officers nor the school administrators contacted J. D. B.'s grandmother.

The uniformed officer interrupted J. D. B.'s afternoon social studies class, removed J. D. B. from the classroom, and escorted him to a school conference room. There, J. D. B. was met by DiCostanzo, the assistant principal, and the administrative intern. The door to the conference room was closed. With the two police officers and the two administrators present, J. D. B. was questioned for the next 30 to 45 minutes. Prior to the commencement of questioning, J. D. B. was given neither *Miranda* warnings nor the opportunity to speak to his grandmother. Nor was he informed that he was free to leave the room.

Questioning began with small talk—discussion of sports and J. D. B.'s family life. DiCostanzo asked, and J. D. B. agreed, to discuss the events of the prior weekend. Denying any wrongdoing, J. D. B. explained that he had been in the neighborhood where the crimes occurred because he was seeking work mowing lawns. DiCostanzo pressed J. D. B. for additional detail about his efforts to obtain work; asked J. D. B. to explain a prior incident, when one of the victims returned home to find J. D. B. behind her house; and confronted J. D. B. with the stolen camera. The assistant principal urged J. D. B. to "do the right thing," warning J. D. B. that "the truth always comes out in the end."

Eventually, J. D. B. asked whether he would "still be in trouble" if he returned the "stuff." In response, DiCostanzo explained that return of the stolen items would be helpful, but "this thing is going to court" regardless. ("[W]hat's done is done[;] now you need to help yourself by making it right"). DiCostanzo then warned that he may need to seek a secure custody order if he believed that J. D. B. would continue to break into other homes. When J. D. B. asked what a secure custody order was, DiCostanzo explained that "it's where you get sent to juvenile detention before court."

After learning of the prospect of juvenile detention, J. D. B. confessed that he and a friend were responsible for the break-ins. DiCostanzo only then informed J. D. B. that he could refuse to answer the investigator's questions and that he was free to leave. Asked whether he understood, J. D. B. nodded and provided further detail, including information about the location of the stolen items. Eventually J. D. B. wrote a statement, at DiCostanzo's request. When the bell rang indicating the end of the schoolday, J. D. B. was allowed to leave to catch the bus home.

B

Two juvenile petitions were filed against J. D. B., each alleging one count of breaking and entering and one count of larceny. J. D. B.'s public defender moved to suppress his statements and the evidence derived therefrom, arguing that suppression was necessary because J. D. B. had been "interrogated by police in a custodial setting without being afforded *Miranda* warning[s]" and because his statements were involuntary under the totality of the circumstances test. After a suppression hearing at which DiCostanzo and J. D. B. testified, the trial court denied the motion, deciding that J. D. B. was not in custody at the time of the schoolhouse interrogation and that his statements were voluntary. As a result, J. D. B. entered a transcript of admission to all four counts, renewing his objection to the denial of his motion to suppress, and the court adjudicated J. D. B. delinquent.

A divided panel of the North Carolina Court of Appeals affirmed. The North Carolina Supreme Court held, over two dissents, that J. D. B. was not in custody when he confessed, "declin[ing] to extend the test for custody to include consideration of the age . . . of an individual subjected to questioning by police."

We granted certiorari to determine whether the *Miranda* custody analysis includes consideration of a juvenile suspect's age.

II

A

Any police interview of an individual suspected of a crime has "coercive aspects to it." Oregon v. Mathiason, 429 U.S. 492, 495 (1977) (per curiam). Only those interrogations that occur while a suspect is in police custody, however, "heighte[n] the

risk" that statements obtained are not the product of the suspect's free choice. Dickerson v. United States, 530 U. S. 428, 435 (2000).

By its very nature, custodial police interrogation entails "inherently compelling pressures." *Miranda*, 384 U. S., at 467. Even for an adult, the physical and psychological isolation of custodial interrogation can undermine the individual's will to resist and compel him to speak where he would not otherwise do so freely. Indeed, the pressure of custodial interrogation is so immense that it "can induce a frighteningly high percentage of people to confess to crimes they never committed." Corley v. United States [Casebook page 697]. That risk is all the more troubling—and recent studies suggest, all the more acute—when the subject of custodial interrogation is a juvenile. See Brief for Center on Wrongful Convictions of Youth et al. as Amici Curiae 21–22 (collecting empirical studies that "illustrate the heightened risk of false confessions from youth").

Recognizing that the inherently coercive nature of custodial interrogation "blurs the line between voluntary and involuntary statements," *Dickerson,* 530 U.S., at 435, this Court in *Miranda* adopted a set of prophylactic measures designed to safeguard the constitutional guarantee against self-incrimination. Prior to questioning, a suspect must be warned that he has a right to remain silent, that any statement he does make may be used as evidence against him, and that he has a right to the presence of an attorney, either retained or appointed. And, if a suspect makes a statement during custodial interrogation, the burden is on the Government to show, as a prerequisite to the statement's admissibility as evidence in the Government's case in chief, that the defendant "voluntarily, knowingly and intelligently" waived his rights. *Miranda*, 384 U.S., at 444.

Because these measures protect the individual against the coercive nature of custodial interrogation, they are required "only where there has been such a restriction on a person's freedom as to render him in custody." Stansbury v. California, 511 U.S. 318, 322 (1994) (per curiam) (quoting Oregon v. Mathiason, 429 U.S. 492, 495 (1977) (per curiam)). As we have repeatedly emphasized, whether a suspect is "in custody" is an objective inquiry.

"Two discrete inquiries are essential to the determination: first, what were the circumstances surrounding the interrogation; and second, given those circumstances, would a reasonable person have felt he or she was at liberty to terminate the interrogation and leave. Once the scene is set and the players' lines and actions are reconstructed, the court must apply an objective test to resolve the ultimate inquiry: was there a formal arrest or restraint on freedom of movement of the degree associated with formal arrest." Thompson v. Keohane, 516 U.S. 99, 112 (1995). See also Yarborough v. Alvarado, 541 U.S. 652, 662–663 (2004); Stansbury, 511 U.S., at 323; Berkemer v. McCarty, 468 U.S. 420, 442, and n. 35 (1984). Rather than demarcate a limited set of relevant circumstances, we have required police officers and courts to "examine all of the circumstances surrounding the interrogation," *Stansbury*, 511 U.S., at 322, including any circumstance that "would have affected how a reasonable person" in the suspect's position "would perceive his or her freedom to leave." On the other hand, the "subjective views harbored by either the interrogating officers or the person being questioned" are irrelevant. Id., at 323. The test, in other words, involves no consideration of the "actual mindset" of the particular suspect subjected to police questioning. *Alvarado,* 541 U.S., at 667.

The benefit of the objective custody analysis is that it is "designed to give clear guidance to the police." *Alvarado,* 541 U.S., at 668. Police must make in-the-moment judgments as to when to administer *Miranda* warnings. By limiting analysis to the objective circumstances of the interrogation, and asking how a reasonable person in the suspect's position would understand his freedom to terminate questioning and leave, the objective test avoids burdening police with the task of anticipating the idiosyncrasies of every individual suspect and divining how those particular traits affect each person's subjective state of mind. See *Alvarado,* 541 U.S., at 668 (officers are under no duty "to consider . . . contingent psychological factors when deciding when suspects should be advised of their *Miranda* rights").

B

The State and its amici contend that a child's age has no place in the custody analysis, no matter how young the child subjected to police questioning. We cannot agree. In some circumstances, a child's age "would have affected how a reasonable person" in the suspect's position "would perceive his or her freedom to leave." *Stansbury,* 511 U.S., at 325. That is, a reasonable child subjected to police questioning will sometimes feel pressured to submit when a reasonable adult would feel free to go. We think it clear that courts can account for that reality without doing any damage to the objective nature of the custody analysis.

A child's age is far "more than a chronological fact." Eddings v. Oklahoma, 455 U.S. 104, 115 (1982); Roper v. Simmons, 543 U.S. 551, 569 (2005). It is a fact that "generates commonsense conclusions about behavior and perception." *Alvarado*, 541 U.S., at 674 (Breyer, J., dissenting). Such conclusions apply broadly to children as a class. And, they are self-evident to anyone who was a child once himself, including any police officer or judge.

Time and again, this Court has drawn these commonsense conclusions for itself. We have observed that children "generally are less mature and responsible than adults," *Eddings*, 455 U.S., at 115–116; that they "often lack the experience, perspective, and judgment to recognize and avoid choices that could be detrimental to them," Bellotti v. Baird, 443 U.S. 622, 635 (1979) (plurality opinion); that they "are more vulnerable or susceptible to . . . outside pressures" than adults, Roper, 543 U.S., at 569; and so on. Addressing the specific context of police interrogation, we have observed that events that "would leave a man cold and unimpressed can overawe and overwhelm a lad in his early teens." Haley v. Ohio, 332 U.S. 596, 599 (1948) (plurality opinion); see also Gallegos v. Colorado, 370 U.S. 49, 54 (1962) ("[N]o matter how sophisticated," a juvenile subject of police interrogation "cannot be compared" to an adult subject). Describing no one child in particular, these observations restate what "any parent knows"— indeed, what any person knows— about children generally. Roper, 543 U.S., at 569.

Our various statements to this effect are far from unique. The law has historically reflected the same assumption that children characteristically lack the capacity to exercise mature judgment and possess only an incomplete ability to understand the world around them. See, e.g., 1 W. Blackstone, Commentaries on the Laws of England *464–*465 (hereinafter Blackstone) (explaining that limits on children's legal capacity under the common law "secure them from hurting themselves by their own improvident acts"). Like this Court's own generalizations, the legal disqualifications placed on children as a class—e.g., limitations on their ability to alienate property, enter a binding contract enforceable against them, and marry without parental consent—exhibit the settled understanding that the differentiating characteristics of youth are universal.

Indeed, even where a "reasonable person" standard otherwise applies, the common law has reflected the reality that children are not adults. In negligence suits, for instance, where liability turns on what an objectively reasonable person would do in the circumstances, "[a]ll American jurisdictions accept the idea that a person's childhood is a relevant circumstance" to be considered. Restatement (Third) of Torts § 10, Comment b, p. 117 (2005); Restatement (Second) of Torts § 283A, Comment b, p. 15 (1963–1964) ("[T]here is a wide basis of community experience upon which it is possible, as a practical matter, to determine what is to be expected of [children]").

As this discussion establishes, "[o]ur history is replete with laws and judicial recognition" that children cannot be viewed simply as miniature adults. *Eddings*, 455 U.S., at 115–116. We see no justification for taking a different course here. So long as the child's age was known to the officer at the time of the interview, or would have been objectively apparent to any reasonable officer, including age as part of the custody analysis requires officers neither to consider circumstances "unknowable" to them, *Berkemer*, 468 U.S., at 430, nor to "anticipat[e] the frailties or idiosyncrasies" of the particular suspect whom they question, *Alvarado*, 541 U.S., at 662. The same "wide basis of community experience" that makes it possible, as an objective matter, "to determine what is to be expected" of children in other contexts, Restatement (Second) of Torts § 283A, at 15; likewise makes it possible to know what to expect of children subjected to police questioning.

In other words, a child's age differs from other personal characteristics that, even when known to police, have no objectively discernible relationship to a reasonable person's understanding of his freedom of action. *Alvarado*, holds, for instance, that a suspect's prior interrogation history with law enforcement has no role to play in the custody analysis because such experience could just as easily lead a reasonable person to feel free to walk away as to feel compelled to stay in place. Because the effect in any given case would be contingent on the psychology of the individual suspect, the Court explained, such experience cannot be considered without compromising the objective nature of the custody analysis. A child's age, however, is different. Precisely because childhood yields objective conclusions like those we have drawn ourselves—among others, that children are "most susceptible to influence," *Eddings*, 455 U. S.,

at 115, and "outside pressures," *Roper*, 543 U.S., at 569—considering age in the custody analysis in no way involves a determination of how youth "subjectively affect[s] the mindset" of any particular child.

In fact, in many cases involving juvenile suspects, the custody analysis would be nonsensical absent some consideration of the suspect's age. This case is a prime example. Were the court precluded from taking J. D. B.'s youth into account, it would be forced to evaluate the circumstances present here through the eyes of a reasonable person of average years. In other words, how would a reasonable adult understand his situation, after being removed from a seventh-grade social studies class by a uniformed school resource officer; being encouraged by his assistant principal to "do the right thing"; and being warned by a police investigator of the prospect of juvenile detention and separation from his guardian and primary caretaker? To describe such an inquiry is to demonstrate its absurdity. Neither officers nor courts can reasonably evaluate the effect of objective circumstances that, by their nature, are specific to children without accounting for the age of the child subjected to those circumstances.

Indeed, although the dissent suggests that concerns "regarding the application of the *Miranda* custody rule to minors can be accommodated by considering the unique circumstances present when minors are questioned in school," (opinion of Alito, J.), the effect of the schoolhouse setting cannot be disentangled from the identity of the person questioned. A student—whose presence at school is compulsory and whose disobedience at school is cause for disciplinary action—is in a far different position than, say, a parent volunteer on school grounds to chaperone an event, or an adult from the community on school grounds to attend a basketball game. Without asking whether the person "questioned in school" is a "minor," the coercive effect of the schoolhouse setting is unknowable.

Our prior decision in *Alvarado* in no way undermines these conclusions. In that case, we held that a state-court decision that failed to mention a 17–year-old's age as part of the *Miranda* custody analysis was not objectively unreasonable under the deferential standard of review set forth by the Antiterrorism and Effective Death Penalty Act of 1996 (AEDPA), 110 Stat. 1214. [W]e observed that accounting for a juvenile's age in the *Miranda* custody analysis "could be viewed as creating a subjective inquiry," 541 U.S., at 668. We said nothing, however, of whether such a view would be correct under the law. Cf. Renico v. Lett, 559 U.S. ___, ___, n. 3 (2010) (slip op., at 11, n. 3) ("[W]hether the [state court] was right or wrong is not the pertinent question under AEDPA"). To the contrary, Justice O'Connor's concurring opinion explained that a suspect's age may indeed "be relevant to the 'custody' inquiry." *Alvarado,* 541 U.S., at 669.

Reviewing the question de novo today, we hold that so long as the child's age was known to the officer at the time of police questioning, or would have been objectively apparent to a reasonable officer, its inclusion in the custody analysis is consistent with the objective nature of that test. This is not to say that a child's age will be a determinative, or even a significant, factor in every case. (O'Connor, J., concurring) (explaining that a state-court decision omit-

ting any mention of the defendant's age was not unreasonable under AEDPA's deferential standard of review where the defendant "was almost 18 years old at the time of his interview"). It is, however, a reality that courts cannot simply ignore.

III

The State and its amici offer numerous reasons that courts must blind themselves to a juvenile defendant's age. None is persuasive.

To start, the State contends that a child's age must be excluded from the custody inquiry because age is a personal characteristic specific to the suspect himself rather than an "external" circumstance of the interrogation. Despite the supposed significance of this distinction, however, at oral argument counsel for the State suggested without hesitation that at least some undeniably personal characteristics—for instance, whether the individual being questioned is blind—are circumstances relevant to the custody analysis. Thus, the State's quarrel cannot be that age is a personal characteristic, without more.

The State further argues that age is irrelevant to the custody analysis because it "go[es] to how a suspect may internalize and perceive the circumstances of an interrogation." But the same can be said of every objective circumstance that the State agrees is relevant to the custody analysis: Each circumstance goes to how a reasonable person would "internalize and perceive" every other. Indeed, this is the very reason that we ask whether the objective circumstances "add up to custody," *Keohane*, 516 U.S., at 113, instead of evaluating the circumstances one by one.

In the same vein, the State and its amici protest that the "effect of . . . age on [the] perception of custody is internal," or "psychological." But the whole point of the custody analysis is to determine whether, given the circumstances, "a reasonable person [would] have felt he or she was . . . at liberty to terminate the interrogation and leave." *Keohane,* 516 U.S., at 112. Because the *Miranda* custody inquiry turns on the mindset of a reasonable person in the suspect's position, it cannot be the case that a circumstance is subjective simply because it has an "internal" or "psychological" impact on perception. Were that so, there would be no objective circumstances to consider at all.

Relying on our statements that the objective custody test is "designed to give clear guidance to the police," *Alvarado,* 541 U.S., at 668, the State next argues that a child's age must be excluded from the analysis in order to preserve clarity. Similarly, the dissent insists that the clarity of the custody analysis will be destroyed unless a "one-size-fits-all reasonable-person test" applies. In reality, however, ignoring a juvenile defendant's age will often make the inquiry more artificial, and thus only add confusion. And in any event, a child's age, when known or apparent, is hardly an obscure factor to assess. Though the State and the dissent worry about gradations among children of different ages, that concern cannot justify ignoring a child's age altogether. Just as police officers are competent to account for other objective circumstances that are a matter of degree such as the length of questioning or the number of officers present, so too are they competent to evaluate the effect of relative age. * * * The same is true of judges, including

those whose childhoods have long since passed. In short, officers and judges need no imaginative powers, knowledge of developmental psychology, training in cognitive science, or expertise in social and cultural anthropology to account for a child's age. They simply need the common sense to know that a 7–year-old is not a 13–year-old and neither is an adult.

There is, however, an even more fundamental flaw with the State's plea for clarity and the dissent's singular focus on simplifying the analysis: Not once have we excluded from the custody analysis a circumstance that we determined was relevant and objective, simply to make the fault line between custodial and noncustodial "brighter." Indeed, were the guiding concern clarity and nothing else, the custody test would presumably ask only whether the suspect had been placed under formal arrest. But we have rejected that "more easily administered line," recognizing that it would simply "enable the police to circumvent the constraints on custodial interrogations established by *Miranda.*"

Finally, the State and the dissent suggest that excluding age from the custody analysis comes at no cost to juveniles' constitutional rights because the due process voluntariness test independently accounts for a child's youth. To be sure, that test permits consideration of a child's age, and it erects its own barrier to admission of a defendant's inculpatory statements at trial. See *Haley,* 332 U.S., at 599–601. But *Miranda*'s procedural safeguards exist precisely because the voluntariness test is an inadequate barrier when custodial interrogation is at stake. See *Dickerson,* 530 U.S., at 442 ("[R]eliance on the traditional totality-of-the-circumstances test raise[s] a risk of overlooking an involuntary custodial confession"). To hold, as the State requests, that a child's age is never relevant to whether a suspect has been taken into custody—and thus to ignore the very real differences between children and adults—would be to deny children the full scope of the procedural safeguards that *Miranda* guarantees to adults.

———

The question remains whether J. D. B. was in custody when police interrogated him. We remand for the state courts to address that question, this time taking account of all of the relevant circumstances of the interrogation, including J. D. B.'s age at the time. The judgment of the North Carolina Supreme Court is reversed, and the case is remanded for proceedings not inconsistent with this opinion.

It is so ordered.

JUSTICE ALITO, with whom THE CHIEF JUSTICE, JUSTICE SCALIA, AND JUSTICE THOMAS join, dissenting.

The Court's decision in this case may seem on first consideration to be modest and sensible, but in truth it is neither. It is fundamentally inconsistent with one of the main justifications for the *Miranda* rule: the perceived need for a clear rule that can be easily applied in all cases. And today's holding is not needed to protect the constitutional rights of minors who are questioned by the police.

Miranda's prophylactic regime places a high value on clarity and certainty. Dissatisfied with the highly fact-specific constitutional rule against the admission of in-voluntary confessions, the *Miranda* Court set down rigid standards that often require courts to ignore personal characteristics that may be highly relevant to a particular suspect's actual susceptibility to police pressure. This rigidity, however, has brought with it one of *Miranda*'s principal strengths—"the ease and clarity of its application" by law enforcement officials and courts. See Moran v. Burbine, 475 U.S. 412, 425–426 (1986). A key contributor to this clarity, at least up until now, has been *Miranda*'s objective reasonable-person test for determining custody.

Miranda's custody requirement is based on the proposition that the risk of unconstitutional coercion is heightened when a suspect is placed under formal arrest or is subjected to some functionally equivalent limitation on freedom of movement. When this custodial threshold is reached, *Miranda* warnings must precede police questioning. But in the interest of simplicity, the custody analysis considers only whether, under the circumstances, a hypothetical reasonable person would consider himself to be confined.

Many suspects, of course, will differ from this hypothetical reasonable person. Some, including those who have been hardened by past interrogations, may have no need for *Miranda* warnings at all. And for other suspects—those who are unusually sensitive to the pressures of police questioning—*Miranda* warnings may come too late to be of any use. That is a necessary consequence of *Miranda*'s rigid standards, but it does not mean that the constitutional rights of these especially sensitive suspects are left unprotected. A vulnerable defendant can still turn to the constitutional rule against actual coercion and contend that that his confession was extracted against his will.

Today's decision shifts the *Miranda* custody determination from a one-size-fits-all reasonable-person test into an inquiry that must account for at least one individualized characteristic—age—that is thought to correlate with susceptibility to coercive pressures. Age, however, is in no way the only personal characteristic that may correlate with pliability, and in future cases the Court will be forced to choose between two unpalatable alternatives. It may choose to limit today's decision by arbitrarily distinguishing a suspect's age from other personal characteristics—such as intelligence, education, occupation, or prior experience with law enforcement—that may also correlate with susceptibility to coercive pressures. Or, if the Court is unwilling to draw these arbitrary lines, it will be forced to effect a fundamental transformation of the *Miranda* custody test—from a clear, easily applied prophylactic rule into a highly fact-intensive standard resembling the voluntariness test that the *Miranda* Court found to be unsatisfactory.

For at least three reasons, there is no need to go down this road. First, many minors subjected to police interrogation are near the age of majority, and for these suspects the one-size-fits-all *Miranda* custody rule may not be a bad fit. Second, many of the difficulties in applying the *Miranda* custody rule to minors arise because of the unique circumstances present when the police conduct interrogations at school. The *Miranda* custody rule has always taken into account the setting in which questioning occurs, and accounting for the school setting in such cases will address many of these problems. Third, in cases like the one now before us, where the suspect is especially young, courts applying the constitu-tional voluntariness standard can take special care to ensure that incriminating statements were not obtained through coercion.

Safeguarding the constitutional rights of minors does not require the extreme makeover of *Miranda* that today's decision may portend.

I

* * *

II

* * *

A

* * * I do not dispute that many suspects who are under 18 will be more susceptible to police pressure than the average adult. * * * It is no less a "reality," however, that many persons over the age of 18 are also more susceptible to police pressure than the hypothetical reasonable person. Yet the *Miranda* custody standard has never accounted for the personal characteristics of these or any other individual defendants.

Indeed, it has always been the case under *Miranda* that the unusually meek or compliant are subject to the same fixed rules, including the same custody requirement, as those who are unusually resistant to police pressure. *Berkemer,* 468 U.S., at 442, and n. 35 ("[O]nly relevant inquiry is how a reasonable man in the suspect's position would have understood his situation"). *Miranda*'s rigid standards are both overinclusive and underinclusive. They are overinclusive to the extent that they provide a windfall to the most hardened and savvy of suspects, who often have no need for *Miranda*'s protections. And *Miranda*'s requirements are underinclusive to the extent that they fail to account for "frailties," "idiosyncrasies," and other individualized considerations that might cause a person to bend more easily during a confrontation with the police. Members of this Court have seen this rigidity as a major weakness in *Miranda*'s "code of rules for confessions." See 384 U.S., at 504 (Harlan, J., dissenting). But if it is, then the weakness is an inescapable consequence of the *Miranda* Court's decision to supplement the more holistic voluntariness requirement with a one-size-fits-all prophylactic rule.

That is undoubtedly why this Court's *Miranda* cases have never before mentioned "the suspect's age" or any other individualized consideration in applying the custody standard. See *Alvarado*, supra, at 666. And unless the *Miranda* custody rule is now to be radically transformed into one that takes into account the wide range of individual characteristics that are relevant in determining whether a confession is voluntary, the Court must shoulder the burden of explaining why age is different from these other personal characteristics.

Why, for example, is age different from intelligence? Suppose that an officer, upon going to a school to question a student, is told by the principal that the student has an I. Q. of 75 and is in a special-education class. Are those facts more or less important than the student's age in determining whether he or she felt at liberty to terminate the interrogation and leave? An I. Q. score, like age, is more than just a number. And an individual's intelligence can also yield "conclusions" similar to those "we have drawn ourselves" in cases far afield of *Miranda*. Compare ibid. (relying on Eddings v. Oklahoma, 455 U.S. 104 (1982), and Roper v. Simmons, 543 U.S. 551 (2005)), with Smith v. Texas, 543 U.S. 37, 44–45 (2004) (per curiam).

How about the suspect's cultural background? Suppose the police learn (or should have learned) that a suspect they wish to question is a recent immigrant from a country in which dire consequences often befall any person who dares to attempt to cut short any meeting with the police. Is this really less relevant than the fact that a suspect is a month or so away from his 18th birthday?

The defendant's education is another personal characteristic that may generate "conclusions about behavior and perception." Under today's decision, why should police officers and courts "blind themselves" to the fact that a suspect has only a fifth-grade education?. Alternatively, what if the police know or should know that the suspect is a college-educated man with law school training? How are these individual considerations meaningfully different from age in their "relationship to a reasonable person's understanding of his freedom of action"? Ante, at 11. The Court proclaims that "[a] child's age . . . is different," but the basis for this ipse dixit is dubious.

I have little doubt that today's decision will soon be cited by defendants—and perhaps by prosecutors as well—for the proposition that all manner of other individual characteristics should be treated like age and taken into account in the *Miranda* custody calculus. * * *

In time, the Court will have to confront these issues, and it will be faced with a difficult choice. It may choose to distinguish today's decision and adhere to the arbitrary proclamation that "age . . . is different." Or it may choose to extend today's holding and, in doing so, further undermine the very rationale for the *Miranda* regime.

B

If the Court chooses the latter course, then a core virtue of *Miranda*—the "ease and clarity of its application"—will be lost. However, even today's more limited departure from *Miranda*'s one-size-fits-all reasonable-person test will produce the very consequences that prompted the *Miranda* Court to abandon exclusive reliance on the voluntariness test in the first place: The Court's test will be hard for the police to follow, and it will be hard for judges to apply.

The Court holds that age must be taken into account when it "was known to the officer at the time of the interview," or when it "would have been objectively apparent" to a reasonable officer. The first half of this test overturns the rule that the initial determination of custody does not depend on the "subjective views harbored by . . . interrogating officers." *Stansbury*, 511 U.S., at 323. The second half will generate time-consuming satellite litigation over a reasonable officer's perceptions. When, as here, the interrogation takes place in school, the inquiry may be relatively simple. But not all police questioning of minors takes place in schools. In many cases, courts will presumably have to make findings as to whether a particular suspect had a sufficiently youthful look to alert a reasonable officer to the possibility that the suspect was under 18, or whether a reasonable officer would have recognized that a suspect's I. D. was a fake. The inquiry will be both "time-consuming and disruptive" for the police and the courts. See *Berkemer*, 468 U.S., at 432 (refusing to modify the custody test based on similar considerations). It will also be made all the more complicated by the fact that a suspect's dress and manner will often be different when the issue is litigated in court than it was at the time of the interrogation.

Even after courts clear this initial hurdle, further problems will likely emerge as judges attempt to put themselves in the shoes of the average 16–year-old, or 15–year-old, or 13–year-old, as the case may be. Consider, for example, a 60–year-old judge attempting to make a custody determination through the eyes of a hypothetical, average 15–year-old. Forty-five years of personal experience and societal change separate this judge from the days when he or she was 15 years old. And this judge may or may not have been an average 15–year-old. The Court's answer to these difficulties is to state that "no imaginative powers, knowledge of developmental psychology, [or] training in cognitive science" will be necessary. Judges "simply need the common sense," the Court assures, "to know that a 7–year-old is not a 13–year-old and neither is an adult." It is obvious, however, that application of the Court's new rule demands much more than this.

Take a fairly typical case in which today's holding may make a difference. A 16–year-old moves to suppress incriminating statements made prior to the administration of *Miranda* warnings. The circumstances are such that, if the defendant were at least 18, the court would not find that he or she was in custody, but the defendant argues that a reasonable 16–year-old would view the situation differently. The judge will not have the luxury of merely saying: "It is common sense that a 16–year-old is not an 18–year-old. Motion granted." Rather, the judge will be required to determine whether the differences between a typical 16–year-old and a typical 18–year-old with respect to susceptibility to the pressures of interrogation are sufficient to change the outcome of the custody determination. Today's opinion contains not a word of actual guidance as to how judges are supposed to go about making that determination.

C

* * *

III

The Court's decision greatly diminishes the clarity and administrability that have long been recognized as "principal advantages" of *Miranda*'s prophylactic requirements. But what is worse, the Court takes this step unnecessarily, as there are other, less disruptive tools available to ensure that minors are not coerced into confessing.

As an initial matter, the difficulties that the Court's standard introduces will likely yield little added protection for most juvenile defendants. Most juveniles who are subjected to police interrogation are teenagers nearing the age of majority. These defendants' reactions to police pressure are unlikely to be much different from the reaction of a typical 18–year-old in similar circumstances. A one-size-fits-all *Miranda* custody rule thus provides a roughly reasonable fit for these defendants.

In addition, many of the concerns that petitioner raises regarding the application of the *Miranda* custody rule to minors can be accommodated by considering the unique circumstances present when minors are questioned in school. The *Miranda* custody rule has always taken into account the setting in which questioning occurs, restrictions on a suspect's freedom of movement, and the presence of police officers or other authority figures. It can do so here as well.

Finally, in cases like the one now before us, where the suspect is much younger than the typical juvenile defendant, courts should be instructed to take particular care to ensure that incriminating statements were not obtained involuntarily. The voluntariness inquiry is flexible and accommodating by nature, and the Court's precedents already make clear that "special care" must be exercised in applying the voluntariness test where the confession of a "mere child" is at issue. *Haley*, 332 U.S., at 599 (plurality opinion). If *Miranda*'s rigid, one-size-fits-all standards fail to account for the unique needs of juveniles, the response should be to rigorously apply the constitutional rule against coercion to ensure that the rights of minors are protected. There is no need to run *Miranda* off the rails.

———

I respectfully dissent.

5. How Complete and Accurate Must the Warnings Be?

Page 741. Add at the end of the section.

Ambiguity About the Right to Have an Attorney Present
Throughout the Questioning: Florida v. Powell

FLORIDA v. POWELL
Supreme Court of the United States, 2010
130 S.Ct. 1195

JUSTICE GINSBURG **delivered the opinion of the Court.**

In a pathmarking decision, Miranda v. Arizona, the Court held that an individual must be "clearly informed," prior to custodial questioning, that he has, among other rights, "the right to consult with a lawyer and to have the lawyer with him during interrogation." The question presented in this case is whether advice that a suspect has "the right to talk to a lawyer before answering any of [the law enforcement officers'] questions," and that he can invoke this right "at any time ... *1200 during th[e] interview," satisfies *Miranda*. We hold that it does.

I

On August 10, 2004, law enforcement officers in Tampa, Florida, seeking to apprehend respondent Kevin Dewayne Powell in connection with a robbery investigation, entered an apartment rented by Powell's girlfriend. After spotting Powell coming from a bedroom, the officers searched the room and discovered a loaded nine-millimeter handgun under the bed. Ibid.

The officers arrested Powell and transported him to the Tampa Police headquarters. Once there, and before asking Powell any questions, the officers read Powell the standard Tampa Police Department Consent and Release Form 310. The form states:

"You have the right to remain silent. If you give up the right to remain silent, anything you say can be used against you in court. You have the right to talk to a lawyer before answering any of our questions. If you cannot afford to hire a lawyer, one will be appointed for you without cost and before any questioning. You have the right to use any of these rights at any time you want during this interview."

Acknowledging that he had been informed of his rights, that he "underst[oo]d them," and that he was "willing to talk" to the officers, Powell signed the form. He then admitted that he owned the handgun found in the apartment. Powell knew he was prohibited from possessing a gun because he had previously been convicted of a felony, but said he had nevertheless purchased and carried the firearm for his protection.

Powell was charged in state court with possession of a weapon by a prohibited possessor * * *. Contending that the *Miranda* warnings were deficient because they did not adequately convey his right to the presence of an attorney during questioning, he moved to suppress his inculpatory statements. The trial court denied the motion, concluding that the officers had properly notified Powell of his right to counsel. A jury convicted Powell of the gun-possession charge.

On appeal, the Florida Second District Court of Appeal held that the trial court should have suppressed Powell's statements. The *Miranda* warnings, the appellate court concluded, did not "adequately inform [Powell] of his ... right to have an attorney present throughout [the] interrogation." Considering the issue to be "one of great public importance," the court certified the following question to the Florida Supreme Court:

"Does the failure to provide express advice of the right to the presence of counsel during questioning vitiate *Miranda* warnings which advise of both (A) the right to talk to a lawyer 'before questioning' and (B) the 'right to use' the right to consult a lawyer 'at any time' during questioning?"

Surveying decisions of this Court as well as Florida precedent, the Florida Supreme Court answered the certified question in the affirmative. "Both *Miranda* and article I, section 9 of the Florida Constitution," the Florida High Court noted, "require that a suspect be clearly informed of the right to have a lawyer present during questioning." The court found that the advice Powell received was misleading because it suggested that Powell could "only consult with an attorney before questioning" and did not convey Powell's entitlement to counsel's presence throughout the interrogation. Nor, in the court's view, did the final catchall warning— "[y]ou have the right to use any of these rights at any time you want during this interview"—cure the defect the court perceived in the right-to-counsel advice: "The catch-all phrase did not supply the missing warning of the right to have counsel present during police questioning," the court stated, for "a right that has never been expressed cannot be reiterated."

* * *

We granted certiorari, and now reverse the judgment of the Florida Supreme Court.

II5TC

We first address Powell's contention that this Court lacks jurisdiction to hear this case because the Florida Supreme Court, by relying not only on *Miranda* but also on the Florida Constitution, rested its decision on an adequate and independent state ground. * * *

[W]e announced, in Michigan v. Long, 463 U.S. 1032, 1040–1041 (1983), the following presumption:

"[W]hen ... a state court decision fairly appears to rest primarily on federal law, or to be interwoven with the federal law, and when the adequacy and independence of any possible state law ground is not clear from the face of the opinion, we will accept as the most reasonable explanation that the state court decided the case the way it did because it believed that federal law required it to do so."

At the same time, we adopted a plain-statement rule to avoid the presumption: "If the state court decision indicates clearly and expressly that it is alternatively based on bona fide separate, adequate, and independent grounds, we, of course, will not undertake to review the decision."

Under the *Long* presumption, we have jurisdiction to entertain this case. Although invoking Florida's Constitution and precedent in addition to this Court's decisions, the Florida Supreme Court treated state and federal law as interchangeable and interwoven; the court at no point expressly asserted that state-law sources gave Powell rights distinct from, or broader than, those delineated in *Miranda*.

* * *

Powell notes that "state courts are absolutely free to interpret state constitutional provisions to accord greater protection to individual rights than do similar provisions of the United States Constitution." Powell is right in this regard. Nothing in our decision today, we emphasize, trenches on the Florida Supreme Court's authority to impose, based on the State's Constitution, any additional protections against coerced confessions it deems appropriate. But because the Florida Supreme Court's decision does not "indicat[e] clearly and expressly that it is alternatively based on bona fide separate, adequate, and independent [state] grounds," *Long*, we have jurisdiction to decide this case.

III

A

* * *

[In *Miranda*] we stated, as "an absolute prerequisite to interrogation," that an individual held for questioning "must be clearly informed that he has the right to consult with a lawyer and to have the lawyer with him during interrogation." The question before us is whether the warnings Powell received satisfied this requirement.

The four warnings *Miranda* requires are invariable, but this Court has not dictated the words in which the essential information must be conveyed. See California v. Prysock, 453 U.S. 355, 359, (1981) (per curiam) ("This Court has never indicat-ed that the rigidity of *Miranda* extends to the precise formulation of the warnings given a criminal defendant."). The inquiry is simply whether the warnings reasonably convey to a suspect his rights as required by *Miranda*.

B

[JUSTICE GINSBURG discusses the facts and results in California v. Prysock and Duckworth v. Eagan, both at page 741 of the Casebook].

The Tampa officers * * * informed Powell that he had "the right to talk to a lawyer before answering any of [their] questions" and "the right to use any of [his] rights at any time [he] want[ed] during th[e] interview." The first statement communicated that Powell could consult with a lawyer before answering any particular question, and the second statement confirmed that he could exercise that right while the interrogation was underway. In combination, the two warnings reasonably conveyed Powell's right to have an attorney present, not only at the outset of interrogation, but at all times.

To reach the opposite conclusion, i.e., that the attorney would not be present throughout the interrogation, the suspect would have to imagine an unlikely scenario: To consult counsel, he would be obliged to exit and reenter the interrogation room between each query. A reasonable suspect in a custodial setting who has just been read his rights, we believe, would not come to the counterintuitive conclusion that he is obligated, or allowed, to hop in and out of the holding area to seek his attorney's advice. Instead, the suspect would likely assume that he must stay put in the interrogation room and that his lawyer would be there with him the entire time.

The Florida Supreme Court found the warning misleading because it believed the temporal language—that Powell could "talk to a lawyer before answering any of [the officers'] questions"—suggested Powell could consult with an attorney only before the interrogation started. In context, however, the term "before" merely conveyed when Powell's right to an attorney became effective—namely, before he answered any questions at all. Nothing in the words used indicated that counsel's presence would be restricted after the questioning commenced. Instead, the warning communicated that the right to counsel carried forward to and through the interrogation: Powell could seek his attorney's advice before responding to "any of [the officers'] questions" and "at any time ... during th[e] interview." Although the warnings were not the clearest possible formulation of *Miranda's* right-to-counsel advisement, they were sufficiently comprehensive and comprehensible when given a commonsense reading.

Pursuing a different line of argument, Powell points out that most jurisdictions in Florida and across the Nation expressly advise suspects of the right to have counsel present both before and during interrogation. If we find the advice he received adequate, Powell suggests, law enforcement agencies, hoping to obtain uninformed waivers, will be tempted to end-run *Miranda* by amending their warnings to introduce ambiguity. But as the United States explained as amicus curiae in support of the State of Florida, "law enforcement agencies have little reason to assume the litigation risk of experimenting with novel *Miranda* formulations"; instead, it is "desirable police practice" and "in law enforcement's own

interest" to state warnings with maximum clarity.

For these reasons, "all ... federal law enforcement agencies explicitly advise ... suspect[s] of the full contours of each [*Miranda*] right, including the right to the presence of counsel during questioning." The standard warnings used by the Federal Bureau of Investigation are exemplary. They provide, in relevant part: "You have the right to talk to a lawyer for advice before we ask you any questions. You have the right to have a lawyer with you during questioning." This advice is admirably informative, but we decline to declare its precise formulation necessary to meet *Miranda's* requirements. Different words were used in the advice Powell received, but they communicated the same essential message.

———

For the reasons stated, the judgment of the Supreme Court of Florida is reversed, and the case is remanded for further proceedings not inconsistent with this opinion.

It is so ordered.

JUSTICE STEVENS, **with whom** JUSTICE BREYER **joins as to Part II, dissenting.**

Today, the Court decides a case in which the Florida Supreme Court held a local police practice violated the Florida Constitution. The Court's power to review that decision is doubtful at best; moreover, the Florida Supreme Court has the better view on the merits.

I

[JUSTICE STEVENS argues that the Florida Supreme Court's decision was independently grounded in Florida law and therefore that the Supreme Court did not have jurisdiction to hear the case.]

II

* * *

In this case, the form regularly used by the Tampa police warned Powell that he had "the right to talk to a lawyer before answering any of our questions." This informed him only of the right to consult with a lawyer before questioning, the very right the *Miranda* Court identified as insufficient to protect the Fifth Amendment privilege. The warning did not say anything about the right to have counsel present during interrogation. Although we have never required "rigidity in the form of the required warnings," California v. Prysock, this is, I believe, the first time the Court has approved a warning which, if given its natural reading, entirely omitted an essential element of a suspect's rights.

Despite the failure of the warning to mention it, in the Court's view the warning "reasonably conveyed" to Powell that he had the right to a lawyer's presence during the interrogation. The Court cobbles together this conclusion from two elements of the warning. First, the Court assumes the warning regarding Powell's right "to talk to a lawyer before answering any of [the officers'] questions" conveyed that "Powell could consult with a lawyer before answering any particular question." Second, in the Court's view, the addition of a catchall clause at the end of the recitation of rights "confirmed" that Powell could use his right to consult an attorney "while the interrogation was underway."

The more natural reading of the warning Powell was given, which (1) contained a temporal limit and (2) failed to mention his right to the presence of counsel in the interrogation room, is that Powell only had the right to consult with an attorney before the interrogation began, not that he had the right to have an attorney with him during questioning. * * *

When the relevant clause of the warning in this case is given its most natural reading, the catchall clause does not meaningfully clarify Powell's rights. It communicated that Powell could exercise the previously listed rights at any time. Yet the only previously listed right was the "right to talk to a lawyer *before* answering any of [the officers'] questions." Informing Powell that he could exercise, at any time during the interview, the right to talk to a lawyer *before* answering any questions did not reasonably convey the right to talk to a lawyer *after* answering some questions, much less implicitly inform Powell of his right to have a lawyer with him at all times during interrogation. An intelligent suspect could reasonably conclude that all he was provided was a one-time right to consult with an attorney, not a right to have an attorney present with him in the interrogation room at all times.

The Court relies on Duckworth v. Eagan, and *Prysock*, but in neither case did the warning at issue completely omit one of a suspect's rights. In *Prysock*, the warning regarding the right to an appointed attorney contained no temporal limitation, which clearly distinguishes that case from Powell's. In *Duckworth*, the suspect was explicitly informed that he had the right "to talk to a lawyer for advice before we ask you any questions, and to have him with you during questioning," and that he had "this right to the advice and presence of a lawyer even if you cannot afford to hire one." The warning thus conveyed in full the right to appointed counsel before and during the interrogation. Although the warning was arguably undercut by the addition of a statement that an attorney would be appointed "if and when you go to court," the Court found the suspect was informed of his full rights and the warning simply added additional, truthful information regarding when counsel would be appointed. Unlike the *Duckworth* warning, Powell's warning did not convey his *Miranda* rights in full with the addition of some arguably misleading statement. Rather, the warning entirely failed to inform him of the separate and distinct right "to have counsel present during any questioning."

In sum, the warning at issue in this case did not reasonably convey to Powell his right to have a lawyer with him during the interrogation. * * * In determining that the warning implied what it did not say, it is the Court "that is guilty of attaching greater importance to the form of the *Miranda* ritual than to the substance of the message it is intended to con-

vey." *Prysock*, 453 U.S., at 366 (STEVENS, J., dissenting).

III

Whether we focus on Powell's particular case, or the use of the warning form as the standard used in one jurisdiction, it is clear that the form is imperfect. As the majority's decision today demonstrates, reasonable judges may well differ over the question whether the deficiency is serious enough to violate the Federal Constitution. That difference of opinion, in my judgment, falls short of providing a justification for reviewing this case when the judges of the highest court of the State have decided the warning is insufficiently protective of the rights of the State's citizens. In my view, respect for the independence of state courts, and their authority to set the rules by which their citizens are protected, should result in a dismissal of this petition.

I respectfully dissent.

E. Waiver of *Miranda* Rights

2. Waiver After Invocation of *Miranda* Rights

Page 755. Add at the end of the page.

Right to Silence Must Be Clearly Invoked; Waiver Can Be Implied From the Confession Itself; and Interrogation After Warnings Is Permissible So Long As Waiver Is Ultimately Found: Berghuis v. Thompkins

The following case takes up a number of important questions concerning waiver of *Miranda* rights. The case concerns specifically whether the *Miranda* right to silence is invoked by remaining silent. But the Court also provides important rules on when a waiver of *Miranda* rights can be found in the absence of an invocation.

BERGHUIS v. THOMPKINS

Supreme Court of the United States, 2010
130 S.Ct. 2250

Justice Kennedy delivered the opinion of the Court

The United States Court of Appeals for the Sixth Circuit, in a habeas corpus proceeding challenging a Michigan conviction for first-degree murder and certain other offenses, ruled that * * * a statement by the accused, relied on at trial by the prosecution, had been elicited in violation of Miranda v. Arizona. [That contention] had been rejected in Michigan courts and in the habeas corpus proceedings before the United States District Court. Certiorari was granted to review the decision by the Court of Appeals on both points. The warden of a Michigan correctional facility is the petitioner here, and Van Chester Thompkins, who was convicted, is the respondent.

I

A

On January 10, 2000, a shooting occurred outside a mall in Southfield, Michigan. Among the victims was Samuel Morris, who died from multiple gunshot wounds. The other victim, Frederick France, recovered from his injuries and later testified. Thompkins, who was a suspect, fled. About one year later he was found in Ohio and arrested there.

Two Southfield police officers traveled to Ohio to interrogate Thompkins, then awaiting transfer to Michigan. The interrogation began around 1:30 p.m. and lasted about three hours. The interrogation was conducted in a room that was 8 by 10 feet, and Thompkins sat in a chair that resembled a school desk (it had an arm on it that swings around to provide a surface to write on). At the beginning of the interrogation, one of the officers, Detective Helgert, presented Thompkins with a form derived from the *Miranda* rule. It stated:

"NOTIFICATION OF CONSTITUTIONAL RIGHTS AND STATEMENT

"1. You have the right to remain silent.

"2. Anything you say can and will be used against you in a court of law.

"3. You have a right to talk to a lawyer before answering any questions and you have the right to have a lawyer present with you while you are answering any questions.

"4. If you cannot afford to hire a lawyer, one will be appointed to represent you before any questioning, if you wish one.

"5. You have the right to decide at any time before or during questioning to use your right to remain silent and your right to talk with a lawyer while you are being questioned."

Helgert asked Thompkins to read the fifth warning out loud. Thompkins complied. Helgert later said this was to ensure that Thompkins could read, and Helgert concluded that Thompkins understood English. Helgert then read the other four *Miranda* warnings out loud and asked Thompkins to sign the form to demonstrate that he understood his rights. Thompkins declined to sign the form. The record contains conflicting evidence about whether Thompkins then verbally confirmed that he understood the rights listed on the form.

Officers began an interrogation. At no point during the interrogation did Thompkins say that he wanted to remain silent, that he did not want to talk with the police, or that he wanted an attorney. Thompkins was "[l]argely" silent during the interrogation, which lasted about three hours. He did give a few limited verbal responses, however, such as "yeah," "no," or "I don't know." And on occasion he communicated by nodding his head. Thompkins also said that he "didn't want a peppermint" that was offered to him by the police and that the chair he was "sitting in was hard."

About 2 hours and 45 minutes into the interrogation, Helgert asked Thompkins, "Do you believe in God?" Thompkins made eye contact with Helgert and said "Yes," as his eyes "well[ed] up with tears." Helgert asked, "Do you pray to God?" Thompkins said "Yes." Helgert asked, "Do you pray to God to forgive you for shooting that boy down?" Thompkins answered "Yes" and looked away. Thompkins refused to make a written confession, and the interrogation ended about 15 minutes later.

Thompkins was charged with first-degree murder, assault with intent to commit murder, and certain firearms-related offenses. He moved to suppress the statements made during the interrogation. He argued that he had invoked his Fifth Amendment right to remain silent, requiring police to end the interrogation at once, see Michigan v. Mosley, that he had not waived his right to remain silent, and that his inculpatory statements were involuntary. The trial court denied the motion. [Thompkins was convicted. His state appeals were rejected]

B

Thompkins filed a petition for a writ of habeas corpus in the United States District Court for the Eastern District of Michigan. The District Court rejected Thompkins's *Miranda* [claim]. It noted that, under the Anti-

terrorism and Effective Death Penalty Act of 1996 (AEDPA), a federal court cannot grant a petition for a writ of habeas corpus unless the state court's adjudication of the merits was "contrary to, or involved an unreasonable application of, clearly established Federal law." 28 U.S.C. § 2254(d)(1). The District Court reasoned that Thompkins did not invoke his right to remain silent and was not coerced into making statements during the interrogation. It held further that the Michigan Court of Appeals was not unreasonable in determining that Thompkins had waived his right to remain silent.

The United States Court of Appeals for the Sixth Circuit reversed * * *. The Court of Appeals ruled that the state court, in rejecting Thompkins's *Miranda* claim, unreasonably applied clearly established federal law and based its decision on an unreasonable determination of the facts. See 28 U.S.C. § 2254(d). The Court of Appeals acknowledged that a waiver of the right to remain silent need not be express, as it can be "inferred from the actions and words of the person interrogated." 547 F.3d, at 582 (quoting North Carolina v. Butler) [Casebook page 743]. The panel held, nevertheless, that the state court was unreasonable in finding an implied waiver in the circumstances here. The Court of Appeals found that the state court unreasonably determined the facts because "the evidence demonstrates that Thompkins was silent for two hours and forty-five minutes." According to the Court of Appeals, Thompkins's "persistent silence for nearly three hours in response to questioning and repeated invitations to tell his side of the story offered a clear and unequivocal message to the officers: Thompkins did not wish to waive his rights."

* * *

II

* * *

III

The *Miranda* Court formulated a warning that must be given to suspects before they can be subjected to custodial interrogation. The substance of the warning still must be given to suspects today. * * *

All concede that the warning given in this case was in full compliance with these requirements. The dispute centers on the response—or nonresponse—from the suspect.

A

Thompkins makes various arguments that his answers to questions from the detectives were inadmissible. He first contends that he invoked his privilege to remain silent by not saying anything for a sufficient period of time, so the interrogation should have ceased before he made his inculpatory statements.

This argument is unpersuasive. In the context of invoking the *Miranda* right to counsel, the Court in Davis v. United States [Casebook page 754], held that a suspect must do so "unambiguously." If an accused makes a statement concerning the right to counsel "that is ambiguous or equivocal" or makes no statement, the police are not required to end the interrogation, or ask questions to clarify whether the accused wants to invoke his or her *Miranda* rights.

The Court has not yet stated whether an invocation of the right to remain silent can be ambiguous or equivocal, but there is no principled reason to adopt different standards for determining when an accused has invoked the *Miranda* right to remain silent and the *Miranda* right to counsel at issue in *Davis*. Both protect the privilege against compulsory self-incrimination, by requiring an interrogation to cease when either right is invoked.

There is good reason to require an accused who wants to invoke his or her right to remain silent to do so unambiguously. A requirement of an unambiguous invocation of *Miranda* rights results in an objective inquiry that avoids difficulties of proof and provides guidance to officers on how to proceed in the face of ambiguity. *Davis*. If an ambiguous act, omission, or statement could require police to end the interrogation, police would be required to make difficult decisions about an accused's unclear intent and face the consequence of suppression if they guess wrong. Suppression of a voluntary confession in these circumstances would place a significant burden on society's interest in prosecuting criminal activity. Treating an ambiguous or equivocal act, omission, or statement as an invocation of *Miranda* rights might add marginally to *Miranda's* goal of dispelling the compulsion inherent in custodial interrogation. But as *Miranda* holds, full comprehension of the rights to remain silent and request an attorney are sufficient to dispel whatever coercion is inherent in the interrogation process.

Thompkins did not say that he wanted to remain silent or that he did not want to talk with the police. Had he made either of these simple, unambiguous statements, he would have invoked his right to cut off questioning. Michigan v. Mosley [Casebook page 752]. Here he did neither, so he did not invoke his right to remain silent.

B

We next consider whether Thompkins waived his right to remain silent. Even absent the accused's invocation of the right to remain silent, the accused's statement during a custodial interrogation is inadmissible at trial unless the prosecution can establish that the accused in fact knowingly and voluntarily waived *Miranda* rights when making the statement. The waiver inquiry "has two distinct dimensions": waiver must be "voluntary in the sense that it was the product of a free and deliberate choice rather than intimidation, coercion, or deception," and "made with a full awareness of both the nature of the right being abandoned and the consequences of the decision to abandon it." Moran v. Burbine [Casebook, page 748].

Some language in *Miranda* could be read to indicate that waivers are difficult to establish absent an explicit written waiver or a formal, express oral statement. *Miranda* said "a valid waiver will not be presumed simply from the silence of the accused after warnings are given or simply from the fact that a confession was in fact eventually obtained." In addition, the *Miranda* Court stated that "a heavy burden rests on the government to demonstrate that the defendant knowingly and intelligently waived his privilege against self-incrimination and his right to retained or appointed counsel."

The course of decisions since *Miranda*, informed by the application of *Miranda* warnings in the whole course of law enforcement, demonstrates that waivers can be established even absent formal or express statements of waiver that would be expected in, say, a judicial hearing to determine if a guilty plea has been properly entered. The main purpose of *Miranda* is to ensure that an accused is advised of and understands the right to remain silent and the right to counsel. Thus, "[i]f anything, our subsequent cases have reduced the impact of the *Miranda* rule on legitimate law enforcement while reaffirming the decision's core ruling

that unwarned statements may not be used as evidence in the prosecution's case in chief." Dickerson v. United States [Casebook page 691].

One of the first cases to decide the meaning and import of *Miranda* with respect to the question of waiver was North Carolina v. Butler. The Butler Court, after discussing some of the problems created by the language in *Miranda*, established certain important propositions. *Butler* interpreted the *Miranda* language concerning the "heavy burden" to show waiver, in accord with usual principles of determining waiver, which can include waiver implied from all the circumstances. And in a later case, the Court stated that this "heavy burden" is not more than the burden to establish waiver by a preponderance of the evidence. Colorado v. Connelly [Casebook page 744].

The prosecution therefore does not need to show that a waiver of *Miranda* rights was express. * * * *Butler* made clear that a waiver of *Miranda* rights may be implied through "the defendant's silence, coupled with an understanding of his rights and a course of conduct indicating waiver." The Court in *Butler* therefore retreated from the language and tenor of the *Miranda* opinion, which suggested that the Court would require that a waiver be specifically made.

If the State establishes that a *Miranda* warning was given and the accused made an uncoerced statement, this showing, standing alone, is insufficient to demonstrate a valid waiver of *Miranda* rights. The prosecution must make the additional showing that the accused understood these rights. Where the prosecution shows that a *Miranda* warning was given and that it was understood by the accused, an accused's uncoerced statement establishes an implied waiver of the right to remain silent.

Although *Miranda* imposes on the police a rule that is both formalistic and practical when it prevents them from interrogating suspects without first providing them with a *Miranda* warning, it does not impose a formalistic waiver procedure that a suspect must follow to relinquish those rights. As a general proposition, the law can presume that an individual who, with a full understanding of his or her rights, acts in a manner inconsistent with their exercise has made a deliberate choice to relinquish the protection those rights afford. See, *Connelly,* ("There is obviously no reason to require more in the way of a 'voluntariness' inquiry in the *Miranda* waiver context than in the [due process] confession context"). * * * As *Butler* recognized, *Miranda* rights can therefore be waived through means less formal than a typical waiver on the record in a courtroom, given the practical constraints and necessities of interrogation and the fact that *Miranda's* main protection lies in advising defendants of their rights.

The record in this case shows that Thompkins waived his right to remain silent. * * * First, there is no contention that Thompkins did not understand his rights; and from this it follows that he knew what he gave up when he spoke. There was more than enough evidence in the record to conclude that Thompkins understood his *Miranda* rights. Thompkins received a written copy of the *Miranda* warnings; Detective Helgert determined that Thompkins could read and understand English; and Thompkins was given time to read the warnings. Thompkins, furthermore, read aloud the fifth warning,

which stated that "you have the right to decide at any time before or during questioning to use your right to remain silent and your right to talk with a lawyer while you are being questioned." He was thus aware that his right to remain silent would not dissipate after a certain amount of time and that police would have to honor his right to be silent and his right to counsel during the whole course of interrogation. Those rights, the warning made clear, could be asserted at any time. Helgert, moreover, read the warnings aloud.

Second, Thompkins's answer to Detective Helgert's question about whether Thompkins prayed to God for forgiveness for shooting the victim is a "course of conduct indicating waiver" of the right to remain silent. *Butler.* If Thompkins wanted to remain silent, he could have said nothing in response to Helgert's questions, or he could have unambiguously invoked his *Miranda* rights and ended the interrogation. The fact that Thompkins made a statement about three hours after receiving a *Miranda* warning does not overcome the fact that he engaged in a course of conduct indicating waiver. Police are not required to rewarn suspects from time to time. Thompkins's answer to Helgert's question about praying to God for forgiveness for shooting the victim was sufficient to show a course of conduct indicating waiver. This is confirmed by the fact that before then Thompkins had given sporadic answers to questions throughout the interrogation.

Third, there is no evidence that Thompkins's statement was coerced. Thompkins does not claim that police threatened or injured him during the interrogation or that he was in any way fearful. The interrogation was conducted in a standard-sized room in the middle of the afternoon. It is true that apparently he was in a straight-backed chair for three hours, but there is no authority for the proposition that an interrogation of this length is inherently coercive. Indeed, even where interrogations of greater duration were held to be improper, they were accompanied, as this one was not, by other facts indicating coercion, such as an incapacitated and sedated suspect, sleep and food deprivation, and threats. The fact that Helgert's question referred to Thompkins's religious beliefs also did not render Thompkins's statement involuntary. The Fifth Amendment privilege is not concerned with moral and psychological pressures to confess emanating from sources other than official coercion. In these circumstances, Thompkins knowingly and voluntarily made a statement to police, so he waived his right to remain silent.

C

Thompkins next argues that, even if his answer to Detective Helgert could constitute a waiver of his right to remain silent, the police were not allowed to question him until they obtained a waiver first. *Butler* forecloses this argument. The *Butler* Court held that courts can infer a waiver of *Miranda* rights "from the actions and words of the person interrogated." This principle would be inconsistent with a rule that requires a waiver at the outset. The *Butler* Court thus rejected the rule proposed by the *Butler* dissent, which would have "requir[ed] the police to obtain an express waiver of [*Miranda* rights] before proceeding with interrogation." This holding also makes sense given that the primary protection afforded suspects subjected to custodial interrogation is the

Miranda warnings themselves. The *Miranda* rule and its requirements are met if a suspect receives adequate *Miranda* warnings, understands them, and has an opportunity to invoke the rights before giving any answers or admissions. Any waiver, express or implied, may be contradicted by an invocation at any time. If the right to counsel or the right to remain silent is invoked at any point during questioning, further interrogation must cease.

Interrogation provides the suspect with additional information that can put his or her decision to waive, or not to invoke, into perspective. As questioning commences and then continues, the suspect has the opportunity to consider the choices he or she faces and to make a more informed decision, either to insist on silence or to cooperate. When the suspect knows that *Miranda* rights can be invoked at any time, he or she has the opportunity to reassess his or her immediate and long-term interests. Cooperation with the police may result in more favorable treatment for the suspect; the apprehension of accomplices; the prevention of continuing injury and fear; beginning steps towards relief or solace for the victims; and the beginning of the suspect's own return to the law and the social order it seeks to protect.

In order for an accused's statement to be admissible at trial, police must have given the accused a *Miranda* warning. If that condition is established, the court can proceed to consider whether there has been an express or implied waiver of *Miranda* rights. In making its ruling on the admissibility of a statement made during custodial questioning, the trial court, of course, considers whether there is evidence to support the conclusion that, from the whole course of questioning, an express or implied waiver has been established. Thus, after giving a *Miranda* warning, police may interrogate a suspect who has neither invoked nor waived his or her *Miranda* rights. On these premises, it follows the police were not required to obtain a waiver of Thompkins's *Miranda* rights before commencing the interrogation.

D

In sum, a suspect who has received and understood the *Miranda* warnings, and has not invoked his *Miranda* rights, waives the right to remain silent by making an uncoerced statement to the police. Thompkins did not invoke his right to remain silent and stop the questioning. Understanding his rights in full, he waived his right to remain silent by making a voluntary statement to the police. The police, moreover, were not required to obtain a waiver of Thompkins's right to remain silent before interrogating him. The state court's decision rejecting Thompkins's *Miranda* claim was thus correct under de novo review and therefore necessarily reasonable under the more deferential AEDPA standard of review.

JUSTICE SOTOMAYOR, with whom JUSTICE STEVENS, JUSTICE GINSBURG, and JUSTICE BREYER join, dissenting.

The Court concludes today that a criminal suspect waives his right to remain silent if, after sitting tacit and uncommunicative through nearly three hours of police interrogation, he utters a few one-word responses. The Court also concludes that a suspect who wishes to guard his right to remain silent against such a finding of "waiver" must, counterintuitively, speak—and must do so with sufficient precision to satisfy a clear-state-

ment rule that construes ambiguity in favor of the police. Both propositions mark a substantial retreat from the protection against compelled self-incrimination that *Miranda* has long provided during custodial interrogation. * * * .

I

* * *

The strength of Thompkins' *Miranda* claims depends in large part on the circumstances of the 3–hour interrogation, at the end of which he made inculpatory statements later introduced at trial. The Court's opinion downplays record evidence that Thompkins remained almost completely silent and unresponsive throughout that session. * * * The record contains no indication that the officers sought or obtained an express waiver.

* * *

II

A

This Court's decisions subsequent to *Miranda* have emphasized the prosecution's "heavy burden" in proving waiver. We have also reaffirmed that a court may not presume waiver from a suspect's silence or from the mere fact that a confession was eventually obtained. See North Carolina v. Butler.

* * *

That Thompkins did not make the inculpatory statements at issue until after approximately 2 hours and 45 minutes of interrogation serves as strong evidence against waiver. *Miranda* and *Butler* expressly preclude the possibility that the inculpatory statements themselves are sufficient to establish waiver.

In these circumstances, Thompkins' "actions and words" preceding the inculpatory statements simply do not evidence a "course of conduct indicating waiver" sufficient to carry the prosecution's burden. See *Butler.* Although the Michigan court stated that Thompkins "sporadically" participated in the interview, that court's opinion and the record before us are silent as to the subject matter or context of even a single question to which Thompkins purportedly responded, other than the exchange about God and the statements respecting the peppermint and the chair. Unlike in *Butler,* Thompkins made no initial declaration akin to "I will talk to you." Indeed, Michigan and the United States concede that no waiver occurred in this case until Thompkins responded "yes" to the questions about God. I believe it is objectively unreasonable under our clearly established precedents to conclude the prosecution met its "heavy burden" of proof on a record consisting of three one-word answers, following 2 hours and 45 minutes of silence punctuated by a few largely nonverbal responses to unidentified questions.

B

Perhaps because our prior *Miranda* precedents so clearly favor Thompkins, the Court today goes beyond AEDPA's deferential standard of review and announces a new general principle of law. Any new rule, it must be emphasized, is unnecessary to the disposition of this case. If, in the Court's view, the Michigan court did not unreasonably apply our *Miranda* precedents in denying Thompkins relief, it should simply say so and reverse the Sixth Circuit's judgment on that ground. * * * No necessity exists to justify the Court's broad announcement today.

The Court concludes that when *Miranda* warnings have been given and

understood, "an accused's uncoerced statement establishes an implied waiver of the right to remain silent." More broadly still, the Court states that, "[a]s a general proposition, the law can presume that an individual who, with a full understanding of his or her rights, acts in a manner inconsistent with their exercise has made a deliberate choice to relinquish the protection those rights afford."

These principles flatly contradict our longstanding views that "a valid waiver will not be presumed . . . simply from the fact that a confession was in fact eventually obtained," *Miranda,* and that "[t]he courts must presume that a defendant did not waive his rights," *Butler.* Indeed, we have in the past summarily reversed a state-court decision that inverted *Miranda*'s antiwaiver presumption, characterizing the error as "readily apparent." Tague v. Louisiana [Casebook, page 743]. At best, the Court today creates an unworkable and conflicting set of presumptions that will undermine *Miranda*'s goal of providing "concrete constitutional guidelines for law enforcement agencies and courts to follow," At worst, it overrules sub silentio an essential aspect of the protections *Miranda* has long provided for the constitutional guarantee against self-incrimination.

* * *

Today's dilution of the prosecution's burden of proof to the bare fact that a suspect made inculpatory statements after *Miranda* warnings were given and understood takes an unprecedented step away from the "high standards of proof for the waiver of constitutional rights" this Court has long demanded. When waiver is to be inferred during a custodial interrogation, there are sound reasons to require evidence beyond inculpatory statements themselves. *Miranda* and our subsequent cases are premised on the idea that custodial interrogation is inherently coercive. Requiring proof of a course of conduct beyond the inculpatory statements themselves is critical to ensuring that those statements are voluntary admissions and not the dubious product of an overborne will.

* * *

III

Thompkins separately argues that his conduct during the interrogation invoked his right to remain silent, requiring police to terminate questioning. * * * I would not reach this question because Thompkins is in any case entitled to relief as to waiver. But even if Thompkins would not prevail on his invocation claim under AEDPA's deferential standard of review, I cannot agree with the Court's much broader ruling that a suspect must clearly invoke his right to silence by speaking. Taken together with the Court's reformulation of the prosecution's burden of proof as to waiver, today's novel clear-statement rule for invocation invites police to question a suspect at length—notwithstanding his persistent refusal to answer questions—in the hope of eventually obtaining a single inculpatory response which will suffice to prove waiver of rights. * * *

A

Thompkins' claim for relief under AEDPA rests on the clearly established federal law of *Miranda* and *Mosley.* In *Miranda,* the Court concluded that "[i]f [an] individual indicates in any manner, at any time prior to or during questioning, that he wishes to remain silent, the interrogation must cease.... [A]ny state-

ment taken after the person invokes his privilege cannot be other than the product of compulsion, subtle or otherwise." In *Mosley,* the Court said that * * * "the admissibility of statements obtained after the person in custody has decided to remain silent depends under *Miranda* on whether his right to cut off questioning was scrupulously honored."

Because this Court has never decided whether *Davis'* clear-statement rule applies to an invocation of the right to silence, Michigan contends, there was no clearly established federal law prohibiting the state court from requiring an unambiguous invocation. * * *

Under AEDPA's deferential standard of review, it is indeed difficult to conclude that the state court's application of our precedents was objectively unreasonable. Although the duration and consistency of Thompkins' refusal to answer questions throughout the 3–hour interrogation provide substantial evidence in support of his claim, Thompkins did not remain absolutely silent, and this Court has not previously addressed whether a suspect can invoke the right to silence by remaining uncooperative and nearly silent for 2 hours and 45 minutes.

B

The Court, however, eschews this narrow ground of decision, instead extending *Davis* to hold that police may continue questioning a suspect until he unambiguously invokes his right to remain silent. Because Thompkins neither said "he wanted to remain silent" nor said "he did not want to talk with the police," the Court concludes, he did not clearly invoke his right to silence.

I disagree with this novel application of *Davis.* Neither the rationale nor holding of that case compels today's result. *Davis* involved the right to counsel, not the right to silence. The Court in *Davis* reasoned that extending *Edwards'* "rigid" prophylactic rule to ambiguous requests for a lawyer would transform *Miranda* into a "wholly irrational obstacle to legitimate police investigative activity" by "needlessly preventing the police from questioning a suspect in the absence of counsel even if he did not wish to have a lawyer present." But *Miranda* itself "distinguished between the procedural safeguards triggered by a request to remain silent and a request for an attorney." *Mosley.* * * * The different effects of invoking the rights are consistent with distinct standards for invocation. To the extent *Mosley* contemplates a more flexible form of prophylaxis than Edwards—and, in particular, does not categorically bar police from reapproaching a suspect who has invoked his right to remain silent—*Davis'* concern about "wholly irrational obstacles" to police investigation applies with less force.

* * *

In my mind, a more appropriate standard for addressing a suspect's ambiguous invocation of the right to remain silent is the constraint *Mosley* places on questioning a suspect who has invoked that right: The suspect's "right to cut off questioning" must be "scrupulously honored." Such a standard is necessarily precautionary and fact specific. The rule would acknowledge that some statements or conduct are so equivocal that police may scrupulously honor a suspect's rights without terminating questioning—for instance, if a suspect's actions are reasonably understood to indicate a willingness to listen before deciding whether to respond. But other statements or actions—in particular, when a suspect sits silent throughout prolonged interrogation, long past the point when he could be deciding whether to respond—cannot reasonably be understood other than as an invocation of the right to remain silent. Under such circumstances, "scrupulous" respect for the suspect's rights will require police to terminate questioning under *Mosley.*

To be sure, such a standard does not provide police with a bright-line rule. But, as we have previously recognized, *Mosley* itself does not offer clear guidance to police about when and how interrogation may continue after a suspect invokes his rights. Given that police have for nearly 35 years applied *Mosley's* fact-specific standard in questioning suspects who have invoked their right to remain silent; that our cases did not during that time resolve what statements or actions suffice to invoke that right; and that neither Michigan nor the Solicitor General have provided evidence in this case that the status quo has proved unworkable, I see little reason to believe today's clear-statement rule is necessary to ensure effective law enforcement.

Davis' clear-statement rule is also a poor fit for the right to silence. Advising a suspect that he has a "right to remain silent" is unlikely to convey that he must speak (and must do so in some particular fashion) to ensure the right will be protected. By contrast, telling a suspect he has the right to the presence of an attorney, and that if he cannot afford an attorney one will be appointed for him prior to any questioning if he so desires implies the need for speech to exercise that right. *Davis'* requirement that a suspect must "clearly reques[t] an attorney" to terminate questioning thus aligns with a suspect's likely understanding of the *Miranda* warnings in a way today's rule does not. The Court suggests Thompkins could have employed the "simple, unambiguous" means of saying "he wanted to remain silent" or "did not want to talk with the police." But the *Miranda* warnings give no hint that a suspect should use those magic words, and there is little reason to believe police—who have ample incentives to avoid invocation—will provide such guidance.

Conversely, the Court's concern that police will face "difficult decisions about an accused's unclear intent" and suffer the consequences of "guessing wrong," is misplaced. If a suspect makes an ambiguous statement or engages in conduct that creates uncertainty about his intent to invoke his right, police can simply ask for clarification. It is hardly an unreasonable burden for police to ask a suspect, for instance, "Do you want to talk to us?" * * * Given this straightforward mechanism by which police can "scrupulously honor" a suspect's right to silence, today's clear-statement rule can only be seen as accepting as tolerable the certainty that some poorly expressed requests to remain silent will be disregarded, without any countervailing benefit. * * *

The Court asserts in passing that treating ambiguous statements or acts as an invocation of the right to silence will only "marginally "serve *Miranda's* goals. Experience suggests the contrary. In the 16 years since *Davis* was decided, ample evidence has accrued that criminal suspects often use equivocal or colloquial language in attempting to invoke their right to silence. * * * For these reasons, I believe a precautionary requirement that police scrupulously honor a suspect's right to cut off questioning is a more faithful application of our precedents than the Court's awkward and needless extension of *Davis*.

———

Today's decision turns *Miranda* upside down. Criminal suspects must now unambiguously invoke their right to remain silent—which, counterintuitively, requires them to speak. At the same time, suspects will be legally presumed to have waived their rights even if they have given no clear expression of their intent to do so. Those results, in my view, find no basis in *Miranda* or our subsequent cases and are inconsistent with the fair-trial principles on which those precedents are grounded. Today's broad new rules are all the more unfortunate because they are unnecessary to the disposition of the case before us. I respectfully dissent.

Page 765. Add after the section on *Minnick v. Mississippi*.

The Requirement of Continuous Custody for Edwards Protection: Maryland v. Shatzer

MARYLAND v. SHATZER

Supreme Court of the United States, 2010
130 S.Ct. 1213

JUSTICE SCALIA **delivered the opinion of the Court.**

We consider whether a break in custody ends the presumption of involuntariness established in Edwards v. Arizona.

I

In August 2003, a social worker assigned to the Child Advocacy Center in the Criminal Investigation Division of the Hagerstown Police Department referred to the department allegations that respondent Michael Shatzer, Sr., had sexually abused his 3–year-old son. At that time, Shatzer was incarcerated at the Maryland Correctional Institution–Hagerstown, serving a sentence for an unrelated child-sexual-abuse offense. Detective Shane Blankenship was assigned to the investigation and interviewed Shatzer at the correctional institution on August 7, 2003. Before asking any questions, Blankenship reviewed Shatzer's *Miranda* rights with him, and obtained a written waiver of those rights. When Blankenship explained that he was there to question Shatzer about sexually abusing his son, Shatzer expressed confusion— he had thought Blankenship was an attorney there to discuss the prior crime for which he was incarcerated. Blankenship clarified the purpose of his visit, and Shatzer declined to speak without an attorney. Accordingly, Blankenship ended the interview, and Shatzer was released back into the general prison population.

Shortly thereafter, Blankenship closed the investigation.

Two years and six months later, the same social worker referred more specific allegations to the department about the same incident involving Shatzer. Detective Paul Hoover, from the same division, was assigned to the investigation. He and the social worker interviewed the victim, then eight years old, who described the incident in more detail. With this new information in hand, on March 2, 2006, they went to the Roxbury Correctional Institute, to which Shatzer had since been transferred, and interviewed Shatzer in a maintenance room outfitted with a desk and three chairs. Hoover explained that he wanted to ask Shatzer about the alleged incident involving Shatzer's son. Shatzer was surprised because he thought that the investigation had been closed, but Hoover explained they had opened a new file. Hoover then read Shatzer his *Miranda* rights and obtained a written waiver on a standard department form.

Hoover interrogated Shatzer about the incident for approximately 30 minutes. Shatzer denied ordering his son to perform fellatio on him, but admitted to masturbating in front of his son from a distance of less than three feet. Before the interview ended, Shatzer agreed to Hoover's request that he submit to a polygraph examination. At no point during the interrogation did Shatzer request to speak with an attorney or refer to his prior refusal to answer questions without one.

Five days later, on March 7, 2006, Hoover and another detective met with Shatzer at the correctional facility to administer the polygraph examination. After reading Shatzer his *Miranda* rights and obtaining a written waiver, the other detective administered the test and concluded that Shatzer had failed. When the detectives then questioned Shatzer, he became upset, started to cry, and incriminated himself by saying, "I didn't force him. I didn't force him." After making this inculpatory statement, Shatzer requested an attorney, and Hoover promptly ended the interrogation.

The State's Attorney for Washington County charged Shatzer with second-degree sexual offense, sexual child abuse, second-degree assault, and contributing to conditions rendering a child in need of assistance. Shatzer moved to suppress his March 2006 statements pursuant to *Edwards*. The trial court held a suppression hearing and later denied Shatzer's motion. The *Edwards* protections did not apply, it reasoned, because Shatzer had experienced a break in custody for *Miranda* purposes between the 2003 and 2006 interrogations. [Shatzer was convicted and appealed.]

Over the dissent of two judges, the Court of Appeals of Maryland reversed and remanded. The court held that "the passage of time alone is insufficient to [end] the protections afforded by *Edwards*," and that, assuming, arguendo, a break-in-custody exception to *Edwards* existed, Shatzer's release back into the general prison population between

interrogations did not constitute a break in custody.

II

* * *

The rationale of *Edwards* is that once a suspect indicates that "he is not capable of undergoing [custodial] questioning without advice of counsel," "any subsequent waiver that has come at the authorities' behest, and not at the suspect's own instigation, is itself the product of the 'inherently compelling pressures' and not the purely voluntary choice of the suspect." Arizona v. Roberson. Under this rule, a voluntary *Miranda* waiver is sufficient at the time of an initial attempted interrogation to protect a suspect's right to have counsel present, but it is not sufficient at the time of subsequent attempts if the suspect initially requested the presence of counsel. The implicit assumption, of course, is that the subsequent requests for interrogation pose a significantly greater risk of coercion. That increased risk results not only from the police's persistence in trying to get the suspect to talk, but also from the continued pressure that begins when the individual is taken into custody as a suspect and sought to be interrogated—pressure likely to "increase as custody is prolonged," Minnick v. Mississippi. The *Edwards* presumption of involuntariness ensures that police will not take advantage of the mounting coercive pressures of prolonged police custody, by repeatedly attempting to question a suspect who previously requested counsel until the suspect is badgered into submission.

* * *

It is easy to believe that a suspect may be coerced or badgered into abandoning his earlier refusal to be questioned without counsel in * * * a case in which the suspect has been arrested for a particular crime and is held in uninterrupted pretrial custody while that crime is being actively investigated. After the initial interrogation, and up to and including the second one, hc rcmains cut off from his normal life and companions, "thrust into" and isolated in an "unfamiliar," "police-dominated atmosphere," *Miranda,* where his captors "appear to control [his] fate," Illinois v. Perkins. * * *

When * * * a suspect has been released from his pretrial custody and has returned to his normal life for some time before the later attempted interrogation, there is little reason to think that his change of heart regarding interrogation without counsel has been coerced. He has no longer been isolated. He has likely been able to seek advice from an attorney, family members, and friends. And he knows from his earlier experience that he need only demand counsel to bring the interrogation to a halt; and that investigative custody does not last indefinitely. In these circumstances, it is far fetched to think that a police officer's asking the suspect whether he would like to waive his *Miranda* rights will any more wear down the accused than did the first such request at the original attempted interrogation—which is of course not deemed coercive. His change of heart is less likely attributable to "badgering" than it is to the fact that further deliberation in familiar surroundings has caused him to believe (rightly or wrongly) that cooperating with the investigation is in his interest. Uncritical extension of *Edwards* to this situation would not significantly increase the number of genuinely coerced confessions excluded. The justification for a conclu-

sive presumption disappears when application of the presumption will not reach the correct result most of the time.

At the same time that extending the *Edwards* rule yields diminished benefits, extending the rule also increases its costs: the in-fact voluntary confessions it excludes from trial, and the voluntary confessions it deters law enforcement officers from even trying to obtain. * * *

The only logical endpoint of *Edwards* disability is termination of *Miranda* custody and any of its lingering effects. Without that limitation—and barring some purely arbitrary time-limit—every *Edwards* prohibition of custodial interrogation of a particular suspect would be eternal. The prohibition applies, of course, when the subsequent interrogation pertains to a different crime, *Roberson,* supra, when it is conducted by a different law enforcement authority, *Minnick,* and even when the suspect has met with an attorney after the first interrogation, ibid. And it not only prevents questioning ex ante; it would render invalid ex post, confessions invited and obtained from suspects who (unbeknownst to the interrogators) have acquired *Edwards* immunity previously in connection with any offense in any jurisdiction. In a country that harbors a large number of repeat offenders, this consequence is disastrous.

We conclude that such an extension of *Edwards* is not justified; we have opened its protective umbrella far enough. The protections offered by *Miranda,* which we have deemed sufficient to ensure that the police respect the suspect's desire to have an attorney present the first time police interrogate him, adequately ensure that result when a suspect who initially requested counsel is reinterrogated after a break in custody that is of sufficient duration to dissipate its coercive effects.

If Shatzer's return to the general prison population qualified as a break in custody (a question we address in Part III, infra), there is no doubt that it lasted long enough (2½ years) to meet that durational requirement. But what about a break that has lasted only one year? Or only one week? It is impractical to leave the answer to that question for clarification in future case-by-case adjudication; law enforcement officers need to know, with certainty and beforehand, when renewed interrogation is lawful. And while it is certainly unusual for this Court to set forth precise time limits governing police action, it is not unheard-of. In County of Riverside v. McLaughlin, 500 U.S. 44 (1991), we specified 48 hours as the time within which the police must comply with the requirement * * * that a person arrested without a warrant be brought before a magistrate to establish probable cause for continued detention.

Like *McLaughlin*, this is a case in which the requisite police action (there, presentation to a magistrate; here, abstention from further interrogation) has not been prescribed by statute but has been established by opinion of this Court. We think it appropriate to specify a period of time to avoid the consequence that continuation of the *Edwards* presumption will not reach the correct result most of the time. It seems to us that period is 14 days. That provides plenty of time for the suspect to get reacclimated to his normal life, to consult with friends and counsel, and to shake off any residual coercive effects of his prior custody.

The 14–day limitation meets Shatzer's concern that a break-in-custody rule lends itself to police abuse. He envisions that once a suspect invokes his *Miranda* right to counsel, the police will release the suspect briefly (to end the *Edwards* presumption) and then promptly bring him back into custody for reinterrogation. But once the suspect has been out of custody long enough (14 days) to eliminate its coercive effect, there will be nothing to gain by such gamesmanship—nothing, that is, except the entirely appropriate gain of being able to interrogate a suspect who has made a valid waiver of his *Miranda* rights.

Shatzer argues that ending the *Edwards* protections at a break in custody will undermine *Edwards'* purpose to conserve judicial resources. To be sure, we have said that "[t]he merit of the *Edwards* decision lies in the clarity of its command and the certainty of its application." *Minnick.* But clarity and certainty are not goals in themselves. They are valuable only when they reasonably further the achievement of some substantive end-here, the exclusion of compelled confessions. Confessions obtained after a 2–week break in custody and a waiver of *Miranda* rights are most unlikely to be compelled, and hence are unreasonably excluded. In any case, a break-in-custody exception will dim only marginally, if at all, the bright-line nature of *Edwards*. In every case involving *Edwards*, the courts must determine whether the suspect was in custody when he requested counsel and when he later made the statements he seeks to suppress. Now, in cases where there is an alleged break in custody, they simply have to repeat the inquiry for the time between the initial invocation and reinterrogation. In most cases that determination will be easy. And when it is determined that the defendant pleading *Edwards* has been out of custody for two weeks before the contested interrogation, the court is spared the fact-intensive inquiry into whether he ever, anywhere, asserted his Miranda right to counsel.

III

The facts of this case present an additional issue. * * *

Here, we are addressing the interim period during which a suspect was not interrogated, but was subject to a baseline set of restraints imposed pursuant to a prior conviction. Without minimizing the harsh realities of incarceration, we think lawful imprisonment imposed upon conviction of a crime does not create the coercive pressures identified in *Miranda.*

Interrogated suspects who have previously been convicted of crime live in prison. When they are released back into the general prison population, they return to their accustomed surroundings and daily routine-they regain the degree of control they had over their lives prior to the interrogation. Sentenced prisoners, in contrast to the *Miranda* paradigm, are not isolated with their accusers. They live among other inmates, guards, and workers, and often can receive visitors and communicate with people on the outside by mail or telephone.

Their detention, moreover, is relatively disconnected from their prior unwillingness to cooperate in an investigation. The former interrogator has no power to increase the duration of incarceration, which was determined at sentencing. And even where the possibility of parole exists, the former interrogator has no apparent power to decrease the time

served. This is in stark contrast to the circumstances faced by the defendants in *Edwards, Roberson,* and *Minnick,* whose continued detention as suspects rested with those controlling their interrogation, and who confronted the uncertainties of what final charges they would face, whether they would be convicted, and what sentence they would receive.

* * *

IV

A few words in response to Justice STEVENS' concurrence: It claims we ignore that "[w]hen police tell an indigent suspect that he has the right to an attorney" and then "reinterrogate" him without providing a lawyer, "the suspect is likely to feel that the police lied to him and that he really does not have any right to a lawyer." The fallacy here is that we are not talking about "reinterrogating" the suspect; we are talking about asking his permission to be interrogated. An officer has in no sense lied to a suspect when, after advising, as *Miranda* requires, "You have the right to remain silent, and if you choose to speak you have the right to the presence of an attorney," he promptly ends the attempted interrogation because the suspect declines to speak without counsel present, and then, two weeks later, reapproaches the suspect and asks, "Are you now willing to speak without a lawyer present?"

The concern that motivated the *Edwards* line of cases is that the suspect will be coerced into saying yes. That concern guides our decision today. Contrary to the concurrence's conclusion, there is no reason to believe a suspect will view confession as "the only way to end his interrogation" when, before the interrogation begins, he is told that he can avoid it by simply requesting that he not be interrogated without counsel present—an option that worked before. If, as the concurrence argues will often be the case, a break in custody does not change the suspect's mind, he need only say so.

The concurrence also accuses the Court of "ignor[ing] that when a suspect asks for counsel, until his request is answered, there are still the same inherently compelling pressures of custodial interrogation on which the *Miranda* line of cases is based." We do not ignore these pressures; nor do we suggest that they disappear when custody is recommenced after a break. But if those pressures are merely "the same" as before, then *Miranda* provides sufficient protection—as it did before. The *Edwards* presumption of involuntariness is justified only in circumstances where the coercive pressures have increased so much that suspects' waivers of *Miranda* rights are likely to be involuntary most of the time. Contrary to the concurrence's suggestion, it is only in those narrow circumstances—when custody is unbroken—that the Court has concluded a fresh set of *Miranda* warnings is not sufficient.

* * *

Because Shatzer experienced a break in *Miranda* custody lasting more than two weeks between the first and second attempts at interrogation, *Edwards* does not mandate suppression of his March 2006 statements. Accordingly, we reverse the judgment of the Court of Appeals of Maryland, and remand the case for further proceedings not inconsistent with this opinion.

It is so ordered.

JUSTICE THOMAS, concurring in part and concurring in the judgment.

I join Part III of the Court's opinion, which holds that release into the general prison population constitutes a break in custody. I do not join the Court's decision to extend the presumption of involuntariness established in Edwards v. Arizona for 14 days after custody ends.

It is not apparent to me that the presumption of involuntariness the Court recognized in *Edwards* is justifiable even in the custodial setting to which *Edwards* applies it. Accordingly, I would not extend the *Edwards* rule beyond the circumstances present in *Edwards* itself. But even if one believes that the Court is obliged to apply *Edwards* to any case involving continuing custody, the Court's opinion today goes well beyond that. It extends the presumption of involuntariness *Edwards* applies in custodial settings to interrogations that occur after custody ends.

The Court concedes that this extension, like the *Edwards* presumption itself, is not constitutionally required. The Court nevertheless defends the extension as a judicially created prophylaxis against compelled confessions. * * *

Our precedents insist that judicially created prophylactic rules like those in *Edwards* and *Miranda* maintain "the closest possible fit" between the rule and the Fifth Amendment interests they seek to protect. United States v. Patane. The Court's 14–day rule does not satisfy this test. The Court relates its 14–day rule to the Fifth Amendment simply by asserting that 14 days between release and recapture should provide "plenty of time for the suspect ... to shake off any residual coercive effects of his prior custody."

This ipse dixit does not explain why extending the *Edwards* presumption for 14 days following a break in custody—as opposed to 0, 10, or 100 days—provides the "closest possible fit" with the Self–Incrimination Clause. Nor does it explain how the benefits of a prophylactic 14–day rule (either on its own terms or compared with other possible rules) "outweigh its costs" (which would include the loss of law enforcement information as well as the exclusion of confessions that are in fact voluntary).

To be sure, the Court's rule has the benefit of providing a bright line. But * * * an otherwise arbitrary rule is not justifiable merely because it gives clear instruction to law enforcement officers.

As the Court concedes, "clarity and certainty are not goals in themselves. They are valuable only when they reasonably further the achievement of some substantive end—here, the exclusion of compelled confessions" that the Fifth Amendment prohibits. The Court's arbitrary 14–day rule fails this test, even under the relatively permissive criteria set forth in our precedents. Accordingly, I do not join that portion of the Court's opinion.

JUSTICE STEVENS, concurring in the judgment.

While I agree that the presumption from Edwards v. Arizona is not "eternal," and does not mandate suppression of Shatzer's statement made after a 2½–year break in custody, I do not agree with the Court's newly announced rule: that *Edwards* always ceases to apply when there is a 14–day break in custody.

* * *

I

The most troubling aspect of the Court's time-based rule is that it disregards the compulsion caused by a second (or third, or fourth) interrogation of an indigent suspect who was told that if he requests a lawyer, one will be provided for him. When police tell an indigent suspect that he has the right to an attorney, that he is not required to speak without an attorney present, and that an attorney will be provided to him at no cost before questioning, the police have made a significant promise. If they cease questioning and then reinterrogate the suspect 14 days later without providing him with a lawyer, the suspect is likely to feel that the police lied to him and that he really does not have any right to a lawyer.

* * * When police have not honored an earlier commitment to provide a detainee with a lawyer, the detainee likely will understand his (expressed) wishes to have been ignored and may well see further objection as futile and confession (true or not) as the only way to end his interrogation. Cf. Cooper v. Dupnik, 963 F.2d 1220, 1225 (C.A.9 1992) (en banc) (describing an elaborate police task force plan to ignore a suspect's requests for counsel, on the theory that such would induce hopelessness and thereby elicit an admission). Simply giving a fresh set of *Miranda* warnings will not reassure a suspect who has been denied the counsel he has clearly requested that his rights have remained untrammeled.

II

The Court never explains why its rule cannot depend on, in addition to a break in custody and passage of time, a concrete event or state of affairs, such as the police having honored their commitment to provide counsel. Instead, the Court simply decides to create a time-based rule, and in so doing, disregards much of the analysis upon which *Edwards* and subsequent decisions were based. * * * The Court ignores the effects not of badgering but of reinterrogating a suspect who took the police at their word that he need not answer questions without an attorney present. The Court, moreover, ignores that when a suspect asks for counsel, until his request is answered, there are still the same "inherently compelling" pressures of custodial interrogation on which the *Miranda* line of cases is based and that the concern about compulsion is especially serious for a detainee who has requested a lawyer, an act that signals his inability to cope with the pressures of custodial interrogation.

Instead of deferring to these well-settled understandings of the *Edwards* rule, the Court engages in its own speculation that a 14–day break in custody eliminates the compulsion that animated *Edwards*. But its opinion gives no strong basis for believing that this is the case. * * * A 14–day break in custody does not change the fact that custodial interrogation is inherently compelling. It is unlikely to change the fact that a detainee "considers himself unable to deal with the pressures of custodial interrogation without legal assistance." *Roberson*. And in some instances, a 14–day break in custody may make matters worse when a suspect understands his (expressed) wishes to have been ignored and thus may well see further objection as futile and confession (true or not) as the only way to end his interrogation.

* * *

The many problems with the Court's new rule are exacerbated in the very situation in this case: a suspect who is in prison. Even if, as the Court assumes, a trip to one's home significantly changes the *Edwards* calculus, a trip to one's prison cell is not the same. A prisoner's freedom is severely limited, and his entire life remains subject to government control. Such an environment is not conducive to "shak[ing] off any residual coercive effects of his prior custody." Nor can a prisoner easily "seek advice from an attorney, family members, and friends," especially not within 14 days; prisoners are frequently subject to restrictions on communications. Nor, in most cases, can he live comfortably knowing that he cannot be badgered by police; prison is not like a normal situation in which a suspect is in control, and need only shut his door or walk away to avoid police badgering. * * * The Court ignores these realities of prison, and instead rests its argument on the supposition that a prisoner's "detention . . . is relatively disconnected from their prior unwillingness to cooperate in an investigation." But that is not necessarily the case. Prisoners are uniquely vulnerable to the officials who control every aspect of their lives; prison guards may not look kindly upon a prisoner who refuses to cooperate with police. And cooperation frequently is relevant to whether the prisoner can obtain parole. Moreover, even if it is true as a factual matter that a prisoner's fate is not controlled by the police who come to interrogate him, how is the prisoner supposed to know that? * * *

III

Because, at the very least, we do not know whether Shatzer could obtain a lawyer, and thus would have felt that police had lied about providing one, I cannot join the Court's opinion. I concur in today's judgment, however, on another ground: Even if Shatzer could not consult a lawyer and the police never provided him one, the 2½–year break in custody is a basis for treating the second interrogation as no more coercive than the first. Neither a break in custody nor the passage of time has an inherent, curative power. But certain things change over time. An indigent suspect who took police at their word that they would provide an attorney probably will feel that he has been denied the counsel he has clearly requested when police begin to question him, without a lawyer, only 14 days later. But, when a suspect has been left alone for a significant period of time, he is not as likely to draw such conclusions when the police interrogate him again. It is concededly impossible to determine with precision where to draw such a line. In the case before us, however, the suspect was returned to the general prison population for 2½ years. I am convinced that this period of time is sufficient. I therefore concur in the judgment.

CHAPTER FIVE

THE RIGHT TO COUNSEL

■ ■ ■

IV. THE SCOPE OF THE RIGHT

Page 854. Add this New Section.

D. CIVIL CONTEMPT PROCEEDINGS

The Sixth Amendment right to counsel is limited by its terms to criminal prosecutions. The following case considers whether the Due Process Clause guarantees a right to counsel in a civil contempt proceeding that leads to the defendant's incarceration.

TURNER v. ROGERS

Supreme Court of the United States, 2011.
2011 WL 2437010

Justice Breyer delivered the opinion of the Court.

South Carolina's Family Court enforces its child support orders by threatening with incarceration for civil contempt those who are (1) subject to a child support order, (2) able to comply with that order, but (3) fail to do so. We must decide whether the Fourteenth Amendment's Due Process Clause requires the State to provide counsel (at a civil contempt hearing) to an indigent person potentially faced with such incarceration. We conclude that where as here the custodial parent (entitled to receive the support) is unrepresented by counsel, the State need not provide counsel to the noncustodial parent (required to provide the sup-

port). But we attach an important caveat, namely, that the State must nonetheless have in place alternative procedures that assure a fundamentally fair determination of the critical incarceration-related question, whether the supporting parent is able to comply with the support order.

I

A

South Carolina family courts enforce their child support orders in part through civil contempt proceedings. Each month the family court clerk reviews outstanding child support orders, identifies those in which the supporting parent has fallen

87

more than five days behind, and sends that parent an order to "show cause" why he should not be held in contempt. The "show cause" order and attached affidavit refer to the relevant child support order, identify the amount of the arrearage, and set a date for a court hearing. At the hearing that parent may demonstrate that he is not in contempt, say, by showing that he is not able to make the required payments. If he fails to make the required showing, the court may hold him in civil contempt. And it may require that he be imprisoned unless and until he purges himself of contempt by making the required child support payments (but not for more than one year regardless).

B

In June 2003 a South Carolina family court entered an order, which * * * required petitioner, Michael Turner, to pay $51.73 per week to respondent, Rebecca Rogers, to help support their child. * * * Over the next three years, Turner repeatedly failed to pay the amount due and was held in contempt on five occasions. The first four times he was sentenced to 90 days' imprisonment, but he ultimately paid the amount due (twice without being jailed, twice after spending two or three days in custody). The fifth time he did not pay but completed a 6–month sentence.

After his release in 2006 Turner remained in arrears. On March 27, 2006, the clerk issued a new "show cause" order. And after an initial postponement due to Turner's failure to appear, Turner's civil contempt hearing took place on January 3, 2008. Turner and Rogers were present, each without representation by counsel.

The hearing was brief. The court clerk said that Turner was $5,728.76 behind in his payments. The judge asked Turner if there was "anything you want to say." Turner replied,

"Well, when I first got out, I got back on dope. I done meth, smoked pot and everything else, and I paid a little bit here and there. And, when I finally did get to working, I broke my back, back in September. I filed for disability and SSI. And, I didn't get straightened out off the dope until I broke my back and laid up for two months. And, now I'm off the dope and everything. I just hope that you give me a chance. I don't know what else to say. I mean, I know I done wrong, and I should have been paying and helping her, and I'm sorry. I mean, dope had a hold to me."

The judge then said, "[o]kay," and asked Rogers if she had anything to say. After a brief discussion of federal benefits, the judge stated,

"If there's nothing else, this will be the Order of the Court. I find the Defendant in willful contempt. I'm [going to] sentence him to twelve months in the Oconee County Detention Center. He may purge himself of the contempt and avoid the sentence by having a zero balance on or before his release. I've also placed a lien on any SSI or other benefits."

The judge added that Turner would not receive good-time or work credits, but "[i]f you've got a job, I'll make you eligible for work release." Ibid. When Turner asked why he could not receive good-time or work credits, the judge said, "[b]ecause that's my ruling."

The court made no express finding concerning Turner's ability to pay his arrearage (though Turner's wife had voluntarily submitted a copy of Turner's application for disability benefits). Nor did the judge ask any followup questions or otherwise address the ability-to-pay issue. After the hearing, the judge filled out a prewritten form titled "Order for Contempt of Court," which included the statement:

> "Defendant (was) (was not) gainfully employed and/or (had) (did not have) the ability to make these support payments when due."

But the judge left this statement as is without indicating whether Turner was able to make support payments.

C

While serving his 12–month sentence, Turner, with the help of pro bono counsel, appealed. He claimed that the Federal Constitution entitled him to counsel at his con tempt hearing. The South Carolina Supreme Court * * * rejected his "right to counsel" claim. The court pointed out that civil contempt differs significantly from criminal contempt. The former does not require all the "constitutional safeguards" applicable in criminal proceedings. And the right to government-paid counsel, the Supreme Court held, was one of the "safeguards" not required.

Turner sought certiorari. In light of differences among state courts (and some federal courts) on the applicability of a "right to counsel" in civil contempt proceedings enforcing child support orders, we granted the writ.

II

Respondents argue that this case is moot. * * * The short, conclusive answer to respondents' mootness claim, however, is that this case is not moot because it falls within a special category of disputes that are "capable of repetition" while "evading review." A dispute falls into that category, and a case based on that dispute remains live, if "(1) the challenged action [is] in its duration too short to be fully litigated prior to its cessation or expiration, and (2) there [is] a reasonable expectation that the same complaining party [will] be subjected to the same action again." Weinstein v. Bradford, 423 U.S. 147, 149 (1975) (per curiam).

* * *

III

A

We must decide whether the Due Process Clause grants an indigent defendant, such as Turner, a right to state-appointed counsel at a civil contempt proceeding, which may lead to his incarceration. This Court's precedents provide no definitive answer to that question. This Court has long held that the Sixth Amendment grants an indigent defendant the right to state-appointed counsel in a criminal case. Gideon v. Wainwright, 372 U.S. 335 (1963). And we have held that this same rule applies to criminal contempt proceedings (other than summary proceedings). United States v. Dixon, 509 U.S. 688, 696 (1993).

But the Sixth Amendment does not govern civil cases. Civil contempt differs from criminal contempt in that it seeks only to coerce the defendant to do what a court had previously ordered him to do. A court may not impose punishment "in a civil contempt proceeding when it is clearly established that the alleged contemnor is unable to comply with the terms of the order." Hicks v. Feiock, 485 U.S. 624, 638, n. 9 (1988). And once a civil contemnor complies with the underlying order, he is purged of the contempt and is free.

Consequently, the Court has made clear (in a case not involving the right to counsel) that, where civil contempt is at issue, the Fourteenth Amendment's Due Process Clause allows a State to provide fewer procedural protections than in a criminal case. Id., at 637–641 (State may place the burden of proving inability to pay on the defendant).

This Court has decided only a handful of cases that more directly concern a right to counsel in civil matters. And the application of those decisions to the present case is not clear. On the one hand, the Court has held that the Fourteenth Amendment requires the State to pay for representation by counsel in a civil "juvenile delinquency" proceeding (which could lead to incarceration). In re Gault, 387 U.S. 1, 35–42 (1967). * * * Further, in Lassiter v. Department of Social Servs. of Durham Cty., 452 U.S. 18 (1981), a case that focused upon civil proceedings leading to loss of parental rights, the Court wrote that the

> "pre-eminent generalization that emerges from this Court's precedents on an indigent's right to appointed counsel is that such a right has been recognized to exist only where the litigant may lose his physical liberty if he loses the litigation." Id., at 25.

And the Court then drew from these precedents "the presumption that an indigent litigant has a right to appointed counsel only when, if he loses, he may be deprived of his physical liberty." Id., at 26–27.

On the other hand, the Court has held that a criminal offender facing revocation of probation and imprisonment does not ordinarily have a right to counsel at a probation revocation hearing. Gagnon v. Scarpelli, 411 U.S. 778 (1973); see also Middendorf v. Henry, 425 U.S. 25 (1976) (no due process right to counsel in summary court-martial proceedings). And, at the same time, Gault, and Lassiter are readily distinguishable. The civil juvenile delinquency proceeding at issue in Gault was "little different" from, and "comparable in seriousness" to, a criminal prosecution. * * * And the Court's statements in Lassiter constitute part of its rationale for denying a right to counsel in that case. We believe those statements are best read as pointing out that the Court previously had found a right to counsel "only" in cases involving incarceration, not that a right to counsel exists in all such cases (a position that would have been difficult to reconcile with Gagnon).

B

Civil contempt proceedings in child support cases constitute one part of a highly complex system designed to assure a noncustodial parent's regular payment of funds typically necessary for the support of his children. Often the family receives welfare support from a state-administered federal program, and the State then seeks reimbursement from the noncustodial parent. Other times the custodial parent (often the mother, but sometimes the father, a grandparent, or another person with custody) does not receive government benefits and is entitled to receive the support payments herself.

The Federal Government has created an elaborate procedural mechanism designed to help both the government and custodial parents to secure the payments to which they are entitled. These systems often rely upon wage withholding, expedited procedures for modifying and enforcing child support orders, and automated data processing. But sometimes States will use contempt orders to ensure that the custodial parent receives support payments or the government receives reimbursement. Although some experts have criticized this last-mentioned procedure, and the Federal Government believes that "the routine use of contempt for non-payment of child support is likely to be an ineffective strategy," the Government also tells us that "coercive enforcement remedies, such as contempt, have a role to play."South Carolina, which relies heavily on contempt proceedings, agrees that they are an important tool.

We here consider an indigent's right to paid counsel at such a contempt proceeding. It is a civil proceeding. And we consequently determine the "specific dictates of due process" by examining the "distinct factors" that this Court has previously found useful in deciding what specific safeguards the Constitution's Due Process Clause requires in order to make a civil proceeding fundamentally fair. Mathews v. Eldridge, 424 U.S. 319, 335 (1976) (considering fairness of an administrative proceeding). As relevant here those factors include (1) the nature of "the private interest that will be affected," (2) the comparative "risk" of an "erroneous deprivation" of that interest with and without "additional or substitute procedural safeguards," and (3) the nature and magnitude of any countervailing interest in not providing "additional or substitute procedural requirement[s]."

The "private interest that will be affected" argues strongly for the right to counsel that Turner advocates.

That interest consists of an indigent defendant's loss of personal liberty through imprisonment. The interest in securing that freedom, the freedom "from bodily restraint," lies "at the core of the liberty protected by the Due Process Clause." Foucha v. Louisiana, 504 U.S. 71, 80 (1992). And we have made clear that its threatened loss through legal proceedings demands "due process protection." Addington v. Texas, 441 U.S. 418, 425 (1979).

Given the importance of the interest at stake, it is obviously important to assure accurate decisionmaking in respect to the key "ability to pay" question. Moreover, the fact that ability to comply marks a dividing line between civil and criminal contempt, Hicks, reinforces the need for accuracy. That is because an incorrect decision (wrongly classifying the contempt proceeding as civil) can increase the risk of wrongful incarceration by depriving the defendant of the procedural protections (including counsel) that the Constitution would demand in a criminal proceeding. And since 70% of child support arrears nationwide are owed by parents with either no reported income or income of $10,000 per year or less, the issue of ability to pay may arise fairly often.

On the other hand, the Due Process Clause does not always require the provision of counsel in civil proceedings where incarceration is threatened. See *Gagnon*, 411 U.S. 778. And in determining whether the Clause requires a right to counsel here, we must take account of opposing interests, as well as consider the probable value of "additional or substitute procedural safeguards." *Mathews*, supra, at 335.

Doing so, we find three related considerations that, when taken together, argue strongly against the Due Process Clause requiring the State to provide indigents with counsel in every proceeding of the kind before us.

First, the critical question likely at issue in these cases concerns, as we have said, the defendant's ability to pay. That question is often closely related to the question of the defendant's indigence. But when the right procedures are in place, indigence can be a question that in many—but not all—cases is sufficiently straightforward to warrant determination prior to providing a defendant with counsel, even in a criminal case. Federal law, for example, requires a criminal defendant to provide information showing that he is indigent, and therefore entitled to state-funded counsel, before he can receive that assistance. See 18 U.S.C. § 3006A(b).

Second, sometimes, as here, the person opposing the defendant at the hearing is not the government represented by counsel but the custodial parent unrepresented by counsel. The custodial parent, perhaps a woman with custody of one or more children, may be relatively poor, unemployed, and unable to afford counsel. Yet she may have encouraged the court to enforce its order through contempt. And the proceeding is ultimately for her benefit.

A requirement that the State provide counsel to the noncustodial parent in these cases could create an asymmetry of representation that would alter significantly the nature of the proceeding. Doing so could mean a degree of formality or delay that would unduly slow payment to those immediately in need. And, perhaps more important for present purposes, doing so could make the proceedings less fair overall, increasing the risk of a decision that would erroneously deprive a family of the support it is entitled to receive. The needs of such families play an important role in our analysis.

Third, as the Solicitor General points out, there is available a set of "substitute procedural safeguards," *Mathews*, 424 U.S., at 335, which, if employed together, can significantly reduce the risk of an erroneous deprivation of liberty. They can do so, moreover, without incurring some of the drawbacks inherent in recognizing an automatic right to counsel. Those safeguards include (1) notice to the defendant that his "ability to pay" is a critical issue in the contempt proceeding; (2) the use of a form (or the equivalent) to elicit relevant financial information; (3) an opportunity at the hearing for the defendant to respond to statements and questions about his financial status, (e.g., those triggered by his responses on the form); and (4) an express finding by the court that the defendant has the ability to pay. In presenting these alternatives, the Government draws upon considerable experience in helping to manage statutorily mandated federal-state efforts to enforce child support orders. It does not claim that they are the only possible alternatives, and this Court's cases suggest, for example, that sometimes assistance other than purely legal assistance (here, say, that of a neutral social worker) can prove constitutionally sufficient. But the Government does claim that these alternatives can assure the "fundamental fairness" of the proceeding even where the State does not pay for counsel for an indigent defendant.

While recognizing the strength of Turner's arguments, we ultimately believe that the three considerations we have just discussed must carry the day. In our view, a categorical right to counsel in proceedings of the kind before us would carry with it disadvantages (in the form of unfairness and delay) that, in terms of ultimate fairness, would deprive it of significant superiority over the alternatives that we have mentioned. We consequently hold that the Due Process Clause does not automatically require the provision of counsel at civil contempt proceedings to an indigent individual who is subject to a child support order, even if that individual faces incarceration (for up to a year). In particular, that Clause does not require the provision of counsel where the opposing parent or other custodian (to whom support funds are owed) is not represented by counsel and the State provides alternative procedural safeguards equivalent to those we have mentioned (adequate notice of the importance of ability to pay, fair opportunity to present, and to dispute, relevant information, and court findings).

We do not address civil contempt proceedings where the underlying child support payment is owed to the State, for example, for reimbursement of welfare funds paid to the parent with custody. Those proceedings more closely resemble debt-collection proceedings. The government is likely to have counsel or some other competent representative. And this kind of proceeding is not before us. Neither do we address what due process requires in an unusually complex case where a defendant "can fairly be represented only by a trained advocate." *Gagnon*, 411 U.S., at 788.

IV

The record indicates that Turner received neither counsel nor the benefit of alternative procedures like those we have described. He did not receive clear notice that his ability to pay would constitute the critical question in his civil contempt proceeding. No one provided him with a form (or the equivalent) designed to elicit information about his financial circumstances. The court did not find that Turner was able to pay his arrearage, but instead left the relevant "finding" section of the contempt order blank. The court nonetheless found Turner in contempt and ordered him incarcerated. Under these circumstances Turner's incarceration violated the Due Process Clause.

We vacate the judgment of the South Carolina Supreme Court and remand the case for further proceedings not inconsistent with this opinion.

It is so ordered.

JUSTICE THOMAS, with whom JUSTICE SCALIA joins, and with whom THE CHIEF JUSTICE and JUSTICE ALITO join [in pertinent part] dissenting.

* * *

I

* * *

A

* * *

B

[T]he Due Process Clause does not provide a right to appointed counsel for all indigent defendants facing incarceration in civil contempt proceedings. Such a reading would render the Sixth Amendment right to counsel—as it is currently understood—superfluous. Moreover, it appears that even cases applying the Court's modern interpretation of due process have not understood it to categorically require appointed counsel in circumstances outside those otherwise covered by the Sixth Amendment.

* * *

II

The majority agrees that the Constitution does not entitle Turner to appointed counsel. But at the invitation of the Federal Government as amicus curiae, the majority holds that his contempt hearing violated the Due Process Clause for an entirely different reason, which the parties have never raised: The family court's procedures "were inadequate to ensure an accurate determination of [Turner's] present ability to pay." I would not reach this issue.

* * *

[I]t is the wise and settled general practice of this Court not to consider an issue in the first instance, much less one raised only by an amicus. This is doubly true when we review the decision of a state court and triply so when the new issue is a constitutional matter.

* * *

* * * The Federal Government's interest in States' child support enforcement efforts may give the Government a valuable perspective, but it does not overcome the strong reasons behind the Court's practice of not considering new issues, raised and addressed only by an amicus, for the first time in this Court.

III

* * *

CHAPTER TEN

TRIAL AND TRIAL-RELATED RIGHTS

■ ■ ■

III. CONSTITUTIONALLY BASED PROOF REQUIREMENTS

C. THE SCOPE OF THE REASONABLE DOUBT REQUIREMENT: WHAT IS AN ELEMENT OF THE CRIME?

Page 1130. Add after the section on Harris v. United States

Construing Criminal Statutes to Distinguish a Sentencing Factor from an Element of the Crime: United States v. O'Brien

UNITED STATES v. O'BRIEN

Supreme Court of the United States, 2010
130 S.Ct. 2169

JUSTICE KENNEDY delivered the opinion of the Court

The Court must interpret, once again, § 924(c) of Title 18 of the United States Code. This provision prohibits the use or carrying of a firearm in relation to a crime of violence or drug trafficking crime, or the possession of a firearm in furtherance of such crimes. § 924(c)(1)(A). A violation of the statute carries a mandatory minimum term of five years' imprisonment, § 924(c)(1)(A)(i); but if the firearm is a machinegun, the statute requires a 30-year mandatory minimum sentence,

§ 924(c)(1)(B)(ii). Whether a firearm was used, carried, or possessed is, as all concede, an element of the offense. At issue here is whether the fact that the firearm was a machinegun is an element to be proved to the jury beyond a reasonable doubt or a sentencing factor to be proved to the judge at sentencing.

In an earlier case the Court determined that an analogous machinegun provision in a previous version of § 924 constituted an element of an offense to be proved to the jury. Castillo v. United States, 530 U.S. 120 (2000). The *Castillo* decision, however, addressed the statute as it existed before congressional amendments

95

made in 1998. And in a case after *Castillo*, the brandishing provision in the post–1998 version of § 924 was held to provide a sentencing factor, not an element of the offense. Harris v. United States [Casebook page 1127]. In light of the 1998 amendments and the *Harris* decision, the question of how to interpret § 924's machinegun provision is considered once more in the instant case.

I

[O'Brien and his co-defendants committed an armed robbery. Three firearms were used during the robbery.] The firearms were a semiautomatic Sig–Sauer pistol, an AK–47 semiautomatic rifle, and a Cobray pistol. The Cobray pistol had been manufactured as, and had the external appearance of, a semiautomatic firearm. According to the Federal Bureau of Investigation, though, it operated as a fully automatic weapon, apparently due to some alteration of its original firing mechanism. Respondents dispute whether the Cobray in fact did operate as a fully automatic weapon.

Respondents were indicted on multiple counts. Relevant here are counts three and four, both of which charged offenses under § 924(c). Count three charged respondents with using a firearm in furtherance of a crime of violence, which carries a statutory minimum of five years' imprisonment. Count four charged respondents in more specific terms, alleging use of a machinegun (the Cobray) in furtherance of a crime of violence, as proscribed by §§ 924(c)(1)(A) and (B)(ii). The latter provision mandates a minimum sentence of 30 years' imprisonment.

The Government moved to dismiss count four on the basis that it would be unable to establish the count be-

yond a reasonable doubt. * * * The Government then maintained that the machinegun provision in § 924(c)(1)(B)(ii) was a sentencing factor, so that, if respondents were convicted of carrying a firearm under count three, the court could determine at sentencing that the particular firearm was a machinegun, thus activating the 30–year mandatory minimum. The District Court dismissed count four, as the Government requested, but rejected the Government's position that the machinegun provision was a sentencing enhancement to be determined by the court at sentencing once there was a conviction on count three. It ruled that the machinegun provision states an element of a crime. Thus, to invoke the 30–year minimum sentence, the Government was required to charge in the indictment, and then prove to the jury, that the Cobray was a machinegun.

* * * The Government appealed the District Court's ruling that the § 924 machinegun provision constitutes an element of an offense instead of a sentencing factor. [The Court of Appeals agreed with the district court that the machinegun provision constituted an element of the crime.]

II

Elements of a crime must be charged in an indictment and proved to a jury beyond a reasonable doubt. Sentencing factors, on the other hand, can be proved to a judge at sentencing by a preponderance of the evidence. See McMillan v. Pennsylvania [Casebook page 1117]. Though one exception has been established, see Almendarez–Torres v. United States, [Casebook page 1118], "[i]t is unconstitutional for a legislature to remove from the jury the assessment of facts that increase the prescribed range of penalties to which a criminal defendant is exposed." Apprendi v. New Jersey. In other words, while sentencing factors may guide or confine a judge's discretion in sentencing an offender within the range prescribed by statute, judge-found sentencing factors cannot increase the maximum sentence a defendant might otherwise receive based purely on the facts found by the jury.

Subject to this constitutional constraint, whether a given fact is an element of the crime itself or a sentencing factor is a question for Congress. When Congress is not explicit, as is often the case because it seldom directly addresses the distinction between sentencing factors and elements, courts look to the provisions and the framework of the statute to determine whether a fact is an element or a sentencing factor. In examining whether the machinegun provision in § 924 is an element or a sentencing factor, the analysis must begin with this Court's previous examination of the question in *Castillo*.

In *Castillo*, the Court considered a prior version of § 924, which provided:

"(c)(1) Whoever, during and in relation to any crime of violence or drug trafficking crime . . . , uses or carries a firearm, shall, in addition to the punishment provided for such crime of violence or drug trafficking crime, be sentenced to imprisonment for five years, and if the firearm is a short-barreled rifle [or a] short-barreled shotgun to imprisonment for ten years, and if the firearm is a machinegun, or a destructive device, or is equipped with a firearm silencer or firearm muffler, to imprisonment for thirty

years. . . ." 18 U.S.C. § 924(c)(1) (1988 ed., Supp. V).

In determining whether the machinegun provision in the just-quoted version of § 924 constituted an element or a sentencing factor, the Court in *Castillo* observed that the bare statutory language was "neutral." It examined five factors directed at determining congressional intent: (1) language and structure, (2) tradition, (3) risk of unfairness, (4) severity of the sentence, and (5) legislative history. The Court unanimously concluded that the machinegun provision provided an element of an offense, noting that the first four factors favored treating it as such while legislative history did not significantly favor either side.

III

A

Section 924(c) was amended to its current form in 1998. The instant case concerns the post–1998 (and current) version of the statute, which provides:

"(A) Except to the extent that a greater minimum sentence is otherwise provided by this subsection or by any other provision of law, any person who, during and in relation to any crime of violence or drug trafficking crime . . . uses or carries a firearm, or who, in furtherance of any such crime, possesses a firearm, shall, in addition to the punishment provided for such crime of violence or drug trafficking crime—

"(i) be sentenced to a term of imprisonment of not less than 5 years;

"(ii) if the firearm is brandished, be sentenced to a term of imprisonment of not less than 7 years; and "(iii) if the firearm is discharged, be sentenced to a term of imprisonment of not less than 10 years.

"(B) If the firearm possessed by a person convicted of a violation of this subsection—

"(i) is a short-barreled rifle, short-barreled shotgun, or semiautomatic assault weapon, the person shall be sentenced to a term of imprisonment of not less than 10 years; or

"(ii) is a machinegun or a destructive device, or is equipped with a firearm silencer or firearm muffler, the person shall be sentenced to a term of imprisonment of not less than 30 years." 18 U.S.C. § 924(c)(1) (2006 ed.).

The 1998 amendment did make substantive changes to the statute, to be discussed below; but for purposes of the present case the most apparent effect of the amendment was to divide what was once a lengthy principal sentence into separate subparagraphs. This Court's observation in considering the first *Castillo* factor, that "Congress placed the element 'uses or carries a firearm' and the word 'machinegun' in a single sentence, not broken up with dashes or separated into subsections," no longer holds true. Aside from this new structure, however, the 1998 amendment of § 924 did nothing to affect the second through fifth *Castillo* factors. Each of the factors, except for legislative history (which, assuming its relevance, remains relatively silent), continues to favor the conclusion that the machinegun provision is an element of an offense.

Legal tradition and past congressional practice are the second *Castillo* factor. The factor is to be consulted when, as here, a statute's text is unclear as to whether certain

facts constitute elements or sentencing factors. Sentencing factors traditionally involve characteristics of the offender—such as recidivism, cooperation with law enforcement, or acceptance of responsibility. Characteristics of the offense itself are traditionally treated as elements, and the use of a machinegun under § 924(c) lies closest to the heart of the crime at issue. This is no less true today than it was 10 years ago in *Castillo*. Unsurprisingly, firearm type is treated as an element in a number of statutes, as numerous gun crimes make substantive distinctions between weapons such as pistols and machineguns.

The Government counters that this tradition or pattern has evolved since the version of § 924(c) under review in *Castillo* was enacted. The Government contends that the Federal Sentencing Guidelines altered the tradition by treating the possession of a firearm as a sentencing factor. Brief for United States 23 (citing United States Sentencing Commission, Guidelines Manual § 2K2.1(a)(5) (Nov.1998) (raising base offense level "if the offense involved a firearm")).

The argument is not persuasive. The Sentencing Reform Act of 1984, establishing the Federal Sentencing Guidelines, was enacted four years before the version of § 924 under review in *Castillo*. * * * The Guidelines were explicitly taken into account when this Court analyzed the traditions in *Castillo*.

The third *Castillo* factor, potential unfairness, was unchanged by the restructuring of § 924. The Court explained in *Castillo* that treating the machinegun provision as a sentencing factor "might unnecessarily produce a conflict between the judge and the jury" because "a jury may well have to decide which of several weapons" a defendant used. The concern was that the judge may not know which weapon the jurors determined a defendant used, and "a judge's later, sentencing-related decision that the defendant used the machinegun, rather than, say, the pistol, might conflict with the jury's belief that he actively used the pistol." This same concern arises under the current version of § 924, where jurors might have to determine which among several weapons a defendant used, carried, or possessed in furtherance of a crime.

* * *

The fourth *Castillo* factor, the severity of the sentence accompanying a finding that a defendant carried a machinegun under § 924, was also unaffected by the statute's restructuring. A finding that a defendant carried a machinegun under § 924, in contrast to some less dangerous firearm, vaults a defendant's mandatory minimum sentence from 5 to 30 years, or from 7 to 30 years if, as in this case, the firearm was brandished. This is not akin to the "incremental changes in the minimum" that one would "expect to see in provisions meant to identify matters for the sentencing judge's consideration," *Harris* (from 5 years to 7 years); it is a drastic, sixfold increase that strongly suggests a separate substantive crime.

There is one substantive difference between the old and new versions of § 924 that might bear on this fourth factor. The previous version of § 924 provided mandatory sentences: 5 years for using or carrying a firearm and 30 years if the firearm is a machinegun, for example. The current statute provides only mandatory minimums: not less than 5 years for using or possessing a firearm; not less than 7 for brandishing it; and not

less than 30 if the firearm is a machinegun. The Government argues that this difference is critical because a 30-year sentence is conceivable under the statute even without a finding that the particular weapon is a machinegun.

This is a distinction in theory, perhaps, but not in practice. Neither the Government nor any party or amicus has identified a single defendant whose conviction under § 924 for possessing or brandishing a nonspecific firearm led to a sentence approaching the 30-year sentence that is required when the firearm is a machinegun. Respondents advise, without refutation, that most courts impose the mandatory minimum of 7 years' imprisonment for brandishing a nonspecific weapon and the longest sentence that has come to the litigants' or the Court's attention is 14 years. Indeed, in the instant case, Burgess received the statutory minimum 7-year sentence, and O'Brien received only 18 months more than that. Once the machinegun enhancement was off the table, the Government itself did not seek anything approaching 30-year terms, instead requesting 12-year terms for each respondent.

The immense danger posed by machineguns, the moral depravity in choosing the weapon, and the substantial increase in the minimum sentence provided by the statute support the conclusion that this prohibition is an element of the crime, not a sentencing factor. It is not likely that Congress intended to remove the indictment and jury trial protections when it provided for such an extreme sentencing increase. Perhaps Congress was not concerned with parsing the distinction between elements and sentencing factors, a matter more often discussed by the courts when discussing the proper allocation of functions between judge and jury. Instead, it likely was more focused on deterring the crime by creating the mandatory minimum sentences. But the severity of the increase in this case counsels in favor of finding that the prohibition is an element, at least absent some clear congressional indication to the contrary.

The fifth factor considered in *Castillo* was legislative history, and the Court there found it to be of little help. The 1998 amendment has its own legislative record * * * but the parties accurately observe that it is silent as to congressional consideration of the distinction between elements and sentencing factors. This silence is not neutral, however, because as explained below, it tends to counsel against finding that Congress made a substantive change to this statutory provision.

Four of the five factors the Court relied upon in *Castillo* point in the same direction they did 10 years ago. How the 1998 amendment affects the remaining factor—the provision's language and structure—requires closer examination.

B

* * *

There are three principal differences between the previous and current versions of § 924(c): two substantive changes and a third regarding the stylistic structure of the statute. The first difference, as discussed above, * * * is that the amendment changed what were once mandatory sentences into mandatory minimum sentences. A person convicted of the primary offense of using or carrying a firearm during a crime of violence was once to "be

sentenced to imprisonment for five years," but under the current version he or she is to "be sentenced to a term of imprisonment of not less than 5 years."

The second difference is that the amended version includes the word "possesses" in addition to "uses or carries" in its principal paragraph, and then adds the substantive provisions in §§ 924(c)(1)(A)(ii) and (iii), which provide mandatory minimums for brandishing (7 years) and discharging (10 years) the firearm. These provisions are new substantive additions to the text of the previous version, which provided a bare 5–year mandatory minimum for any offender who "use[d] or carrie[d] a firearm," without concern for how the firearm was used.

* * * Neither of these substantive changes suggests that Congress meant to transform the machinegun provision from an element into a sentencing factor.

The Government stresses a third, structural, difference in the statute, pointing out that the machinegun provision now resides in a separate subsection, § 924(c)(1)(B), whereas it once resided in the principal paragraph that unmistakably lists offense elements. This structural or stylistic change, though, does not provide a clear indication that Congress meant to alter its treatment of machineguns as an offense element. A more logical explanation for the restructuring is that it broke up a lengthy principal paragraph, which exceeded 250 words * * * into a more readable statute. This is in step with current legislative drafting guidelines, which advise drafters to break lengthy statutory provisions into separate subsections that can be read more easily.

* * *

To be sure, there are some arguments in favor of treating the machinegun provision as a sentencing factor. The current structure of § 924(c) is more favorable to that interpretation than was true in *Castillo*, particularly because the machinegun provision is now positioned between the sentencing factors provided in (A)(ii) and (iii), and the recidivist provisions in (C)(i) and (ii), which are typically sentencing factors as well. *See Almendarez–Torres*. These points are overcome, however, by the substantial weight of the other *Castillo* factors and the principle that Congress would not enact so significant a change without a clear indication of its purpose to do so. * * * The analysis and holding of *Castillo* control this case. The machinegun provision in § 924(c)(1)(B)(ii) is an element of an offense.

The judgment of the Court of Appeals is affirmed.

JUSTICE STEVENS, concurring.

A "sentencing factor" may serve two very different functions. As a historical matter, the term has described a fact that a trial judge might rely upon when choosing a specific sentence within the range authorized by the legislature. In that setting, the judge has broad discretion in determining both the significance of the factor and whether it has been established by reliable evidence.

In the 1970's and 1980's, as part of a national effort to enact tougher sentences, a new type of "sentencing factor" emerged. Since then the term has been used to describe facts, found by the judge by a preponderance of the evidence, that have the effect of imposing mandatory limits on a sentencing judge's discretion.

When used as an element of a mandatory sentencing scheme, a sentencing factor is the functional equivalent of an element of the criminal offense itself. In these circumstances, I continue to believe the Constitution requires proof beyond a reasonable doubt of this "factor."

I

We first encountered the use of a "sentencing factor" in the mandatory minimum context in McMillan v. Pennsylvania, [where the Court] reasoned that because visible possession of a firearm was a mere "sentencing factor," rather than an element of any of the specified offenses defined by the legislature, the protections afforded by cases like In re Winship [Casebook page 1107] did not apply.

* * *

The majority opinion in *McMillan* can fairly be described as pathmarking, but unlike one of its predecessors, it pointed in the wrong direction. * * * I continue to believe that *McMillan* was incorrectly decided.

II

Not only was *McMillan* wrong the day it was decided, but its reasoning has been substantially undermined—if not eviscerated—by the development of our Sixth Amendment jurisprudence in more recent years. We now understand that it is unconstitutional under the Sixth Amendment for a legislature to remove from the jury the assessment of facts that increase the prescribed range of penalties to which a criminal defendant is exposed. Apprendi v. New Jersey. Harmonizing *Apprendi* with our existing Sixth Amendment jurisprudence, we explained that "any fact that increases the penalty for a crime beyond the prescribed statutory maximum must be submitted to a jury, and proved beyond a reasonable doubt.'' In other words, we narrowed our holding to those facts that effectively raised the ceiling on the offense, but did not then consider whether the logic of our holding applied also to those facts necessary to set the floor of a particular sentence.

As JUSTICE THOMAS eloquently explained in his dissent in Harris v. United States, the reasoning in our decision in *Apprendi* applies with equal force in the context of mandatory minimums. There is, quite simply, no reason to distinguish between facts that trigger punishment in excess of the statutory maximum and facts that trigger a mandatory minimum. This case vividly illustrates the point. It is quite plain that there is a world of difference between the 8 1/2–year sentence and the 7–year sentence the judge imposed on the defendants in this case and the 30–year sentence mandated by the machinegun finding under 18 U.S.C. § 924(c)(1)(B).

Mandatory minimums may have a particularly acute practical effect in this type of statutory scheme which contains an implied statutory maximum of life. There is, in this type of case, no ceiling; there is only a floor below which a sentence cannot fall. * * *

* * * *McMillan* and *Harris* should be overruled, at least to the extent that they authorize judicial factfinding on a preponderance of the evidence standard of facts that expose a defendant to a greater punishment than what is otherwise legally prescribed Any such fact is the functional equivalent of an element of the offense.

III

In my view, the simplest, and most correct, solution to the case before us would be to recognize that any fact mandating the imposition of a sentence more severe than a judge would otherwise have discretion to impose should be treated as an element of the offense. The unanimity of our decision today does not imply that *McMillan* is safe from a direct challenge to its foundation.

JUSTICE THOMAS, **concurring in the judgment.**

* * *

In my view, it makes no difference whether the sentencing fact vaults a defendant's mandatory minimum sentence by many years, or only incrementally changes it by a few. Nor does it make a difference whether the sentencing fact involves characteristics of the offender or characteristics of the offense, or which direction the other factors in the Court's five-factor test may tilt. One question decides the matter: If a sentencing fact either raises the floor or raises the ceiling of the range of punishments to which a defendant is exposed, it is, by definition an element.

Without a finding that a defendant used a machinegun, the penalty range for a conviction under § 924(c)(1)(A)(i) is five years to life imprisonment. But once that finding is added, the penalty range becomes harsher—30 years to life imprisonment, § 924(c)(1)(B)(ii)—thus exposing a defendant to greater punishment than what is otherwise legally prescribed. As a consequence, it is ultimately beside the point whether as a matter of statutory interpretation the machinegun enhancement is a sentencing factor. As a constitutional matter, because it establishes a harsher range of punishments, it must be treated as an element of a separate, aggravated offense that is submitted to a jury and proved beyond a reasonable doubt.

Because the Court reaches this same conclusion based on its analysis of a five-factor test, I concur in the judgment.

IV. TRIAL BY JURY

D. JURY SELECTION AND COMPOSITION

5. The Use of Peremptory Challenges

b. Constitutional Limits on Peremptory Challenges

Page 1216. Add after the section on Snyder v. Louisiana.

Review of Demeanor–Based Grounds of Exclusion When the Court Did Not Personally Observe the Voir Dire: Thaler v. Haynes

Note that because the following case is a review of a habeas petition, the standard for review of a state court determination is extremely deferential. The question is not whether the state court misinterpreted Federal law. The question is whether the state court ignored *clearly established* Federal law. [See generally Casebook Chapter 13]. In reading the case, consider whether the Court would actually rule that, under *Batson*, a trial court cannot uphold a demeanor-based exclusion of the juror unless the court was present at the voir dire.

THALER v. HAYNES

Supreme Court of the United States, 2010
130 S.Ct. 1171

Per Curiam

This case presents the question whether any decision of this Court "clearly establishes" that a judge, in ruling on an objection to a peremptory challenge under Batson v. Kentucky, must reject a demeanor-based explanation for the challenge unless the judge personally observed and recalls the aspect of the prospective juror's demeanor on which the explanation is based. The Court of Appeals appears to have concluded that either *Batson* itself or Snyder v. Louisiana, [Casebook page 1213] clearly established such a rule, but the Court of Appeals read far too much into

those decisions, and its holding, if allowed to stand, would have important implications. We therefore * * * reverse the judgment of the Court of Appeals.

I

Respondent was tried in a Texas state court for the murder of a police officer, and the State sought the death penalty. During voir dire, two judges presided at different stages. Judge Harper presided when the attorneys questioned the prospective jurors individually, but Judge Wallace took over when peremptory challenges were exercised. When the prosecutor struck an African–American juror named Owens, respondent's attorney raised a *Batson* objection. Judge Wallace determined that respondent had made out a prima facie case under *Batson*, and the prosecutor then offered a race-neutral explanation that was based on Owens' demeanor during individual questioning. Specifically, the prosecutor asserted that Owens' demeanor had been "somewhat humorous" and not "serious" and that her "body language" had belied her "true feeling." Based on his observations of Owens during questioning by respondent's attorney, the prosecutor stated, he believed that she "had a predisposition" and would not look at the possibility of imposing a death sentence "in a neutral fashion." Respondent's attorney did not dispute the prosecutor's characterization of Owens' demeanor, but he asserted that her answers on the jury questionnaire "show[ed] that she was a juror who [was] leaning towards the State's case." After considering the prosecutor's explanation and the arguments of defense counsel, Judge Wallace stated that the prosecutor's reason for the strike was "race-neutral" and denied the *Batson* objection without further explanation.

The case proceeded to trial, respondent was convicted and sentenced to death, and the Texas Court of Criminal Appeals affirmed the conviction. Rejecting respondent's argument that "a trial judge who did not witness the actual voir dire cannot, as a matter of law, fairly evaluate a *Batson* challenge," the Court of Criminal Appeals wrote:

"There are many factors which a trial judge—even one who did not preside over the voir dire examinations—can consider in determining whether the opponent of the peremptory strikes has met his burden. These include the nature and strength of the parties' arguments during the *Batson* hearing and the attorneys' demeanor and credibility. And, when necessary, a trial judge who has not witnessed the voir dire may refer to the record."

With respect to the strike of juror Owens, the court held that Judge Wallace's acceptance of the prosecutor's explanation was not clearly erroneous and noted that "[t]he record does reflect that Owens was congenial and easygoing during voir dire and that her attitude was less formal than that of other veniremembers." This Court denied respondent's petition for a writ of certiorari.

After the Texas courts denied his application for state habeas relief, respondent filed a federal habeas petition. The District Court denied the petition and observed that this Court had never held that the deference to state-court factual determinations that is mandated by the federal habeas statute is inapplicable when the judge ruling on a *Batson* objection did not observe the jury selection.

A panel of the Court of Appeals granted a certificate of appealability with respect to respondent's *Batson* objections * * *. In its opinion granting the certificate, the panel discussed our opinion in *Snyder* at length and then concluded:

"Under *Snyder's* application of *Batson*, . . . an appellate court applying *Batson* arguably should find clear error when the record reflects that the trial court was not able to verify the aspect of the juror's demeanor upon which the prosecutor based his or her peremptory challenge."

When the same panel later ruled on the merits of respondent's *Batson* claim regarding juror Owens, the court adopted the rule that it had previously termed "arguabl[e]." The court concluded that the decisions of the state courts were not owed "AEDPA deference" in this case "because the state courts engaged in pure appellate fact-finding for an issue that turns entirely on demeanor." Ibid. The court then held that

"no court, including ours, can now engage in a proper adjudication of the defendant's demeanor-based *Batson* challenge as to prospective juror Owens because we will be relying solely on a paper record and would thereby contravene *Batson* and its clearly-established 'factual inquiry' requirement."

II

Respondent cannot obtain federal habeas relief under 28 U.S.C. § 2254(d)(1) unless he can show that the decision of the Texas Court of Criminal Appeals "was contrary to, or involved an unreasonable application of, clearly established Federal law, as determined by the Supreme Court." A legal principle is "clearly established" within the meaning of this provision only when it is embodied in a holding of this Court. * * *

III

In holding that respondent is entitled to a new trial, the Court of Appeals cited two decisions of this Court, *Batson* and *Snyder*, but neither of these cases held that a demeanor-based explanation for a peremptory challenge must be rejected unless the judge personally observed and recalls the relevant aspect of the prospective juror's demeanor.

The Court of Appeals appears to have concluded that *Batson* supports its decision because *Batson* requires

a judge ruling on an objection to a peremptory challenge to "undertake a sensitive inquiry into such circumstantial and direct evidence of intent as may be available." This general requirement, however, did not clearly establish the rule on which the Court of Appeals' decision rests. *Batson* noted the need for a judge ruling on an objection to a peremptory challenge to "tak[e] into account all possible explanatory factors in the particular case." Thus, where the explanation for a peremptory challenge is based on a prospective juror's demeanor, the judge should take into account, among other things, any observations of the juror that the judge was able to make during the voir dire. But *Batson* plainly did not go further and hold that a demeanor-based explanation must be rejected if the judge did not observe or cannot recall the juror's demeanor.

Nor did we establish such a rule in *Snyder*. In that case, the judge who presided over the voir dire also ruled on the *Batson* objections, and thus we had no occasion to consider how *Batson* applies when different judges preside over these two stages of the jury selection process. The part of *Snyder* on which the Court of Appeals relied concerned a very different problem. The prosecutor in that case asserted that he had exercised a peremptory challenge for two reasons, one of which was based on demeanor (i.e., that the juror had appeared to be nervous), and the trial judge overruled the *Batson* objection without explanation. We concluded that the record refuted the explanation that was not based on demeanor and, in light of the particular circumstances of the case, held that the peremptory challenge could not be sustained on the demeanor-based ground, which might not have figured in the trial judge's unexplained ruling. Nothing in this analysis supports the blanket rule on which the decision below appears to rest.

The opinion in *Snyder* did note that when the explanation for a peremptory challenge "invoke[s] a juror's demeanor," the trial judge's "first hand observations" are of great importance. And in explaining why we could not assume that the trial judge had credited the claim that the juror was nervous, we noted that, because the peremptory challenge was not exercised until some time after the juror was questioned, the trial judge might not have recalled the juror's demeanor. These observa-

tions do not suggest that, in the absence of a personal recollection of the juror's demeanor, the judge could not have accepted the prosecutor's explanation. Indeed, *Snyder* quoted the observation in Hernandez v. New York, 500 U.S. 352, 365 (1991), that the best evidence of the intent of the attorney exercising a strike is often that attorney's demeanor.

Accordingly, we hold that no decision of this Court clearly establishes the categorical rule on which the Court of Appeals appears to have relied, and we therefore reverse the judgment and remand the case for proceedings consistent with this opinion. * * *

V. THE IMPARTIALITY OF THE TRIBUNAL AND THE INFLUENCE OF THE PRESS

B. CONTROLLING THE MEDIA'S IMPACT

1. Controlling Access to Courts; Public Trials

Page 1267. Add after the section on Waller v. Georgia

Sixth Amendment Limitation on Excluding Public From Juror Voir Dire: Presley v. Georgia

PRESLEY v. GEORGIA

Supreme Court of the United States, 2010
130 S.Ct. 721

Per Curiam

After a jury trial in the Superior Court of DeKalb County, Georgia, petitioner Eric Presley was convicted of a cocaine trafficking offense. The conviction was affirmed by the Supreme Court of Georgia. Presley seeks certiorari, claiming his Sixth and Fourteenth Amendment right to a public trial was violated when the trial court excluded the public from

the voir dire of prospective jurors. The Supreme Court of Georgia's affirmance contravened this Court's clear precedents. Certiorari and petitioner's motion for leave to proceed in forma pauperis are now granted, and the judgment is reversed.

Before selecting a jury in Presley's trial, the trial court noticed a lone courtroom observer. The court explained that prospective jurors were about to enter and instructed the man that he was not allowed in the courtroom and had to leave that floor of the courthouse entirely. The court then questioned the man and learned he was Presley's uncle. The court reiterated its instruction:

> "Well, you still can't sit out in the audience with the jurors. You know, most of the afternoon actually we're going to be picking a jury. And we may have a couple of pre-trial matters, so you're welcome to come in after we ... complete selecting the jury this afternoon. But, otherwise, you would have to leave the sixth floor, because jurors will be all out in the hallway in a few moments. That applies to everybody who's got a case."

Presley's counsel objected to "the exclusion of the public from the courtroom," but the court explained, "[t]here just isn't space for them to sit in the audience." When Presley's counsel requested "some accommodation," the court explained its ruling further:

> "Well, the uncle can certainly come back in once the trial starts. There's no, really no need for the uncle to be present during jury selection.... [W]e have 42 jurors coming up. Each of those rows will be occupied by jurors. And his uncle cannot sit and intermingle with members of the jury panel. But, when the trial starts, the opening statements and other matters, he can certainly come back into the courtroom."

After Presley was convicted, he moved for a new trial based on the exclusion of the public from the juror voir dire. At a hearing on the motion, Presley presented evidence showing that 14 prospective jurors could have fit in the jury box and the remaining 28 could have fit entirely on one side of the courtroom, leaving adequate room for the public. The trial court denied the motion, commenting that it preferred to seat jurors throughout the entirety of the courtroom, and "it's up to the individual judge to decide ... what's comfortable." The court continued: "It's totally up to my discretion whether or not I want family members in the courtroom to intermingle with the jurors and sit directly behind the jurors where they might overhear some inadvertent comment or conversation." On appeal, the Court of Appeals of Georgia agreed, finding "[t]here was no abuse of discretion here, when the trial court explained the need to exclude spectators at the voir dire stage of the proceedings and when members of the public were invited to return afterward."

The Supreme Court of Georgia granted certiorari and affirmed, with two justices dissenting. After finding "the trial court certainly had an overriding interest in ensuring that potential jurors heard no inherently prejudicial remarks from observers during voir dire," the Supreme Court of Georgia rejected Presley's argument that the trial court was required to consider alternatives to closing the courtroom. It noted that "the United States Supreme Court [has] not provide[d] clear guidance regarding whether a court must, sua sponte, advance its own alternatives to [closure]," and the court ruled that "Presley was obliged to present the court with any alternatives that he wished the court to consider." When no alternatives are offered, it concluded, "there is no abuse of discretion in the court's failure to sua sponte advance its own alternatives."

This Court's rulings with respect to the public trial right rest upon two different provisions of the Bill of Rights, both applicable to the States via the Due Process Clause of the Fourteenth Amendment. The Sixth Amendment directs, in relevant part, that "[i]n all criminal prosecutions, the accused shall enjoy the right to a speedy and public trial...." The Court in In re Oliver, 333 U.S. 257, 273 (1948), made it clear that this right extends to the States. The Sixth Amendment right, as the quoted language makes explicit, is the right of the accused.

The Court has further held that the public trial right extends beyond the accused and can be invoked under the First Amendment. Press–Enterprise Co. v. Superior Court of Cal., Riverside Cty., 464 U.S. 501 (1984) (*Press-Enterprise I*). This requirement, too, is binding on the States. Ibid.

The case now before the Court is brought under the Sixth Amendment, for it is the accused who invoked his right to a public trial. An initial question is whether the right to a public trial in criminal cases extends to the jury selection phase of trial, and in particular the voir dire of prospective jurors. In the First Amendment context that question was answered in *Press-Enterprise I*. The Court there held that the voir dire of prospective jurors must be open to the public under the First Amendment. Later in the same Term as Press–Enterprise I, the Court considered a Sixth Amendment case concerning whether the public trial right extends to a pretrial hearing on a motion to suppress certain evidence. Waller v. Georgia, 467 U.S. 39 (1984). The *Waller* Court relied heavily upon *Press-Enterprise I* in finding that the Sixth Amendment right to a public trial extends beyond the actual proof at trial. It ruled that the pretrial suppression hearing must be open to the public because "there can be little doubt that the explicit Sixth Amendment right of the accused is no less protective of a public trial than the implicit First Amendment right of the press and public."

While *Press-Enterprise I* was heavily relied upon in *Waller*, the jury selection issue in the former case was resolved under the First, not the Sixth, Amendment. In the instant case, the question then arises whether it is so well settled that the Sixth Amendment right extends to jury voir dire that this Court may proceed by summary disposition.

The point is well settled under *Press-Enterprise I* and *Waller*. The extent to which the First and Sixth Amendment public trial rights are coextensive is an open question, and it is not necessary here to speculate whether or in what circumstances the reach or protections of one might be greater than the other. Still, there is no legitimate reason, at least in the context of juror selection proceedings, to give one who asserts a First Amendment privilege greater rights to insist on public proceedings than the accused has. "Our cases have uniformly recognized the public-trial guarantee as one created for the benefit of the defendant." Gannett Co. v. DePasquale, 443 U.S. 368, 380 (1979). There could be no explanation for barring the accused from raising a constitutional right that is unmistakably for his or her benefit. That rationale suffices to resolve the instant matter. The Supreme Court of Georgia was correct in assuming that the Sixth Amendment right to a public trial extends to the voir dire of prospective jurors.

While the accused does have a right to insist that the voir dire of the jurors be public, there are exceptions to this general rule. "[T]he right to an open trial may give way in certain cases to other rights or interests, such as the defendant's right to a fair trial or the government's interest in inhibiting disclosure of sensitive information." *Waller*. "Such circumstances will be rare, however, and the balance of interests must be struck with special care." Ibid. *Waller* provided standards for courts to apply before excluding the public from any stage of a criminal trial:

"[T]he party seeking to close the hearing must advance an overriding interest that is likely to be prejudiced, the closure must be no broader than necessary to protect that interest, the trial court must consider reasonable alternatives to closing the proceeding, and it must make findings adequate to support the closure."

In upholding exclusion of the public at juror voir dire in the instant case, the Supreme Court of Georgia concluded, despite our explicit statements to the contrary, that trial courts need not consider alternatives to closure absent an opposing party's proffer of some alternatives. While the Supreme Court of Georgia concluded this was an open question under this Court's precedents, the statement in *Waller* that "the trial court must consider reasonable alternatives to closing the proceeding" settles the point. If that statement leaves any room for doubt, the Court was more explicit in *Press-Enterprise I*:

"Even with findings adequate to support closure, the trial court's orders denying access to voir dire testimony failed to consider whether alternatives were available to protect the interests of the prospective jurors that the trial court's orders sought to guard. Absent consideration of alternatives to closure, the trial court could not constitutionally close the voir dire."

The conclusion that trial courts are required to consider alternatives to closure even when they are not offered by the parties is clear not only from this Court's precedents but also from the premise that "[t]he process of juror selection is itself a matter of importance, not simply to the adversaries but to the criminal justice system." Id. The public has a right to be present whether or not any party has asserted the right. In *Press-Enterprise I*, for instance, neither the defendant nor the prosecution requested an open courtroom during juror voir dire proceedings; in fact, both specifically argued in favor of keeping the transcript of the proceedings confidential. The Court, nonetheless, found it was error to close the courtroom.

Trial courts are obligated to take every reasonable measure to accommodate public attendance at criminal trials. Nothing in the record shows that the trial court could not have accommodated the public at Presley's trial. Without knowing the precise circumstances, some possibilities include reserving one or more rows for the public; dividing the jury venire panel to reduce courtroom congestion; or instructing prospective jurors not to engage or interact with audience members.

Petitioner also argues that, apart from failing to consider alternatives to closure, the trial court erred because it did not even identify any overriding interest likely to be prejudiced absent the closure of voir dire. There is some merit to this complaint. The generic risk of jurors overhearing prejudicial remarks, unsubstantiated by any specific threat or incident, is inherent whenever members of the public are present during the selection of jurors. If broad concerns of this sort were sufficient to override a defendant's constitutional right to a public trial, a court could exclude the public from jury selection almost as a matter of course. * * *

There are no doubt circumstances where a judge could conclude that threats of improper communications with jurors or safety concerns are concrete enough to warrant closing voir dire. But in those cases, the particular interest, and threat to that interest, must "be articulated along with findings specific enough that a reviewing court can determine whether the closure order was properly entered." *Press-Enterprise I, supra*, at 510, 104 S.Ct. 819; see also Press–Enterprise Co. v. Superior Court of Cal., County of Riverside, 478 U.S. 1, 15, 106 S.Ct. 2735, 92 L.Ed.2d 1 (1986) ("The First Amendment right of access cannot be overcome by the conclusory assertion that publicity might deprive the defendant of [the right to a fair trial]").

We need not rule on this second claim of error, because even assuming, arguendo, that the trial court had an overriding interest in closing voir dire, it was still incumbent upon it to consider all reasonable alternatives to closure. It did not, and that is all this Court needs to decide.

The Supreme Court of Georgia's judgment is reversed, and the case is remanded for further proceedings not inconsistent with this opinion.

JUSTICE THOMAS, **with whom** JUSTICE SCALIA **joins, dissenting.**

* * *

The Court correctly notes that *Waller* answers whether a "defendant's Sixth Amendment right to a public trial applies to a suppression hearing" (not to jury voir dire), and that *Press-Enterprise I* interprets the public's First Amendment right to attend jury voir dire, so neither *Waller* nor *Press-Enterprise I* expressly answers the question here. That acknowledgment should have eliminated any basis for disposing of this case summarily; the Court should reserve that procedural option for cases that our precedents govern squarely and directly.

* * *

The Court chides the Supreme Court of Georgia for "conclud[ing], despite our explicit statements to the contrary, that trial courts need not consider alternatives to closure absent an opposing party's proffer of some alternatives." But neither *Waller* nor *Press-Enterprise I* expressly holds that jury voir dire is covered by the Sixth Amendment's "[P]ublic [T]rial" Clause. Accordingly, it is not obvious that the "alternatives to closure" language in those opinions governs this case.

* * *

VII. THE RIGHT TO EFFECTIVE ASSISTANCE OF COUNSEL

A. INEFFECTIVENESS AND PREJUDICE

3. Assessing Counsel's Effectiveness

Page 1323. Add the following cases after the section on Rompilla v. Beard

The Duty to Investigate Mitigating Evidence in a Capital Case—the Relevance of ABA Standards: Bobby v. Van Hook.

BOBBY v. VAN HOOK

Supreme Court of the United States, 2009
130 S.Ct. 13

Per Curiam.

The Court of Appeals for the Sixth Circuit granted habeas relief to Robert Van Hook on the ground that he did not receive effective assistance of counsel during the sentencing phase of his capital trial. Because we think it clear that Van Hook's attorneys met the constitutional minimum of competence under the correct standard, we * * * reverse.

I

On February 18, 1985, Van Hook went to a Cincinnati bar that catered to homosexual men, hoping to find someone to rob. He approached David Self, and after the two spent several hours drinking together they left for Self's apartment. There Van Hook lured Self into a vulnerable position and attacked him, first strangling him until he was unconscious, then killing him with a kitchen knife and mutilating his body. Before fleeing with Self's valuables, Van Hook attempted to cover his tracks, stuffing the knife and other items into the body and smearing fingerprints he had left behind. Six weeks later, police found him in Florida, where he confessed.

Van Hook was indicted in Ohio for aggravated murder, with one capital specification, and aggravated robbery. He waived his right to a jury trial, and a three-judge panel found him guilty of both charges and the capital specification. At the sentencing hearing, the defense called eight mitigation witnesses, and Van Hook himself gave an unsworn statement. After weighing the aggravating and mitigating circumstances, the trial court imposed the death penalty. The Ohio courts affirmed on direct appeal, and we denied certiorari. * * *

Van Hook filed this federal habeas petition in 1995. The District Court denied relief on all 17 of his claims. * * * [A panel of the Sixth Circuit Court of Appeals]—relying on guidelines published by the American Bar Association (ABA) in 2003—granted relief to Van Hook on the sole ground that his lawyers performed deficiently in investigating and presenting mitigating evidence. The State petitioned for a writ of certiorari. We grant the petition and reverse.

II

Because Van Hook filed his federal habeas petition before April 24, 1996, the provisions of the Antiterrorism and Effective Death Penalty Act of 1996 do not apply. Even without the Act's added layer of deference to state-court judgments, we cannot agree with the Court of Appeals that Van Hook is entitled to relief.

A

The Sixth Amendment entitles criminal defendants to the effective assistance of counsel—that is, representation that does not fall "below an objective standard of reasonableness" in light of "prevailing professional norms." Strickland v. Washington. That standard is necessarily a general one. No particular set of detailed rules for counsel's conduct can satisfactorily take account of the variety of circumstances faced by defense counsel or the range of legitimate decisions regarding how best to represent a criminal defendant. Restatements of professional standards, we have recognized, can be useful as "guides" to what reasonableness entails, but only to the extent they describe the professional norms prevailing when the representation took place.

The Sixth Circuit ignored this limiting principle, relying on ABA guidelines announced 18 years after Van Hook went to trial. The ABA standards in effect in 1985 described defense counsel's duty to investigate both the merits and mitigating circumstances in general terms: "It is the duty of the lawyer to conduct a prompt investigation of the circumstances of the case and to explore all avenues leading to facts relevant to the merits of the case and the penalty in the event of conviction." 1 ABA Standards for Criminal Justice 4–4.1, p. 4–53 (2d ed.1980). The accompanying two-page commentary noted that defense counsel have "a substantial and important role to perform in raising mitigating factors," and that "[i]nformation concerning the defendant's background, education, employment record, mental and emotional stability, family relationships, and the like, will be relevant, as will mitigating circumstances surrounding the commission of the offense itself."

Quite different are the ABA's 131–page "Guidelines" for capital defense counsel, published in 2003, on which the Sixth Circuit relied. Those directives expanded what had been (in the 1980 Standards) a broad outline of defense counsel's duties in all criminal cases into detailed prescriptions for legal representation of capital defendants. They discuss the duty to investigate mitigating evidence in exhaustive detail, specifying what attorneys should look for, where to look, and when to begin. They include, for example, the requirement that counsel's investigation cover every period of the defendant's life from "the moment of conception," and that counsel contact "virtually everyone . . . who knew [the defendant] and his family" and obtain records "concerning not only the client, but also his parents, grandparents, siblings, and children." Judging counsel's conduct in the 1980's on the basis of these 2003 Guidelines—without even pausing to consider whether they reflected the prevailing professional practice at the time of the trial—was error.

To make matters worse, the Court of Appeals (following Circuit precedent) treated the ABA's 2003 Guidelines not merely as evidence of what reasonably diligent attorneys would do, but as inexorable commands with which all capital defense counsel "must fully comply." *Strickland* stressed, however, that "American Bar Association standards and the like" are "only guides" to what reasonableness means, not its definition. We have since regarded them as such. *See* Wiggins v. Smith, 539 U.S. 510 (2003). What we have said of state requirements is a fortiori true of standards set by private organizations: "[W]hile States are free to impose whatever specific rules they see fit to ensure that criminal defendants are well represented, we have held that the Federal Constitution imposes one general requirement: that counsel make objectively reasonable choices." Roe v. Flores–Ortega, 528 U.S. 470, 479 (2000).

B

Van Hook insists that the Sixth Circuit's missteps made no difference because his counsel were ineffective even under professional standards prevailing at the time. He is wrong.

Like the Court of Appeals, Van Hook first contends that his attorneys began their mitigation investigation too late, waiting until he was found guilty—only days before the sentencing hearing—to dig into his background. But the record shows they started much sooner. Between Van Hook's indictment and his trial less than three months later, they contacted their lay witnesses early and often: They spoke nine times with his mother (beginning within a week after the indictment), once with both parents together, twice with an aunt who lived with the family and often cared for Van Hook as a child, and three times with a family friend whom Van Hook visited immediately after the crime. As for their expert witnesses, they were in touch with one more than a month before trial, and they met with the other for two hours a week before the trial court reached

its verdict. Moreover, after reviewing his military history, they met with a representative of the Veterans Administration seven weeks before trial and attempted to obtain his medical records. And they looked into enlisting a mitigation specialist when the trial was still five weeks away. The Sixth Circuit, in short, was simply incorrect in saying Van Hook's lawyers waited until the "last minute."

Nor was the scope of counsel's investigation unreasonable. The Sixth Circuit said Van Hook's attorneys found only "a little information about his traumatic childhood experience," but that is a gross distortion. The trial court learned, for instance, that Van Hook (whose parents were both "heavy drinkers") started drinking as a toddler, began "barhopping" with his father at age 9, drank and used drugs regularly with his father from age 11 forward, and continued abusing drugs and alcohol into adulthood. The court also heard that Van Hook grew up in a " 'combat zone' ": He watched his father beat his mother weekly, saw him hold her at gun-and knife-point, "observed" episodes of "sexual violence" while sleeping in his parents' bedroom, and was beaten himself at least once. It learned that Van Hook, who had "fantasies about killing and war" from an early age, was deeply upset when his drug and alcohol abuse forced him out of the military, and attempted suicide five times (including a month before the murder). And although the experts agreed that Van Hook did not suffer from a "mental disease or defect," the trial court learned that Van Hook's borderline personality disorder and his consumption of drugs and alcohol the day of the crime impaired "his ability to refrain from the [crime]," and that his "explo[sion]" of "senseless and bizarre brutality" may have resulted from what one expert termed a "homosexual panic."

Despite all the mitigating evidence the defense did present, Van Hook and the Court of Appeals fault his counsel for failing to find more. What his counsel did discover, the argument goes, gave them "reason to suspect that much worse details existed," and that suspicion should have prompted them to interview other family members—his stepsister, two uncles, and two aunts—as well as a psychiatrist who once treated his mother, all of whom "could have helped his counsel narrate the true story of Van Hook's childhood experiences." But there comes a point at which evidence from more distant relatives can reasonably be expected to be only cumulative, and the search for it distractive from more important duties. * * * And given all the evidence they unearthed from those closest to Van Hook's upbringing and the experts who reviewed his history, it was not unreasonable for his counsel not to identify and interview every other living family member or every therapist who once treated his parents. This is not a case in which the defendant's attorneys failed to act while potentially powerful mitigating evidence stared them in the face, cf. Wiggins, or would have been apparent from documents any reasonable attorney would have obtained, cf. Rompilla v. Beard, 545 U.S. 374 (2005). It is instead a case, like Strickland itself, in which defense counsel's decision not to seek more mitigating evidence from the defendant's background than was already in hand fell well within the range of professionally reasonable judgments.

What is more, even if Van Hook's counsel performed deficiently by fail-

ing to dig deeper, he suffered no prejudice as a result. * * * Only two witnesses even arguably would have added new, relevant information: One of Van Hook's uncles noted that Van Hook's mother was temporarily committed to a psychiatric hospital, and Van Hook's stepsister mentioned that his father hit Van Hook frequently and tried to kill Van Hook's mother. But the trial court had already heard—from Van Hook's mother herself—that she had been "under psychiatric care" more than once. And it was already aware that his father had a violent nature, had attacked Van Hook's mother, and had beaten Van Hook at least once. Neither the Court of Appeals nor Van Hook has shown why the minor additional details the trial court did not hear would have made any difference.

On the other side of the scales, moreover, was the evidence of the aggravating circumstance the trial court found: that Van Hook committed the murder alone in the course of an aggravated robbery. Van Hook's confession made clear, and he never subsequently denied, both that he was the sole perpetrator of the crime and that his intention from beginning to end was to rob Self at some point in their evening's activities. Nor did he arrive at that intention on a whim: Van Hook had previously pursued the same strategy—of luring homosexual men into secluded settings to rob them—many times since his teenage years, and he employed it again even after Self's murder in the weeks before his arrest. Although Van Hook apparently deviated from his original plan once the offense was underway—going beyond stealing Self's goods to killing him and disfiguring the dead body—that hardly helped his cause. The Sixth Circuit, which focused on the *number* of aggravating factors instead of their *weight*, gave all this evidence short shrift, leading it to overstate further the effect additional mitigating evidence might have had.

* * *

The judgment of the Court of Appeals is reversed, and the case is remanded for further proceedings consistent with this opinion.

JUSTICE ALITO, concurring.

I join the Court's per curiam opinion but emphasize my understanding that the opinion in no way suggests that the American Bar Association's Guidelines for the Appointment and Performance of Defense Counsel in Death Penalty Cases have special relevance in determining whether an attorney's performance meets the standard required by the Sixth Amendment. The ABA is a venerable organization with a history of service to the bar, but it is, after all, a private group with limited membership. The views of the association's members, not to mention the views of the members of the advisory committee that formulated the 2003 Guidelines, do not necessarily reflect the views of the American bar as a whole. It is the responsibility of the courts to determine the nature of the work that a defense attorney must do in a capital case in order to meet the obligations imposed by the Constitution, and I see no reason why the ABA Guidelines should be given a privileged position in making that determination.

Detailed and Fact–Intensive Review Under AEDPA of Claim of Ineffectiveness for Failure to Investigated and Present Mitigating Evidence at the Penalty Phase: Cullen v. Pinholster

CULLEN v. PINHOLSTER
Supreme Court of the United States, 2011.
131 S.Ct. 1388

JUSTICE THOMAS delivered the opinion of the Court.

[Note: Justices Ginsburg and Kagan join only Part II of Justice Thomas's opinion]

Scott Lynn Pinholster and two accomplices broke into a house in the middle of the night and brutally beat and stabbed to death two men who happened to interrupt the burglary. A jury convicted Pinholster of first-degree murder, and he was sentenced to death.

After the California Supreme Court twice unanimously denied Pinholster habeas relief, a Federal District Court held an evidentiary hearing and granted Pinholster habeas relief under 28 U.S.C. § 2254. The District Court concluded that Pinholster's trial counsel had been constitutionally ineffective at the penalty phase of trial. Sitting en banc, the Court of Appeals for the Ninth Circuit affirmed. Considering the new evidence adduced in the District Court hearing, the Court of Appeals held that the California Supreme Court's decision "was contrary to, or involved an unreasonable application of, clearly established Federal law." § 2254(d)(1). We granted certiorari and now reverse.

I

A

On the evening of January 8, 1982, Pinholster solicited Art Corona and

Paul David Brown to help him rob Michael Kumar, a local drug dealer. On the way, they stopped at Lisa Tapar's house, where Pinholster put his buck knife through her front door and scratched a swastika into her car after she refused to talk to him. The three men, who were all armed with buck knives, found no one at Kumar's house, broke in, and began ransacking the home. They came across only a small amount of marijuana before Kumar's friends, Thomas Johnson and Robert Beckett, arrived and shouted that they were calling the police.

Pinholster and his accomplices tried to escape through the rear door, but Johnson blocked their path. Pinholster backed Johnson onto the patio, demanding drugs and money and repeatedly striking him in the chest. Johnson dropped his wallet on the ground and stopped resisting. Beckett then came around the corner, and Pinholster attacked him, too, stabbing him repeatedly in the chest. Pinholster forced Beckett to the ground, took both men's wallets, and began kicking Beckett in the head. Meanwhile, Brown stabbed Johnson in the chest, burying his knife to the hilt. Johnson and Beckett died of their wounds.

Corona drove the three men to Pinholster's apartment. While in the car, Pinholster and Brown exulted, "We got 'em, man, we got 'em good."Ibid. At the apartment, Pinholster washed his knife, and the three split the proceeds of the robbery: $23 and one quarter-ounce of marijuana. Although Pinholster instructed Corona to "lay low," Corona turned himself in to the police two weeks later. Pinholster was arrested shortly thereafter and threatened to kill Corona if he did not keep quiet about the burglary and murders. Corona

later became the State's primary witness. The prosecution brought numerous charges against Pinholster, including two counts of first-degree murder.

B

The California trial court appointed Harry Brainard and Wilbur Dettmar to defend Pinholster on charges of first-degree murder, robbery, and burglary. Before their appointment, Pinholster had rejected other attorneys and insisted on representing himself. During that time, the State had mailed Pinholster a letter in jail informing him that the prosecution planned to offer aggravating evidence during the penalty phase of trial to support a sentence of death.

The guilt phase of the trial began on February 28, 1984. Pinholster testified on his own behalf and presented an alibi defense. He claimed that he had broken into Kumar's house alone at around 8 p.m. on January 8, 1982, and had stolen marijuana but denied killing anyone. Pinholster asserted that later that night around 1 a.m., while he was elsewhere, Corona went to Kumar's house to steal more drugs and did not return for three hours. Pinholster told the jury that he was a "professional robber," not a murderer. He boasted of committing hundreds of robberies over the previous six years but insisted that he always used a gun, never a knife. The jury convicted Pinholster on both counts of first-degree murder.

Before the penalty phase, Brainard and Dettmar moved to exclude any aggravating evidence on the ground that the prosecution had failed to provide notice of the evidence to be introduced, as required by Cal.Penal Code Ann. § 190.3. At a hearing on April 24, Dettmar argued that, in reliance on the lack of notice, he was "not presently prepared to offer anything by way of mitigation." He acknowledged, however, that the prosecutor "possibly ha[d] met the [notice] requirement." The trial court asked whether a continuance might be helpful, but Dettmar declined, explaining that he could not think of a mitigation witness other than Pinholster's mother and that additional time would not "make a great deal of difference." Three days later, after hearing testimony, the court found that Pinholster had received notice while representing himself and denied the motion to exclude.

The penalty phase was held before the same jury that had convicted Pinholster. The prosecution produced eight witnesses, who testified about Pinholster's history of threatening and violent behavior, including resisting arrest and assaulting police officers, involvement with juvenile gangs, and a substantial prison disciplinary record. Defense counsel called only Pinholster's mother, Burnice Brashear. She gave an account of Pinholster's troubled childhood and adolescent years, discussed Pinholster's siblings, and described Pinholster as "a perfect gentleman at home." Defense counsel did not call a psychiatrist, though they had consulted Dr. John Stalberg at least six weeks earlier. Dr. Stalberg noted Pinholster's "psychopathic personality traits," diagnosed him with antisocial personality disorder, and concluded that he "was not under the influence of extreme mental or emotional disturbance" at the time of the murders.

After 2½ days of deliberation, the jury unanimously voted for death on each of the two murder counts. On mandatory appeal, the California Supreme Court affirmed the judgment.

C

In August 1993, Pinholster filed his first state habeas petition. Represented by new counsel, Pinholster alleged, inter alia, ineffective assistance of counsel at the penalty phase of his trial. He alleged that Brainard and Dettmar had failed to adequately investigate and present mitigating evidence, including evidence of mental disorders. Pinholster supported this claim with school, medical, and legal records, as well as declarations from family members, Brainard, and Dr. George Woods, a psychiatrist who diagnosed Pinholster with bipolar mood disorder and seizure disorders. Dr. Woods criticized Dr. Stalberg's report as incompetent, unreliable, and inaccurate. The California Supreme Court unanimously and summarily denied Pinholster's penalty-phase ineffective-assistance claim "on the substantive ground that it is without merit."

Pinholster filed a federal habeas petition in April 1997. He reiterated his previous allegations about penalty-phase ineffective assistance and also added new allegations that his trial counsel had failed to furnish Dr. Stalberg with adequate background materials. In support of the new allegations, Dr. Stalberg provided a declaration stating that in 1984, Pinholster's trial counsel had provided him with only some police reports and a 1978 probation report. Dr. Stalberg explained that, had he known about the material that had since been gathered by Pinholster's habeas counsel, he would have conducted "further inquiry" before concluding that Pinholster suffered only from a personality disorder. He noted that Pinholster's school records showed evidence of "some degree of brain damage." Dr. Stalberg did not, however, retract his earlier diagnosis. The parties stipulated that this declaration had never been submitted to the California Supreme Court, and the federal petition was held in abeyance to allow Pinholster to go back to state court.

In August 1997, Pinholster filed his second state habeas petition, this time including Dr. Stalberg's declaration and requesting judicial notice of the documents previously submitted in support of his first state habeas petition. His allegations of penalty-phase ineffective assistance of counsel mirrored those in his federal habeas petition. The California Supreme Court again unanimously and summarily denied the petition "on the substantive ground that it is without merit."

Having presented Dr. Stalberg's declaration to the state court, Pinholster returned to the District Court. In November 1997, he filed an amended petition for a writ of habeas corpus. His allegations of penalty-phase ineffective assistance of counsel were identical to those in his second state habeas petition. [The district court held an evidentiary hearing.] Before the hearing, the State deposed Dr. Stalberg, who stated that none of the new material he reviewed altered his original diagnosis. Dr. Stalberg disagreed with Dr. Woods' conclusion that Pinholster suffers from bipolar disorder. Pinholster did not call Dr. Stalberg to testify at the hearing. He presented two new medical experts: Dr. Sophia Vinogradov, a psychiatrist who diagnosed Pinholster with organic personality syndrome and ruled out antisocial personality disorder, and Dr. Donald Olson, a pediatric neurologist who suggested that Pinholster suffers from partial epilepsy and brain injury. The State called Dr. F. David Rudnick, a psychiatrist

who, like Dr. Stalberg, diagnosed Pinholster with antisocial personality disorder and rejected any diagnosis of bipolar disorder.

D

The District Court granted habeas relief [on grounds of ineffective assistance of counsel]. Over a dissent, a panel of the Court of Appeals for the Ninth Circuit reversed. On rehearing en banc, the Court of Appeals vacated the panel opinion and affirmed the District Court's grant of habeas relief. The en banc court held that that new evidence from the hearing could be considered in assessing whether the California Supreme Court's decision "was contrary to, or involved an unreasonable application of, clearly established Federal law" under § 2254(d)(1). Taking the District Court evidence into account, the en banc court determined that the California Supreme Court unreasonably applied Strickland v. Washington, 466 U.S. 668 (1984), in denying Pinholster's claim of penalty-phase ineffective assistance of counsel.

Three judges dissented and rejected the majority's conclusion that the District Court hearing was not barred by § 2254(e)(2). Limiting its review to the state-court record, the dissent concluded that the California Supreme Court did not unreasonably apply *Strickland*.

We granted certiorari to resolve two questions. First, whether review under § 2254(d)(1) permits consideration of evidence introduced in an evidentiary hearing before the federal habeas court. Second, whether the Court of Appeals properly granted Pinholster habeas relief on his claim of penalty-phase ineffective assistance of counsel.

II

We first consider the scope of the record for a § 2254(d)(1) inquiry. The State argues that review is limited to the record that was before the state court that adjudicated the claim on the merits. Pinholster contends that evidence presented to the federal habeas court may also be considered. We agree with the State.

A

As amended by AEDPA, 28 U.S.C. § 2254 sets several limits on the power of a federal court to grant an application for a writ of habeas corpus on behalf of a state prisoner. Section 2254(a) permits a federal court to entertain only those applications alleging that a person is in state custody "in violation of the Constitution or laws or treaties of the United States." Sections 2254(b) and (c) provide that a federal court may not grant such applications unless, with certain exceptions, the applicant has exhausted state remedies.

If an application includes a claim that has been "adjudicated on the merits in State court proceedings," § 2254(d), an additional restriction applies. Under § 2254(d), that application "shall not be granted with respect to [such a] claim . . . unless the adjudication of the claim":

> "(1) resulted in a decision that was contrary to, or involved an unreasonable application of, clearly established Federal law, as determined by the Supreme Court of the United States; or

> "(2) resulted in a decision that was based on an unreasonable determination of the facts in light of the evidence presented in the State court proceeding."

* * *

We now hold that review under § 2254(d)(1) is limited to the record that was before the state court that adjudicated the claim on the merits. Section 2254(d)(1) refers, in the past tense, to a state-court adjudication that "resulted in" a decision that was contrary to, or "involved" an unreasonable application of, established law. This backward-looking language requires an examination of the state-court decision at the time it was made. It follows that the record under review is limited to the record in existence at that same time i.e., the record before the state court.

This understanding of the text is compelled by the broader context of the statute as a whole, which demonstrates Congress' intent to channel prisoners' claims first to the state courts. Section 2254(b) requires that prisoners must ordinarily exhaust state remedies before filing for federal habeas relief. It would be contrary to that purpose to allow a petitioner to overcome an adverse state-court decision with new evidence introduced in a federal habeas court and reviewed by that court in the first instance effectively de novo.

Limiting § 2254(d)(1) review to the state-court record is consistent with our precedents interpreting that statutory provision. Our cases emphasize that review under § 2254(d)(1) focuses on what a state court knew and did. State-court decisions are measured against this Court's precedents as of "the time the state court renders its decision." Lockyer v. Andrade, 538 U.S. 63, 71–72 (2003). To determine whether a particular decision is "contrary to" then-established law, a federal court must consider whether the decision "applies a rule that contradicts [such] law" and how the decision "confronts [the] set of facts" that were before the state court. Williams v. Taylor, 529 U.S. 362, 405, 406

(2000). * * * It would be strange to ask federal courts to analyze whether a state court's adjudication resulted in a decision that unreasonably applied federal law to facts not before the state court.

B

* * *

Although state prisoners may sometimes submit new evidence in federal court, AEDPA's statutory scheme is designed to strongly discourage them from doing so. Provisions like §§ 2254(d)(1) and (e)(2) ensure that federal courts sitting in habeas are not an alternative forum for trying facts and issues which a prisoner made insufficient effort to pursue in state proceedings. See Wainwright v. Sykes, 433 U.S. 72, 90 (1977) ("[T]he state trial on the merits [should be] the 'main event,' so to speak, rather than a 'tryout on the road' for what will later be the determinative federal habeas hearing").

C

Accordingly, we conclude that the Court of Appeals erred in considering the District Court evidence in its review under § 2254(d)(1). Although we might ordinarily remand for a properly limited review, the Court of Appeals also ruled, in the alternative, that Pinholster merited habeas relief even on the state-court record alone. Remand is therefore inappropriate, and we turn next to a review of the state-court record.

III

The Court of Appeals' alternative holding was also erroneous. Pinholster has failed to demonstrate that the California Supreme Court unreasonably applied clearly established federal law to his penalty-phase ineffective-assistance claim on the state-

court record. Section 2254(d) prohibits habeas relief.

A

* * *

* * * Even taking the approach most favorable to Pinholster, and reviewing only whether the California Supreme Court was objectively unreasonable in the second state habeas proceeding, we find that Pinholster has failed to satisfy § 2254(d)(1).

B

There is no dispute that the clearly established federal law here is Strickland v. Washington. In *Strickland*, this Court made clear that "the purpose of the effective assistance guarantee of the Sixth Amendment is not to improve the quality of legal representation . . . [but] simply to ensure that criminal defendants receive a fair trial." Thus, "[t]he benchmark for judging any claim of ineffectiveness must be whether counsel's conduct so undermined the proper functioning of the adversarial process that the trial cannot be relied on as having produced a just result." The Court acknowledged that "[t]here are countless ways to provide effective assistance in any given case," and that "[e]ven the best criminal defense attorneys would not defend a particular client in the same way."

Our review of the California Supreme Court's decision is * * * "doubly deferential." Knowles v. Mirzayance, 129 S.Ct. 1411, 1413 (2009). We take a highly deferential look at counsel's performance, through the deferential lens of § 2254(d). Pinholster must demonstrate that it was necessarily unreasonable for the California Supreme Court to conclude: (1) that he had not overcome the strong presumption of competence; and (2) that he had failed to undermine confidence in the jury's sentence of death.

C

1

Pinholster has not shown that the California Supreme Court's decision that he could not demonstrate deficient performance by his trial counsel necessarily involved an unreasonable application of federal law. In arguing to the state court that his counsel performed deficiently, Pinholster contended that they should have pursued and presented additional evidence about: his family members and their criminal, mental, and substance abuse problems; his schooling; and his medical and mental health history, including his epileptic disorder. To support his allegation that his trial counsel had "no reasonable tactical basis" for the approach they took, Pinholster relied on statements his counsel made at trial. When arguing the motion to exclude the State's aggravating evidence at the penalty phase for failure to comply with Cal.Penal Code Ann. § 190.3, Dettmar, one of Pinholster's counsel, contended that because the State did not provide notice, he "[was] not presently prepared to offer anything by way of mitigation." In response to the trial court's inquiry as to whether a continuance might be helpful, Dettmar noted that the only mitigation witness he could think of was Pinholster's mother. Additional time, Dettmar stated, would not "make a great deal of difference."

We begin with the premise that "under the circumstances, the challenged action[s] might be considered sound trial strategy." *Strickland,* supra, at 689. The Court of Appeals dissent described one possible strategy:

"[Pinholster's attorneys] were fully aware that they would have to deal with mitigation sometime during the course of the trial, did spend considerable time and effort investigating avenues for mitigation[,] and made a reasoned professional judgment that the best way to serve their client would be to rely on the fact that they never got [the required § 190.3] notice and hope the judge would bar the state from putting on their aggravation witnesses." 590 F.3d, at 701–702 (opinion of Kozinski, C.J.).

Further, if their motion was denied, counsel were prepared to present only Pinholster's mother in the penalty phase to create sympathy not for Pinholster, but for his mother. After all, the "family sympathy" mitigation defense was known to the defense bar in California at the time and had been used by other attorneys. Rather than displaying neglect, we presume that Dettmar's arguments were part of this trial strategy.

The state-court record supports the idea that Pinholster's counsel acted strategically to get the prosecution's aggravation witnesses excluded for lack of notice, and if that failed, to put on Pinholster's mother. Other statements made during the argument regarding the motion to exclude suggest that defense counsel were trying to take advantage of a legal technicality and were not truly surprised. Brainard and Dettmar acknowledged that the prosecutor had invited them on numerous occasions to review Pinholster's state prison file but argued that such an invitation did not meet with the "strict demands" of § 190.3. Dettmar admitted that the prosecutor, "being as thorough as she is, possibly ha[d] met the requirement." But if so, he wanted her "to make that representation to the court."

Timesheets indicate that Pinholster's trial counsel investigated mitigating evidence. Long before the guilty verdict, Dettmar talked with Pinholster's mother and contacted a psychiatrist. On February 26, two months before the penalty phase started, he billed six hours for "[p]reparation argument, death penalty phase." Brainard, who merely assisted Dettmar for the penalty phase, researched epilepsy and also interviewed Pinholster's mother. We know that Brainard likely spent additional time, not reflected in these entries, preparing Pinholster's brother, Terry, who provided some mitigation testimony about Pinholster's background during the guilt phase.

The record also shows that Pinholster's counsel confronted a challenging penalty phase with an unsympathetic client, which limited their feasible mitigation strategies. By the end of the guilt phase, the jury had observed Pinholster glory in his criminal disposition and "hundreds of robberies." During his cross-examination, Pinholster laughed or smirked when he told the jury that his "occupation" was "a crook," when he was asked whether he had threatened a potential witness, and when he described thwarting police efforts to recover a gun he had once used. He bragged about being a "professional robber." To support his defense, Pinholster claimed that he used only guns not knives to commit his crimes. But during cross-examination, Pinholster admitted that he had previously been convicted of using a knife in a kidnaping. Pinholster also said he was a white supremacist and that he frequently carved swastikas into other people's property as "a sideline to robbery."

Trial counsel's psychiatric expert, Dr. Stalberg, had concluded that Pinholster showed no significant signs or symptoms of mental disorder or defect other than his "psychopathic personality traits." Dr. Stalberg was aware of Pinholster's hyperactivity as a youngster, hospitalization at age 14 for incorrigibility, alleged epileptic disorder, and history of drug dependency. Nevertheless, Dr. Stalberg told counsel that Pinholster did not appear to suffer from brain damage, was not significantly intoxicated or impaired on the night in question, and did not have an impaired ability to appreciate the criminality of his conduct.

Given these impediments, it would have been a reasonable penalty-phase strategy to focus on evoking sympathy for Pinholster's mother. In fact, such a family sympathy defense is precisely how the State understood defense counsel's strategy. The prosecutor carefully opened her cross-examination of Pinholster's mother with, "I hope you understand I don't enjoy cross-examining a mother of anybody." And in her closing argument, the prosecutor attempted to undercut defense counsel's strategy by pointing out, "Even the most heinous person born, even Adolph Hitler[,] probably had a mother who loved him."

Pinholster's only response to this evidence is a series of declarations from Brainard submitted with Pinholster's first state habeas petition, seven years after the trial. Brainard declares that he has "no recollection" of interviewing any family members (other than Pinholster's mother) regarding penalty-phase testimony, of attempting to secure Pinholster's school or medical records, or of interviewing any former teachers or counselors. Brainard also declares that Dettmar was primarily responsible for mental health issues in the case, but he has "no recollection" of Dettmar ever having secured Pinholster's medical records. Dettmar neither confirmed nor denied Brainard's statements, as he had died by the time of the first state habeas petition.

In sum, Brainard and Dettmar made statements suggesting that they were not surprised that the State intended to put on aggravating evidence, billing records show that they spent time investigating mitigating evidence, and the record demonstrates that they represented a psychotic client whose performance at trial hardly endeared him to the jury. Pinholster has responded to this evidence with only a handful of post-hoc non-denials by one of his lawyers. The California Supreme Court could have reasonably concluded that Pinholster had failed to rebut the presumption of competence mandated by Strickland—here, that counsel had adequately performed at the penalty phase of trial.

2

The Court of Appeals held that the California Supreme Court had unreasonably applied Strickland because Pinholster's attorneys were far more deficient than the attorneys in Wiggins v. Smith, and Rompilla v. Beard [both set forth in Chapter 10 of the Casebook, and in both of which the Supreme Court upheld the petitioner's ineffective assistance claim.] The court drew from those cases a "constitutional duty to investigate" and the principle that "[i]t is prima facie ineffective assistance for counsel to 'abandon[ ] their investigation of [the] petitioner's background after having acquired only rudimentary knowledge of his history from a narrow set of sources,' " (quoting Wig-

gins v. Smith, 539 U.S. 510, 524–525). The court explained that it could not "lightly disregard" a failure to introduce evidence of "excruciating life history" or "nightmarish childhood."

The Court of Appeals misapplied *Strickland* and overlooked "the constitutionally protected independence of counsel and . . . the wide latitude counsel must have in making tactical decisions." 466 U.S., at 689. Beyond the general requirement of reasonableness, "specific guidelines are not appropriate." Id., at 688. * * * The Court of Appeals erred in attributing strict rules to this Court's recent case law.

Nor did the Court of Appeals properly apply the strong presumption of competence that *Strickland* mandates. The court dismissed the dissent's application of the presumption as "fabricat[ing] an excuse that the attorneys themselves could not conjure up." But *Strickland* specifically commands that a court "must indulge [the] strong presumption" that counsel "made all significant decisions in the exercise of reasonable professional judgment." 466 U.S., at 689–690. The Court of Appeals was required not simply to give the attorneys the benefit of the doubt, but to affirmatively entertain the range of possible reasons Pinholster's counsel may have had for proceeding as they did.

Justice SOTOMAYOR questions whether it would have been a reasonable professional judgment for Pinholster's trial counsel to adopt a family-sympathy mitigation defense. She cites no evidence, however, that such an approach would have been inconsistent with the standard of professional competence in capital cases that prevailed in Los Angeles in 1984.

Indeed, she does not contest that, at the time, the defense bar in California had been using that strategy. Justice SOTOMAYOR relies heavily on *Wiggins*, but in that case the defendant's trial counsel specifically acknowledged a standard practice for capital cases in Maryland that was inconsistent with what he had done.

At bottom, Justice SOTOMAYOR's view is grounded in little more than her own sense of "prudence," and what appears to be her belief that the only reasonable mitigation strategy in capital cases is to "help" the jury "understand" the defendant. According to Justice SOTOMAYOR, that Pinholster was an unsympathetic client "compound[ed], rather than excuse[d], counsel's deficiency" in pursuing further evidence "that could explain why Pinholster was the way he was." But it certainly can be reasonable for attorneys to conclude that creating sympathy for the defendant's family is a better idea because the defendant himself is simply unsympathetic.

Justice SOTOMAYOR's approach is flatly inconsistent with *Strickland's* recognition that "[t]here are countless ways to provide effective assistance in any given case." There comes a point where a defense attorney will reasonably decide that another strategy is in order, thus making particular investigations unnecessary. Those decisions are due a heavy measure of deference. The California Supreme Court could have reasonably concluded that Pinholster's counsel made such a reasoned decision in this case.

* * *

D

Even if his trial counsel had performed deficiently, Pinholster also has failed to show that the California Supreme Court must have unreasonably concluded that Pinholster was not prejudiced. "[T]he question is whether there is a reasonable probability that, absent the errors, the sentencer ... would have concluded that the balance of aggravating and mitigating circumstances did not warrant death." *Strickland,* supra, at 695. We therefore reweigh the evidence in aggravation against the totality of available mitigating evidence.

1

We turn first to the aggravating and mitigating evidence that the sentencing jury considered. Here, the same jury heard both the guilt and penalty phases and was instructed to consider all the evidence presented.

The State presented extensive aggravating evidence. As we have already discussed, the jury watched Pinholster revel in his extensive criminal history. Then, during the penalty phase, the State presented evidence that Pinholster had threatened to kill the State's lead witness, assaulted a man with a straight razor, and kidnapped another person with a knife. The State showed that Pinholster had a history of violent outbursts, including striking and threatening a bailiff after a court proceeding at age 17, breaking his wife's jaw, resisting arrest by faking seizures, and assaulting and spitting on police officers. The jury also heard about Pinholster's involvement in juvenile gangs and his substantial disciplinary record in both county and state jails, where he had threatened, assaulted, and thrown urine at guards, and fought with other inmates. While in jail, Pinholster had been segregated for a time due to his propensity for violence and placed on a "special disciplinary diet" reserved only for the most disruptive inmates.

The mitigating evidence consisted primarily of the penalty-phase testimony of Pinholster's mother, Brashear, who gave a detailed account of Pinholster's troubled childhood and adolescence. Early childhood was quite difficult. The family "didn't have lots of money." When he was very young, Pinholster suffered two serious head injuries, first at age 2 or 3 when he was run over by a car, and again at age 4 or 5 when he went through the windshield during a car accident. When he was 5, Pinholster's stepfather moved in and was abusive, or nearly so. Pinholster always struggled in school. He was disruptive in kindergarten and was failing by first grade. He got in fights and would run out of the classroom. In third grade, Pinholster's teacher suggested that he was more than just a "disruptive child." Following tests at a clinic, Pinholster was sent to a school for educationally handicapped children where his performance improved.

At age 10, psychiatrists recommended that Pinholster be sent to a mental institution, although he did not go. Pinholster had continued to initiate fights with his brothers and to act like "Robin Hood" around the neighborhood, "[s]tealing from the rich and giving to the poor." Brashear had thought then that "[s]omething was not working right."

By age 10 or 11, Pinholster was living in boy's homes and juvenile halls. He spent six months when he was 12 in a state mental institution for emotionally handicapped children. By the time he was 18, Pinholster was in county jail, where he was beaten badly. Brashear suspected that the beating caused Pinholster's epilepsy, for which he has been prescribed medication. After a stint in state prison, Pinholster returned home but acted "unusual" and had trouble readjusting to life.

Pinholster's siblings were "basically very good children," although they would get into trouble. His brother, Terry, had been arrested for drunk driving and his sister, Tammy, for public intoxication. Tammy also was arrested for drug possession and was self-destructive and "wild." Pinholster's eldest brother, Alvin, died a fugitive from California authorities.

In addition to Brashear's penalty-phase testimony, Pinholster had previously presented mitigating evidence during the guilt phase from his brother, Terry. Terry testified that Pinholster was "more or less in institutions all his life," suffered from epilepsy, and was "more or less" drunk on the night of the murders.

After considering this aggravating and mitigating evidence, the jury returned a sentence of death. The state trial court found that the jury's determination was "supported overwhelmingly by the weight of the evidence" and added that "the factors in aggravation beyond all reasonable doubt outweigh those in mitigation."

2

There is no reasonable probability that the additional evidence Pinholster presented in his state habeas proceedings would have changed the jury's verdict. The "new" evidence largely duplicated the mitigation evidence at trial. School and medical records basically substantiate the testimony of Pinholster's mother and brother. Declarations from Pinholster's siblings support his mother's testimony that his stepfather was abusive and explain that Pinholster was beaten with fists, belts, and even wooden boards.

To the extent the state habeas record includes new factual allegations or evidence, much of it is of questionable mitigating value. If Pinholster had called Dr. Woods to testify consistently with his psychiatric report, Pinholster would have opened the door to rebuttal by a state expert. The new evidence relating to Pinholster's family—their more serious substance abuse, mental illness, and criminal problems—is also by no means clearly mitigating, as the jury might have concluded that Pinholster was simply beyond rehabilitation.

The remaining new material in the state habeas record is sparse. We learn that Pinholster's brother Alvin died of suicide by drug overdose, and there are passing references to Pinholster's own drug dependency. According to Dr. Stalberg, Pinholster's "school records" apparently evidenced "some degree" of brain damage. Mostly, there are just a few new details about Pinholster's childhood. Pinholster apparently looked like his biological father, whom his grandparents "loathed." Accordingly, whenever his grandparents "spanked or disciplined" the kids, Pinholster "always got the worst of it." Pinholster was mostly unsupervised and "didn't get much love," because his mother and stepfather were always working and "were more concerned with their own lives than the welfare of their kids." Neither parent seemed concerned about Pinholster's schooling. Finally, Pinholster's aunt once saw the children mixing flour and water to make something to eat, although "[m]ost meals consisted of canned spaghetti and foods of that ilk."

Given what little additional mitigating evidence Pinholster presented in state habeas, we cannot say that the California Supreme Court's determination was unreasonable. Having already heard much of what is includ-ed in the state habeas record, the jury returned a sentence of death. Moreover, some of the new testimony would likely have undercut the mitigating value of the testimony by Pinholster's mother. The new material is thus not so significant that, even assuming Pinholster's trial counsel performed deficiently, it was necessarily unreasonable for the California Supreme Court to conclude that Pinholster had failed to show a "substantial" likelihood of a different sentence.

3

[Justice Thomas criticizes the Ninth Circuit's reliance on the prejudice analysis in *Rompilla* and other cases, none of which, according to the Court, were subject to the deferential standard of review required by AEDPA].

* * *

The judgment of the United States Court of Appeals for the Ninth Circuit is reversed.

JUSTICE ALITO, concurring in part and concurring in the judgment.

Although I concur in the Court's judgment, I agree with the conclusion reached in Part I of the dissent, namely, that, when an evidentiary hearing is properly held in federal court, review under 28 U.S.C. § 2254(d)(1) must take into account the evidence admitted at that hearing. * * *

* * *

In this case * * * I would hold that the federal-court hearing should not have been held because respondent did not diligently present his new evidence to the California courts. And I join all but Part II of the opinion of the Court, as I agree that the decision of the state court represented a reasonable application of clearly established Supreme Court precedent in light of the state-court record.

JUSTICE BREYER, concurring in part and dissenting in part.

I join Parts I and II of the Court's opinion. I do not join Part III, for I would send this case back to the Court of Appeals so that it can apply the legal standards that Part II announces to the complex facts of this case.

* * *

JUSTICE SOTOMAYOR, with whom JUSTICE GINSBURG and JUSTICE KAGAN join as to Part II, dissenting.

* * *

I

The Court first holds that, in determining whether a state-court decision is an unreasonable application of Supreme Court precedent under § 2254(d)(1), review is limited to the record that was before the state court that adjudicated the claim on the merits. New evidence adduced at a federal evidentiary hearing is now irrelevant to determining whether a petitioner has satisfied § 2254(d)(1). This holding is unnecessary to promote AEDPA's purposes, and it is inconsistent with the provision's text, the structure of the statute, and our precedents.

A

* * *

B

The majority's interpretation of § 2254(d)(1) finds no support in the provision's text or the statute's structure as a whole.

1

Section 2254(d)(1) requires district courts to ask whether a state-court adjudication on the merits "resulted in a decision that was contrary to, or involved an unreasonable application of, clearly established Federal law, as determined by the Supreme Court of the United States." Because this provision uses "backward-looking language"—i.e., past-tense verbs—the majority believes that it limits review to the state-court record. But both §§ 2254(d)(1) and 2254(d)(2) use "backward-looking language," and § 2254(d)(2)—unlike § 2254(d)(1) —expressly directs district courts to base their review on "the evidence presented in the State court proceeding." If use of the past tense were sufficient to indicate Congress' intent to restrict analysis to the state-court record, the phrase "in light of the evidence presented in the State court proceeding" in § 2254(d)(2) would be superfluous. The majority's construction of § 2254(d)(1) fails to give meaning to Congress' decision to include language referring to the evidence presented to the state court in § 2254(d)(2).

* * *

Unlike my colleagues in the majority, I refuse to assume that Congress simply engaged in sloppy drafting. The inclusion of this phrase in § 2254(d)(2)—coupled with its omission from § 2254(d)(2)'s partner provision, § 2254(d)(1)—provides strong reason to think that Congress did not intend for the § 2254(d)(1) analysis to be limited categorically to "the evidence presented in the State court proceeding."

2

The " 'broader context of the statute as a whole,' " ante, at 1398–1399 (quoting Robinson v. Shell Oil Co., 519 U.S. 337, 341, 117 S.Ct. 843, 136 L.Ed.2d 808 (1997)), reinforces this conclusion. In particular, Congress' decision to include in AEDPA a provision, § 2254(e)(2), that permits federal evidentiary hearings in certain circumstances provides further evidence that Congress did not intend to limit the § 2254(d)(1) inquiry to the state-court record in every case.

* * *

3

* * *

* * * [C]onstruing § 2254(d)(1) to permit consideration of evidence properly introduced in federal court best accords with the text of § 2254(d)(2) and AEDPA's structure as a whole. By interpreting § 2254(d)(1) to prevent nondiligent petitioners from gaming the system— the very purpose of § 2254(e)(2)— the majority potentially has put habeas relief out of reach for diligent petitioners with meritorious claims based on new evidence.

C

* * *

II

I also disagree with the Court's conclusion that the Court of Appeals erred in holding that Pinholster had satisfied § 2254(d)(1) on the basis of the state-court record.

* * *

A

[Justice Sotomayor engages in a detailed and very lengthy discussion of Pinholster's mother's testimony in mitigation, and the additional evidence in mitigation that was presented to the state court on habeas. Her conclusion is that the mitigation evidence presented at trial was extremely weak and that the new evidence presented to the state habeas court provided strong proof of Pinholster's terrible background and his mental illness.]

B

* * *

C

* * *

The majority surmises that counsel decided on a strategy "to get the prosecution's aggravation witnesses excluded for lack of notice, and if that failed, to put on Pinholster's mother." This is the sort of post hoc rationalization for counsel's decision-making that contradicts the available evidence of counsel's actions that courts cannot indulge. The majority's explanation for counsel's conduct contradicts the best available evidence of counsel's actions: Dettmar's frank, contemporaneous statement to the trial judge that he "had not prepared any evidence by way of mitigation." The majority's conjecture that counsel had in fact prepared a mitigation defense, based primarily on isolated entries in counsel's billing records, requires it to assume that Dettmar was lying to the trial judge.

In any event, even if Pinholster's counsel had a strategic reason for their actions, that would not automatically render their actions reasonable. For example, had counsel decided their best option was to move to exclude the aggravating evidence, it would have been unreasonable to forgo a mitigation investigation on the hope that the motion would be granted. With a client's life at stake, it would "flou[t] prudence," Rompilla v. Beard, 545 U.S. 374, 389 (2005), for an attorney to rely on the possibility that the court might preclude aggravating evidence pursuant to a "legal technicality" without any backup plan in place in case the court denied the motion. No reasonable attorney would pursue such a risky strategy. I do not understand the majority to suggest otherwise.

Instead, I understand the majority's conclusion that counsel's actions were reasonable to rest on its belief that they did have a backup plan: a family-sympathy defense. In reaching this conclusion, the majority commits the same *Strickland* error that we corrected, applying § 2254(d)(1), in *Wiggins*: It holds a purportedly "tactical judgment" to be reasonable without assessing "the adequacy of the investigatio[n] supporting [that] judgmen[t]," 539 U.S., at 521. * * *

Wiggins is illustrative of the competence we have required of counsel in a capital case. There, counsel's investigation was limited to three sources: psychological testing, a pre-sentencing report, and Department of Social Services records. The records revealed that the petitioner's mother was an alcoholic, that he displayed emotional difficulties in foster care, that he was frequently absent from school, and that on one occasion, his mother left him alone for days without food. In these circumstances, we concluded, "any reasonably competent attorney would have realized that pursuing these leads was necessary to making an informed choice among possible defenses." Accordingly, we held, the state court's assumption that counsel's investigation was adequate was an unreasonable application of *Strickland*.

This case is remarkably similar to *Wiggins*. As the majority reads the record, counsel's mitigation investigation consisted of talking to Pinholster's mother, consulting with Dr. Stalberg, and researching epilepsy. What little information counsel gleaned from this rudimentary investigation, would have led any reasonable attorney to investigate further. Coun-

sel learned from Pinholster's mother that he attended a class for educationally handicapped children, that a psychologist had recommended placing him in a mental institution, and that he spent time in a state hospital for emotionally handicapped children. They knew that Pinholster had been diagnosed with epilepsy.

Any reasonably competent attorney would have realized that pursuing the leads suggested by this information was necessary to making an informed choice among possible defenses. Yet counsel made no effort to obtain the readily available evidence suggested by the information they learned, such as Pinholster's schooling or medical records, or to contact Pinholster's school authorities. They did not contact Dr. Dubin or the many other health-care providers who had treated Pinholster. Put simply, counsel "failed to act while potentially powerful mitigating evidence stared them in the face." *Bobby v. Van Hook*, 130 S.Ct., at 19.

* * *

"The record of the actual sentencing proceedings underscores the unreasonableness of counsel's conduct by suggesting that their failure to investigate thoroughly resulted from inattention, not reasoned strategic judgment." *Wiggins*, 539 U.S., at 526. Dettmar told the trial judge that he was unprepared to present any mitigation evidence. The mitigation case that counsel eventually put on can be described, at best, as "halfhearted." Ibid. Counsel made no effort to bolster Brashear's self-interested testimony with school or medical records, as the prosecutor effectively emphasized in closing argument. And because they did not pursue obvious leads, they failed to recognize that Brashear's testimony painting Pinholster as the bad apple in a normal, nondeprived family was false.

In denying Pinholster's claim, the California Supreme Court necessarily overlooked *Strickland 's* clearly established admonition that "strategic choices made after less than complete investigation are reasonable precisely to the extent that reasonable professional judgments support the limitations." 466 U.S., at 690–691. As in *Wiggins,* in light of the information available to Pinholster's counsel, it is plain that "reasonable professional judgments" could not have supported their woefully inadequate investigation. Accordingly, the California Supreme Court could not reasonably have concluded that Pinholster had failed to allege that his counsel's investigation was inadequate under *Strickland.*

D

The majority also concludes that the California Supreme Court could reasonably have concluded that Pinholster did not state a claim of prejudice. This conclusion, in light of the overwhelming mitigating evidence that was not before the jury, is wrong. * * *

1

[Counsel at trial] presented little in the way of mitigating evidence, and the prosecutor effectively used their halfhearted attempt to present a mitigation case to advocate for the death penalty. The jury nonetheless took two days to reach a decision to impose a death sentence.

2

The additional mitigating evidence presented to the California Supreme Court "adds up to a mitigation case that bears no relation" to Brashear's unsubstantiated testimony. *Rompilla,* 545 U.S., at 393.

Assuming the evidence presented to the California Supreme Court to be true, as that court was required to do, the new mitigating evidence presented to that court would have shown that Pinholster was raised in "chaos and poverty." The family home was filled with violence. Pinholster's siblings had extremely troubled pasts. There was substantial evidence of "mental disturbance during Mr. Pinholster's childhood and some degree of brain damage."

Dr. Woods concluded that Pinholster's aggressive conduct resulted from bipolar mood disorder. Just months before the murders, a doctor had recommended that Pinholster be sent to a psychiatric institute. Dr. Woods also explained that Pinholster's bizarre behavior before the murders reflected "[a]uditory hallucinations" and "severe psychosis." The available records confirmed that Pinholster suffered from longstanding seizure disorders, which may have been caused by his childhood head injuries.

On this record, I do not see how it can be said that "[t]he 'new' evidence largely duplicated the mitigation evidence at trial." Brashear's self-interested testimony was not confirmed with objective evidence, as the prosecutor highlighted. The new evidence would have "destroyed the [relatively] benign conception of [Pinholster's] upbringing" presented by his mother. *Rompilla,* 545 U.S., at 391. The jury heard no testimony at all that Pinholster likely suffered from brain damage or bipolar mood disorder, and counsel offered no evidence to help the jury understand the likely effect of Pinholster's head injuries or his bizarre behavior on the night of the homicides. The jury heard no testimony recounting the substantial evidence of Pinholster's likely neurological problems. And it heard no medical evidence that Pinholster suffered from epilepsy.

* * *

In many cases, a state court presented with additional mitigation evidence will reasonably conclude that there is no "reasonable probability that, but for counsel's unprofessional errors, the result of the proceeding would have been different." *Strickland*, 466 U.S., at 694. This is not such a case. Admittedly, Pinholster unjustifiably stabbed and killed two people, and his history of violent outbursts and burglaries surely did not endear him to the jury. But the homicides did not appear premeditated. * * * Even on the trial record, it took the jury two days to decide on a penalty. The contrast between the "not persuasive" mitigation case put on by Pinholster's counsel, and the substantial mitigation evidence at their fingertips was stark. Given these considerations, it is not a foregone conclusion, as the majority deems it, that a juror familiar with his troubled background and psychiatric issues would have reached the same conclusion regarding Pinholster's culpability. Fairminded jurists could not doubt that, on the record before the California Supreme Court, "there [was] a reasonable probability that at least one juror would have struck a different balance." *Wiggins*, 539 U.S., at 537.

III

The state-court record on its own was more than adequate to support the Court of Appeals' conclusion that the California Supreme Court could not reasonably have rejected Pinholster's Strickland claim. The additional evidence presented in the federal evi-

dentiary hearing only confirms that conclusion.

A

* * *

B

* * *

In sum, the evidence confirmed what was already apparent from the state-court record: Pinholster's counsel failed to conduct an adequate mitigation investigation, and there was a reasonable probability that at least one juror confronted with the "voluminous" mitigating evidence counsel should have discovered would have voted to spare Pinholster's life. Accordingly, whether on the basis of the state-or federal-court record, the courts below correctly concluded that Pinholster had shown that the California Supreme Court's decision reflected an unreasonable application of Strickland.

I cannot agree with either aspect of the Court's ruling. I fear the consequences of the Court's novel interpretation of § 2254(d)(1) for diligent state habeas petitioners with compelling evidence supporting their claims who were unable, through no fault of their own, to present that evidence to the state court that adjudicated their claims. And the Court's conclusion that the California Supreme Court reasonably denied Pinholster's ineffective-assistance-of-counsel claim overlooks counsel's failure to investigate obvious avenues of mitigation and the contrast between the woefully inadequate mitigation case they presented and the evidence they should and would have discovered. I respectfully dissent.

The Duty to Inform the Defendant About Immigration Consequences of a Conviction: Padilla v. Kentucky

PADILLA v. KENTUCKY

Supreme Court of the United States, 2010
130 S.Ct. 1473

JUSTICE STEVENS **delivered the opinion of the Court.**

Petitioner Jose Padilla, a native of Honduras, has been a lawful permanent resident of the United States for more than 40 years. Padilla served this Nation with honor as a member of the U.S. Armed Forces during the Vietnam War. He now faces deportation after pleading guilty to the transportation of a large amount of marijuana in his tractor-trailer in the Commonwealth of Kentucky.

In this postconviction proceeding, Padilla claims that his counsel not only failed to advise him of this consequence prior to his entering the plea, but also told him that he "did not have to worry about immigration status since he had been in the country so long." Padilla relied on his counsel's erroneous advice when he pleaded guilty to the drug charges that made his deportation virtually mandatory. He alleges that he would have insisted on going to trial if he had not received incorrect advice from his attorney.

Assuming the truth of his allegations, the Supreme Court of Kentucky denied Padilla postconviction relief without the benefit of an evidentiary hearing. The court held that the Sixth Amendment's guarantee of effective assistance of counsel does not protect a criminal defendant from erroneous advice about deportation because it is merely a "collateral" consequence of his conviction. In its view, neither counsel's failure to advise petitioner about the possibility of removal, nor counsel's incorrect advice, could provide a basis for relief.

We granted certiorari to decide whether, as a matter of federal law, Padilla's counsel had an obligation to advise him that the offense to which he was pleading guilty would result in his removal from this country. We agree with Padilla that constitutionally competent counsel would have advised him that his conviction for drug distribution made him subject to automatic deportation. Whether he is entitled to relief depends on whether he has been prejudiced, a matter that we do not address.

I

The landscape of federal immigration law has changed dramatically over the last 90 years. While once there was only a narrow class of deportable offenses and judges wielded broad discretionary authority to prevent deportation, immigration reforms over time have expanded the class of deportable offenses and limited the authority of judges to alleviate the harsh consequences of deportation. The drastic measure of deportation or removal, is now virtually inevitable for a vast number of noncitizens convicted of crimes.

* * *

* * * Under contemporary law, if a noncitizen has committed a removable offense * * * his removal is practically inevitable but for the possible exercise of limited remnants of equitable discretion vested in the Attorney General to cancel removal for noncitizens convicted of particular classes of offenses. See 8 U.S.C. § 1229b. Subject to limited exceptions, this discretionary relief is not available for an offense related to trafficking in a controlled substance. See § 1101(a)(43)(B); § 1228.

These changes to our immigration law have dramatically raised the stakes of a noncitizen's criminal conviction. The importance of accurate legal advice for noncitizens accused of crimes has never been more important. These changes confirm our view that, as a matter of federal law, deportation is an integral part—indeed, sometimes the most important part—of the penalty that may be imposed on noncitizen defendants who plead guilty to specified crimes.

II

* * * The Supreme Court of Kentucky rejected Padilla's ineffectiveness claim on the ground that the advice he sought about the risk of deportation concerned only collateral matters, i.e., those matters not within the sentencing authority of the state trial court. In its view, "collateral consequences are outside the scope of representation required by the Sixth Amendment," and, therefore, the "failure of defense counsel to advise the defendant of possible deportation consequences is not cognizable as a claim for ineffective assistance of counsel." The Kentucky high court is far from alone in this view.

We, however, have never applied a distinction between direct and collateral consequences to define the scope of constitutionally "reasonable professional assistance" required under *Strickland*. Whether that distinction is appropriate is a question we need not consider in this case be-

cause of the unique nature of deportation.

* * *

Deportation as a consequence of a criminal conviction is, because of its close connection to the criminal process, uniquely difficult to classify as either a direct or a collateral consequence. The collateral versus direct distinction is thus ill-suited to evaluating a *Strickland* claim concerning the specific risk of deportation. We conclude that advice regarding deportation is not categorically removed from the ambit of the Sixth Amendment right to counsel. *Strickland* applies to Padilla's claim.

III

Under *Strickland*, we first determine whether counsel's representation "fell below an objective standard of reasonableness." Then we ask whether "there is a reasonable probability that, but for counsel's unprofessional errors, the result of the proceeding would have been different." The first prong-constitutional deficiency-is necessarily linked to the practice and expectations of the legal community: "The proper measure of attorney performance remains simply reasonableness under prevailing professional norms." We long have recognized that "[p]revailing norms of practice as reflected in American Bar Association standards and the like . . . are guides to determining what is reasonable. . . ." Although they are "only guides," and not "inexorable commands," these standards may be valuable measures of the prevailing professional norms of effective representation, especially as these standards have been adapted to deal with the intersection of modern criminal prosecutions and immigration law.

The weight of prevailing professional norms supports the view that counsel must advise her client regarding the risk of deportation. "[A]uthorities of every stripe-including the American Bar Association, criminal defense and public defender organizations, authoritative treatises, and state and city bar publications-universally require defense attorneys to advise as to the risk of deportation consequences for non-citizen clients...." Brief for Legal Ethics, Criminal Procedure, and Criminal Law Professors as Amici Curiae 12–14.

* * *

In the instant case, the terms of the relevant immigration statute are succinct, clear, and explicit in defining the removal consequence for Padilla's conviction. See 8 U.S.C. § 1227(a)(2)(B)(i) ("Any alien who at any time after admission has been convicted of a violation of (or a conspiracy or attempt to violate) any law or regulation of a State, the United States or a foreign country relating to a controlled substance ..., other than a single offense involving possession for one's own use of 30 grams or less of marijuana, is deportable"). Padilla's counsel could have easily determined that his plea would make him eligible for deportation simply from reading the text of the statute, which addresses not some broad classification of crimes but specifically commands removal for all controlled substances convictions except for the most trivial of marijuana possession offenses. Instead, Padilla's counsel provided him false assurance that his conviction would not result in his removal from this country. This is not a hard case in which to find deficiency: The consequences of Padilla's plea could easily be determined from reading the removal statute, his deportation was presump-

tively mandatory, and his counsel's advice was incorrect.

Immigration law can be complex, and it is a legal specialty of its own. Some members of the bar who represent clients facing criminal charges, in either state or federal court or both, may not be well versed in it. There will, therefore, undoubtedly be numerous situations in which the deportation consequences of a particular plea are unclear or uncertain. The duty of the private practitioner in such cases is more limited. When the law is not succinct and straightforward * * * a criminal defense attorney need do no more than advise a noncitizen client that pending criminal charges may carry a risk of adverse immigration consequences. But when the deportation consequence is truly clear, as it was in this case, the duty to give correct advice is equally clear.

Accepting his allegations as true, Padilla has sufficiently alleged constitutional deficiency to satisfy the first prong of *Strickland*. * * *

IV

The Solicitor General has urged us to conclude that *Strickland* applies to Padilla's claim only to the extent that he has alleged affirmative misadvice. In the United States' view, "counsel is not constitutionally required to provide advice on matters that will not be decided in the criminal case ... ," though counsel is required to provide accurate advice if she chooses to discusses these matters.

Respondent and Padilla both find the Solicitor General's proposed rule unpersuasive, although it has support among the lower courts. * * *

A holding limited to affirmative misadvice would invite two absurd results. First, it would give counsel

an incentive to remain silent on matters of great importance, even when answers are readily available. Silence under these circumstances would be fundamentally at odds with the critical obligation of counsel to advise the client of the advantages and disadvantages of a plea agreement. When attorneys know that their clients face possible exile from this country and separation from their families, they should not be encouraged to say nothing at all. Second, it would deny a class of clients least able to represent themselves the most rudimentary advice on deportation even when it is readily available.
* * *

We have given serious consideration to the concerns that the Solicitor General, respondent, and amici have stressed regarding the importance of protecting the finality of convictions obtained through guilty pleas. We confronted a similar "floodgates" concern in Hill v. Lockhart [Text, page 1328], but nevertheless applied *Strickland* to a claim that counsel had failed to advise the client regarding his parole eligibility before he pleaded guilty.

A flood did not follow in that decision's wake. Surmounting *Strickland 's* high bar is never an easy task. Moreover, to obtain relief on this type of claim, a petitioner must convince the court that a decision to reject the plea bargain would have been rational under the circumstances. There is no reason to doubt that lower courts—now quite experienced with applying *Strickland*—can effectively and efficiently use its framework to separate specious claims from those with substantial merit.

It seems unlikely that our decision today will have a significant effect on those convictions already obtained as the result of plea bargains. For at least the past 15 years, professional norms have generally imposed an obligation on counsel to provide advice on the deportation consequences of a client's plea. We should, therefore, presume that counsel satisfied their obligation to render competent advice at the time their clients considered pleading guilty.

Likewise, although we must be especially careful about recognizing new grounds for attacking the validity of guilty pleas, in the 25 years since we first applied *Strickland* to claims of ineffective assistance at the plea stage, practice has shown that pleas are less frequently the subject of collateral challenges than convictions obtained after a trial. Pleas account for nearly 95% of all criminal convictions. But they account for only approximately 30% of the habeas petitions filed. The nature of relief secured by a successful collateral challenge to a guilty plea—an opportunity to withdraw the plea and proceed to trial—imposes its own significant limiting principle: Those who collaterally attack their guilty pleas lose the benefit of the bargain obtained as a result of the plea. Thus, a different calculus informs whether it is wise to challenge a guilty plea in a habeas proceeding because, ultimately, the challenge may result in a less favorable outcome for the defendant, whereas a collateral challenge to a conviction obtained after a jury trial has no similar downside potential.

Finally, informed consideration of possible deportation can only benefit both the State and noncitizen defendants during the plea-bargaining process. By bringing deportation consequences into this process, the defense and prosecution may well be able to reach agreements that better satisfy the interests of both parties. As in this case, a criminal episode may provide the basis for multiple charges, of which only a subset mandate deportation following conviction. Counsel who possess the most rudimentary understanding of the deportation consequences of a particular criminal offense may be able to plea bargain creatively with the prosecutor in order to craft a conviction and sentence that reduce the likelihood of deportation, as by avoiding a conviction for an offense that automatically triggers the removal consequence. At the same time, the threat of deportation may provide the defendant with a powerful incentive to plead guilty to an offense that does not mandate that penalty in exchange for a dismissal of a charge that does.

* * *

V

It is our responsibility under the Constitution to ensure that no criminal defendant-whether a citizen or not-is left to the mercies of incompetent counsel. To satisfy this responsibility, we now hold that counsel must inform her client whether his plea carries a risk of deportation. Our longstanding Sixth Amendment precedents, the seriousness of deportation as a consequence of a criminal plea, and the concomitant impact of deportation on families living lawfully in this country demand no less.

Taking as true the basis for his motion for postconviction relief, we have little difficulty concluding that Padilla has sufficiently alleged that his counsel was constitutionally deficient. Whether Padilla is entitled to relief will depend on whether he can demonstrate prejudice as a result thereof, a question we do not reach because it was not passed on below.

The judgment of the Supreme Court of Kentucky is reversed, and the case is remanded for further proceedings not inconsistent with this opinion.

It is so ordered.

JUSTICE ALITO, with whom THE CHIEF JUSTICE joins, concurring in the judgment.

I concur in the judgment because a criminal defense attorney fails to provide effective assistance * * * if the attorney misleads a noncitizen client regarding the removal consequences of a conviction. In my view, such an attorney must (1) refrain from unreasonably providing incorrect advice and (2) advise the defendant that a criminal conviction may have adverse immigration consequences and that, if the alien wants advice on this issue, the alien should consult an immigration attorney. I do not agree with the Court that the attorney must attempt to explain what those consequences may be. As the Court concedes, "[i]mmigration law can be complex"; "it is a legal specialty of its own"; and "[s]ome members of the bar who represent clients facing criminal charges, in either state or federal court or both, may not be well versed in it." The Court nevertheless holds that a criminal defense attorney must provide advice in this specialized area in those cases in which the law is "succinct and straightforward"—but not, perhaps, in other situations. This vague, halfway test will lead to much confusion and needless litigation.

I

* * * Until today, the longstanding and unanimous position of the federal courts was that reasonable defense counsel generally need only advise a client about the direct consequences of a criminal conviction. While the line between "direct" and "collateral" consequences is not always clear, the collateral-consequences rule expresses an important truth: Criminal defense attorneys have expertise regarding the conduct of criminal proceedings. They are not expected to possess-and very often do not possess-expertise in other areas of the law, and it is unrealistic to expect them to provide expert advice on matters that lie outside their area of training and experience.

This case happens to involve removal, but criminal convictions can carry a wide variety of consequences other than conviction and sentencing, including civil commitment, civil forfeiture, the loss of the right to vote, disqualification from public benefits, ineligibility to possess firearms, dishonorable discharge from the Armed Forces, and loss of business or professional licenses. A criminal conviction may also severely damage a defendant's reputation and thus impair the defendant's ability to obtain future employment or business opportunities. All of those consequences are serious, but this Court has never held that a criminal defense attorney's Sixth Amendment duties extend to providing advice about such matters.

The Court tries to justify its dramatic departure from precedent by pointing to the views of various professional organizations. However, ascertaining the level of professional competence required by the Sixth Amendment is ultimately a task for the courts. Although we may appropriately consult standards promulgated by private bar groups, we cannot delegate to these groups our task of determining what the Constitution commands. See *Strickland*, at 688 (explaining that "[p]revailing norms of practice as reflected in American Bar Association standards ... are guides to determining what is reasonable, but they are only guides"). And we must recognize that such standards may represent only the aspirations of a bar group rather than an empirical assessment of actual practice.

Even if the only relevant consideration were "prevailing professional norms," it is hard to see how those norms can support the duty the Court today imposes on defense counsel. Because many criminal defense attorneys have little understanding of immigration law, it should follow that a criminal defense attorney who refrains from providing immigration advice does not violate prevailing professional norms. But the Court's opinion would not just require defense counsel to warn the client of a general risk of removal; it would also require counsel in at least some cases, to specify what the removal consequences of a conviction would be.

The Court's new approach is particularly problematic because providing advice on whether a conviction for a particular offense will make an alien removable is often quite complex. * * *

* * * To take just a few examples, it may be hard, in some cases, for defense counsel even to determine whether a client is an alien, or whether a particular state disposition will result in a "conviction" for purposes of federal immigration law. The task of offering advice about the immigration consequences of a criminal conviction is further complicated by other problems, including significant variations among Circuit interpretations of federal immigration statutes; the frequency with which

immigration law changes; different rules governing the immigration consequences of juvenile, first-offender, and foreign convictions; and the relationship between the length and type of sentence and the determination whether an alien is subject to removal, eligible for relief from removal, or qualified to become a naturalized citizen.

In short, the professional organizations and guidebooks on which the Court so heavily relies are right to say that "nothing is ever simple with immigration law"—including the determination whether immigration law clearly makes a particular offense removable. ABA Guidebook § 4.65, at 130. I therefore cannot agree with the Court's apparent view that the Sixth Amendment requires criminal defense attorneys to provide immigration advice.

The Court tries to downplay the severity of the burden it imposes on defense counsel by suggesting that the scope of counsel's duty to offer advice concerning deportation consequences may turn on how hard it is to determine those consequences. * * * This approach is problematic for at least four reasons.

First, it will not always be easy to tell whether a particular statutory provision is "succinct, clear, and explicit." How can an attorney who lacks general immigration law expertise be sure that a seemingly clear statutory provision actually means what it seems to say when read in isolation? What if the application of the provision to a particular case is not clear but a cursory examination of case law or administrative decisions would provide a definitive answer?

Second, if defense counsel must provide advice regarding only one of the many collateral consequences of a criminal conviction, many defendants are likely to be misled. To take just one example, a conviction for a particular offense may render an alien excludable but not removable. If an alien charged with such an offense is advised only that pleading guilty to such an offense will not result in removal, the alien may be induced to enter a guilty plea without realizing that a consequence of the plea is that the alien will be unable to reenter the United States if the alien returns to his or her home country for any reason, such as to visit an elderly parent or to attend a funeral. Incomplete legal advice may be worse than no advice at all because it may mislead and may dissuade the client from seeking advice from a more knowledgeable source.

Third, the Court's rigid constitutional rule could inadvertently head off more promising ways of addressing the underlying problem-such as statutory or administrative reforms requiring trial judges to inform a defendant on the record that a guilty plea may carry adverse immigration consequences. * * * A nonconstitutional rule requiring trial judges to inform defendants on the record of the risk of adverse immigration consequences can ensure that a defendant receives needed information without putting a large number of criminal convictions at risk; and because such a warning would be given on the record, courts would not later have to determine whether the defendant was misrepresenting the advice of counsel. Likewise, flexible statutory procedures for withdrawing guilty pleas might give courts appropriate discretion to determine whether the interests of justice would be served by allowing a particular defendant to withdraw a plea entered into on the basis of incomplete information.

Fourth, the Court's decision marks a major upheaval in Sixth Amendment law. This Court decided *Strickland* in 1984, but the majority does not cite a single case, from this or any other federal court, holding that criminal defense counsel's failure to provide advice concerning the removal consequences of a criminal conviction violates a defendant's Sixth Amendment right to counsel. * * * The majority * * * casually dismisses the longstanding and unanimous position of the lower federal courts with respect to the scope of criminal defense counsel's duty to advise on collateral consequences.

* * *

II

While mastery of immigration law is not required by *Strickland*, several considerations support the conclusion that affirmative misadvice regarding the removal consequences of a conviction may constitute ineffective assistance.

First, a rule prohibiting affirmative misadvice regarding a matter as crucial to the defendant's plea decision as deportation appears faithful to the scope and nature of the Sixth Amendment duty this Court has recognized in its past cases. * * * As the Court appears to acknowledge, thorough understanding of the intricacies of immigration law is not "within the range of competence demanded of attorneys in criminal cases." * * * By contrast, reasonably competent attorneys should know that it is not appropriate or responsible to hold themselves out as authorities on a difficult and complicated subject matter with which they are not familiar. Candor concerning the limits of one's professional expertise, in other words, is within the range of duties reasonably expected of defense attorneys in criminal cases. * * *

Second, incompetent advice distorts the defendant's decisionmaking process and seems to call the fairness and integrity of the criminal proceeding itself into question. When a defendant opts to plead guilty without definitive information concerning the likely effects of the plea, the defendant can fairly be said to assume the risk that the conviction may carry indirect consequences of which he or she is not aware. That is not the case when a defendant bases the decision to plead guilty on counsel's express misrepresentation that the defendant will not be removable. In the latter case, it seems hard to say that the plea was entered with the advice of constitutionally competent counsel—or that it embodies a voluntary and intelligent decision to forsake constitutional rights.

Third, a rule prohibiting unreasonable misadvice regarding exceptionally important collateral matters would not deter or interfere with ongoing political and administrative efforts to devise fair and reasonable solutions to the difficult problem posed by defendants who plead guilty without knowing of certain important collateral consequences.

Finally, the conclusion that affirmative misadvice regarding the removal consequences of a conviction can give rise to ineffective assistance would, unlike the Court's approach, not require any upheaval in the law. As the Solicitor General points out, "[t]he vast majority of the lower courts considering claims of ineffective assistance in the plea context have [distinguished] between defense counsel who remain silent and defense counsel who give affirmative misadvice.'' Brief for United States as Amicus Curiae 8 (citing cases). * * *

In concluding that affirmative misadvice regarding the removal consequences of a criminal conviction may constitute ineffective assistance, I do not mean to suggest that the Sixth Amendment does no more than require defense counsel to avoid misinformation. When a criminal defense attorney is aware that a client is an alien, the attorney should advise the client that a criminal conviction may have adverse consequences under the immigration laws and that the client should consult an immigration specialist if the client wants advice on that subject. By putting the client on notice of the danger of removal, such advice would significantly reduce the chance that the client would plead guilty under a mistaken premise.

III

In sum, a criminal defense attorney should not be required to provide advice on immigration law, a complex specialty that generally lies outside the scope of a criminal defense attorney's expertise. On the other hand, any competent criminal defense attorney should appreciate the extraordinary importance that the risk of removal might have in the client's determination whether to enter a guilty plea. Accordingly, unreasonable and incorrect information concerning the risk of removal can give rise to an ineffectiveness claim. In addition, silence alone is not enough to satisfy counsel's duty to assist the client. Instead, an alien defendant's Sixth Amendment right to counsel is satisfied if defense counsel advises the client that a conviction may have immigration consequences, that immigration law is a specialized field, that the attorney is not an immigration lawyer, and that the client should consult an immigration spe-

cialist if the client wants advice on that subject.

JUSTICE SCALIA, with whom JUSTICE THOMAS joins, dissenting.

In the best of all possible worlds, criminal defendants contemplating a guilty plea ought to be advised of all serious collateral consequences of conviction, and surely ought not to be misadvised. The Constitution, however, is not an all-purpose tool for judicial construction of a perfect world; and when we ignore its text in order to make it that, we often find ourselves swinging a sledge where a tack hammer is needed.

* * *

The Sixth Amendment as originally understood and ratified meant only that a defendant had a right to employ counsel, or to use volunteered services of counsel. See, *United States v. Van Duzee*, 140 U.S. 169 (1891). We have held, however, that the Sixth Amendment requires the provision of counsel to indigent defendants at government expense, *Gideon v. Wainwright*, 372 U.S. 335, 344–345 (1963), and that the right to ''the assistance of counsel'' includes the right to effective assistance, *Strickland v. Washington*, 466 U.S. 668, 686 (1984). Even assuming the validity of these holdings, I reject the significant further extension that the Court, and to a lesser extent the concurrence, would create. We have until today at least retained the Sixth Amendment's textual limitation to criminal prosecutions. * * *

There is no basis in text or in principle to extend the constitutionally required advice regarding guilty pleas beyond those matters germane to the criminal prosecution at hand–to wit, the sentence that the plea will produce, the higher sentence that conviction after trial might entail, and the chances of such a conviction. Such matters fall within "the range of competence demanded of attorneys in criminal cases," McMann v. Richardson, 397 U.S. 759, 771 (1970). We have never held, as the logic of the Court's opinion assumes, that once counsel is appointed all professional responsibilities of counsel—even those extending beyond defense against the prosecution—become constitutional commands. Because the subject of the misadvice here was not the prosecution for which Jose Padilla was entitled to effective assistance of counsel, the Sixth Amendment has no application.

* * *

The Court's holding prevents legislation that could solve the problems addressed by today's opinions in a more precise and targeted fashion. If the subject had not been constitutionalized, legislation could specify which categories of misadvice about matters ancillary to the prosecution invalidate plea agreements, what collateral consequences counsel must bring to a defendant's attention, and what warnings must be given. Moreover, legislation could provide consequences for the misadvice, nonadvice, or failure to warn, other than nullification of a criminal conviction after the witnesses and evidence needed for retrial have disappeared. Federal immigration law might provide, for example, that the near-automatic removal which follows from certain criminal convictions will not apply where the conviction rested upon a guilty plea induced by counsel's misadvice regarding removal consequences. Or legislation might put the government to a choice in such circumstances: Either retry the defendant or forgo the removal. But all that has been precluded in favor of today's sledge hammer.

In sum, the Sixth Amendment guarantees adequate assistance of counsel in defending against a pending criminal prosecution. We should limit both the constitutional obligation to provide advice and the consequences of bad advice to that well defined area.

Application of Strickland—and AEDPA Standards of Deference—To Trial Counsel's Failure To Present a Forensic Expert: Harrington v. Richter

HARRINGTON v. RICHTER

Supreme Court of the United States, 2011.
131 S.Ct. 770

JUSTICE KENNEDY **delivered the opinion of the Court.**

The writ of habeas corpus stands as a safeguard against imprisonment of those held in violation of the law. Judges must be vigilant and independent in reviewing petitions for the writ, a commitment that entails substantial judicial resources. Those resources are diminished and misspent, however, and confidence in the writ and the law it vindicates undermined, if there is judicial disregard for the sound and established principles that inform its proper issuance. That judicial disregard is inherent in the opinion of the Court of Appeals for the Ninth Circuit here under review. The Court of Appeals, in disagreement with the contrary conclusions of the Supreme Court of the State of California and of a United States District Court, ordered habeas corpus relief granted to set aside the conviction of Joshua Richter, respondent here. This was clear error.

* * *

I

It is necessary to begin by discussing the details of a crime committed more than a decade and a half ago.

A

Sometime after midnight on December 20, 1994, sheriff's deputies in Sacramento County, California, arrived at the home of a drug dealer named Joshua Johnson. Hours before, Johnson had been smoking marijuana in the company of Richter and two other men, Christian Branscombe and Patrick Klein. When the deputies arrived, however, they found only Johnson and Klein. Johnson was hysterical and covered in blood. Klein was lying on a couch in Johnson's living room, unconscious and bleeding. Klein and Johnson each had been shot twice. Johnson recovered; Klein died of his wounds.

Johnson gave investigators this account: After falling asleep, he awoke to find Richter and Branscombe in his bedroom, at which point Branscombe shot him. Johnson heard more gunfire in the living room and the sound of his assailants leaving. He got up, found Klein bleeding on the living room couch, and called 911. A gun safe, a pistol, and $6,000 cash, all of which had been in the bedroom, were missing.

Evidence at the scene corroborated Johnson's account. Investigators found spent shell casings in the bedroom (where Johnson said he had been shot) and in the living room (where Johnson indicated Klein had been shot). In the living room there were two casings, a .32 caliber and a .22 caliber. One of the bullets recovered from Klein's body was a .32 and the other was a .22. In the bedroom there were two more casings, both .32 caliber. In addition detectives found blood spatter near the living room couch and bloodstains in the bedroom. Pools of blood had collected in the kitchen and the doorway to Johnson's bedroom. Investigators took only a few blood samples from the crime scene. One was from a blood splash on the wall near the bedroom doorway, but no sample was taken from the doorway blood pool itself.

Investigators searched Richter's residence and found Johnson's gun safe, two boxes of .22–caliber ammunition, and a gun magazine loaded with cartridges of the same brand and type as the boxes. A ballistics expert later concluded the .22–caliber bullet that struck Klein and the .22–caliber shell found in the living room matched the ammunition found in Richter's home and bore markings consistent with the model of gun for which the magazine was designed.

Richter and Branscombe were arrested. At first Richter denied involvement. He would later admit taking Johnson's pistol and disposing of it and of the .32–caliber weapon Branscombe used to shoot Johnson and Klein. Richter's counsel produced Johnson's missing pistol, but neither of the guns used to shoot Johnson and Klein was found.

B

Branscombe and Richter were tried together on charges of murder, attempted murder, burglary, and robbery. Only Richter's case is presented here.

The prosecution built its case on Johnson's testimony and on circumstantial evidence. Its opening statement took note of the shell casings found at the crime scene and the ammunition and gun safe found at Richter's residence. Defense counsel offered explanations for the circumstantial evidence and derided Johnson as a drug dealer, a paranoid, and a trigger-happy gun fanatic who had drawn a pistol on Branscombe and Richter the last time he had seen them. And there were inconsistencies in Johnson's story. In his 911 call, for instance, Johnson first said there were four or five men who had broken into his house, not two; and in the call he did not identify Richter and Branscombe among the intruders.

Blood evidence does not appear to have been part of the prosecution's planned case prior to trial, and investigators had not analyzed the few blood samples taken from the crime scene. But the opening statement from the defense led the prosecution to alter its approach. Richter's attorney outlined the theory that Branscombe had fired on Johnson in self-defense and that Klein had been killed not on the living room couch but in the crossfire in the bedroom doorway. Defense counsel stressed deficiencies in the investigation, including the absence of forensic support for the prosecution's version of events.

The prosecution took steps to adjust to the counterattack now disclosed. Without advance notice and over the objection of Richter's attorney, one of the detectives who investigated the shootings testified for the prosecution as an expert in blood pattern evidence. He concluded it

was unlikely Klein had been shot outside the living room and then moved to the couch, given the patterns of blood on Klein's face, as well as other evidence including "high velocity" blood spatter near the couch consistent with the location of a shooting. The prosecution also offered testimony from a serologist. She testified the blood sample taken near the pool by the bedroom door could be Johnson's but not Klein's.

Defense counsel's cross-examination probed weaknesses in the testimony of these two witnesses. The detective who testified on blood patterns acknowledged that his inferences were imprecise, that it was unlikely Klein had been lying down on the couch when shot, and that he could not say the blood in the living room was from either of Klein's wounds. Defense counsel elicited from the serologist a concession that she had not tested the bedroom blood sample for cross-contamination. She said that if the year-old sample had degraded, it would be difficult to tell whether blood of Klein's type was also present in the sample.

For the defense, Richter's attorney called seven witnesses. Prominent among these was Richter himself. Richter testified he and Branscombe returned to Johnson's house just before the shootings in order to deliver something to one of Johnson's roommates. By Richter's account, Branscombe entered the house alone while Richter waited in the driveway; but after hearing screams and gunshots, Richter followed inside. There he saw Klein lying not on the couch but in the bedroom doorway, with Johnson on the bed and Branscombe standing in the middle of the room. According to Richter, Branscombe said he shot at Johnson and Klein after they attacked him. Other defense witnesses provided some corroboration for Richter's story. His former girlfriend, for instance, said she saw the gun safe at Richter's house shortly before the shootings.

The jury returned a verdict of guilty on all charges. Richter was sentenced to life without parole. On appeal, his conviction was affirmed. The California Supreme Court denied a petition for review, and Richter did not file a petition for certiorari with this Court. His conviction became final.

C

Richter later petitioned the California Supreme Court for a writ of habeas corpus. He asserted a number of grounds for relief, including ineffective assistance of counsel. As relevant here, he claimed his counsel was deficient for failing to present expert testimony on serology, pathology, and blood spatter patterns, testimony that, he argued, would disclose the source of the blood pool in the bedroom doorway. This, he contended, would bolster his theory that Johnson had moved Klein to the couch.

He offered affidavits from three types of forensic experts. First, he provided statements from two blood serologists who said there was a possibility Klein's blood was intermixed with blood of Johnson's type in the sample taken from near the pool in the bedroom doorway. Second, he provided a statement from a pathologist who said the blood pool was too large to have come from Johnson given the nature of his wounds and his own account of his actions while waiting for the police. Third, he provided a statement from an expert in bloodstain analysis who said the absence of "a large number of satellite droplets" in photographs of the area around the blood in the bedroom doorway was inconsistent with the blood pool coming from Johnson as he stood in the doorway. Richter argued this evidence established the possibility that the blood in the bedroom doorway came from Klein, not Johnson. If that were true, he argued, it would confirm his account, not Johnson's. The California Supreme Court denied Richter's petition in a one-sentence summary order. Richter did not seek certiorari from this Court.

After the California Supreme Court issued its summary order denying relief, Richter filed a petition for habeas corpus in United States District Court for the Eastern District of California. He reasserted the claims in his state petition. The District Court denied his petition, and a three-judge panel of the Court of Appeals for the Ninth Circuit affirmed. The Court of Appeals granted rehearing en banc and reversed the District Court's decision.

As a preliminary matter, the Court of Appeals questioned whether 28 U.S.C. § 2254(d) was applicable to Richter's petition, since the California Supreme Court issued only a summary denial when it rejected his *Strickland* claims; but it determined the California decision was unreasonable in any event and that Richter was entitled to relief. The court held Richter's trial counsel was deficient for failing to consult experts on blood evidence in determining and pursuing a trial strategy and in preparing to rebut expert evidence the prosecution might—and later did—offer. Four judges dissented from the en banc decision. We granted certiorari.

II

The statutory authority of federal courts to issue habeas corpus relief for persons in state custody is provided by 28 U.S.C. § 2254, as amended by the Antiterrorism and Effective Death Penalty Act of 1996 (AEDPA). The text of § 2254(d) states:

"An application for a writ of habeas corpus on behalf of a person in custody pursuant to the judgment of a State court shall not be granted with respect to any claim that was adjudicated on the merits in State court proceedings unless the adjudication of the claim—"

"(1) resulted in a decision that was contrary to, or involved an unreasonable application of, clearly established Federal law, as determined by the Supreme Court of the United States"; or

"(2) resulted in a decision that was based on an unreasonable determination of the facts in light of the evidence presented in the State court proceeding."

As an initial matter, it is necessary to decide whether § 2254(d) applies when a state court's order is unaccompanied by an opinion explaining the reasons relief has been denied. [The Court holds that the AEDPA does apply because the claim was adjudicated on the merits—an opinion with written reasons is not required.]

III

Federal habeas relief may not be granted for claims subject to § 2254(d) unless it is shown that the earlier state court's decision "was contrary to" federal law then clearly established in the holdings of this Court, § 2254(d)(1); or that it "involved an unreasonable application of" such law, § 2254(d)(1); or that it "was based on an unreasonable determination of the facts" in light of the record before the state court, § 2254(d)(2).

The Court of Appeals relied on the second of these exceptions to § 2254(d)'s relitigation bar, the exception in § 2254(d)(1) permitting relitigation where the earlier state decision resulted from an "unreasonable application of" clearly established federal law. In the view of the Court of Appeals, the California Supreme Court's decision on Richter's ineffective-assistance claim unreasonably applied the holding in *Strickland*. The Court of Appeals' lengthy opinion, however, discloses an improper understanding of § 2254(d)'s unreasonableness standard and of its operation in the context of a *Strickland* claim.

The pivotal question is whether the state court's application of the *Strickland* standard was unreasonable. This is different from asking whether defense counsel's performance fell below *Strickland's* standard. Were that the inquiry, the analysis would be no different than if, for example, this Court were adjudicating a *Strickland* claim on direct review of a criminal conviction in a United States district court. Under AEDPA, though, it is a necessary premise that the two questions are different. * * * A state court must be granted a deference and latitude that are not in operation when the case involves review under the Strickland standard itself.

A state court's determination that a claim lacks merit precludes federal habeas relief so long as "fairminded jurists could disagree" on the correctness of the state court's decision. Yarborough v. Alvarado, 541 U.S. 652, 664 (2004). And as this Court has explained, "[E]valuating whether a rule application was unreasonable requires considering the rule's specificity. The more general the rule, the more leeway courts have in reaching outcomes in case-by-case determinations." It is not an unreasonable application of clearly established Federal law for a state court to decline to apply a specific legal rule that has not been squarely established by this Court.

Here it is not apparent how the Court of Appeals' analysis would have been any different without AEDPA. The court explicitly conducted a de novo review, and after finding a *Strickland* violation, it declared, without further explanation, that the "state court's decision to the contrary constituted an unreasonable application of *Strickland.*" AEDPA demands more. Under § 2254(d), a habeas court must determine what arguments or theories supported or, as here, could have supported, the state court's decision; and then it must ask whether it is possible fairminded jurists could disagree that those arguments or theories are inconsistent with the holding in a prior decision of this Court. * * *

If this standard is difficult to meet, that is because it was meant to be. As amended by AEDPA, § 2254(d) stops short of imposing a complete bar on federal court relitigation of claims already rejected in state proceedings. It preserves authority to issue the writ in cases where there is no possibility fairminded jurists could disagree that the state court's decision conflicts with this Court's precedents. It goes no farther. Section 2254(d) reflects the view that habeas corpus is a guard against extreme malfunctions in the state criminal justice systems, not a substitute for ordinary error correction through appeal. As a condition for obtaining habeas corpus from a federal court, a state prisoner must show that the state court's ruling on the claim being presented in federal court was so lacking in justification that there was an error well understood and comprehended in existing law beyond any possibility for fairminded disagreement.

* * *

IV

The conclusion of the Court of Appeals that Richter demonstrated an unreasonable application by the state court of the Strickland standard now must be discussed. To have been entitled to relief from the California Supreme Court, Richter had to show both that his counsel provided deficient assistance and that there was prejudice as a result.

* * * A court considering a claim of ineffective assistance must apply a strong presumption that counsel's representation was within the wide range of reasonable professional assistance. The challenger's burden is to show that counsel made errors so serious that counsel was not functioning as the "counsel" guaranteed the defendant by the Sixth Amendment.

With respect to prejudice, a challenger must demonstrate a reasonable probability that, but for counsel's unprofessional errors, the result of the proceeding would have been different. A reasonable probability is a probability sufficient to undermine confidence in the outcome. It is not enough to show that the errors had some conceivable effect on the outcome of the proceeding. Counsel's errors must be so serious as to deprive the defendant of a fair trial, a trial whose result is reliable.

* * *

A

With respect to defense counsel's performance, the Court of Appeals held that because Richter's attorney had not consulted forensic blood experts or introduced expert evidence, the California Supreme Court could not reasonably have concluded counsel provided adequate representation. This conclusion was erroneous.

1

The Court of Appeals first held that Richter's attorney rendered constitutionally deficient service because he did not consult blood evidence experts in developing the basic strategy for Richter's defense or offer their testimony as part of the principal case for the defense. *Strickland*, however, permits counsel to make a reasonable decision that makes particular investigations unnecessary. It was at least arguable that a reasonable attorney could decide to forgo inquiry into the blood evidence in the circumstances here.

Criminal cases will arise where the only reasonable and available defense strategy requires consultation with experts or introduction of expert evidence, whether pretrial, at trial, or both. There are, however, countless ways to provide effective assistance in any given case. Even the best criminal defense attorneys would not defend a particular client in the same way. Rare are the situations in which the wide latitude counsel must have in making tactical decisions will be limited to any one technique or approach. It can be assumed that in some cases counsel would be deemed ineffective for failing to consult or rely on experts, but even that formulation is sufficiently general that state courts would have wide latitude in applying it. Here it would be well within the bounds of a reasonable judicial determination for the state court to conclude that de-fense counsel could follow a strategy that did not require the use of experts regarding the pool in the doorway to Johnson's bedroom.

From the perspective of Richter's defense counsel when he was preparing Richter's defense, there were any number of hypothetical experts—specialists in psychiatry, psychology, ballistics, fingerprints, tire treads, physiology, or numerous other disciplines and subdisciplines—whose insight might possibly have been useful. An attorney can avoid activities that appear "distractive from more important duties." Bobby v. Van Hook, 130 S.Ct. 13, 19 (2009) (per curiam). Counsel was entitled to formulate a strategy that was reasonable at the time and to balance limited resources in accord with effective trial tactics and strategies.

In concluding otherwise the Court of Appeals failed to reconstruct the circumstances of counsel's challenged conduct and evaluate the conduct from counsel's perspective at the time. In its view Klein's location was "the single most critical issue in the case" given the differing theories of the prosecution and the defense, and the source of the blood in the doorway was therefore of central concern. But it was far from a necessary conclusion that this was evident at the time of the trial. There were many factual differences between prosecution and defense versions of the events on the night of the shootings. It is only because forensic evidence has emerged concerning the source of the blood pool that the issue could with any plausibility be said to stand apart. Reliance on "the harsh light of hindsight" to cast doubt on a trial that took place now more than 15 years ago is precisely what *Strickland* and AEDPA seek to prevent.

Even if it had been apparent that expert blood testimony could support Richter's defense, it would be reasonable to conclude that a competent attorney might elect not to use it. The Court of Appeals opinion for the en banc majority rests in large part on a hypothesis that reasonably could have been rejected. The hypothesis is that without jeopardizing Richter's defense, an expert could have testified that the blood in Johnson's doorway could not have come from Johnson and could have come from Klein, thus suggesting that Richter's version of the shooting was correct and Johnson's a fabrication. This theory overlooks the fact that concentrating on the blood pool carried its own serious risks. If serological analysis or other forensic evidence demonstrated that the blood came from Johnson alone, Richter's story would be exposed as an invention. An attorney need not pursue an investigation that would be fruitless, much less one that might be harmful to the defense. Here Richter's attorney had reason to question the truth of his client's account, given, for instance, Richter's initial denial of involvement and the subsequent production of Johnson's missing pistol.

It would have been altogether reasonable to conclude that this concern justified the course Richter's counsel pursued. Indeed, the Court of Appeals recognized this risk insofar as it pertained to the suggestion that counsel should have had the blood evidence tested. But the court failed to recognize that making a central issue out of blood evidence would have increased the likelihood of the prosecution's producing its own evidence on the blood pool's origins and composition; and once matters proceeded on this course, there was a serious risk that expert evidence could destroy Richter's case. Even apart from this danger, there was the possibility that expert testimony could shift attention to esoteric matters of forensic science, distract the jury from whether Johnson was telling the truth, or transform the case into a battle of the experts.

True, it appears that defense counsel's opening statement itself inspired the prosecution to introduce expert forensic evidence. But the prosecution's evidence may well have been weakened by the fact that it was assembled late in the process; and in any event the prosecution's response shows merely that the defense strategy did not work out as well as counsel had hoped, not that counsel was incompetent.

To support a defense argument that the prosecution has not proved its case it sometimes is better to try to cast pervasive suspicion of doubt than to strive to prove a certainty that exonerates. All that happened here is that counsel pursued a course that conformed to the first option. If this case presented a de novo review of *Strickland*, the foregoing might well suffice to reject the claim of inadequate counsel, but that is an unnecessary step. The Court of Appeals must be reversed if there was a reasonable justification for the state court's decision. In light of the record here there was no basis to rule that the state court's determination was unreasonable.

The Court of Appeals erred in dismissing strategic considerations like these as an inaccurate account of counsel's actual thinking. Although courts may not indulge post hoc rationalization for counsel's decision-making that contradicts the available evidence of counsel's actions, neither may they insist counsel confirm every aspect of the strategic basis for his or her actions. There is a "strong presumption" that counsel's attention to certain issues to the exclusion of others reflects trial tactics rather than "sheer neglect." Yarborough v. Gentry, 540 U.S. 1, 8 (2003) (per curiam). After an adverse verdict at trial even the most experienced counsel may find it difficult to resist asking whether a different strategy might have been better, and, in the course of that reflection, to magnify their own responsibility for an unfavorable outcome. *Strickland*, however, calls for an inquiry into the objective reasonableness of counsel's performance, not counsel's subjective state of mind.

2

The Court of Appeals also found that Richter's attorney was constitutionally deficient because he had not expected the prosecution to offer expert testimony and therefore was unable to offer expert testimony of his own in response.

The Court of Appeals erred in suggesting counsel had to be prepared for "any contingency." *Strickland* does not guarantee perfect representation, only a reasonably competent attorney. * * * Just as there is no expectation that competent counsel will be a flawless strategist or tactician, an attorney may not be faulted for a reasonable miscalculation or lack of foresight or for failing to prepare for what appear to be remote possibilities.

Here, Richter's attorney was mistaken in thinking the prosecution would not present forensic testimony. But the prosecution itself did not expect to make that presentation and had made no preparations for doing

so on the eve of trial. For this reason alone, it is at least debatable whether counsel's error was so fundamental as to call the fairness of the trial into doubt.

Even if counsel should have foreseen that the prosecution would offer expert evidence, Richter would still need to show it was indisputable that *Strickland* required his attorney to act upon that knowledge. Attempting to establish this, the Court of Appeals held that defense counsel should have offered expert testimony to rebut the evidence from the prosecution. But *Strickland* does not enact Newton's third law for the presentation of evidence, requiring for every prosecution expert an equal and opposite expert from the defense.

In many instances cross-examination will be sufficient to expose defects in an expert's presentation. When defense counsel does not have a solid case, the best strategy can be to say that there is too much doubt about the State's theory for a jury to convict. And while in some instances "even an isolated error" can support an ineffective-assistance claim if it is "sufficiently egregious and prejudicial," Murray v. Carrier, 477 U.S. 478, 496 (1986), it is difficult to establish ineffective assistance when counsel's overall performance indicates active and capable advocacy. Here Richter's attorney represented him with vigor and conducted a skillful cross-examination. As noted, defense counsel elicited concessions from the State's experts and was able to draw attention to weaknesses in their conclusions stemming from the fact that their analyses were conducted long after investigators had left the crime scene. For all of these reasons, it would have been reasonable to find that Richter had not shown his attorney was deficient under *Strickland*.

B

The Court of Appeals further concluded that Richter had established prejudice under *Strickland* given the expert evidence his attorney could have introduced. It held that the California Supreme Court would have been unreasonable in concluding otherwise. This too was error.

In assessing prejudice under *Strickland,* the question is not whether a court can be certain counsel's performance had no effect on the outcome or whether it is possible a reasonable doubt might have been established if counsel acted differently. Instead, *Strickland* asks whether it is "reasonably likely" the result would have been different. * * * The likelihood of a different result must be substantial, not just conceivable.

It would not have been unreasonable for the California Supreme Court to conclude Richter's evidence of prejudice fell short of this standard. His expert serology evidence established nothing more than a theoretical possibility that, in addition to blood of Johnson's type, Klein's blood may also have been present in a blood sample taken near the bedroom doorway pool. At trial, defense counsel extracted a concession along these lines from the prosecution's expert. The pathology expert's claim about the size of the blood pool could be taken to suggest only that the wounded and hysterical Johnson erred in his assessment of time or that he bled more profusely than estimated. And the analysis of the purported blood pattern expert indicated no more than that Johnson was not standing up when the blood pool formed.

It was also reasonable to find Richter had not established prejudice given that he offered no evidence directly challenging other conclusions reached by the prosecution's experts. For example, there was no dispute that the blood sample taken near the doorway pool matched Johnson's blood type. The California Supreme Court reasonably could have concluded that testimony about patterns that form when blood drips to the floor or about the rate at which Johnson was bleeding did not undermine the results of chemical tests indicating blood type. Nor did Richter provide any direct refutation of the State's expert testimony describing how blood spatter near the couch suggested a shooting in the living room and how the blood patterns on Klein's face were inconsistent with Richter's theory that Klein had been killed in the bedroom doorway and moved to the couch.

There was, furthermore, sufficient conventional circumstantial evidence pointing to Richter's guilt. It included the gun safe and ammunition found at his home; his flight from the crime scene; his disposal of the .32–caliber gun and of Johnson's pistol; his shifting story concerning his involvement; the disappearance prior to the arrival of the law enforcement officers of the .22–caliber weapon that killed Klein; the improbability of Branscombe's not being wounded in the shootout that resulted in a combined four bullet wounds to Johnson and Klein; and the difficulties the intoxicated and twice-shot Johnson would have had in carrying the body of a dying man from bedroom doorway to living room couch, not to mention the lack of any obvious reason for him to do so. There was ample basis for the California Supreme Court to think any real possibility of Richter's being acquitted was eclipsed by the remaining evidence pointing to guilt.

The California Supreme Court's decision on the merits of Richter's *Strickland* claim required more deference than it received. Richter was not entitled to the relief ordered by the Court of Appeals. The judgment is reversed, and the case is remanded for further proceedings consistent with this opinion.

Justice KAGAN took no part in the consideration or decision of this case.

JUSTICE GINSBURG, **concurring in the judgment.**

In failing even to consult blood experts in preparation for the murder trial, Richter's counsel, I agree with the Court of Appeals, "was not functioning as the 'counsel' guaranteed the defendant by the Sixth Amendment." Strickland v. Washington, 466 U.S. 668, 687 (1984). The strong force of the prosecution's case, however, was not significantly reduced by the affidavits offered in support of Richter's habeas petition. I would therefore not rank counsel's lapse "so serious as to deprive [Richter] of a fair trial, a trial whose result is reliable." For that reason, I concur in the Court's judgment.

Application of Strickland and AEDPA Review Standards to Counsel's Conduct When a Guilty Plea Is Entered Early in the Proceedings: Premo v. Moore

PREMO v. MOORE

Supreme Court of the United States, 2011
131 S.Ct. 733

JUSTICE KENNEDY **delivered the opinion of the Court.**

This case calls for determinations parallel in some respects to those discussed in today's opinion in Harrington v. Richter, 131 S.Ct. 770. [set forth in this Supplement.] Here, as in *Richter*, the Court reviews a decision of the Court of Appeals for the Ninth Circuit granting federal habeas corpus relief in a challenge to a state criminal conviction. Here, too, the case turns on the proper implementation of one of the stated premises for issuance of federal habeas corpus relief contained in 28 U.S.C. § 2254(d), the instruction that federal habeas corpus relief may not be granted with respect to any claim a state court has adjudicated on the merits unless, among other exceptions, the state court's decision denying relief involves "an unreasonable application" of "clearly established Federal law, as determined by the Supreme Court of the United States." And, as in *Richter*, the relevant clearly established law derives from Strickland v. Washington, 466 U.S. 668, (1984), which provides the standard for inadequate assistance of counsel under the Sixth Amendment. *Richter* involves a California conviction and addresses the adequacy of representation when counsel did not consult or use certain experts in pretrial preparation and at trial. The instant case involves an unrelated Oregon conviction and concerns the adequacy of representation in providing an assessment of a plea bargain without first seeking suppression of a confession assumed to have been improperly obtained.

I

On December 7, 1995, respondent Randy Moore and two confederates attacked Kenneth Rogers at his home and bloodied him before tying him with duct tape and throwing him in the trunk of a car. They drove into the Oregon countryside, where Moore shot Rogers in the temple, killing him.

Afterwards, Moore and one of his accomplices told two people—Moore's brother and the accomplice's girlfriend—about the crimes. According to Moore's brother, Moore and his accomplice admitted:

"[T]o make an example and put some scare into Mr. Rogers ... , they had blind-folded him [and] duct taped him and put him in the trunk of the car and took him out to a place that's a little remote.... [T]heir intent was to leave him there and make him walk home ... [Moore] had taken the revolver from Lonnie and at the time he had taken it, Mr. Rogers had slipped backwards on the mud and the gun discharged."

Moore and his accomplice repeated this account to the police. On the advice of counsel Moore agreed to plead no contest to felony murder in exchange for a sentence of 300 months, the minimum sentence allowed by law for the offense.

Moore later filed for postconviction relief in an Oregon state court, alleging that he had been denied his right to effective assistance of counsel. He complained that his lawyer had not filed a motion to suppress his confession to police in advance of the lawyer's advice that Moore considered before accepting the plea offer. After an evidentiary hearing, the Oregon court concluded a "motion to suppress would have been fruitless" in light of the other admissible confession by Moore, to which two witnesses could testify. As the court

noted, Moore's trial counsel explained why he did not move to exclude Moore's confession to police:

"Mr. Moore and I discussed the possibility of filing a Motion to Suppress and concluded that it would be unavailing, because ... he had previously made a full confession to his brother and to [his accomplice's girlfriend], either one of whom could have been called as a witness at any time to repeat his confession in full detail."

Counsel added that he had made Moore aware of the possibility of being charged with aggravated murder, which carried a potential death sentence, as well as the possibility of a sentence of life imprisonment without parole. The intense and serious abuse to the victim before the shooting might well have led the State to insist on a strong response. In light of these facts the Oregon court concluded Moore had not established ineffective assistance of counsel under *Strickland*.

Moore filed a petition for habeas corpus in the United States District Court for the District of Oregon, renewing his ineffective-assistance claim. The District Court denied the petition, finding sufficient evidence to support the Oregon court's conclusion that suppression would not have made a difference.

A divided panel of the United States Court of Appeals for the Ninth Circuit reversed. In its view the state court's conclusion that counsel's action did not constitute ineffective assistance was an unreasonable application of clearly established law in light of *Strickland* and was contrary to Arizona v. Fulminante, 499 U.S. 279 (1991). Six judges dissented from denial of rehearing en banc.

We granted certiorari.

II

[Justice Kennedy reviews the AEDPA, which allows habeas relief only if the state court determination "(1) resulted in a decision that was contrary to, or involved an unreasonable application of, clearly established Federal law, as determined by the Supreme Court of the United States.; or (2) resulted in a decision that was based on an unreasonable determination of the facts in light of the evidence presented in the State court proceeding."] Relevant here is § 2254(d)(1)'s exception permitting relitigation where the earlier state decision resulted from an unreasonable application of clearly established federal law. The applicable federal law consists of the rules for determining when a criminal defendant has received inadequate representation as defined in *Strickland*.

[Justice Kennedy discusses the *Strickland* requirements—that the petitioner must show both that counsel was ineffectiveness and that the ineffectiveness was prejudicial.]

Surmounting *Strickland's* high bar is never an easy task. An ineffective-assistance claim can function as a way to escape rules of waiver and forfeiture and raise issues not presented at trial or in pretrial proceedings, and so the *Strickland* standard must be applied with scrupulous care, lest intrusive post-trial inquiry threaten the integrity of the very adversary process the right to counsel is meant to serve. Even under de novo review, the standard for judging counsel's representation is a most deferential one. Unlike a later reviewing court, the attorney observed the relevant proceedings, knew of materials outside the record, and interacted with the client, with opposing counsel, and with the judge. It is all too tempting to second-guess counsel's assistance after conviction or adverse sentence. The question is whether an attorney's representation amounted to incompetence under prevailing professional norms, not whether it deviated from best practices or most common custom.

Establishing that a state court's application of *Strickland* was unreasonable under § 2254(d) is all the more difficult. * * * The *Strickland* standard is a general one, so the range of reasonable applications is substantial. Federal habeas courts must guard against the danger of equating unreasonableness under *Strickland* with unreasonableness under § 2254(d). When § 2254(d) applies, the question is not whether counsel's actions were reasonable. The question is whether there is any reasonable argument that counsel satisfied *Strickland's* deferential standard.

III

The question becomes whether Moore's counsel provided ineffective assistance by failing to seek suppression of Moore's confession to police before advising Moore regarding the plea. Finding that any "motion to suppress would have been fruitless," the state postconviction court concluded that Moore had not received ineffective assistance of counsel. The state court did not specify whether this was because there was no deficient performance under *Strickland* or because Moore suffered no *Strickland* prejudice, or both. To overcome the limitation imposed by § 2254(d), the Court of Appeals had to conclude that both findings would have involved an unreasonable application of clearly established federal law. In finding that this standard was met, the Court of Appeals erred, for the state-court decision was not an unreasonable application of either part of the *Strickland* rule.

A

The Court of Appeals was wrong to accord scant deference to counsel's judgment, and doubly wrong to conclude it would have been unreasonable to find that the defense attorney qualified as counsel for Sixth Amendment purposes. Counsel gave this explanation for his decision to discuss the plea bargain without first challenging Moore's confession to the police: that suppression would serve little purpose in light of Moore's other full and admissible confession, to which both his brother and his accomplice's girlfriend could testify. The state court would not have been unreasonable to accept this explanation.

Counsel also justified his decision by asserting that any motion to suppress was likely to fail. Reviewing the reasonableness of that justification is complicated by the possibility that petitioner forfeited one argument that would have supported its position: The Court of Appeals assumed that a motion would have succeeded because the warden did not argue otherwise. Of course that is not the same as a concession that no competent attorney would think a motion to suppress would have failed, which is the relevant question under *Strickland*. It is unnecessary to consider whether counsel's second justification was reasonable, however, since the first and independent explanation—that suppression would have been futile—confirms that his representation was adequate under *Strickland*, or at least that it would have been reasonable for the state court to reach that conclusion.

Acknowledging guilt and accepting responsibility by an early plea respond to certain basic premises in the law and its function. Those principles are eroded if a guilty plea is too easily set aside based on facts and circumstances not apparent to a competent attorney when actions and advice leading to the plea took place. Plea bargains are the result of complex negotiations suffused with uncertainty, and defense attorneys must make careful strategic choices in balancing opportunities and risks. The opportunities, of course, include pleading to a lesser charge and obtaining a lesser sentence, as compared with what might be the outcome not only at trial but also from a later plea offer if the case grows stronger and prosecutors find stiffened resolve. A risk, in addition to the obvious one of losing the chance for a defense verdict, is that an early plea bargain might come before the prosecution finds its case is getting weaker, not stronger. The State's case can begin to fall apart as stories change, witnesses become unavailable, and new suspects are identified.

These considerations make strict adherence to the *Strickland* standard all the more essential when reviewing the choices an attorney made at the plea bargain stage. Failure to respect the latitude Strickland requires can create at least two problems in the plea context. First, the potential for the distortions and imbalance that can inhere in a hindsight perspective may become all too real. The art of negotiation is at least as nuanced as the art of trial advocacy and it presents questions farther removed from immediate judicial supervision. There are, moreover, special difficulties in evaluating the basis for counsel's judgment: An attorney often has insights borne of past dealings with the same prosecutor or court, and the record at the pretrial stage is never as full as it is after a trial. In determining how searching and exacting their review must be, habeas courts must respect their limited role in determining whether there was manifest deficiency in light of information then available to counsel. AEDPA compounds the imperative of judicial caution.

Second, ineffective-assistance claims that lack necessary foundation may bring instability to the very process the inquiry seeks to protect. *Strickland* allows a defendant to escape rules of waiver and forfeiture. Prosecutors must have assurance that a plea will not be undone years later because of infidelity to the requirements of AEDPA and the teachings of *Strickland*. The prospect that a plea deal will afterwards be unraveled when a court second-guesses counsel's decisions while failing to accord the latitude *Strickland* mandates or disregarding the structure dictated by AEDPA could lead prosecutors to forgo plea bargains that would benefit defendants, a result favorable to no one.

Whether before, during, or after trial, when the Sixth Amendment applies, the formulation of the standard is the same: reasonable competence in representing the accused. In applying and defining this standard substantial deference must be accorded to counsel's judgment. But at different stages of the case that deference may be measured in different ways.

In the case of an early plea, neither the prosecution nor the defense may know with much certainty what course the case may take. It follows that each side, of necessity, risks consequences that may arise from contingencies or circumstances yet unperceived. The absence of a developed or an extensive record and the circumstance that neither the prosecution nor the defense case has been well defined create a particular risk that an after-the-fact assessment will run counter to the deference that must be accorded counsel's judgment and perspective when the plea was negotiated, offered, and entered.

Prosecutors in the present case faced the cost of litigation and the risk of trying their case without Moore's confession to the police. Moore's counsel could reasonably believe that a swift plea bargain would allow Moore to take advantage of the State's aversion to these hazards. And whenever cases involve multiple defendants, there is a chance that prosecutors might convince one defendant to testify against another in exchange for a better deal. Moore's plea eliminated that possibility and ended an ongoing investigation. Delaying the plea for further proceedings would have given the State time to uncover additional incriminating evidence that could have formed the basis of a capital prosecution. It must be remembered, after all, that Moore's claim that it was an accident when he shot the victim through the temple might be disbelieved.

It is not clear how the successful exclusion of the confession would have affected counsel's strategic calculus. The prosecution had at its disposal two witnesses able to relate another confession. True, Moore's brother and the girlfriend of his accomplice might have changed their accounts in a manner favorable to Moore. But the record before the state court reveals no reason to believe that either witness would violate the legal obligation to convey the content of Moore's confession. And to the extent that his accomplice's girlfriend had an ongoing interest in the matter, she might have been tempted to put more blame, not less, on Moore. Then, too, the accomplices themselves might have decided to implicate Moore to a greater extent than his own confession did, say by indicating that Moore shot the victim deliberately, not accidentally. All these possibilities are speculative. What counsel knew at the time was that the existence of the two witnesses to an additional confession posed a serious strategic concern.

Moore's prospects at trial were thus anything but certain. Even now, he does not deny any involvement in the kidnaping and killing. In these circumstances, and with a potential capital charge lurking, Moore's counsel made a reasonable choice to opt for a quick plea bargain. At the very least, the state court would not have been unreasonable to so conclude.

The Court of Appeals' contrary holding rests on a case that did not involve ineffective assistance of counsel: Arizona v. Fulminante, 499 U.S. 279 (1991). To reach that result, it transposed that case into a novel context; and novelty alone—at least insofar as it renders the relevant rule less than "clearly established"—provides a reason to reject it under AEDPA. And the transposition is improper even on its own terms. According to the Court of Appeals, "*Fulminante* stands for the proposition that the admission of an additional confession ordinarily reinforces and corroborates the others and is therefore prejudicial." * * * But Fulminante may not be so incorporated into the Strickland performance inquiry.

A state-court adjudication of the performance of counsel under the Sixth Amendment cannot be "contrary to" *Fulminante*, for *Fulminante*—which involved the admission of an involuntary confession in violation of the Fifth Amendment— says nothing about the Strickland standard of effectiveness. The *Fulminante* prejudice inquiry presumes a constitutional violation, whereas *Strickland* seeks to define one. The state court accepted counsel's view that seeking to suppress Moore's second confession would have been "fruitless." It would not have been unreasonable to conclude that counsel could incorporate that view into his assessment of a plea offer, a subject with which *Fulminante* is in no way concerned.

* * *

B

The Court of Appeals further concluded that it would have been unreasonable for the state postconviction court to have found no prejudice in counsel's failure to suppress Moore's confession to police. To prevail on prejudice before the state court Moore had to demonstrate a reasonable probability that, but for counsel's errors, he would not have pleaded guilty and would have insisted on going to trial.

Deference to the state court's prejudice determination is all the more significant in light of the uncertainty inherent in plea negotiations described above: The stakes for defendants are high, and many elect to limit risk by forgoing the right to assert their innocence. A defendant who accepts a plea bargain on counsel's advice does not necessarily suffer prejudice when his counsel fails to seek suppression of evidence, even if it would be reversible error for the court to admit that evidence.

The state court here reasonably could have determined that Moore would have accepted the plea agreement even if his second confession had been ruled inadmissible. By the time the plea agreement cut short investigation of Moore's crimes, the State's case was already formidable and included two witnesses to an admissible confession. Had the prosecution continued to investigate, its case might well have become stronger. At the same time, Moore faced grave punishments. His decision to plead no contest allowed him to avoid a possible sentence of life without parole or death. The bargain counsel struck was thus a favorable one—the statutory minimum for the charged offense—and the decision to forgo a challenge to the confession may have been essential to securing that agreement.

Once again the Court of Appeals reached a contrary conclusion by pointing to *Fulminante* * * * . And again there is no sense in which the state court's finding could be contrary to *Fulminante*, for *Fulminante* says nothing about prejudice for *Strickland* purposes, nor does it contemplate prejudice in the plea bargain context. [See the discussion of *Fulminante* and harmless error at page 1595 of the Casebook.]

The Court of Appeals appears to have treated *Fulminante* as a per se rule of prejudice, or something close to it, in all cases involving suppressible confessions. It is not. In *Fulminante* five Justices made the uncontroversial observation that many confessions are powerful evidence. *Fulminante 's* prejudice analysis arose on direct review following an acknowledged constitutional error at trial. The State therefore had the burden of showing that it was clear beyond a reasonable doubt that a rational jury would have found the defendant guilty absent

the error. That standard cannot apply to determinations of whether inadequate assistance of counsel prejudiced a defendant who entered into a plea agreement. Many defendants reasonably enter plea agreements even though there is a significant probability—much more than a reasonable doubt—that they would be acquitted if they proceeded to trial. Thus, the question in the present case is not whether Moore was sure beyond a reasonable doubt that he would still be convicted if the extra confession were suppressed. It is whether Moore established the reasonable probability that he would not have entered his plea but for his counsel's deficiency, and more to the point, whether a state court's decision to the contrary would be unreasonable.

* * *

The State gave no indication that its felony-murder prosecution depended on the admission of the police confession, and Moore does not now deny that he kidnapped and killed Rogers. Given all this, an unconstitutional admission of Moore's confession to police might well have been found harmless even on direct review if Moore had gone to trial after the denial of a suppression motion.

Other than for its discussion of the basic proposition that a confession is often powerful evidence, *Fulminante* is not relevant to the present case. The state postconviction court reasonably could have concluded that Moore was not prejudiced by counsel's actions. Under AEDPA, that finding ends federal review.

* * *

IV

There are certain differences between inadequate assistance of counsel claims in cases where there was a full trial on the merits and those, like this one, where a plea was entered even before the prosecution decided upon all of the charges. A trial provides the full written record and factual background that serve to limit and clarify some of the choices counsel made. Still, hindsight cannot suffice for relief when counsel's choices were reasonable and legitimate based on predictions of how the trial would proceed.

Hindsight and second guesses are also inappropriate, and often more so, where a plea has been entered without a full trial or, as in this case, even before the prosecution decided on the charges. The added uncertainty that results when there is no extended, formal record and no actual history to show how the charges have played out at trial works against the party alleging inadequate assistance. Counsel, too, faced that uncertainty. There is a most substantial burden on the claimant to show ineffective assistance. The plea process brings to the criminal justice system a stability and a certainty that must not be undermined by the prospect of collateral challenges in cases not only where witnesses and evidence have disappeared, but also in cases where witnesses and evidence were not presented in the first place. The substantial burden to show ineffective assistance of counsel, the burden the claimant must meet to avoid the plea, has not been met in this case.

The state postconviction court's decision involved no unreasonable application of Supreme Court precedent. Because the Court of Appeals erred in finding otherwise, its judgment is reversed, and the case is remanded for further proceedings consistent with this opinion.

Justice KAGAN took no part in the consideration or decision of this case.

JUSTICE GINSBURG, **concurring in the judgment.**

To prevail under the prejudice requirement of *Strickland v. Washington*, a petitioner for federal habeas corpus relief must demonstrate a reasonable probability that, but for counsel's errors, he would not have pleaded guilty and would have insisted on going to trial. As Moore's counsel confirmed at oral argument, Moore never declared that, better informed, he would have resisted the plea bargain and opted for trial. For that reason, I concur in the Court's judgment.

4. Assessing Prejudice

Page 1327. Add the following cases after the section on Lockhart v. Fretwell

Failure to Present Mitigating Evidence of Combat Trauma at the Sentencing Phase of a Capital Trial: Analysis of Ineffectiveness and Prejudice: Porter v. McCollum

PORTER v. McCOLLUM

Supreme Court of the United States 2009
130 S.Ct. 447

Per Curiam

Petitioner George Porter is a veteran who was both wounded and decorated for his active participation in two major engagements during the Korean War; his combat service unfortunately left him a traumatized, changed man. His commanding officer's moving description of those two battles was only a fraction of the mitigating evidence that his counsel failed to discover or present during the penalty phase of his trial in 1988.

In this federal postconviction proceeding, the District Court held that Porter's lawyer's failure to adduce that evidence violated his Sixth Amendment right to counsel and granted his application for a writ of habeas corpus. The Court of Appeals for the Eleventh Circuit reversed, on the ground that the Florida Supreme Court's determination that Porter was not prejudiced by any deficient performance by his counsel was a reasonable application of Strickland v. Washington. Like the District Court, we are persuaded that it was objectively unreasonable to conclude there was no reasonable probability the sentence would have been different if the sentencing judge and jury had heard the significant mitigation evidence that Porter's counsel neither uncovered nor presented. We

therefore * * * reverse the judgment of the Court of Appeals.

I

Porter was convicted of two counts of first-degree murder for the shooting of his former girlfriend, Evelyn Williams, and her boyfriend Walter Burrows. He was sentenced to death on the first count but not the second.

In July 1986, as his relationship with Williams was ending, Porter threatened to kill her and then left town. When he returned to Florida three months later, he attempted to see Williams but her mother told him that Williams did not want to see him. He drove past Williams' house each of the two days prior to the shooting, and the night before the murder he visited Williams, who called the police. Porter then went to two cocktail lounges and spent the night with a friend, who testified Porter was quite drunk by 11 p.m. Early the next morning, Porter shot Williams in her house. Burrows struggled with Porter and forced him outside where Porter shot him.

Porter represented himself, with standby counsel, for most of the pretrial proceedings and during the beginning of his trial. Near the completion of the State's case in chief,

Porter pleaded guilty. He thereafter changed his mind about representing himself, and his standby counsel was appointed as his counsel for the penalty phase. During the penalty phase, the State attempted to prove four aggravating factors: Porter had been "previously convicted" of another violent felony (i.e., in Williams' case, killing Burrows, and in his case, killing Williams); the murder was committed during a burglary; the murder was committed in a cold, calculated, and premeditated manner; and the murder was especially heinous, atrocious, or cruel. The defense put on only one witness, Porter's ex-wife, and read an excerpt from a deposition. The sum total of the mitigating evidence was inconsistent testimony about Porter's behavior when intoxicated and testimony that Porter had a good relationship with his son. Although his lawyer told the jury that Porter "has other handicaps that weren't apparent during the trial" and Porter was not "mentally healthy," he did not put on any evidence related to Porter's mental health.

The jury recommended the death sentence for both murders. The trial court found that the State had proved all four aggravating circumstances for the murder of Williams but that only the first two were established with respect to Burrows' murder. The trial court found no mitigating circumstances and imposed a death sentence for Williams' murder only. On direct appeal, the Florida Supreme Court affirmed the sentence over the dissent of two justices, but struck the heinous, atrocious, or cruel aggravating factor. The court found the State had not carried its burden on that factor because the "record is consistent with the hypothesis that Porter's was a crime of passion, not a crime that was meant to be deliberately and extraordinarily painful." The two dissenting justices would have reversed the penalty because the evidence of drunkenness, "combined with evidence of Porter's emotionally charged, desperate, frustrated desire to meet with his former lover, is sufficient to render the death penalty disproportional punishment in this instance."

In 1995, Porter filed a petition for postconviction relief in state court, claiming his penalty-phase counsel failed to investigate and present mitigating evidence. The court conducted a 2–day evidentiary hearing, during which Porter presented extensive mitigating evidence, all of which was apparently unknown to his penalty-phase counsel. Unlike the evidence presented during Porter's penalty hearing, which left the jury knowing hardly anything about him other than the facts of his crimes, the new evidence described his abusive childhood, his heroic military service and the trauma he suffered because of it, his long-term substance abuse, and his impaired mental health and mental capacity.

The depositions of his brother and sister described the abuse Porter suffered as a child. Porter routinely witnessed his father beat his mother, one time so severely that she had to go to the hospital and lost a child. Porter's father was violent every weekend, and by his siblings' account, Porter was his father's favorite target, particularly when Porter tried to protect his mother. On one occasion, Porter's father shot at him for coming home late, but missed and just beat Porter instead. According to his brother, Porter attended classes for slow learners and left school when he was 12 or 13.

To escape his horrible family life, Porter enlisted in the Army at age 17 and fought in the Korean War. His company commander, Lieutenant Colonel Sherman Pratt, testified at Porter's postconviction hearing. Porter was with the 2d Division, which had advanced above the 38th parallel to Kunu-ri when it was attacked by Chinese forces. Porter suffered a gunshot wound to the leg during the advance but was with the unit for the battle at Kunu-ri. While the Eighth Army was withdrawing, the 2d Division was ordered to hold off the Chinese advance, enabling the bulk of the Eighth Army to live to fight another day. As Colonel Pratt described it, the unit "went into position there in bitter cold night, terribly worn out, terribly weary, almost like zombies because we had been in constant—for five days we had been in constant contact with the enemy fighting our way to the rear, little or no sleep, little or no food, literally as I say zombies." The next morning, the unit engaged in a "fierce hand-to-hand fight with the Chinese" and later that day received permission to withdraw, making Porter's regiment the last unit of the Eighth Army to withdraw.

Less than three months later, Porter fought in a second battle, at Chip'yong-ni. His regiment was cut off from the rest of the Eighth Army and defended itself for two days and two nights under constant fire. After the enemy broke through the perimeter and overtook defensive positions on high ground, Porter's company was charged with retaking those positions. In the charge up the hill, the soldiers "were under direct open fire of the enemy forces on top of the hill. They immediately came under mortar, artillery, machine gun, and every other kind of fire you can imag-

ine and they were just dropping like flies as they went along." Porter's company lost all three of its platoon sergeants, and almost all of the officers were wounded. Porter was again wounded and his company sustained the heaviest losses of any troops in the battle, with more than 50% casualties. Colonel Pratt testified that these battles were "very trying, horrifying experiences," particularly for Porter's company at Chip'yong-ni. Porter's unit was awarded the Presidential Unit Citation for the engagement at Chip'yong-ni, and Porter individually received two Purple Hearts and the Combat Infantryman Badge, along with other decorations.

Colonel Pratt testified that Porter went absent without leave (AWOL) for two periods while in Korea. He explained that this was not uncommon, as soldiers sometimes became disoriented and separated from the unit, and that the commander had decided not to impose any punishment for the absences. In Colonel Pratt's experience, an "awful lot of [veterans] come back nervous wrecks. Our [veterans'] hospitals today are filled with people mentally trying to survive the perils and hardships [of] . . . the Korean War," particularly those who fought in the battles he described.

When Porter returned to the United States, he went AWOL for an extended period of time. He was sentenced to six months' imprisonment for that infraction, but he received an honorable discharge. After his discharge, he suffered dreadful nightmares and would attempt to climb his bedroom walls with knives at night. Porter's family eventually removed all of the knives from the house. According to Porter's brother, Porter developed a serious drinking problem and began drinking so heavily that he would get into fights and not remember them at all.

In addition to this testimony regarding his life history, Porter presented an expert in neuropsychology, Dr. Dee, who had examined Porter and administered a number of psychological assessments. Dr. Dee concluded that Porter suffered from brain damage that could manifest in impulsive, violent behavior. At the time of the crime, Dr. Dee testified, Porter was substantially impaired in his ability to conform his conduct to the law and suffered from an extreme mental or emotional disturbance, two statutory mitigating circumstances. Dr. Dee also testified that Porter had substantial difficulties with reading, writing, and memory, and that these cognitive defects were present when he was evaluated for competency to stand trial. Although the State's experts reached different conclusions regarding the statutory mitigators, each expert testified that he could not diagnose Porter or rule out a brain abnormality.

The trial judge who conducted the state postconviction hearing, without determining counsel's deficiency, held that Porter had not been prejudiced by the failure to introduce any of that evidence. He found that Porter had failed to establish any statutory mitigating circumstances, and that the nonstatutory mitigating evidence would not have made a difference in the outcome of the case. He discounted the evidence of Porter's alcohol abuse because it was inconsistent and discounted the evidence of Porter's abusive childhood because he was 54 years old at the time of the trial. He also concluded that Porter's periods of being AWOL would have reduced the impact of Porter's military service to "inconsequential proportions." Finally, he held that even

considering all three categories of evidence together, the "trial judge and jury still would have imposed death."

The Florida Supreme Court affirmed. * * *

Porter thereafter filed his federal habeas petition. The District Court * * * first determined that counsel's performance had been deficient because "penalty-phase counsel did little, if any investigation . . . and failed to effectively advocate on behalf of his client before the jury." It then determined that counsel's deficient performance was prejudicial, finding that the state court's decision was contrary to clearly established law in part because the state court failed to consider the entirety of the evidence when reweighing the evidence in mitigation, including the trial evidence suggesting that "this was a crime of passion, that [Porter] was drinking heavily just hours before the murders, or that [Porter] had a good relationship with his son."

The Eleventh Circuit reversed. It held the District Court had failed to appropriately defer to the state court's factual findings with respect to Porter's alcohol abuse and his mental health. The Court of Appeals then separately considered each category of mitigating evidence and held it was not unreasonable for the state court to discount each category as it did. Porter petitioned for a writ of certiorari. We grant the petition and reverse with respect to the Court of Appeals' disposition of Porter's ineffective-assistance claim.

II

* * * Porter is entitled to relief only if the state court's rejection of his claim of ineffective assistance of counsel was "contrary to, or involved an unreasonable application of"

Strickland, or it rested "on an unreasonable determination of the facts in light of the evidence presented in the State court proceeding." 28 U.S.C. § 2254(d).

Because the state court did not decide whether Porter's counsel was deficient, we review this element of Porter's *Strickland* claim de novo. It is unquestioned that under the prevailing professional norms at the time of Porter's trial, counsel had an obligation to conduct a thorough investigation of the defendant's background. The investigation conducted by Porter's counsel clearly did not satisfy those norms.

Although Porter had initially elected to represent himself, his standby counsel became his counsel for the penalty phase a little over a month prior to the sentencing proceeding before the jury. It was the first time this lawyer had represented a defendant during a penalty-phase proceeding. At the postconviction hearing, he testified that he had only one short meeting with Porter regarding the penalty phase. He did not obtain any of Porter's school, medical, or military service records or interview any members of Porter's family. In Wiggins v. Smith, 539 U.S. 510 (2003), we held counsel "fell short of . . . professional standards" for not expanding their investigation beyond the presentence investigation report and one set of records they obtained, particularly "in light of what counsel actually discovered" in the records. Here, counsel did not even take the first step of interviewing witnesses or requesting records. Beyond that, like the counsel in *Wiggins*, he ignored pertinent avenues for investigation of which he should have been aware. The court-ordered competency evaluations, for example, collectively reported Porter's very few years of reg-

ular school, his military service and wounds sustained in combat, and his father's "over-disciplin[e]." As an explanation, counsel described Porter as fatalistic and uncooperative. But he acknowledged that although Porter instructed him not to speak with Porter's ex-wife or son, Porter did not give him any other instructions limiting the witnesses he could interview.

Counsel thus failed to uncover and present any evidence of Porter's mental health or mental impairment, his family background, or his military service. The decision not to investigate did not reflect reasonable professional judgment. Porter may have been fatalistic or uncooperative, but that does not obviate the need for defense counsel to conduct some sort of mitigation investigation.

III

Because we find Porter's counsel deficient, we must determine whether the Florida Supreme Court unreasonably applied *Strickland* in holding Porter was not prejudiced by that deficiency. Under *Strickland*, a defendant is prejudiced by his counsel's deficient performance if "there is a reasonable probability that, but for counsel's unprofessional errors, the result of the proceeding would have been different." * * *

This is not a case in which the new evidence "would barely have altered the sentencing profile presented to the sentencing judge." *Strickland.* The judge and jury at Porter's original sentencing heard almost nothing that would humanize Porter or allow them to accurately gauge his moral culpability. They learned about Porter's turbulent relationship with Williams, his crimes, and almost nothing else. Had Porter's counsel been effective, the judge and jury would have learned of the "kind of troubled history we have declared relevant to assessing a defendant's moral culpability." *Wiggins*. They would have heard about (1) Porter's heroic military service in two of the most critical-and horrific-battles of the Korean War, (2) his struggles to regain normality upon his return from war, (3) his childhood history of physical abuse, and (4) his brain abnormality, difficulty reading and writing, and limited schooling. See Penry v. Lynaugh, 492 U.S. 302, 319 (1989) (" '[E]vidence about the defendant's background and character is relevant because of the belief, long held by this society, that defendants who commit criminal acts that are attributable to a disadvantaged background . . . may be less culpable' "). Instead, they heard absolutely none of that evidence, evidence which might well have influenced the jury's appraisal of Porter's moral culpability.

* * *

The Florida Supreme Court's decision that Porter was not prejudiced by his counsel's failure to conduct a thorough—or even cursory—investigation is unreasonable. The Florida Supreme Court either did not consider or unreasonably discounted the mitigation evidence adduced in the postconviction hearing. Under Florida law, mental health evidence that does not rise to the level of establishing a statutory mitigating circumstance may nonetheless be considered by the sentencing judge and jury as mitigating. * * * . Yet neither the postconviction trial court nor the Florida Supreme Court gave any consideration for the purpose of nonstatutory mitigation to Dr. Dee's testimony regarding the existence of a brain abnormality and cognitive defects. While the State's experts identified

perceived problems with the tests that Dr. Dee used and the conclusions that he drew from them, it was not reasonable to discount entirely the effect that his testimony might have had on the jury or the sentencing judge.

Furthermore, the Florida Supreme Court, following the state postconviction court, unreasonably discounted the evidence of Porter's childhood abuse and military service. It is unreasonable to discount to irrelevance the evidence of Porter's abusive childhood, especially when that kind of history may have particular salience for a jury evaluating Porter's behavior in his relationship with Williams. It is also unreasonable to conclude that Porter's military service would be reduced to "inconsequential proportions," simply because the jury would also have learned that Porter went AWOL on more than one occasion. Our Nation has a long tradition of according leniency to veterans in recognition of their service, especially for those who fought on the front lines as Porter did. Moreover, the relevance of Porter's extensive combat experience is not only that he served honorably under extreme hardship and gruesome conditions, but also that the jury might find mitigating the intense stress and mental and emotional toll that combat took on Porter. The evidence that he was AWOL is consistent with this theory of mitigation and does not impeach or diminish the evidence of his service. To conclude otherwise reflects a failure to engage with what Porter actually went through in Korea.

* * * Although the burden is on petitioner to show he was prejudiced by his counsel's deficiency, the Florida Supreme Court's conclusion that

Porter failed to meet this burden was an unreasonable application of our clearly established law. We do not require a defendant to show "that counsel's deficient conduct more likely than not altered the outcome" of his penalty proceeding, but rather that he establish "a probability suffi-cient to undermine confidence in [that] outcome." *Strickland*. This Porter has done.

* * * The judgment of the Court of Appeals is reversed, and the case is remanded for further proceedings consistent with this opinion.

Prejudice Must Be Assessed By What Evidence—Including Damaging Evidence—Would Have Been Admitted Had Defense Counsel Acted Effectively: Wong v. Belmontes

WONG v. BELMONTES

Supreme Court of the United States, 2009
130 S.Ct. 383

Per Curiam.

In 1981, in the course of a burgla-ry, Fernando Belmontes bludgeoned Steacy McConnell to death, striking her in the head 15 to 20 times with a steel dumbbell bar. After the murder, Belmontes and his accomplices stole McConnell's stereo, sold it for $100, and used the money to buy beer and drugs for the night.

Belmontes was convicted of mur-der and sentenced to death in state court. Unsuccessful on direct appeal and state collateral review, Bel-montes sought federal habeas relief, which the District Court denied. The Court of Appeals [found] that Bel-montes suffered ineffective assistance of counsel during the sentencing phase of his trial. The District Court had previously denied relief on that ground, finding that counsel for Bel-montes had performed deficiently under Ninth Circuit precedent, but that Belmontes could not establish prejudice under Strickland v. Wash-ington. The Court of Appeals agreed that counsel's performance was defi-cient, but disagreed with the District Court with respect to prejudice, de-termining that counsel's errors un-dermined confidence in the penalty phase verdict. We disagree with the Court of Appeals as to prejudice, grant the State's petition for certiora-ri, and reverse.

I

* * *

The challenge confronting Bel-montes' lawyer, John Schick, was very specific. Substantial evidence in-dicated that Belmontes had commit-ted a prior murder, and the prose-cution was eager to introduce that evidence during the penalty phase of the McConnell trial. The evidence of the prior murder was extensive, including eyewitness testimony, Bel-montes' own admissions, and Bel-montes' possession of the murder weapon and the same type of am-munition used to kill the victim.

The evidence, furthermore, was potentially devastating. It would have shown that two years before Steacy McConnell's death, police found Jer-ry Howard's body in a secluded area. Howard had been killed execution style, with a bullet to the back of the head. The authorities suspected Bel-montes, but on the eve of trial the State's witnesses refused to cooper-ate (Belmontes' mother had begged one not to testify). The prosecution therefore believed it could not prove Belmontes guilty of murder beyond a reasonable doubt. What the prosecution could prove, even without the recalcitrant witnesses, was that Belmontes possessed the gun used to murder Howard. So the State offered, and Belmontes accepted, a no-contest plea to accessory after the fact to voluntary manslaughter.

But Belmontes had not been shy about discussing the murder, boasting to several people that he had killed Howard. * * *

Schick understood the gravity of this aggravating evidence, and he built his mitigation strategy around the overriding need to exclude it. California evidentiary rules, Schick knew, offered him an argument to exclude the evidence, but those same rules made clear that the evidence would come in for rebuttal if Schick opened the door. Schick thus had "grave concerns" that, even if he succeeded initially in excluding the prior murder evidence, it would still be admitted if his mitigation case swept too broadly. Accordingly, Schick decided to proceed cautiously, structuring his mitigation arguments and witnesses to limit that possibility.

As Schick expected, the prosecution was ready to admit this evidence during the *386 sentencing phase. Schick moved to exclude the evidence, arguing that the State should be allowed to tell the jury only that Belmontes had been convicted of being an accessory after the fact to voluntary manslaughter-nothing more. Schick succeeded in keeping the prosecution from presenting the damaging evidence in its sentencing case in chief, but his client remained at risk: The trial court indicated the evidence would come in for rebuttal

or impeachment if Schick opened the door.

* * *

II

* * *

The Ninth Circuit determined that a reasonably competent lawyer would have introduced more mitigation evidence, on top of what Schick had already presented. For purposes of our prejudice analysis, we accept that conclusion and proceed to consider whether there is a reasonable probability that a jury presented with this additional mitigation evidence would have returned a different verdict.

In evaluating that question, it is necessary to consider all the relevant evidence that the jury would have had before it if Schick had pursued the different path—not just the mitigation evidence Schick could have presented, but also the Howard murder evidence that almost certainly would have come in with it. Thus, to establish prejudice, Belmontes must show a reasonable probability that the jury would have rejected a capital sentence after it weighed the entire body of mitigating evidence (including the additional testimony Schick could have presented) against the entire body of aggravating evidence (including the Howard murder evidence). Belmontes cannot meet this burden.

We begin with the mitigating evidence Schick did present during the sentencing phase. That evidence was substantial.* * *

All told, Schick put nine witnesses on the stand over a span of two days, and elicited a range of testimony on Belmontes' behalf. A number of those witnesses highlighted Belmontes' "terrible" childhood. They testified that his father was an alcoholic and extremely abusive. Belmontes' grandfather described the one-bedroom house where Belmontes spent much of his childhood as a "chicken coop." Belmontes did not do well in school; he dropped out in the ninth grade. His younger sister died when she was only 10 months old. And his grandmother died tragically when she drowned in her swimming pool.

Family members also testified that, despite these difficulties, Belmontes maintained strong relationships with his grandfather, grandmother, mother, and sister. And Belmontes' best friend offered the insights of a close friend and confidant.

Schick also called witnesses who detailed Belmontes' religious conversion while in state custody on the accessory charge. These witnesses told stories about Belmontes' efforts advising other inmates in his detention center's religious program, to illustrate that he could live a productive and meaningful life in prison. They described his success working as part of a firefighting crew, detailing his rise from lowest man on the team to second in command. Belmontes' assistant chaplain even said that he would use Belmontes as a regular part of his prison counseling program if the jury handed down a life sentence.

Belmontes himself bolstered these accounts by testifying about his childhood and religious conversion, both at sentencing and during allocution. Belmontes described his childhood as "pretty hard," but took responsibility for his actions, telling the jury that he did not want to use his background "as a crutch[,] to say I am in a situation now ... because of that." .

* * * More evidence, the Court of Appeals * * * concluded, would have made a difference; in particular, more evidence to "humanize" Belmontes, as that court put it no fewer than 11 times in its opinion. The Court determined that the failure to put on this evidence prejudiced Belmontes.

There are two problems with this conclusion: Some of the evidence was merely cumulative of the humanizing evidence Schick actually presented; adding it to what was already there would have made little difference. Other evidence proposed by the Ninth Circuit would have put into play aspects of Belmontes' character that would have triggered admission of the powerful Howard evidence in rebuttal. This evidence would have made a difference, but in the wrong direction for Belmontes. In either event, Belmontes cannot establish Strickland prejudice.

First, the cumulative evidence. In the Court of Appeals' view, Belmontes should have presented more humanizing evidence about Belmontes' "difficult childhood" and highlighted his "positive attributes." As for his difficult childhood, Schick should have called witnesses to testify that "when Belmontes was five years old, his 10–month-old sister died of a brain tumor," that he "exhibited symptoms of depression" after her death, that his grandmother suffered from "alcoholism and prescription drug addiction," and that both his immediate and extended family lived in a state of "constant strife." As for his positive attributes, Schick should have produced testimony about Belmontes' "strong character as a child in the face of adversity." Ibid. Schick should have illustrated that Belmontes was "kind, responsible, and likeable"; that he "got along well with his siblings" and was "respectful towards his grandparents despite their disapproval of his mixed racial background"; and that he "participated in community activities, kept up in school and got along with his teachers before [an] illness, and made friends easily."

But as recounted above * * * Schick did put on substantial mitigation evidence, much of it targeting the same "humanizing" theme the Ninth Circuit highlighted. The sentencing jury was thus well acquainted with Belmontes' background and potential humanizing features. Additional evidence on these points would have offered an insignificant benefit, if any at all.

The Ninth Circuit also determined that both the evidence Schick presented and the additional evidence it proposed would have carried greater weight if Schick had submitted expert testimony. Such testimony could "make connections between the various themes in the mitigation case and explain to the jury how they could have contributed to Belmontes's involvement in criminal activity." But the body of mitigating evidence the Ninth Circuit would have required Schick to present was neither complex nor technical. It required only that the jury make logical connections of the kind a layperson is well equipped to make. The jury simply did not need expert testimony to understand the "humanizing" evidence; it could use its common sense or own sense of mercy.

What is more, expert testimony discussing Belmontes' mental state, seeking to explain his behavior, or putting it in some favorable context would have exposed Belmontes to the Howard evidence. * * *

If, for example, an expert had testified that Belmontes had a " 'high likelihood of a . . . nonviolent adjustment to a prison setting,' " as Belmontes suggested an expert might, the question would have immediately arisen: "What was his propensity toward violence to begin with? Does evidence of another murder alter your view?" Expert testimony explaining why the jury should feel sympathy, as opposed simply to facts that might elicit that response, would have led to a similar rejoinder: "Is such sympathy equally appropriate for someone who committed a second murder?" Any of this testimony from an expert's perspective would have made the Howard evidence fair game.

Many of Belmontes' other arguments fail for the same reason. He argues that the jury should have been told that he suffered an "extended bout with rheumatic fever," which led to "emotional instability, impulsivity, and impairment of the neurophysiological mechanisms for planning and reasoning." But the cold, calculated nature of the Howard murder and Belmontes' subsequent bragging about it would have served as a powerful counterpoint.

The type of "more-evidence-is-better" approach advocated by Belmontes and the Court of Appeals might seem appealing-after all, what is there to lose? But here there was a lot to lose. A heavyhanded case to portray Belmontes in a positive light, with or without experts, would have invited the strongest possible evidence in rebuttal—the evidence that Belmontes was responsible for not one but two murders.

Belmontes counters that some of the potential mitigating evidence might not have opened the door to the prior murder evidence. The Court of Appeals went so far as to state, without citation, that "[t]here would be no basis for suggesting that [expert testimony] would be any different if the expert were informed that Belmontes committed two murders rather than one." But it is surely pertinent in assessing expert testimony "explain[ing] . . . involvement in criminal activity," to know what criminal activity was at issue. And even if the number of murders were as irrelevant as the Ninth Circuit asserted, the fact that these two murders were so different in character made each of them highly pertinent in evaluating expert testimony of the sort envisioned by the Court of Appeals.

* * *

In balancing the mitigating factors against the aggravators, the Court of Appeals repeatedly referred to the aggravating evidence the State presented as "scant." That characterization misses *Strickland's* point that the reviewing court must consider all the evidence—the good and the bad—when evaluating prejudice. Here, the worst kind of bad evidence would have come in with the good. The only reason it did not was because Schick was careful in his mitigation case. The State's aggravation evidence could only be characterized as "scant" if one ignores the "elephant in the courtroom"—Belmontes' role in the Howard murder—that would have been presented had Schick submitted the additional mitigation evidence.

Even on the record before it—which did not include the Howard murder—the state court determined that Belmontes "was convicted on extremely strong evidence that he committed an intentional murder of extraordinary brutality." * * * The Ninth Circuit saw the murder differ-

ently. It viewed the circumstances of the crime as only "conceivably significant" as an aggravating factor. In particular, the Court of Appeals concluded that "[t]he crime here did not involve . . . needless suffering on the part of the victim."

We agree with the state court's characterization of the murder, and simply cannot comprehend the assertion by the Court of Appeals that this case did not involve "needless suffering." The jury saw autopsy photographs showing Steacy McConnell's mangled head, her skull crushed by 15 to 20 blows from a steel dumbbell bar the jury found to have been wielded by Belmontes. McConnell's corpse showed numerous "defensive bruises and contusions on [her] hands, arms, and feet," which "plainly evidenced a desperate struggle for life at [Belmontes'] hands." Belmontes left McConnell to die, but officers found her still fighting for her life before ultimately succumbing to the injuries caused by the blows from Belmontes. The jury also heard that this savage murder was committed solely to prevent interference with a burglary that netted Belmontes $100 he used to buy beer and drugs for the night. McConnell suffered, and it was clearly needless.

Some of the error below may be traced to confusion about the appropriate standard and burden of proof. * * * In explaining its prejudice determination, the Ninth Circuit concluded that "[t]he aggravating evidence, even with the addition of evidence that Belmontes murdered Howard, is not strong enough, in light of the mitigating evidence that could have been adduced, to rule out a sentence of life in prison." But

Strickland does not require the State to "rule out" a sentence of life in prison to prevail. Rather, *Strickland* places the burden on the defendant, not the State, to show a "reasonable probability" that the result would have been different. Under a proper application of the *Strickland* standard,

Belmontes cannot carry this burden.

* * *

The judgment of the Court of Appeals for the Ninth Circuit is reversed, and the case is remanded for further proceedings consistent with this opinion.

[The concurring opinion of JUSTICE STEVENS is omitted.]

Defense Counsel's Argument at the Penalty Phase of a Capital Trial, Stressing the Severity of the Crimes, Was Not Prejudicial: Smith v. Spisak

SMITH v. SPISAK

Supreme Court of the United States, 2010
130 S.Ct. 676

JUSTICE BREYER **delivered the opinion of the Court**.

Frank G. Spisak, Jr., the respondent, was convicted in an Ohio trial court of three murders and two attempted murders. He was sentenced to death. He filed a habeas corpus petition in federal court, claiming that constitutional errors occurred at his trial. * * * Spisak claimed that he suffered significant harm as a result of his counsel's inadequate closing argument at the penalty phase of the proceeding. See Strickland v. Washington. The Federal Court of Appeals accepted these arguments and ordered habeas relief. We now reverse the Court of Appeals.

I

In 1983, an Ohio jury convicted Spisak of three murders and two attempted murders at Cleveland State University in 1982. The jury recommended, and the judge imposed, a death sentence. * * *

II

[The Court found that habeas relief was improperly granted on Spisak's

challenge to the jury instruction at the penalty phase.]

III

Spisak's second claim is that his counsel's closing argument at the sentencing phase of his trial was so inadequate as to violate the Sixth Amendment. To prevail, Spisak must show both that "counsel's representation fell below an objective standard of reasonableness," *Strickland,* and that there is a "reasonable probability that, but for counsel's unprofessional errors, the result of the proceeding would have been different," id.

* * *

In his closing argument at the penalty phase, Spisak's counsel described Spisak's killings in some detail. He acknowledged that Spisak's admiration for Hitler inspired his crimes. He portrayed Spisak as "sick," "twisted," and "demented." And he said that Spisak was "never going to be any different." He then pointed out that all the experts had testified that Spisak suffered from some degree of mental illness. And, after a fairly lengthy and rambling disquisition about his own decisions about calling expert witnesses and preparing them, counsel argued that, even if Spisak was not legally insane so as to warrant a verdict of not guilty by reason of insanity, he nonetheless was sufficiently mentally ill to lessen his culpability to the point where he should not be executed. Counsel also told the jury that, when weighing Spisak's mental illness against the "substantial" aggravating factors present in the case, the jurors should draw on their own sense of "pride" for living in "a humane society" made up of "a humane people." That humanity, he said, required the jury to weigh the evidence "fairly" and to be "loyal to that oath" the jurors had taken to uphold the law.

Spisak and his supporting amici say that this argument was constitutionally inadequate because: (1) It overly emphasized the gruesome nature of the killings; (2) it overly emphasized Spisak's threats to continue his crimes; (3) it understated the facts upon which the experts based their mental illness conclusions; (4) it said little or nothing about any other possible mitigating circumstance; and (5) it made no explicit request that the jury return a verdict against death.

We assume for present purposes that Spisak is correct that the closing argument was inadequate. We nevertheless find no "reasonable probability" that a better closing argument without these defects would have made a significant difference.

Any different, more adequate closing argument would have taken place in the following context: Spisak admitted that he had committed three murders and two other shootings. Spisak's defense at the guilt phase of the trial consisted of an effort by counsel to show that Spisak was not guilty by reason of insanity. And counsel, apparently hoping to demonstrate Spisak's mentally defective condition, called him to the stand.

Spisak testified that he had shot and killed Horace Rickerson, Timothy Sheehan, and Brian Warford. He also admitted that he had shot and tried to kill John Hardaway, and shot at Coletta Dartt. He committed these crimes, he said, because he was a follower of Adolf Hitler, who was Spisak's "spiritual leader" in a "war" for "survival" of "the Aryan people." He said that he had purchased guns and stockpiled ammunition to further this war. And he had hoped to "create terror" at Cleveland State University, because it was "one of the prime targets" where the "Jews and the system . . . are brainwashing the youth."

Spisak then said that in February 1982 he had shot Rickerson, who was black, because Rickerson had made a sexual advance on Spisak in a university bathroom. He expressed satisfaction at having "eliminated that particular threat . . . to me and to the white race." In June he saw a stranger, John Hardaway, on a train platform and shot him seven times because he had been looking for a black person to kill as "blood atonement" for a recent crime against two white women. He added that he felt "good" after shooting Hardaway because he had "accomplished something," but later felt "[k]ind of bad" when he learned that Hardaway had survived. In August 1982, Spisak shot at Coletta Dartt because, he said, he heard her "making some derisive remarks about us," meaning the Nazi Party. Later that August, he shot and killed Timothy Sheehan because he "thought he was one of those Jewish professors ... that liked to hang around in the men's room and seduce and pervert and subvert the young people that go there." Spisak added that he was "sorry about that" murder because he later learned Sheehan "wasn't Jewish like I thought he was." And three days later, while on a "search and destroy mission," he shot and killed Brian Warford, a young black man who "looked like he was almost asleep" in a bus shelter, to fulfill his "duty" to "inflict the maximum amount of casualties on the enemies."

Spisak also testified that he would continue to commit similar crimes if he had the chance. He said about Warford's murder that he "didn't want to get caught that time because I wanted to be able to do it again and again and again and again." In a letter written to a friend, he called the murders of Rickerson and Warford "the finest thing I ever did in my whole life" and expressed a wish that he "had a human submachine gun right now so I could exterminate" black men "and watch them scream and twitch in agony." And he testified that, if he still had his guns, he would escape from jail, "go out and continue the war I started," and "continue to inflict the maximum amount of damage on the enemies as I am able to do."

The State replied by attempting to show that Spisak was lying in his testimony about the Nazi-related motives for these crimes. The State contended instead that the shootings were motivated by less unusual purposes, such as robbery.

The defense effort to show that Spisak was not guilty by reason of insanity foundered when the trial judge refused to instruct the jury to consider that question and excluded expert testimony regarding Spisak's mental state. The defense's expert witness, Dr. Oscar Markey, had written a report diagnosing Spisak as suffering from a "schizotypal personality disorder" and an "atypical psychotic disorder," and as, at times, "unable to control his impulses to assault." His testimony was somewhat more ambiguous during a voir dire, however. On cross-examination, he conceded that he could not say Spisak failed Ohio's sanity standard at the time of the murders. After Markey made the same concession before the jury, the court granted the prosecution's renewed motion to exclude Markey's testimony and instructed the jury to disregard the testimony that it heard. And the court excluded the defense's proffered reports from other psychologists and psychiatrists who examined Spisak, because none of the reports said that Spisak met the Ohio insanity standard at the time of the crimes.

During the sentencing phase of the proceedings, defense counsel called three expert witnesses, all of whom testified that Spisak suffered from some degree of mental illness. * * *

In light of this background and for the following reasons, we do not find that the assumed deficiencies in defense counsel's closing argument raise "a reasonable probability that," but for the deficient closing, "the result of the proceeding would have been different." *Strickland*. We therefore cannot find the Ohio Supreme Court's decision rejecting Spisak's ineffective-assistance-of-counsel claim to be an "unreasonable application" of the law "clearly established" in *Strickland*. § 2254(d)(1).

First, since the sentencing phase took place immediately following the conclusion of the guilt phase, the jurors had fresh in their minds the government's evidence regarding the killings—which included photographs of the dead bodies, images that formed the basis of defense counsel's vivid descriptions of the crimes—as well as Spisak's boastful and unrepentant confessions and his threats to commit further acts of violence. We therefore do not see how a less descriptive closing argument with fewer disparaging comments about Spisak could have made a significant difference.

Similarly fresh in the jurors' minds was the three defense experts' testimony that Spisak suffered from mental illness. The jury had heard the experts explain the specific facts upon which they had based their conclusions, as well as what they had learned of his family background and his struggles with gender identity. And the jury had heard the experts draw connections between his mental illness and the crimes. We do not see how it could have made a significant difference had counsel gone beyond his actual argument—which emphasized mental illness as a mitigating factor and referred the jury to the experts' testimony—by repeating the facts or connections that the experts had just described.

Nor does Spisak tell us what other mitigating factors counsel might have mentioned. All those he proposes essentially consist of aspects of the "mental defect" factor that the defense experts described.

Finally, in light of counsel's several appeals to the jurors' sense of humanity—he used the words "humane people" and "humane society" 10 times at various points in the argument—we cannot find that a more explicit or more elaborate appeal for mercy could have changed the result, either alone or together with the other circumstances just discussed.
* * *

For these reasons, the judgment of the Court of Appeals for the Sixth Circuit is reversed.

JUSTICE STEVENS, **concurring in part and concurring in the judgment.**

* * *

Petitioner defends Spisak's counsel's closing argument as a reasonable strategic decision "to draw the sting out of the prosecution's argument and gain credibility with the jury by conceding the weaknesses of his own case." I agree that such a strategy is generally a reasonable one and, indeed, was a reasonable strategy under the difficult circumstances of this case. Even Spisak concedes that his counsel "faced an admittedly difficult case in closing argument in the penalty phase." But, surely, a strategy can be executed so poorly as to render even the most reasonable of trial tactics constitutionally deficient under Strickland v. Washington. And this is such a case.

It is difficult to convey how thoroughly egregious counsel's closing argument was without reproducing it in its entirety. The Court's assessment of the closing as "lengthy and rambling" and its brief description of its content does not accurately capture the catastrophe of counsel's failed strategy. Suffice it to say that the argument shares far more in common with a prosecutor's closing than with a criminal defense attorney's. Indeed, the argument was so outrageous that it would have rightly subjected a prosecutor to charges of misconduct. A few examples are in order.

Presumably to take the "sting" out of the prosecution's case, counsel described his client's acts in vivid detail to the jury:

"[Y]ou can smell almost the blood. You can smell, if you will, the urine. You are in a bathroom, and it is death, and you can smell the death . . . and you can feel, the loneliness of that railroad platform . . . and we can all know the terror that [the victim] felt when he turned and looked into those thick glasses and looked into the muzzle of a gun that kept spitting out bullets . . . And we can see a relatively young man cut down with so many years to live, and we could remember his widow, and we certainly can remember looking at his children . . . There are too many family albums. There are too many family portraits dated 1982 that have too many empty spaces. And there is too much terror left in the hearts of those that we call lucky."

Presumably to "gain credibility" with the jury, counsel argued that his client deserved no sympathy for his actions:

"Sympathy, of course, is not part of your consideration. And even if it was, certainly, don't look to him for sympathy, because he demands none. And, ladies and gentlemen, when you turn and look at Frank Spisak, don't look for good deeds, because he has done none. Don't look for good thoughts, because he has none. He is sick, he is twisted. He is demented, and he is never going to be any different."

And then the strategy really broke down: At no point did counsel endeavor to direct his negative statements about his client toward an express appeal for leniency. On the contrary, counsel concluded by telling the jury that "whatever you do, we are going to be proud of you," which I take to mean that, in counsel's view, "either outcome, death or life, would be a valid conclusion."

Spisak's crimes, and the seemingly unmitigated hatred motivating their commission, were truly awful. But that does not excuse a lawyer's duty to represent his client within the bounds of prevailing professional norms. The mere fact that counsel, laudably, may have had a "strategy" to build rapport with the jury and lessen the impact of the prosecution's case, does not excuse counsel's utter failure to achieve either of these objectives through his closing argument. In short, counsel's argument grossly transgressed the bounds of what constitutionally competent counsel would have done in a similar situation.

III

* * * As JUSTICE BREYER'S discussion in Part III makes vividly clear, Spisak's own conduct alienated and ostracized the jury, and his crimes were monstrous. In my judgment even the most skillful of closing arguments— even one befitting Clarence Darrow—would not have created a reasonable probability of a different outcome in this case. * * *

CHAPTER ELEVEN

SENTENCING

■ ■ ■

I. INTRODUCTION

D. CONSTITUTIONAL LIMITATIONS ON PUNISHMENT

2. Eighth Amendment Limitations on Sentencing

Page 1422. Add after the section on the death penalty

Categorical Constitutional Limitation on Sentencing in a Non–Capital Case: Graham v. Florida

In the following case, the majority combines its proportionality analysis for non-capital sentences with its categorical rules barring capital sentences for certain offenses or offenders.

GRAHAM v. FLORIDA
Supreme Court of the United States, 2010
130 S.Ct. 2011

JUSTICE KENNEDY **delivered the opinion of the Court.**

The issue before the Court is whether the Constitution permits a juvenile offender to be sentenced to life in prison without parole for a nonhomicide crime. The sentence was imposed by the State of Florida. Petitioner challenges the sentence under the Eighth Amendment's Cruel and Unusual Punishments Clause, made applicable to the States by the Due Process Clause of the Fourteenth Amendment.

I

Petitioner is Terrance Jamar Graham. He was born on January 6,

1987. Graham's parents were addicted to crack cocaine, and their drug use persisted in his early years. Graham was diagnosed with attention deficit hyperactivity disorder in elementary school. He began drinking alcohol and using tobacco at age 9 and smoked marijuana at age 13.

In July 2003, when Graham was age 16, he and three other school-age youths attempted to rob a barbeque restaurant in Jacksonville, Florida. One youth, who worked at the restaurant, left the back door unlocked just before closing time. Graham and another youth, wearing masks, entered through the unlocked door. Graham's masked accomplice twice struck the restaurant manager in the back of the head with a metal bar. When the manager started yelling at the assailant and Graham, the two youths ran out and escaped in a car driven by the third accomplice. The restaurant manager required stitches for his head injury. No money was taken.

Graham was arrested for the robbery attempt. Under Florida law, it is within a prosecutor's discretion whether to charge 16– and 17–year-olds as adults or juveniles for most felony crimes. Graham's prosecutor elected to charge Graham as an adult. The charges against Graham were armed burglary with assault or battery, a first-degree felony carrying a maximum penalty of life imprisonment without the possibility of parole; and attempted armed-robbery, a second-degree felony carrying a maximum penalty of 15 years' imprisonment.

On December 18, 2003, Graham pleaded guilty to both charges under a plea agreement. Graham wrote a letter to the trial court. After reciting "this is my first and last time getting in trouble," he continued "I've decided to turn my life around." Graham said "I made a promise to God and myself that if I get a second chance, I'm going to do whatever it takes to get to the [National Football League]."

The trial court accepted the plea agreement. The court withheld adjudication of guilt as to both charges and sentenced Graham to concurrent 3–year terms of probation. Graham was required to spend the first 12 months of his probation in the coun-

ty jail, but he received credit for the time he had served awaiting trial, and was released on June 25, 2004.

Less than 6 months later, on the night of December 2, 2004, Graham again was arrested. The State's case was as follows: Earlier that evening, Graham participated in a home invasion robbery. His two accomplices were Meigo Bailey and Kirkland Lawrence, both 20–year-old men. According to the State, at 7 p.m. that night, Graham, Bailey, and Lawrence knocked on the door of the home where Carlos Rodriguez lived. Graham, followed by Bailey and Lawrence, forcibly entered the home and held a pistol to Rodriguez's chest. For the next 30 minutes, the three held Rodriguez and another man, a friend of Rodriguez, at gunpoint while they ransacked the home searching for money. Before leaving, Graham and his accomplices barricaded Rodriguez and his friend inside a closet.

The State further alleged that Graham, Bailey, and Lawrence, later the same evening, attempted a second robbery, during which Bailey was shot. Graham, who had borrowed his father's car, drove Bailey and Lawrence to the hospital and left them there. As Graham drove away, a police sergeant signaled him to stop. Graham continued at a high speed but crashed into a telephone pole. He tried to flee on foot but was apprehended. Three handguns were found in his car.

When detectives interviewed Graham, he denied involvement in the crimes. He said he encountered Bailey and Lawrence only after Bailey had been shot. One of the detectives told Graham that the victims of the home invasion had identified him. He asked Graham, "Aside from the two robberies tonight how many more were you involved in?" Graham responded, "Two to three before tonight." The night that Graham allegedly committed the robbery, he was 34 days short of his 18th birthday.

On December 13, 2004, Graham's probation officer filed with the trial court an affidavit asserting that Graham had violated the conditions of his probation by possessing a firearm, committing crimes, and associating with persons engaged in criminal activity. The trial court held hearings on Graham's violations about a year later, in December 2005 and January 2006. The judge who presided was not the same judge who had accepted Graham's guilty plea to the earlier offenses.

Graham maintained that he had no involvement in the home invasion robbery; but, even after the court underscored that the admission could expose him to a life sentence on the earlier charges, he admitted violating probation conditions by fleeing. The State presented evidence related to the home invasion, including testimony from the victims. The trial court noted that Graham, in admitting his attempt to avoid arrest, had acknowledged violating his probation. The court further found that Graham had violated his probation by committing a home invasion robbery, by possessing a firearm, and by associating with persons engaged in criminal activity.

The trial court held a sentencing hearing. Under Florida law the minimum sentence Graham could receive absent a downward departure by the judge was 5 years' imprisonment. The maximum was life imprisonment. Graham's attorney requested the minimum nondeparture sentence of 5 years. A presentence report prepared by the Florida Department of Corrections recommended that Graham receive an even lower sentence—at most 4 years' imprisonment. The State recommended that Graham receive 30 years on the armed burglary count and 15 years on the attempted armed robbery count.

After hearing Graham's testimony, the trial court explained the sentence it was about to pronounce:

"Mr. Graham, as I look back on your case, yours is really candidly a sad situation. You had, as far as I can tell, you have quite a family structure. You had a lot of people who wanted to try and help you get your life turned around including the court system, and you had a judge who took the step to try and give you direction through his probation order to give you a chance to get back onto track. And at the time you seemed through your letters that that is exactly what you wanted to do. And I don't know why it is that you threw your life away. I don't know why.

"But you did, and that is what is so sad about this today is that you have actually been given a chance to get through this, the original charge, which were very serious charges to begin with.... The attempted robbery with a weapon was a very serious charge.

* * *

"And I don't understand why you would be given such a great opportunity to do something with your life and why you would throw it away. The only thing that I can rationalize is that you decided that this is how you were going to lead your life and that there is nothing that we can do for you. And as the state pointed out, that this is an escalating pattern of criminal conduct on your part and that we can't help you any further. We can't do anything to deter you. * * *

"So then it becomes a focus, if I can't do anything to help you, if I can't do anything to get you back on the right path, then I have to start focusing on the community and trying to protect the community from your actions. * * *

The trial court found Graham guilty of the earlier armed burglary and attempted armed robbery charges. It sentenced him to the maximum sentence authorized by law on each charge: life imprisonment for the armed burglary and 15 years for the attempted armed robbery. Because Florida has abolished its parole system, a life sentence gives a defendant no possibility of release unless he is granted executive clemency.

Graham filed a motion in the trial court challenging his sentence under the Eighth Amendment. The motion was deemed denied after the trial court failed to rule on it within 60 days. The First District Court of Appeal of Florida affirmed, concluding that Graham's sentence was not grossly disproportionate to his crimes. The court took note of the seriousness of Graham's offenses and their violent nature, as well as the fact that they "were not committed by a pre-teen, but a seventeen-year-old who was ultimately sentenced at the age of nineteen." The court concluded further that Graham was incapable of rehabilitation. Although Graham "was given an unheard of probationary sentence for a life felony, ... wrote a letter expressing his remorse and promising to refrain from the commission of further crime, and ... had a strong family

structure to support him," the court noted, he "rejected his second chance and chose to continue committing crimes at an escalating pace." The Florida Supreme Court denied review. We granted certiorari.

II

The Eighth Amendment states: "Excessive bail shall not be required, nor excessive fines imposed, nor cruel and unusual punishments inflicted." * * * The concept of proportionality is central to the Eighth Amendment. Embodied in the Constitution's ban on cruel and unusual punishments is the "precept of justice that punishment for crime should be graduated and proportioned to [the] offense." Weems v. United States, 217 U.S. 349, 367 (1910).

The Court's cases addressing the proportionality of sentences fall within two general classifications. The first involves challenges to the length of term-of-years sentences given all the circumstances in a particular case. The second comprises cases in which the Court implements the proportionality standard by certain categorical restrictions on the death penalty.

In the first classification the Court considers all of the circumstances of the case to determine whether the sentence is unconstitutionally excessive. Under this approach, the Court has held unconstitutional a life without parole sentence for the defendant's seventh nonviolent felony, the crime of passing a worthless check. Solem v. Helm. In other cases, however, it has been difficult for the challenger to establish a lack of proportionality. A leading case is Harmelin v. Michigan, in which the offender was sentenced under state law to life without parole for possessing a large quantity of cocaine. A closely divided Court upheld the sentence. The controlling opinion concluded that the Eighth Amendment contains a "narrow proportionality principle," that "does not require strict proportionality between crime and sentence" but rather "forbids only extreme sentences that are 'grossly disproportionate' to the crime." (KENNEDY, J., concurring in part and concurring in judgment). Again closely divided, the Court rejected a challenge to a sentence of 25 years to life for the theft of a few golf clubs under California's so-called three-strikes recidivist sentencing scheme. Ewing v. California. The Court has also upheld a sentence of life with the possibility of parole for a defendant's third nonviolent felony, the crime of obtaining money by false pretenses, Rummel v. Estelle, and a sentence of 40 years for possession of marijuana with intent to distribute and distribution of marijuana, Hutto v. Davis, 454 U.S. 370 (1982).

The controlling opinion in *Harmelin* explained its approach for determining whether a sentence for a term of years is grossly disproportionate for a particular defendant's crime. A court must begin by comparing the gravity of the offense and the severity of the sentence. "[I]n the rare case in which [this] threshold comparison ... leads to an inference of gross disproportionality" the court should then compare the defendant's sentence with the sentences received by other offenders in the same jurisdiction and with the sentences imposed for the same crime in other jurisdictions. If this comparative analysis "validate[s] an initial judgment that [the] sentence is grossly disproportionate," the sentence is cruel and unusual.

The second classification of cases has used categorical rules to define Eighth Amendment standards. The previous cases in this classification involved the death penalty. The classification in turn consists of two subsets, one considering the nature of the offense, the other considering the characteristics of the offender. With respect to the nature of the offense, the Court has concluded that capital punishment is impermissible for nonhomicide crimes against individuals. In cases turning on the characteristics of the offender, the Court has adopted categorical rules prohibiting the death penalty for defendants who committed their crimes before the age of 18, Roper v. Simmons, 543 U.S. 551 (2005), or whose intellectual functioning is in a low range, Atkins v. Virginia, 536 U.S. 304 (2002).

In the cases adopting categorical rules the Court has taken the following approach. The Court first considers objective indicia of society's standards, as expressed in legislative enactments and state practice to determine whether there is a national consensus against the sentencing practice at issue. Next, guided by the standards elaborated by controlling precedents and by the Court's own understanding and interpretation of the Eighth Amendment's text, history, meaning, and purpose, the Court must determine in the exercise of its own independent judgment whether the punishment in question violates the Constitution. *Roper*.

The present case involves an issue the Court has not considered previously: a categorical challenge to a term-of-years sentence. The approach in cases such as *Harmelin* and *Ewing* is suited for considering a gross proportionality challenge to a particular defendant's sentence, but here a sentencing practice itself is in question. This case implicates a particular type of sentence as it applies to an entire class of offenders who have committed a range of crimes. As a result, a threshold comparison between the severity of the penalty and the gravity of the crime does not advance the analysis. Here, in addressing the question presented, the appropriate analysis is the one used in cases that involved the categorical approach.

III

A

The analysis begins with objective indicia of national consensus. The clearest and most reliable objective evidence of contemporary values is the legislation enacted by the country's legislatures. Six jurisdictions do not allow life without parole sentences for any juvenile offenders. Seven jurisdictions permit life without parole for juvenile offenders, but only for homicide crimes. Thirty-seven States as well as the District of Columbia permit sentences of life without parole for a juvenile nonhomicide offender in some circumstances. Federal law also allows for the possibility of life without parole for offenders as young as 13. Relying on this metric, the State and its amici argue that there is no national consensus against the sentencing practice at issue.

This argument is incomplete and unavailing. There are measures of consensus other than legislation. Actual sentencing practices are an important part of the Court's inquiry into consensus. Here, an examination of actual sentencing practices in jurisdictions where the sentence in question is permitted by statute discloses a consensus against its use. Although these statutory schemes contain no explicit prohibition on sentences of life without parole for juvenile nonhomicide offenders, those sentences are most infrequent. According to a recent study, nationwide there are only 109 juvenile offenders serving sentences of life without parole for nonhomicide offenses. See P. Annino, D. Rasmussen, & C. Rice, Juvenile Life without Parole for Non–Homicide Offenses: Florida Compared to Nation 2 (Sept. 14, 2009) (hereinafter Annino).

The State contends that this study's tally is inaccurate because it does not count juvenile offenders who were convicted of both a homicide and a nonhomicide offense, even when the offender received a life without parole sentence for the nonhomicide. This distinction is unpersuasive. Juvenile offenders who committed both homicide and nonhomicide crimes present a different situation for a sentencing judge than juvenile offenders who committed no homicide. It is difficult to say that a defendant who receives a life sentence on a nonhomicide offense but who was at the same time convicted of homicide is not in some sense being punished in part for the homicide when the judge makes the sentencing determination. The instant case concerns only those juvenile offenders sentenced to life without parole solely for a nonhomicide offense.

Florida further criticizes this study because the authors were unable to obtain complete information on some States and because the study was not peer reviewed. The State does not, however, provide any data of its own. Although in the first instance it is for the litigants to provide data to aid the Court, we have been able to supplement the study's findings. * * * [A]dding the individuals counted by the study to those we have been able to locate independently, there are 129 juvenile nonhomicide offenders serving life without parole sentences. A significant majority of those, 77 in total, are serving sentences imposed in Florida. The other 52 are imprisoned in just 10 States—California, Delaware, Iowa, Louisiana, Mississippi, Nebraska, Nevada, Oklahoma, South Carolina, and Virginia—and in the federal system. Thus, only 12 jurisdictions nationwide in fact impose life without parole sentences on juvenile nonhomicide offenders—and most of those impose the sentence quite rarely—while 26 States as well as the District of Columbia do not impose them despite apparent statutory authorization.

* * *

The evidence of consensus is not undermined by the fact that many jurisdictions do not prohibit life without parole for juvenile nonhomicide offenders. * * * Many States have chosen to move away from juvenile court systems and to allow juveniles to be transferred to, or charged directly in, adult court under certain circumstances. Once in adult court, a juvenile offender may receive the same sentence as would be given to an adult offender, including a life without parole sentence. But the fact that transfer and direct charging laws make life without parole possible for some juvenile nonhomicide offenders does not justify a judgment that many States intended to subject such offenders to life without parole sentences.

For example, under Florida law a child of any age can be prosecuted as an adult for certain crimes and can be sentenced to life without parole. The State acknowledged at oral argument that even a 5–year-old, theoretically, could receive such a sentence

under the letter of the law. All would concede this to be unrealistic, but the example underscores that the statutory eligibility of a juvenile offender for life without parole does not indicate that the penalty has been endorsed through deliberate, express, and full legislative consideration. Similarly, the many States that allow life without parole for juvenile nonhomicide offenders but do not impose the punishment should not be treated as if they have expressed the view that the sentence is appropriate. The sentencing practice now under consideration is exceedingly rare. And "it is fair to say that a national consensus has developed against it." *Atkins*.

B

Community consensus, while "entitled to great weight," is not itself determinative of whether a punishment is cruel and unusual. In accordance with the constitutional design, "the task of interpreting the Eighth Amendment remains our responsibility." *Roper*. The judicial exercise of independent judgment requires consideration of the culpability of the offenders at issue in light of their crimes and characteristics, along with the severity of the punishment in question. In this inquiry the Court also considers whether the challenged sentencing practice serves legitimate penological goals.

Roper established that because juveniles have lessened culpability they are less deserving of the most severe punishments. As compared to adults, juveniles have a "lack of maturity and an underdeveloped sense of responsibility"; they "are more vulnerable or susceptible to negative influences and outside pressures, including peer pressure"; and their characters are "not as well formed." These salient characteristics mean that "[i]t is difficult even for expert psychologists to differentiate between the juvenile offender whose crime reflects unfortunate yet transient immaturity, and the rare juvenile offender whose crime reflects irreparable corruption." Accordingly, "juvenile offenders cannot with reliability be classified among the worst offenders." A juvenile is not absolved of responsibility for his actions, but his transgression is not as morally reprehensible as that of an adult.

No recent data provide reason to reconsider the Court's observations in Roper about the nature of juveniles. As petitioner's amici point out, developments in psychology and brain science continue to show fundamental differences between juvenile and adult minds. For example, parts of the brain involved in behavior control continue to mature through late adolescence. Juveniles are more capable of change than are adults, and their actions are less likely to be evidence of "irretrievably depraved character" than are the actions of adults. *Roper*. It remains true that "[f]rom a moral standpoint it would be misguided to equate the failings of a minor with those of an adult, for a greater possibility exists that a minor's character deficiencies will be reformed." Ibid. These matters relate to the status of the offenders in question; and it is relevant to consider next the nature of the offenses to which this harsh penalty might apply.

The Court has recognized that defendants who do not kill, intend to kill, or foresee that life will be taken are categorically less deserving of the most serious forms of punishment than are murderers. Tison v. Arizona, 481 U.S. 137 (1987). There is a line between homicide and other serious violent offenses against the individual. Serious nonhomicide crimes "may be devastating in their harm ... but in terms of moral depravity and of the injury to the person and to the public, ... they cannot be compared to murder in their severity and irrevocability." * * * Although an offense like robbery or rape is a serious crime deserving serious punishment, those crimes differ from homicide crimes in a moral sense.

It follows that, when compared to an adult murderer, a juvenile offender who did not kill or intend to kill has a twice diminished moral culpability. The age of the offender and the nature of the crime each bear on the analysis.

As for the punishment, life without parole is the second most severe penalty permitted by law. It is true that a death sentence is unique in its severity and irrevocability; yet life without parole sentences share some characteristics with death sentences that are shared by no other sentences. The State does not execute the offender sentenced to life without parole, but the sentence alters the offender's life by a forfeiture that is irrevocable. It deprives the convict of the most basic liberties without giving hope of restoration, except perhaps by executive clemency—the remote possibility of which does not mitigate the harshness of the sentence. As one court observed in overturning a life without parole sentence for a juvenile defendant, this sentence "means denial of hope; it means that good behavior and character improvement are immaterial; it means that whatever the future might hold in store for the mind and spirit of [the convict], he will remain in prison for the rest of his days." Naovarath v. State, 105 Nev. 525, 526, 779 P.2d 944 (1989).

* * *

Life without parole is an especially harsh punishment for a juvenile. Under this sentence a juvenile offender will on average serve more years and a greater percentage of his life in prison than an adult offender. A 16–year-old and a 75–year-old each sentenced to life without parole receive the same punishment in name only. This reality cannot be ignored.

The penological justifications for the sentencing practice are also relevant to the analysis. Criminal punishment can have different goals, and choosing among them is within a legislature's discretion. It does not follow, however, that the purposes and effects of penal sanctions are irrelevant to the determination of Eighth Amendment restrictions. A sentence lacking any legitimate penological justification is by its nature disproportionate to the offense. With respect to life without parole for juvenile nonhomicide offenders, none of the goals of penal sanctions that have been recognized as legitimate—retribution, deterrence, incapacitation, and rehabilitation—provides an adequate justification.

Retribution is a legitimate reason to punish, but it cannot support the sentence at issue here. Society is entitled to impose severe sanctions on a juvenile nonhomicide offender to express its condemnation of the crime and to seek restoration of the moral imbalance caused by the offense. But the heart of the retribution rationale is that a criminal sentence must be directly related to the personal culpability of the criminal offender. And as *Roper* observed, "[w]hether viewed as an attempt to express the community's moral outrage or as an attempt

to right the balance for the wrong to the victim, the case for retribution is not as strong with a minor as with an adult." The case becomes even weaker with respect to a juvenile who did not commit homicide. *Roper* found that "[r]etribution is not proportional if the law's most severe penalty is imposed" on the juvenile murderer. The considerations underlying that holding support as well the conclusion that retribution does not justify imposing the second most severe penalty on the less culpable juvenile nonhomicide offender.

Deterrence does not suffice to justify the sentence either. *Roper* noted that "the same characteristics that render juveniles less culpable than adults suggest . . . that juveniles will be less susceptible to deterrence." Because juveniles' lack of maturity and underdeveloped sense of responsibility often result in impetuous and ill-considered actions and decisions, they are less likely to take a possible punishment into consideration when making decisions. This is particularly so when that punishment is rarely imposed. That the sentence deters in a few cases is perhaps plausible, but this argument does not overcome other objections. Even if the punishment has some connection to a valid penological goal, it must be shown that the punishment is not grossly disproportionate in light of the justification offered. Here, in light of juvenile nonhomicide offenders' diminished moral responsibility, any limited deterrent effect provided by life without parole is not enough to justify the sentence.

Incapacitation, a third legitimate reason for imprisonment, does not justify the life without parole sentence in question here. Recidivism is a serious risk to public safety, and so incapacitation is an important goal. But while incapacitation may be a legitimate penological goal sufficient to justify life without parole in other contexts, it is inadequate to justify that punishment for juveniles who did not commit homicide. To justify life without parole on the assumption that the juvenile offender forever will be a danger to society requires the sentencer to make a judgment that the juvenile is incorrigible. The characteristics of juveniles make that judgment questionable. "It is difficult even for expert psychologists to differentiate between the juvenile offender whose crime reflects unfortunate yet transient immaturity, and the rare juvenile offender whose crime reflects irreparable corruption." *Roper.* As one court concluded in a challenge to a life without parole sentence for a 14–year-old, "incorrigibility is inconsistent with youth." Workman v. Commonwealth, 429 S.W.2d 374, 378 (Ky.1968).

Here one cannot dispute that this defendant posed an immediate risk, for he had committed, we can assume, serious crimes early in his term of supervised release and despite his own assurances of reform. Graham deserved to be separated from society for some time in order to prevent what the trial court described as an "escalating pattern of criminal conduct," but it does not follow that he would be a risk to society for the rest of his life. Even if the State's judgment that Graham was incorrigible were later corroborated by prison misbehavior or failure to mature, the sentence was still disproportionate because that judgment was made at the outset. A life without parole sentence improperly denies the juvenile offender a chance to demonstrate growth and maturity. Incapacitation cannot override all other considerations, lest the Eighth Amendment's rule against disproportionate sentences be a nullity.

Finally there is rehabilitation, a penological goal that forms the basis of parole systems. The concept of rehabilitation is imprecise; and its utility and proper implementation are the subject of a substantial, dynamic field of inquiry and dialogue. It is for legislatures to determine what rehabilitative techniques are appropriate and effective.

A sentence of life imprisonment without parole, however, cannot be justified by the goal of rehabilitation. The penalty forswears altogether the rehabilitative ideal. By denying the defendant the right to reenter the community, the State makes an irrevocable judgment about that person's value and place in society. This judgment is not appropriate in light of a juvenile nonhomicide offender's capacity for change and limited moral culpability. A State's rejection of rehabilitation, moreover, goes beyond a mere expressive judgment. As one amicus notes, defendants serving life without parole sentences are often denied access to vocational training and other rehabilitative services that are available to other inmates. For juvenile offenders, who are most in need of and receptive to rehabilitation, the absence of rehabilitative opportunities or treatment makes the disproportionality of the sentence all the more evident.

In sum, penological theory is not adequate to justify life without parole for juvenile nonhomicide offenders. This determination; the limited culpability of juvenile nonhomicide offenders; and the severity of life without parole sentences all lead to the conclusion that the sentencing practice under consideration is cruel and unusual. This Court now holds that for a juvenile offender who did not commit homicide the Eighth Amendment forbids the sentence of life without parole. This clear line is necessary to prevent the possibility that life without parole sentences will be imposed on juvenile nonhomicide offenders who are not sufficiently culpable to merit that punishment. Because "[t]he age of 18 is the point where society draws the line for many purposes between childhood and adulthood," those who were below that age when the offense was committed may not be sentenced to life without parole for a nonhomicide crime. *Roper*.

A State is not required to guarantee eventual freedom to a juvenile offender convicted of a nonhomicide crime. What the State must do, however, is give defendants like Graham some meaningful opportunity to obtain release based on demonstrated maturity and rehabilitation. It is for the State, in the first instance, to explore the means and mechanisms for compliance. It bears emphasis, however, that while the Eighth Amendment forbids a State from imposing a life without parole sentence on a juvenile nonhomicide offender, it does not require the State to release that offender during his natural life. Those who commit truly horrifying crimes as juveniles may turn out to be irredeemable, and thus deserving of incarceration for the duration of their lives. The Eighth Amendment does not foreclose the possibility that persons convicted of nonhomicide crimes committed before adulthood will remain behind bars for life. It does forbid States from making the judgment at the outset that those offenders never will be fit to reenter society.

C

Categorical rules tend to be imperfect, but one is necessary here. * * * [A] categorical rule gives all juvenile nonhomicide offenders a chance to demonstrate maturity and reform. The juvenile should not be deprived of the opportunity to achieve maturity of judgment and self-recognition of human worth and potential. In *Roper*, that deprivation resulted from an execution that brought life to its end. Here, though by a different dynamic, the same concerns apply. Life in prison without the possibility of parole gives no chance for fulfillment outside prison walls, no chance for reconciliation with society, no hope. Maturity can lead to that considered reflection which is the foundation for remorse, renewal, and rehabilitation. A young person who knows that he or she has no chance to leave prison before life's end has little incentive to become a responsible individual. In some prisons, moreover, the system itself becomes complicit in the lack of development. As noted above, * * * it is the policy in some prisons to withhold counseling, education, and rehabilitation programs for those who are ineligible for parole consideration. A categorical rule against life without parole for juvenile nonhomicide offenders avoids the perverse consequence in which the lack of maturity that led to an offender's crime is reinforced by the prison term.

Terrance Graham's sentence guarantees he will die in prison without any meaningful opportunity to obtain release, no matter what he might do to demonstrate that the bad acts he committed as a teenager are not representative of his true character, even if he spends the next half century attempting to atone for his crimes and learn from his mistakes. The

State has denied him any chance to later demonstrate that he is fit to rejoin society based solely on a non-homicide crime that he committed while he was a child in the eyes of the law. This the Eighth Amendment does not permit.

D

There is support for our conclusion in the fact that, in continuing to impose life without parole sentences on juveniles who did not commit homicide, the United States adheres to a sentencing practice rejected the world over. This observation does not control our decision. The judgments of other nations and the international community are not dispositive as to the meaning of the Eighth Amendment. But the climate of international opinion concerning the acceptability of a particular punishment is also not irrelevant. The Court has looked beyond our Nation's borders for support for its independent conclusion that a particular punishment is cruel and unusual. [Justice Kennedy cites a string of Eighth Amendment death penalty cases including *Roper* and *Atkins*.]

Today we continue that longstanding practice in noting the global consensus against the sentencing practice in question. A recent study concluded that only 11 nations authorize life without parole for juvenile offenders under any circumstances; and only 2 of them, the United States and Israel, ever impose the punishment in practice. See M. Leighton & C. de la Vega, Sentencing Our Children to Die in Prison: Global Law and Practice 4 (2007). An updated version of the study concluded that Israel's "laws allow for parole review of juvenile offenders serving life terms," but expressed reservations about how that parole review is implemented. But

even if Israel is counted as allowing life without parole for juvenile offenders, that nation does not appear to impose that sentence for nonhomicide crimes; all of the seven Israeli prisoners whom commentators have identified as serving life sentences for juvenile crimes were convicted of homicide or attempted homicide. See Amnesty International, Human Rights Watch, The Rest of Their Lives: Life without Parole for Child Offenders in the United States 106, n. 322 (2005).

Thus, as petitioner contends and respondent does not contest, the United States is the only Nation that imposes life without parole sentences on juvenile nonhomicide offenders. * * *

The State's amici stress that no international legal agreement that is binding on the United States prohibits life without parole for juvenile offenders and thus urge us to ignore the international consensus. These arguments miss the mark. The question before us is not whether international law prohibits the United States from imposing the sentence at issue in this case. The question is whether that punishment is cruel and unusual. In that inquiry, "the overwhelming weight of international opinion against" life without parole for nonhomicide offenses committed by juveniles "provide[s] respected and significant confirmation for our own conclusions." *Roper*.

* * * The Court has treated the laws and practices of other nations and international agreements as relevant to the Eighth Amendment not because those norms are binding or controlling but because the judgment of the world's nations that a particular sentencing practice is inconsistent with basic principles of decency dem-

onstrates that the Court's rationale has respected reasoning to support it.

_____

The Constitution prohibits the imposition of a life without parole sentence on a juvenile offender who did not commit homicide. A State need not guarantee the offender eventual release, but if it imposes a sentence of life it must provide him or her with some realistic opportunity to obtain release before the end of that term. The judgment of the First District Court of Appeal of Florida affirming Graham's conviction is reversed, and the case is remanded for further proceedings not inconsistent with this opinion.

JUSTICE STEVENS, **with whom** JUSTICE GINSBURG **and** JUSTICE SOTOMAYOR **join, concurring.**

In his dissenting opinion, JUSTICE THOMAS argues that today's holding is not entirely consistent with the controlling opinions in * * * Ewing v. California, Harmelin v. Michigan, and Rummel v. Estelle. Given that "evolving standards of decency" have played a central role in our Eighth Amendment jurisprudence for at least a century, see Weems v. United States, 217 U.S. 349, 373–378 (1910), this argument suggests the dissenting opinions in those cases more accurately describe the law today than does JUSTICE THOMAS' rigid interpretation of the Amendment. Society changes. Knowledge accumulates. We learn, sometimes, from our mistakes. Punishments that did not seem cruel and unusual at one time may, in the light of reason and experience, be found cruel and unusual at a later time; unless we are to abandon the moral commitment embodied in the Eighth Amendment, proportionality

review must never become effectively obsolete.

While JUSTICE THOMAS would apparently not rule out a death sentence for a $50 theft by a 7–year-old, the Court wisely rejects his static approach to the law. Standards of decency have evolved since 1980. They will never stop doing so.

CHIEF JUSTICE ROBERTS, **concurring in the judgment.**

I agree with the Court that Terrance Graham's sentence of life without parole violates the Eighth Amendment's prohibition on "cruel and unusual punishments." Unlike the majority, however, I see no need to invent a new constitutional rule of dubious provenance in reaching that conclusion. Instead, my analysis is based on an application of this Court's precedents, in particular (1) our cases requiring "narrow proportionality" review of noncapital sentences and (2) our conclusion in Roper v. Simmons that juvenile offenders are generally less culpable than adults who commit the same crimes.

* * *

I

* * *

A

Graham's case arises at the intersection of two lines of Eighth Amendment precedent. The first consists of decisions holding that the Cruel and Unusual Punishments Clause embraces a "narrow proportionality principle" that we apply, on a case-by-case basis, when asked to review noncapital sentences. This "narrow proportionality principle" does not grant judges blanket authority to second-guess decisions made by legislatures or sentencing courts. On the contrary, a reviewing court will only "rarely" need "to engage in extended analysis to determine that a sentence is not constitutionally disproportionate," *Solem*, and "successful challenges" to noncapital sentences will be all the more exceedingly rare.

We have not established a clear or consistent path for courts to follow in applying the highly deferential "narrow proportionality" analysis. We have, however, emphasized the primacy of the legislature in setting sentences, the variety of legitimate penological schemes, the state-by-state diversity protected by our federal system, and the requirement that review be guided by objective, rather than subjective, factors. *Harmelin* (opinion of KENNEDY, J.). Most importantly, however, we have explained that the Eighth Amendment "does not require strict proportionality between crime and sentence"; rather, it forbids only extreme sentences that are "grossly disproportionate" to the crime.

* * *

Only in "the rare case in which a threshold comparison of the crime committed and the sentence imposed leads to an inference of gross disproportionality" should courts proceed to an "intrajurisdictional" comparison of the sentence at issue with those imposed on other criminals in the same jurisdiction, and an "interjurisdictional" comparison with sentences imposed for the same crime in other jurisdictions. *Solem.* If these subsequent comparisons confirm the inference of gross disproportionality, courts should invalidate the sentence as a violation of the Eighth Amendment.

B

The second line of precedent relevant to assessing Graham's sentence consists of our cases acknowledging that juvenile offenders are generally—though not necessarily in every case—less morally culpable than adults who commit the same crimes. This insight animated our decision in Thompson v. Oklahoma, 487 U.S. 815 (1988), in which we invalidated a capital sentence imposed on a juvenile who had committed his crime under the age of 16. More recently, in *Roper*, we extended the prohibition on executions to those who committed their crimes before the age of 18.

Both *Thompson* and *Roper* arose in the unique context of the death penalty, a punishment that our Court has recognized "must be limited to those offenders who commit a narrow category of the most serious crimes and whose extreme culpability makes them the most deserving of execution." *Roper's* prohibition on the juvenile death penalty followed from our conclusion that "[t]hree general differences between juveniles under 18 and adults demonstrate that juvenile offenders cannot with reliability be classified among the worst offenders." These differences are a lack of maturity and an underdeveloped sense of responsibility, a heightened susceptibility to negative influences and outside pressures, and the fact that the character of a juvenile is "more transitory" and "less fixed" than that of an adult. Together, these factors establish the "diminished culpability of juveniles," and "render suspect any conclusion" that juveniles are among "the worst offenders" for whom the death penalty is reserved.

Today, the Court views *Roper* as providing the basis for a new categorical rule that juveniles may never receive a sentence of life without parole for nonhomicide crimes. I disagree. In *Roper*, the Court tailored its analysis of juvenile characteristics to the specific question whether juvenile offenders could constitutionally be subject to capital punishment. Our answer that they could not be sentenced to death was based on the explicit conclusion that they "cannot with reliability be classified among the worst offenders."

This conclusion does not establish that juveniles can never be eligible for life without parole. A life sentence is of course far less severe than a death sentence, and we have never required that it be imposed only on the very worst offenders, as we have with capital punishment. Treating juvenile life sentences as analogous to capital punishment is at odds with our longstanding view that "the death penalty is different from other punishments in kind rather than degree." * * *

But the fact that *Roper* does not support a categorical rule barring life sentences for all juveniles does not mean that a criminal defendant's age is irrelevant to those sentences. On the contrary, our cases establish that the "narrow proportionality" review applicable to noncapital cases itself takes the personal "culpability of the offender" into account in examining whether a given punishment is proportionate to the crime. There is no reason why an offender's juvenile status should be excluded from the analysis. * * *

II

Applying the "narrow proportionality" framework to the particular facts of this case, I conclude that Graham's sentence of life without parole violates the Eighth Amendment.

A

I begin with the threshold inquiry comparing the gravity of Graham's conduct to the harshness of his penalty. There is no question that the crime for which Graham received his life sentence—armed burglary of a nondomicil with an assault or battery—is a serious crime deserving serious punishment. So too is the home invasion robbery that was the basis of Graham's probation violation. But these crimes are certainly less serious than other crimes, such as murder or rape.

As for Graham's degree of personal culpability, he committed the relevant offenses when he was a juvenile—a stage at which, *Roper* emphasized, one's "culpability or blameworthiness is diminished, to a substantial degree, by reason of youth and immaturity." * * * Graham's youth made him relatively more likely to engage in reckless and dangerous criminal activity than an adult; it also likely enhanced his susceptibility to peer pressure. There is no reason to believe that Graham should be denied the general presumption of diminished culpability that *Roper* indicates should apply to juvenile offenders. If anything, Graham's in-court statements—including his request for a second chance so that he could "do whatever it takes to get to the NFL"—underscore his immaturity.

The fact that Graham committed the crimes that he did proves that he was dangerous and deserved to be punished. But it does not establish that he was particularly dangerous—at least relative to the murderers and rapists for whom the sentence of life without parole is typically reserved. On the contrary, his lack of prior criminal convictions, his youth and immaturity, and the difficult circumstances of his upbringing noted by the majority, all suggest that he was markedly less culpable than a typical adult who commits the same offenses.

Despite these considerations, the trial court sentenced Graham to life in prison without the possibility of parole. * * * No one in Graham's case other than the sentencing judge appears to have believed that Graham deserved to go to prison for life.

Based on the foregoing circumstances, I conclude that there is a strong inference that Graham's sentence of life imprisonment without parole was grossly disproportionate in violation of the Eighth Amendment. I therefore proceed to the next steps of the proportionality analysis.

B

Both intrajurisdictional and interjurisdictional comparisons of Graham's sentence confirm the threshold inference of disproportionality.

Graham's sentence was far more severe than that imposed for similar violations of Florida law, even without taking juvenile status into account. For example, individuals who commit burglary or robbery offenses in Florida receive average sentences of less than 5 years and less than 10 years, respectively. Unsurprisingly, Florida's juvenile criminals receive similarly low sentences—typically less than five years for burglary and less than seven years for robbery. Graham's life without parole sentence was far more severe than the average sentence imposed on those convicted of murder or manslaughter, who typically receive under 25 years in prison. * * *

Finally, the inference that Graham's sentence is disproportionate is further validated by comparison to the sentences imposed in other domestic jurisdictions. As the majority opinion explains, Florida is an outlier in its willingness to impose sentences of life without parole on juveniles convicted of nonhomicide crimes.

III

So much for Graham. But what about Milagro Cunningham, a 17–year-old who beat and raped an 8–year-old girl before leaving her to die under 197 pounds of rock in a recycling bin in a remote landfill? Or Nathan Walker and Jakaris Taylor, the Florida juveniles who together with their friends gang-raped a woman and forced her to perform oral sex on her 12–year-old son? The fact that Graham cannot be sentenced to life without parole for his conduct says nothing whatever about these offenders, or others like them who commit nonhomicide crimes far more reprehensible than the conduct at issue here. The Court uses Graham's case as a vehicle to proclaim a new constitutional rule—applicable well beyond the particular facts of Graham's case—that a sentence of life without parole imposed on any juvenile for any nonhomicide offense is unconstitutional. This categorical conclusion is as unnecessary as it is unwise.

A holding this broad is unnecessary because the particular conduct and circumstances at issue in the case before us are not serious enough to justify Graham's sentence. In reaching this conclusion, there is no need for the Court to decide whether that same sentence would be constitutional if imposed for other more heinous nonhomicide crimes.

A more restrained approach is especially appropriate in light of the Court's apparent recognition that it is perfectly legitimate for a juvenile to receive a sentence of life without parole for committing murder. This means that there is nothing inherently unconstitutional about imposing sentences of life without parole on juvenile offenders; rather, the constitutionality of such sentences depends on the particular crimes for which they are imposed. But if the constitutionality of the sentence turns on the particular crime being punished, then the Court should limit its holding to the particular offenses that Graham committed here, and should decline to consider other hypothetical crimes not presented by this case.

In any event, the Court's categorical conclusion is also unwise. Most importantly, it ignores the fact that some nonhomicide crimes—like the ones committed by Milagro Cunningham, Nathan Walker, and Jakaris Taylor—are especially heinous or grotesque, and thus may be deserving of more severe punishment.

* * *

JUSTICE THOMAS, **with whom** JUSTICE SCALIA **joins, and with whom** JUSTICE ALITO **joins as to Parts I and III, dissenting.**

The Court holds today that it is "grossly disproportionate" and hence unconstitutional for any judge or jury to impose a sentence of life without parole on an offender less than 18 years old, unless he has committed a homicide. Although the text of the Constitution is silent regarding the permissibility of this sentencing practice, and although it would not have offended the standards that prevailed at the founding, the Court insists that the standards of American society have evolved such that the Constitution now requires its prohibition.

The news of this evolution will, I think, come as a surprise to the American people. Congress, the District of Columbia, and 37 States allow judges and juries to consider this sentencing practice in juvenile nonhomicide cases, and those judges and juries have decided to use it in the very worst cases they have encountered.

The Court does not conclude that life without parole itself is a cruel and unusual punishment. It instead rejects the judgments of those legislatures, judges, and juries regarding what the Court describes as the "moral" question of whether this sentence can ever be "proportionat[e]" when applied to the category of offenders at issue here.

I am unwilling to assume that we, as members of this Court, are any more capable of making such moral judgments than our fellow citizens. Nothing in our training as judges qualifies us for that task, and nothing in Article III gives us that authority.

I respectfully dissent.

I

* * *

II

A

* * *

[T]he Court has held that the [Cruel and Unusual Punishment] Clause authorizes it to proscribe not only methods of punishment that qualify as "cruel and unusual," but also any punishment that the Court deems "grossly disproportionate" to the crime committed. This latter interpretation is entirely the Court's creation. As has been described elsewhere at length, there is virtually no indication that the Cruel and Unusual Punishments Clause originally was understood to require proportionality in sentencing. See *Harmelin* (opinion of SCALIA, J.). Here, it suffices to recall just two points. First, the Clause does not expressly refer to proportionality or invoke any synonym for that term, even though the Framers were familiar with the concept, as evidenced by several founding-era state constitutions that required (albeit without defining) proportional punishments. In addition, the penal statute adopted by the First Congress demonstrates that proportionality in sentencing was not considered a constitutional command. * * *

The Court has nonetheless invoked proportionality to declare that capital punishment—though not unconstitutional per se—is categorically too harsh a penalty to apply to certain types of crimes and certain classes of offenders. See Coker v. Georgia, 433 U.S. 584(1977) (plurality opinion) (rape of an adult woman); Kennedy v. Louisiana, 128 S.Ct. 2641 (2008) (rape of a child); Enmund v. Florida, 458 U.S. 782 (1982) (felony murder in which the defendant participated in the felony but did not kill or intend to kill); Thompson v. Oklahoma, 487 U.S. 815 (1988) (plurality opinion) (juveniles under 16); Roper v. Simmons, 543 U.S. 551 (2005) (juveniles under 18); Atkins v. Virginia, 536 U.S. 304 (2002) (mentally retarded offenders). In adopting these categorical proportionality rules, the Court intrudes upon areas that the Constitution reserves to other (state and federal) organs of government. * * *

The Court has nonetheless adopted categorical rules that shield entire classes of offenses and offenders from the death penalty on the theory that "evolving standards of decency" require this result. The Court has offered assurances that these standards can be reliably measured by " 'objective indicia' " of "national consensus," such as state and federal legislation, jury behavior, and (surprisingly, given that we are talking about "national" consensus) international opinion. Yet even assuming that is true, the Framers did not provide for the constitutionality of a particular type of punishment to turn on a "snapshot of American public opinion" taken at the moment a case is decided. By holding otherwise, the Court pretermits in all but one direction the evolution of the standards it describes * * * .

But the Court is not content to rely on snapshots of community consensus in any event. Instead, it reserves the right to reject the evidence of consensus it finds whenever its own "independent judgment" points in a different direction. The Court thus openly claims the power not only to approve or disapprove of democratic choices in penal policy based on evidence of how society's standards have evolved, but also on the basis of the Court's "independent" perception of how those standards should evolve, which depends on what the Court concedes is "necessarily a moral judgment" regarding the propriety of a given punishment in today's society.

The categorical proportionality review the Court employs in capital cases thus lacks a principled foundation. The Court's decision today is significant because it does not merely apply this standard—it remarkably expands its reach. For the first time in its history, the Court declares an entire class of offenders immune from a noncapital sentence using the categorical approach it previously reserved for death penalty cases alone.

B

Until today, the Court has based its categorical proportionality rulings on the notion that the Constitution gives special protection to capital defendants because the death penalty is a uniquely severe punishment that must be reserved for only those who are "most deserving of execution." Of course, the Eighth Amendment itself makes no distinction between capital and noncapital sentencing, but the "bright line" the Court drew between the two penalties has for many years served as the principal justification for the Court's willingness to reject democratic choices regarding the death penalty.

Today's decision eviscerates that distinction. "Death is different" no longer. * * * No reliable limiting principle remains to prevent the Court from immunizing any class of offenders from the law's third, fourth, fifth, or fiftieth most severe penalties as well.

The Court's departure from the "death is different" distinction is especially mystifying when one considers how long it has resisted crossing that divide. Indeed, for a time the Court declined to apply proportionality principles to noncapital sentences at all * * *. Even when the Court broke from that understanding in its 5–to–4 decision in Solem v. Helm (striking down as "grossly disproportionate" a life-without-parole sentence imposed on a defendant for passing a worthless check), the Court did so only as applied to the facts of that case; it announced no categorical rule. Moreover, the Court soon cabined *Solem's* rationale. The controlling opinion in the Court's very next noncapital proportionality case emphasized that principles of federalism require substantial deference to legislative choices regarding the proper length of prison sentences. *Harmelin*. That opinion thus concluded that "successful challenges to the proportionality of [prison] sentences [would be] exceedingly rare."

They have been rare indeed. In the 28 years since *Solem*, the Court has considered just three such challenges and has rejected them all, see Ewing v. California; Lockyer v. Andrade; *Harmelin*, *supra*, largely on the theory that criticisms of the "wisdom, cost-efficiency, and effectiveness" of term-of-years prison sentences are "appropriately directed at the legislature[s]," not the courts. *Ewing.* * * *

Remarkably, the Court today does more than return to *Solem's* case-by-case proportionality standard for noncapital sentences; it hurtles past it to impose a categorical proportionality rule banning life-without-parole sentences not just in this case, but in every case involving a juvenile nonhomicide offender, no matter what the circumstances. Neither the Eighth Amendment nor the Court's precedents justify this decision.

III

The Court asserts that categorical proportionality review is necessary here merely because Graham asks for a categorical rule, and because the Court thinks clear lines are a good idea. I find those factors wholly insufficient to justify the Court's break from past practice. First, the Court fails to acknowledge that a petitioner seeking to exempt an entire category of offenders from a sentencing practice carries a much heavier burden than one seeking case-specific relief under *Solem*. Unlike the petitioner in *Solem*, Graham must establish not only that his own life-without-parole sentence is "grossly disproportionate," but also that such a sentence is always grossly disproportionate whenever it is applied to a juvenile nonhomicide offender, no matter how heinous his crime. Second, even applying the Court's categorical "evolving standards" test, neither objective evidence of national consensus nor the notions of culpability on which the Court's "independent judgment" relies can justify the categorical rule it declares here.

A

According to the Court, proper Eighth Amendment analysis "begins with objective indicia of national consensus," and "[t]he clearest and most reliable objective evidence of contemporary values is the legislation enacted by the country's legislatures." As such, the analysis should end quickly, because a national "consensus" in favor of the Court's result simply does not exist. The laws of all 50 States, the Federal Government, and the District of Columbia provide that juveniles over a certain age may be tried in adult court if charged with certain crimes. Forty-five States, the Federal Government, and the District of Columbia expose juvenile offenders charged in adult court to the very same range of punishments faced by adults charged with the same crimes. Eight of those States do not make life-without-parole sentences available for any nonhomicide offender, regardless of age. All remaining jurisdictions—the Federal Government, the other 37 States, and the District—authorize life-without-parole sentences for certain nonhomicide offenses, and authorize the imposition of such sentences on persons under 18. Only five States prohibit juvenile offenders from receiving a life-without-parole sentence that could be imposed on an adult convicted of the same crime.

No plausible claim of a consensus against this sentencing practice can be made in light of this overwhelming legislative evidence. The sole fact that federal law authorizes this practice singlehandedly refutes the claim

that our Nation finds it morally repugnant. * * *

Undaunted, however, the Court brushes this evidence aside as "incomplete and unavailing," declaring that "[t]here are measures of consensus other than legislation." This is nothing short of stunning. Most importantly, federal civilian law approves this sentencing practice. And although the Court has never decided how many state laws are necessary to show consensus, the Court has never banished into constitutional exile a sentencing practice that the laws of a majority, let alone a supermajority, of States expressly permit.

* * *

B

The Court nonetheless dismisses existing legislation, pointing out that life-without-parole sentences are rarely imposed on juvenile nonhomicide offenders—129 times in recent memory by the Court's calculation, spread out across 11 States and the federal courts. Based on this rarity of use, the Court proclaims a consensus against the practice, implying that laws allowing it either reflect the consensus of a prior, less civilized time or are the work of legislatures tone-deaf to moral values of their constituents that this Court claims to have easily discerned from afar.

* * *

[T]he Court is wrong to equate a jurisdiction's disuse of a legislatively authorized penalty with its moral opposition to it. The fact that the laws of a jurisdiction permit this sentencing practice demonstrates, at a minimum, that the citizens of that jurisdiction find tolerable the possibility that a jury of their peers could impose a life-without-parole sentence on a juvenile whose nonhomicide crime is sufficiently depraved.

The recent case of 16–year-old Keighton Budder illustrates this point. Just weeks before the release of this opinion, an Oklahoma jury sentenced Budder to life without parole after hearing evidence that he viciously attacked a 17–year-old girl who gave him a ride home from a party. Budder allegedly put the girl's head " 'into a headlock and sliced her throat,' " raped her, stabbed her about 20 times, beat her, and pounded her face into the rocks alongside a dirt road. Miraculously, the victim survived.

Budder's crime was rare in its brutality. The sentence the jury imposed was also rare. According to the study relied upon by this Court, Oklahoma had no such offender in its prison system before Budder's offense. Without his conviction, therefore, the Court would have counted Oklahoma's citizens as morally opposed to life-without-parole sentences for juveniles nonhomicide offenders.

Yet Oklahoma's experience proves the inescapable flaw in that reasoning: Oklahoma citizens have enacted laws that allow Oklahoma juries to consider life-without-parole sentences in juvenile nonhomicide cases. Oklahoma juries invoke those laws rarely—in the unusual cases that they find exceptionally depraved. I cannot agree with the Court that Oklahoma citizens should be constitutionally disabled from using this sentencing practice merely because they have not done so more frequently. If anything, the rarity of this penalty's use underscores just how judicious sentencing judges and juries across the country have been in invoking it.

* * *

In the end, however, objective factors such as legislation and the frequency of a penalty's use are merely ornaments in the Court's analysis, window dressing that accompanies its judicial fiat. By the Court's own decree, "[c]ommunity consensus . . . is not itself determinative." Only the independent moral judgment of this Court is sufficient to decide the question.

* * *

IV

* * *

V

The ultimate question in this case is not whether a life-without-parole sentence fits the crime at issue here or the crimes of juvenile nonhomicide offenders more generally, but to whom the Constitution assigns that decision. The Florida Legislature has concluded that such sentences should be available for persons under 18 who commit certain crimes, and the trial judge in this case decided to impose that legislatively authorized sentence here. Because a life-without-parole prison sentence is not a "cruel and unusual" method of punishment under any standard, the Eighth Amendment gives this Court no authority to reject those judgments.

It would be unjustifiable for the Court to declare otherwise even if it could claim that a bare majority of state laws supported its independent moral view. The fact that the Court categorically prohibits life-without-parole sentences for juvenile nonhomicide offenders in the face of an overwhelming legislative majority in favor of leaving that sentencing option available under certain cases simply illustrates how far beyond any cognizable constitutional principle the Court has reached to ensure that its own sense of morality and retributive justice pre-empts that of the people and their representatives.

I agree with JUSTICE STEVENS that "[w]e learn, sometimes, from our mistakes." Perhaps one day the Court will learn from this one.

[The short dissenting opinion of JUSTICE ALITO is omitted].

II.　GUIDELINES SNTENCING

D.　SUPREME COURT CONSTRUCTION OF THE SENTENCING GUIDELINES

2.　Application of Advisory Guidelines After Booker

Page 1463. Add after Kimbrough

Rehabilitation and Guidelines Sentencing: United States v. Tapia

In Tapia v. United States, 2011 WL 2369395 (2011), Justice Kagan wrote for a unanimous court as it held that 18 U.S.C. 3582(a) does not permit a sentencing court to impose or lengthen a prison term in order to foster a defendant's rehabilitation. The Court found the language of the statute to clearly support its holding but added the following: "A court commits no error by discussing the opportunities for rehabilitation within prison or the benefits of specific treatment or training programs. To the contrary, a court properly may address a person who is about to begin a prison term about these important matters. And * * * a court may urge the BOP [Bureau of Prisons] to place an offender in a prison treatment program."

Page 1475. Add at the end of the section.

Considering Post–Sentence Rehabilitation When a Sentence Is Vacated on Appeal: Pepper v. United States.

In Pepper v. United States, 131 S.Ct. 1229 (2011), the Court considered whether the Sentencing Guidelines allow a district court, when called on to resentence a defendant, to further reduce the sentence on the basis of post-sentence rehabilitation. After pleading guilty to drug charges, Pepper was sentenced under the Federal Sentencing Guidelines to a term of imprisonment followed by five years of supervised release. That sentence was entered before the Supreme Court's decision in United States v. Booker, which found the Guidelines to be advisory, not mandatory. Pepper's sentence was reversed in light of Booker and his case was remanded to the district court. At resentencing Pepper testified that he was no longer a drug addict, having completed a 500–hour drug treatment program while in prison; that he was enrolled in community college and had achieved very good grades; and that he was working part time. Pepper's father testified that he and his son were no longer estranged, and Pepper's probation officer testified that a 24–month sentence would be reasonable in light of Pepper's substantial assistance, postsentencing rehabilitation, and demonstrated low recidivism risk. The district court sentenced Pepper to 24 months, granting a 40 percent downward departure based, among other things, on Pepper's rehabilitation since his initial sentencing. The court of appeals rejected this sentence, holding that Pepper's postsentencing rehabilitation could not be considered as a factor supporting a downward variance.

The Court, in an opinion by Justice Sotomayor, held that when a defendant's sentence has been set aside on appeal, a district court at resentencing may consider evidence of the defendant's postsentencing rehabilitation, and such evidence may, in appropriate cases, support a downward variance from the now-advisory Guidelines range. She explained as follows:

> This Court has long recognized that sentencing judges "exercise a wide discretion" in the types of evidence they may consider when imposing sentence and that "[h]ighly relevant-if not essential-to [the] selection of an appropriate sentence is the possession of the fullest information possible concerning the defendant's life and characteristics." Williams v. New York, 337 U.S. 241, 246–247 (1949). Congress codified this principle at 18 U.S.C. § 3661, which provides that "[n]o limitation shall be placed on the information" a sentencing court may consider "concerning the [defendant's] background, character, and conduct," and at § 3553(a), which sets forth certain factors that sentencing courts must consider, including "the history and characteristics of the defendant," § 3553(a)(1). * * * Although a separate statutory provision, § 3742(g)(2), prohibits a district court at resentencing from imposing a sentence outside the Federal Sentencing Guidelines range except upon a ground it relied upon at the prior sentencing—thus effectively precluding the court from considering postsentencing rehabilitation for purposes of imposing a non-Guidelines sentence—that provision did not survive our holding in United States v. Booker, 543 U.S. 220 (2005), and we expressly invalidate it today.

Justice Sotomayor parsed the federal sentencing statutes in the following passage:

> Preliminarily, Congress could not have been clearer in directing that "[n]o limitation . . . be placed on the information concerning the background, character, and conduct" of a defendant that a district court may "receive and consider for the purpose of imposing an appropriate sentence." 18 U.S.C. § 3661. The plain language of § 3661 makes no distinction between a defendant's initial sentencing and a subsequent resentencing after a prior sentence has been set aside on appeal. * * * A categorical bar on the consideration of postsentencing rehabilitation evidence would directly contravene Congress' expressed intent in § 3661.

> In addition, evidence of postsentencing rehabilitation may be highly relevant to several of the § 3553(a) factors that Congress has expressly instructed district courts to consider at sentencing. For

example, evidence of postsentencing rehabilitation may plainly be relevant to "the history and characteristics of the defendant." § 3553(a)(1). Such evidence may also be pertinent to "the need for the sentence imposed" to serve the general purposes of sentencing set forth in § 3553(a)(2)—in particular, to "afford adequate deterrence to criminal conduct," "protect the public from further crimes of the defendant," and "provide the defendant with needed educational or vocational training . . . or other correctional treatment in the most effective manner." §§ 3553(a)(2)(B)-(D). Postsentencing rehabilitation may also critically inform a sentencing judge's overarching duty under § 3553(a) to "impose a sentence sufficient, but not greater than necessary" to comply with the sentencing purposes set forth in § 3553(a)(2).

Justice Sotomayor emphasized that Pepper's post-sentencing rehabilitation was plainly relevant to the § 3553 sentencing factors:

> [T]he extensive evidence of Pepper's rehabilitation since his initial sentencing is clearly relevant to the selection of an appropriate sentence in this case. Most fundamentally, evidence of Pepper's conduct since his release from custody in June 2005 provides the most up-to-date picture of Pepper's "history and characteristics." § 3553(a)(1). At the time of his initial sentencing in 2004, Pepper was a 25–year-old drug addict who was unemployed, estranged from his family, and had recently sold drugs as part of a methamphetamine conspiracy. By the time of his second resentencing in 2009, Pepper had been drug-free for nearly five years, had attended college and achieved high grades, was a top employee at his job slated for a promotion, had re-established a relationship with his father, and was married and supporting his wife's daughter. There is no question that this evidence of Pepper's conduct since his initial sentencing constitutes a critical part of the "history and characteristics" of a defendant that Congress intended sentencing courts to consider. § 3553(a).

> Pepper's postsentencing conduct also sheds light on the likelihood that he will engage in future criminal conduct, a central factor that district courts must assess when imposing sentence. See §§ 3553(a)(2)(B)-(C). As recognized by Pepper's probation officer, Pepper's steady employment, as well as his successful completion of a 500–hour drug treatment program and his drug-free condition, also suggest a diminished need for "educational or vocational training . . . or other correctional treatment." § 3553(a)(2)(D). Finally, Pepper's exemplary postsentencing conduct may be taken as the most accurate indicator of his present purposes and tendencies and significantly to suggest the period of restraint and the kind of discipline that ought to be imposed upon him. Accordingly, evidence of Pepper's postsentencing rehabilitation bears directly on the District Court's overarching duty to "impose a sentence sufficient, but not greater than necessary" to serve the purposes of sentencing. § 3553(a).

In sum, the Court of Appeals' ruling prohibiting the District Court from considering any evidence of Pepper's postsentencing rehabilitation at resentencing conflicts with longstanding principles of federal sentencing law and contravenes Congress' directives in §§ 3661 and 3553(a).

Justice Sotomayor then analyzed—in light of Booker—the sentencing statute which on its terms prevents courts from considering post-sentencing rehabilitation when a sentence is set aside on appeal.

18 U.S.C. § 3742(g)(2) states that when a sentence is set aside on appeal, the district court to which the case is remanded:

> "shall not impose a sentence outside the applicable guidelines range except upon a ground that—
>
> > "(A) was specifically and affirmatively included in the written statement of reasons required by section 3553(c) in connection with the previous sentencing of the defendant prior to the appeal"; and
> >
> > "(B) was held by the court of appeals, in remanding the case, to be a permissible ground of departure."

In operation, * * * § 3742(g)(2) effectively forecloses a resentencing court from considering evidence of a defendant's postsentencing rehabilitation for purposes of imposing a non-Guidelines sentence because, as a practical matter, such evidence did not exist at the time of the prior sentencing. As the Government concedes, however, § 3742(g)(2) is invalid after Booker.

As we have explained, Booker held that where judicial factfinding increases a defendant's applicable Sentencing Guidelines range, treating the Guidelines as mandatory in those circumstances would violate the defendant's Sixth Amendment right to be tried by a jury and to have every element of an offense proved by the Government beyond a reasonable doubt. * * *

To remedy the constitutional problem, we rendered the Guidelines effectively advisory by invalidating two provisions of the SRA: 18 U.S.C. § 3553(b)(1), which generally required sentencing courts to impose a sentence within the applicable Guidelines range, and § 3742(e), which prescribed the standard of appellate review, including de novo review of Guidelines departures. We invalidated these provisions even though we recognized that mandatory application of the Guidelines would not always result in a Sixth Amendment violation. Indeed, although the Government suggested in Booker that we render the Guidelines advisory only in cases in which the Constitution prohibits judicial factfinding, we rejected that two-track proposal, reasoning that "Congress would not have authorized a mandatory system in some cases and a non-mandatory system in others, given the administrative complexities that such a system would create."

We did not expressly mention § 3742(g)(2) in Booker, but the rationale we set forth in that opinion for invalidating §§ 3553(b)(1) and 3742(e) applies equally to § 3742(g)(2). As with those provisions, § 3742(g)(2) requires district courts effectively to treat the Guidelines as mandatory in an entire set of cases. Specifically, § 3742(g)(2) precludes a district court on remand from imposing a sentence "outside the applicable guidelines range" except upon a "ground of departure" that was expressly relied upon by the court at the prior sentencing and upheld by the court of appeals. In circumstances in which the district court did not rely upon such a departure ground at the prior sentencing, § 3742(g)(2) would require the court on remand to impose a sentence within the applicable Guidelines range, thus rendering the Guidelines effectively mandatory. Because in a large set of cases, judicial factfinding will increase the applicable Guidelines range beyond that supported solely by the facts established by the jury verdict (or guilty plea), requiring a sentencing judge on remand to apply the Guidelines range, as § 3742(g)(2) does, will often result in a Sixth Amendment violation for the reasons we explained in Booker. Accordingly, as with the provisions in Booker, the proper remedy here is to invalidate § 3742(g)(2).

* * *

Accordingly, we vacate the Eighth Circuit's judgment in respect to Pepper's sentence and remand the case for resentencing consistent with this opinion.

Justice Breyer wrote a separate opinion concurring in part and in the judgment.

Justice Alito also wrote a separate opinion, concurring in part, concurring in the judgment in part, and dissenting in part. Justice Alito criticized the majority's reliance on Williams as a justification for considering post-sentencing rehabilitation.

Anyone familiar with the history of criminal sentencing in this country cannot fail to see the irony in the Court's praise for the sentencing scheme exemplified by Williams v. New York, 337 U.S. 241 (1949). By the time of the enactment of the Sentencing Reform Act in 1984, this scheme had fallen into widespread disrepute. See, e.g., Mistretta v. United States, 488 U.S. 361, 366 (1989) (noting "[f]undamental and widespread dissatisfaction with the uncertainties and the disparities" of this scheme); S.Rep. No. 98–223, p. 62 (1983) ("The shameful disparity in criminal sentences is a major flaw in the existing criminal justice system"). Under this system, each federal district judge was free to implement his or her individual sentencing philosophy, and therefore the sentence imposed in a particular case often depended heavily on the spin of the wheel that determined the judge to whom the case was assigned. See M. Frankel, Criminal Sentences: Law Without Order 5 (1973) ("[T]he almost wholly unchecked and sweeping powers we give to judges in the fashioning of sentences are terrifying and intolerable for a society that professes devotion to the rule of law'').

Some language in today's opinion reads like a paean to that old regime, and I fear that it may be interpreted as sanctioning a move back toward the system that prevailed prior to 1984. If that occurs, I suspect that the day will come when the irrationality of that system is once again seen, and perhaps then the entire Booker line of cases will be reexamined.

Justice Thomas dissented, basically continuing his objection to the Court's remedial opinion in Booker:

In United States v. Booker, the Court rendered the entire Guidelines scheme advisory, a remedy that was ''far broader than necessary to correct constitutional error.'' Kimbrough v. United States, 552 U.S. 85, 114 (2007) (Thomas, J., dissenting). Because there is ''no principled way to apply the Booker remedy,'' I have explained that it is ''best to apply the statute as written, including 18 U.S.C. § 3553(b), which makes the Guidelines mandatory,'' unless doing so would actually violate the Sixth Amendment.

I would apply the Guidelines as written in this case because doing so would not violate the Sixth Amendment. The constitutional problem arises only when a judge makes a finding that raises the sentence beyond the sentence that could have lawfully been imposed by reference to facts found by the jury or admitted by the defendant. Pepper admitted in his plea agreement to involvement with between 1,500 and 5,000 grams of methamphetamine mixture, which carries a sentence of 10 years to life under 21 U.S.C. § 841(b)(1)(A)(viii). Because Pepper has admitted facts that would support a much longer sentence than the 65 months he received, there is no Sixth Amendment problem in this case.

Justice Kagan took no part in the decision in *Pepper*.

CHAPTER TWELVE

DOUBLE JEOPARDY

■ ■ ■

III. ABORTED PROCEEDINGS

B. MISTRIAL DECLARED OVER DEFENDANT'S OBJECTION

2. Manifest Necessity as a Flexible Test

Page 1516. Add at the end of the section on the Manifest Necessity test

Trial Court's Declaring Mistrial Was Not an Unreasonable Application of Manifest Necessity Standard: Renico v. Lett

In evaluating the following case, it is critical to note that the Court is reviewing a habeas corpus petition. On habeas, as the Court indicates, the standard of review for state court determinations is extremely deferential. [See generally Chapter 13 of the Casebook.] Ask yourself if the Court would have ruled differently on the Double Jeopardy question if the case had been on direct appeal.

RENICO v. LETT

Supreme Court of the United States, 2010
130 S.Ct. 1855

CHIEF JUSTICE ROBERTS **delivered the opinion of the Court**.

This case requires us to review the grant of a writ of habeas corpus to a state prisoner under the Antiterrorism and Effective Death Penalty Act of 1996 (AEDPA), 28 U.S.C. § 2254(d). The District Court in this case issued the writ to respondent Reginald Lett on the ground that his Michigan murder conviction violated the Double Jeopardy Clause of the Constitution, and the U.S. Court of Appeals for the Sixth Circuit affirmed. In doing so, however, these courts misapplied AEDPA's deferential standard of review. Because we conclude that the Michigan Supreme Court's application of federal law was not unreasonable, we reverse.

I

On August 29, 1996, an argument broke out in a Detroit liquor store. The antagonists included Adesoji Latona, a taxi driver; Charles Jones, a passenger who claimed he had been wrongfully ejected from Latona's cab; and Reginald Lett, a friend of Jones's. After the argument began, Lett left the liquor store, retrieved a handgun from another friend outside in the parking lot, and returned to the store. He shot Latona twice, once in the head and once in the chest. Latona died from his wounds shortly thereafter.

Michigan prosecutors charged Lett with first-degree murder and possession of a firearm during the commission of a felony. His trial took place in June 1997. From jury selection to jury instructions the trial took less than nine hours, spread over six different days.

The jury's deliberations began on June 12, 1997, at 3:24 p.m., and ran that day until 4 p.m. After resuming its work the next morning, the jury sent the trial court a note—one of seven it sent out in its two days of deliberations—stating that the jurors had "a concern about our voice levels disturbing any other proceedings that might be going on." Later, the jury sent out another note, asking "What if we can't agree? [M]istrial? [R]etrial? [W]hat?"

* * * [A]t 12:45 p.m. the judge called the jury back into the courtroom, along with the prosecutor and defense counsel. Once the jury was seated, the following exchange took place:

"THE COURT: I received your note asking me what if you can't agree? And I have to conclude from that that that is your situation at this time. So, I'd like to ask the fore-

person to identify themselves, please?

"THE FOREPERSON: [Identified herself.]

"THE COURT: Okay, thank you. All right. I need to ask you if the jury is deadlocked; in other words, is there a disagreement as to the verdict?

"THE FOREPERSON: Yes, there is.

"THE COURT: All right. Do you believe that it is hopelessly deadlocked?

"THE FOREPERSON: The majority of us don't believe that—

"THE COURT: (Interposing) Don't say what you're going to say, okay?

"THE FOREPERSON: Oh, I'm sorry.

"THE COURT: I don't want to know what your verdict might be, or how the split is, or any of that. Thank you. Okay? Are you going to reach a unanimous verdict, or not?

"THE FOREPERSON: (No response)

"THE COURT: Yes or no?

"THE FOREPERSON: No, Judge."

The judge then declared a mistrial, dismissed the jury, and scheduled a new trial for later that year. Neither the prosecutor nor Lett's attorney made any objection.

Lett's second trial was held before a different judge and jury in November 1997. This time, the jury was able to reach a unanimous verdict-that Lett was guilty of second-degree murder-after deliberating for only 3 hours and 15 minutes.

Lett appealed his conviction to the Michigan Court of Appeals. He argued that the judge in his first trial had announced a mistrial without any manifest necessity for doing so. Because the mistrial was an error, Lett maintained, the State was barred by the Double Jeopardy Clause of the U.S. Constitution from trying him a second time. The Michigan Court of Appeals agreed with Lett and reversed his conviction.

The State appealed to the Michigan Supreme Court, which reversed the Court of Appeals. The court explained that under our decision in United States v. Perez, 9 Wheat. 579 (1824), a defendant may be retried following the discharge of a deadlocked jury, even if the discharge occurs without the defendant's consent. There is no Double Jeopardy Clause violation in such circumstances, it noted, so long as the trial court exercised its "sound discretion" in concluding that the jury was deadlocked and thus that there was a "manifest necessity" for a mistrial. The court further observed that, under our decision in Arizona v. Washington, 434 U.S. 497 (1978), an appellate court must generally defer to a trial judge's determination that a deadlock has been reached.

After setting forth the applicable law, the Michigan Supreme Court determined that the judge at Lett's first trial had not abused her discretion in declaring the mistrial. The court cited the facts that the jury "had deliberated for at least four hours following a relatively short, and far from complex, trial," that the jury had sent out several notes, "including one that appears to indicate that its discussions may have been particularly heated," and—"[m]ost important"—that the jury foreperson expressly stated that the jury was not going to reach a verdict. Ibid.

Lett petitioned for a federal writ of habeas corpus. Again he argued that the trial court's declaration of a mis-

trial constituted an abuse of discretion because there was no manifest necessity to cut short the jury's deliberations. He further contended that the Michigan Supreme Court's rejection of his double jeopardy claim amounted to "an unreasonable application of . . . clearly established Federal law, as determined by the Supreme Court of the United States," and thus that he was not barred by AEDPA, 28 U.S.C. § 2254(d)(1), from obtaining federal habeas relief. The District Court agreed and granted the writ. On appeal, a divided panel of the U.S. Court of Appeals for the Sixth Circuit affirmed. The State petitioned for review in our Court, and we granted certiorari.

II

It is important at the outset to define the question before us. That question is not whether the trial judge should have declared a mistrial. It is not even whether it was an abuse of discretion for her to have done so—the applicable standard on direct review. The question under AEDPA is instead whether the determination of the Michigan Supreme Court that there was no abuse of discretion was "an unreasonable application of . . . clearly established Federal law." § 2254(d)(1).

We have explained that "an *unreasonable* application of federal law is different from an *incorrect* application of federal law." Williams v. Taylor, 529 U.S. 362, 410 (2000). * * * AEDPA * * * imposes a highly deferential standard for evaluating state-court rulings, and demands that state-court decisions be given the benefit of the doubt.

The "clearly established Federal law" in this area is largely undisputed. In *Perez*, we held that when a judge discharges a jury on the grounds that the jury cannot reach a verdict, the Double Jeopardy Clause does not bar a new trial for the defendant before a new jury. We explained that trial judges may declare a mistrial "whenever, in their opinion, taking all the circumstances into consideration, there is a manifest necessity" for doing so. The decision to declare a mistrial is left to the "sound discretion" of the judge, but "the power ought to be used with the greatest caution, under urgent circumstances, and for very plain and obvious causes." Ibid.

Since *Perez*, we have clarified that the "manifest necessity" standard "cannot be interpreted literally," and that a mistrial is appropriate when there is a " 'high degree' " of necessity. *Washington*. * * *

In particular, "[t]he trial judge's decision to declare a mistrial when he considers the jury deadlocked is . . . accorded great deference by a reviewing court." *Washington*. * * *

The reasons for allowing the trial judge to exercise broad discretion are especially compelling in cases involving a potentially deadlocked jury. There, the justification for deference is that the trial court is in the best position to assess all the factors which must be considered in making a necessarily discretionary determination whether the jury will be able to reach a just verdict if it continues to deliberate. In the absence of such deference, trial judges might otherwise employ coercive means to break the apparent deadlock, thereby creating a significant risk that a verdict may result from pressures inherent in the situation rather than the considered judgment of all the jurors.

This is not to say that we grant *absolute* deference to trial judges in

this context. *Perez* itself noted that the judge's exercise of discretion must be "sound," and we have made clear that "[i]f the record reveals that the trial judge has failed to exercise the 'sound discretion' entrusted to him, the reason for such deference by an appellate court disappears." *Washington*. Thus "if the trial judge acts for reasons completely unrelated to the trial problem which purports to be the basis for the mistrial ruling, close appellate scrutiny is appropriate." Ibid. Similarly, if a trial judge acts irrationally or irresponsibly, his action cannot be condoned.

We have expressly declined to require the "mechanical application" of any "rigid formula" when trial judges decide whether jury deadlock warrants a mistrial. Wade v. Hunter, 336 U.S. 684, 691 (1949). We have also explicitly held that a trial judge declaring a mistrial is not required to make explicit findings of "manifest necessity" nor to "articulate on the record all the factors which informed the deliberate exercise of his discretion." *Washington*. And we have never required a trial judge, before declaring a mistrial based on jury deadlock, to force the jury to deliberate for a minimum period of time, to question the jurors individually, to consult with (or obtain the consent of) either the prosecutor or defense counsel, to issue a supplemental jury instruction, or to consider any other means of breaking the impasse. In 1981, then-Justice Rehnquist noted that this Court had never "overturned a trial court's declaration of a mistrial after a jury was unable to reach a verdict on the ground that the 'manifest necessity' standard had not been met." Winston v. Moore, 452 U.S. 944, 947 (opinion dissenting from denial of certiorari). The same remains true today, nearly 30 years later.

The legal standard applied by the Michigan Supreme Court in this case was whether there was an abuse of the "broad discretion" reserved to the trial judge. This type of general standard triggers another consideration under AEDPA. When assessing whether a state court's application of federal law is unreasonable, the range of reasonable judgment can depend in part on the nature of the relevant rule that the state court must apply. Because AEDPA authorizes federal courts to grant relief only when state courts act unreasonably, it follows that the more general the rule at issue—and thus the greater the potential for reasoned disagreement among fair-minded judges—the more leeway [state] courts have in reaching outcomes in case-by-case determinations.

III

In light of all the foregoing, the Michigan Supreme Court's decision in this case was not unreasonable under AEDPA, and the decision of the Court of Appeals to grant Lett a writ of habeas corpus must be reversed.

The Michigan Supreme Court's adjudication involved a straightforward application of our longstanding precedents to the facts of Lett's case. The court cited our own double jeopardy cases * * * elaborating upon the "manifest necessity" standard for granting a mistrial and noting the broad deference that appellate courts must give trial judges in deciding whether that standard has been met in any given case. It then applied those precedents to the particular facts before it and found no abuse of discretion, especially in light of the length of deliberations after a short

and uncomplicated trial, the jury notes suggesting heated discussions and asking what would happen "if we can't agree," and—"[m]ost important"—"the fact that the jury foreperson expressly stated that the jury was not going to reach a verdict." In these circumstances, it was reasonable for the Michigan Supreme Court to determine that the trial judge had exercised sound discretion in declaring a mistrial.

The Court of Appeals for the Sixth Circuit concluded otherwise. It did not contest the Michigan Supreme Court's description of the objective facts, but disagreed with the inferences to be drawn from them. For example, it speculated that the trial judge may have misinterpreted the jury's notes as signs of discord and deadlock when, read literally, they expressly stated no such thing. It further determined that the judge's brief colloquy with the foreperson may have wrongly implied a false equivalence between "mere disagreement" and "genuine deadlock," and may have given rise to "inappropriate pressure" on her to say that the jury would be unable to reach a verdict. The trial judge's mistakes were so egregious, in the Court of Appeals' view, that the Michigan Supreme Court's opinion finding no abuse of discretion was not only wrong but objectively unreasonable.

The Court of Appeals' interpretation of the trial record is not implausible. * * * After all, the jury only deliberated for four hours, its notes were arguably ambiguous, the trial judge's initial question to the foreperson was imprecise, and the judge neither asked for elaboration of the foreperson's answers nor took any other measures to confirm the foreperson's prediction that a unanimous verdict would not be reached.

But other reasonable interpretations of the record are also possible. Lett's trial was not complex, and there is no reason that the jury would necessarily have needed more than a few hours to deliberate over his guilt. The notes the jury sent to the judge certainly could be read as reflecting substantial disagreement, even if they did not say so outright. Most important, the foreperson expressly told the judge—in response to her unambiguous question "Are you going to reach a unanimous verdict, or not?"—that the jury would be unable to agree.

Given the foregoing facts, the Michigan Supreme Court's decision upholding the trial judge's exercise of discretion—while not necessarily correct—was not objectively unreasonable. Not only are there a number of plausible ways to interpret the record of Lett's trial, but the standard applied by the Michigan Supreme Court—whether the judge exercised sound discretion—is a general one, to which there is no plainly correct or incorrect answer in this case. The Court of Appeals' ruling in Lett's favor failed to grant the Michigan courts the dual layers of deference required by AEDPA and our double jeopardy precedents.[3]

* * *

AEDPA prevents defendants—and federal courts—from using federal habeas corpus review as a vehicle to second-guess the reasonable decisions of state courts. Whether or not the Michigan Supreme Court's opinion reinstating Lett's conviction in this case was correct, it was clearly

not unreasonable. The judgment of the Court of Appeals is reversed, and the case is remanded for further proceedings consistent with this opinion.

JUSTICE STEVENS, with whom JUSTICE SOTOMAYOR joins, and with whom JUSTICE BREYER joins as to Parts I and II, dissenting.

* * *

I

No one disputes that a genuinely deadlocked jury is the classic basis for declaring a mistrial or that such declaration, under our doctrine, does not preclude reprosecution; what is disputed in this case is whether the trial judge took adequate care to ensure the jury was genuinely deadlocked. A long line of precedents from this Court establishes the governing legal principles for resolving this question. Although the Court acknowledges these precedents, it minimizes the heavy burden we have placed on trial courts.

* * *

[W]e have repeatedly reaffirmed that the power to discharge the jury prior to verdict should be reserved for "extraordinary and striking circumstances," *Downum v. United States*, 372 U.S. 734, 736 (1963); that the trial judge may not take this "weighty" step, *Somerville*, unless and until he has "scrupulous[ly]" assessed the situation and "take[n] care to assure himself that [it] warrants action on his part foreclosing the defendant from a poten-

---

3. It is not necessary for us to decide whether the Michigan Supreme Court's decision—or, for that matter, the trial judge's declaration of a mistrial—was right or wrong. The latter question, in particular, is a close one. As Lett points out, at a hearing before the Michigan Court of Appeals, the state prosecutor

expressed the view that the judge had in fact erred in dismissing the jury and declaring a mistrial. The Michigan Supreme Court declined to accept this confession of error, and in any event-for the reasons we have explained-whether the trial judge was right or wrong is not the pertinent question under AEDPA.

tially favorable judgment by the tribunal,'' United States v. Jorn, 400 U.S. 470, 485; that, to exercise sound discretion, the judge may not act ''irrationally,'' ''irresponsibly,'' or ''precipitately'' but must instead act ''deliberately'' and ''careful[ly],'' *Washington*; and that, in view of ''the elusive nature of the problem,'' mechanical rules are no substitute in the double jeopardy mistrial context for the sensitive application of general standards, *Jorn*. * * *

As the Court emphasizes, we have also repeatedly reaffirmed that trial judges have considerable leeway in determining whether the jury is deadlocked, that they are not bound to use specific procedures or to make specific findings, and that reviewing courts must accord broad deference to their decisions. But the reviewing court still has an important role to play; the application of deference ''does not, of course, end the inquiry.'' *Washington*. ''In order to ensure that [the defendant's constitutional] interest is adequately protected, reviewing courts have an obligation to satisfy themselves that, in the words of Mr. Justice Story, the trial judge exercised 'sound discretion' in declaring a mistrial.'' Ibid. ''If the record reveals that the trial judge has failed to exercise the 'sound discretion' entrusted to him, the reason for . . . deference by an appellate court disappears.'' Id. * * *

* * *

II

The Court accurately describes the events leading up to this trial judge's declaration of mistrial, but it glides too quickly over a number of details that, taken together, show her decisionmaking was neither careful nor well considered. If the ''manifest necessity'' and ''sound discretion'' standards are to have any force, we must demand more from our trial courts.

* * *

At 12:45 p.m., the trial judge initiated a colloquy with the foreperson that concluded in the mistrial declaration. Even accounting for the imprecision of oral communication, the judge made an inordinate number of logical and legal missteps during this short exchange. It does not take much exegetical skill to spot them.

The judge began by stating: '' 'I received your note asking me what if you can't agree? And I have to conclude from that that that is your situation at this time.' '' Ante, at ___. This conclusion was a non sequitur. The note asked what would happen if the jury could not agree; it gave no indication that the jury had already reached an irrevocable impasse. The judge ignored the request for information that the note actually contained. Instead, she announced that deadlock was the jury's '' 'situation at this time,' '' thereby prejudging the question she had ostensibly summoned the foreperson to probe: namely, whether the jury was in fact deadlocked.

The judge continued: ''I need to ask you if the jury is deadlocked; in other words, is there a disagreement as to the verdict?'' As the Federal Court of Appeals observed, this question ''improperly conflated deadlock with mere disagreement.'' * * * Disagreement among jurors is perfectly normal and does not come close to approaching the ''imperious necessity'' we have required for their discharge. Downum, 372 U.S., at 736.

The trial judge then modulated her inquiry: ''Do you believe [the jury] is hopelessly deadlocked?'' The foreperson was in the midst of replying, ''The majority of us don't believe that—," when the judge appears to have cut her off. One cannot fault the trial judge for wanting to preserve the secrecy of jury deliberations, but two aspects of the foreperson's truncated reply are notable. First, it tends to show that the foreperson did not feel prepared to declare definitively that the jury was hopelessly deadlocked. If she had been so prepared, then it is hard to see why she would begin her response with a descriptive account of the "majority" viewpoint.

Second, the foreperson's reply suggests the jury may have been leaning toward acquittal. Admittedly, this is crude speculation, but it is entirely possible that the foreperson was in the process of saying, "The majority of us don't believe that he's guilty." Or: "The majority of us don't believe that there is sufficient evidence to prove one of the counts." These possibilities are, I submit, linguistically more probable than something like the following: "The majority of us don't believe that Lett is guilty, whereas a minority of us believe that he is—and we are hopelessly deadlocked on the matter." And they are logically far more probable than something along the lines of, "The majority of us don't believe that we will ever be able to reach a verdict," as the foreperson had been given no opportunity to poll her colleagues on this point. Yet only such implausible endings could have supported a conclusion that it was manifestly necessary to discharge the jury.

The judge then steered the conversation back to the issue of deadlock, asking: "Are you going to reach a unanimous verdict, or not?" After the foreperson hesitated, the judge persisted: "Yes or no?" The foreperson replied: "No, Judge." Ibid. Two aspects of this interchange are also notable. First, the judge's question,

though "very direct," was "actually rather ambiguous," because it gave the foreperson no temporal or legal context within which to understand what was being asked. The foreperson could have easily thought the judge meant, "Are you going to reach a unanimous verdict in the next hour?" or "before the lunch recess?" or "by the end of the day?" Even if the foreperson assumed no time constraint, she could have easily thought the judge meant, "Are you, in your estimation, more likely than not to reach a unanimous verdict?" An affirmative answer to that question would likewise fall far short of manifest necessity.

Second, the foreperson's hesitation suggests a lack of confidence in her position. That alone ought to have called into question the propriety of a mistrial order. * * * Most of the time when we worry about judicial coercion of juries, we worry about judges pressuring them, in the common-law manner, to keep deliberating until they return a verdict they may not otherwise have chosen. This judge exerted pressure so as to prevent the jury from reaching any verdict at all. In so doing, she cut off deliberations well before the point when it was clear they would no longer be fruitful. Recall that prior to summoning the foreperson for their colloquy, the trial judge gave her no opportunity to consult with the other jurors on the matter that would be discussed. So, the foreperson had no solid basis for estimating the likelihood of deadlock. Recall, as well, that almost immediately after sending the judge a note asking what would happen if they disagreed, the jury sent a note asking about lunch. Plainly, this was a group that was prepared to go on with its work.

The judge then declared a mistrial on the spot. Her entire exchange with the foreperson took three minutes, from 12:45 p.m. to 12:48 p.m. The entire jury deliberations took roughly four hours. The judge gave the parties no opportunity to comment on the foreperson's remarks, much less on the question of mistrial. Just as soon as the judge declared a mistrial, she set a new pretrial date, discharged the jury, and concluded proceedings. By 12:50 p.m., everyone was free to take off for the weekend.

In addition to the remarkable haste * * * with which she acted, it is remarkable what the trial judge did not do. Never did the trial judge consider alternatives or otherwise provide evidence that she exercised sound discretion. For example, the judge did not poll the jurors, give an instruction ordering further deliberations, query defense counsel about his thoughts on continued deliberations, or indicate on the record why a mistrial declaration was necessary. Nor did the judge invite any argument or input from the prosecutor, make any findings of fact or provide any statements illuminating her thought process, follow up on the foreperson's final response, or give any evident consideration to the ends of public justice or the balance between the defendant's rights and the State's interests. * * * The judge may not have had a constitutional obligation to take any one of the aforementioned measures, but she did have an obligation to exercise sound discretion and thus to assure herself that the situation warranted action on her part foreclosing the defendant from a potentially favorable judgment by the tribunal.

Add all these factors up, and I fail to see how the trial judge exercised anything resembling "sound discre-

tion" in declaring a mistrial, as we have defined that term. Indeed, I fail to see how a record could disclose much less evidence of sound decisionmaking. Within the realm of realistic, nonpretextual possibilities, this mistrial declaration was about as precipitate as one is liable to find. Despite the multitude of cases involving hung-jury mistrials that have arisen over the years, neither petitioner nor the Court has been able to identify any in which such abrupt judicial action has been upheld. Even the prosecutor felt compelled to acknowledge that the trial court's decision to discharge the jury "clearly was error."

The Michigan Supreme Court's contrary conclusion was unreasonable. * * * It collapses entirely under the weight of the many defects in the trial court's process, virtually all of which the court either overlooked or discounted.

The unreasonableness of the Michigan Supreme Court's decision is highlighted by the decisions of the three other courts that have addressed Lett's double jeopardy claim, each of which ruled in his favor, as well as the dissent filed by two Michigan Supreme Court Justices and the opinion of the State's own prosecutor. This Court's decision unfortunately compounds the deleterious consequences of the Michigan Supreme Court's ruling. Although the trial judge's decision is entitled to great deference, it is not the place of a reviewing court to extract factoids from the record in an attempt to salvage a bad decision.

III

The Court does not really try to vindicate the Michigan Supreme Court on the merits, but instead ascribes today's outcome to the Antiterrorism and Effective Death Penalty Act of 1996 (AEDPA). The foregoing analysis shows why the Michigan Supreme Court's ruling cannot be saved by 28 U.S.C. § 2254(d)(1), however construed. That ruling was not only incorrect but also unreasonable by any fair measure. * * *

[T]he fact that the substantive legal standard applied by the state court "is a general one" has no bearing on the standard of review. * * * General standards are no less binding law than discrete rules.

* * *

I do not agree that AEDPA authorizes "the dual layers of deference" the Court has utilized in this case. There is little doubt that AEDPA directs federal courts to attend to every state-court judgment with utmost care. But the statute never uses the term "deference," and the legislative history makes clear that Congress meant to preserve robust federal-court review. Any attempt to prevent federal courts from exercising independent review of habeas applications would have been a radical reform of dubious constitutionality, and Congress would have spoken with much greater clarity if that had been its intent.

So on two levels, it is absolutely necessary for us to decide whether the Michigan Supreme Court's decision was right or wrong. If a federal judge were firmly convinced that such a decision were wrong, then in my view not only would he have no statutory duty to uphold it, but he might also have a constitutional obligation to reverse it. And regardless of how one conceptualizes the distinction between an incorrect and an "unreasonable" state-court ruling under § 2254(d)(1), one must always determine whether the ruling was wrong to be able to test the magnitude of any error. Substantive and methodological considerations compel federal courts to give habeas claims a full, independent review-and then to decide for themselves. Even under AEDPA, there is no escaping the burden of judgment.

———

In this case, Reginald Lett's constitutional rights were violated when the trial court terminated his first trial without adequate justification and he was subsequently prosecuted for the same offense. The majority does not appear to dispute this point, but it nevertheless denies Lett relief by applying a level of deference to the state court's ruling that effectively effaces the role of the federal courts. Nothing one will find in the United States Code or the United States Reports requires us to turn a blind eye to this manifestly unlawful conviction.

I respectfully dissent.

Chapter Thirteen

Post-Conviction Challenges

■ ■ ■

II. GROUNDS FOR DIRECT ATTACKS ON A CONVICTION

A. INSUFFICIENT EVIDENCE

2. The Standard of Appellate Review of Sufficiency of the Evidence

Page 1585. Add after the section on Wright v. West.

*Court Reviewing Sufficiency of the Evidence Must Consider
All Evidence Admitted at Trial, Even If Erroneously:
McDaniel v. Brown*

McDANIEL v. BROWN

Supreme Court of the United States, 2010
130 S.Ct. 665

Per Curiam.

In Jackson v. Virginia, 443 U.S. 307 (1979), we held that a state prisoner is entitled to habeas corpus relief if a federal judge finds that "upon the record evidence adduced at the trial no rational trier of fact could have found proof of guilt beyond a reasonable doubt." A Nevada jury convicted respondent of rape; the evidence presented included DNA evidence matching respondent's DNA profile. Nevertheless, relying upon a report prepared by a DNA expert over 11 years after the trial, the Federal District Court applied the *Jackson* standard and granted the writ. A divided Court of Appeals affirmed. We granted certiorari to consider whether those courts misapplied *Jackson*. Because the trial record includes both the DNA evidence and other convincing evidence of guilt, we conclude that they clearly did.

I

Around 1 a.m. on January 29, 1994, 9–year-old Jane Doe was brutally raped in the bedroom of her trailer. Respondent Troy Brown was convicted of the crime. During and since his trial, respondent has steadfastly maintained his innocence. He was, however, admittedly intoxicated

212

when the crime occurred, and after he awoke on the following morning he told a friend "he wished that he could remember what did go on or what went on."

Troy and his brother Travis resided near Jane Doe in the same trailer park. Their brother Trent and his wife Raquel lived in the park as well, in a trailer across the street from Jane Doe's. Both Troy and Trent were acquainted with Jane Doe's family; Troy had visited Jane Doe's trailer several times. Jane did not know Travis. The evening of the attack, Jane's mother, Pam, took Jane to Raquel and Trent's trailer to babysit while the three adults went out for about an hour. Raquel and Trent returned at about 7:30 p.m. and took Jane home at about 9:30 p.m. Pam stayed out and ended up drinking and playing pool with Troy at a nearby bar called the Peacock Lounge. Troy knew that Jane and her 4–year-old sister were home alone because he answered the phone at the bar when Jane called for her mother earlier that evening.

Troy consumed at least 10 shots of vodka followed by beer chasers, and was so drunk that he vomited on himself while he was walking home after leaving the Peacock at about 12:15 a.m. Jane called her mother to report the rape at approximately 1 a.m. Although it would have taken a sober man less than 15 minutes to walk home, Troy did not arrive at his trailer until about 1:30 a.m. He was wearing dark jeans, a cowboy hat, a black satin jacket, and boots. Two witnesses saw a man dressed in dark jeans, a cowboy hat, and a black satin jacket stumbling in the road between the two trailers shortly after 1 a.m.

The bedroom where the rape occurred was dark, and Jane was unable to conclusively identify her assailant. When asked whom he reminded her of, she mentioned both Troy and his brother Trent. Several days after the rape, she identified a man she saw on television (Troy) as her assailant*668 but then stated that the man who had sent flowers attacked her. It was Trent and Raquel who had sent her flowers, not Troy. She was unable to identify Troy as her assailant out of a photo lineup, and she could not identify her assailant at trial. The night of the rape, however, she said her attacker was wearing dark jeans, a black jacket with a zipper, boots, and a watch. She also vividly remembered that the man "stunk real, real bad" of "cologne, or some beer or puke or something."

Some evidence besides Jane's inconsistent identification did not inculpate Troy. Jane testified that she thought she had bitten her assailant, but Troy did not have any bite marks on his hands when examined by a police officer approximately four hours after the attack. Jane stated that her assailant's jacket had a zipper (Troy's did not) and that he wore a watch (Troy claimed he did not). Additionally, there was conflicting testimony as to when Troy left the Peacock and when Pam received Jane's call reporting the rape. The witnesses who saw a man stumbling between the two trailers reported a bright green logo on the back of the jacket, but Troy's jacket had a yellow and orange logo. Finally, because Jane thought she had left a night light on when she went to bed, the police suspected the assailant had turned off the light. The only usable fingerprint taken from the light did not match Troy's and the police did not find Troy's fingerprints in the trailer.

Other physical evidence, however, pointed to Troy. The police recovered semen from Jane's underwear and from the rape kit. The State's expert, Renee Romero, tested the former and determined that the DNA matched Troy's and that the probability another person from the general population would share the same DNA (the "random match probability") was only 1 in 3,000,000. Troy's counsel did not call his own DNA expert at trial, although he consulted with an expert in advance who found no problems with Romero's test procedures. At some time before sentencing, Troy's family had additional DNA testing done. That testing showed semen taken from the rape kit matched Troy's DNA, with a random match probability of 1 in 10,000.

[Brown was convicted. His attack on the sufficiency of the evidence was rejected by the state courts and state collateral relief was also denied.]

Respondent thereafter filed this federal habeas petition, claiming there was insufficient evidence to convict him on the sexual assault charges and that the Nevada Supreme Court's rejection of his claim was both contrary to, and an unreasonable application of, *Jackson*. He did not bring a typical *Jackson* claim, however. Rather than argue that the totality of the evidence admitted against him at trial was constitutionally insufficient, he argued that some of the evidence should be excluded from the *Jackson* analysis. In particular, he argued that Romero's testimony related to the DNA evidence was inaccurate and unreliable in two primary respects: Romero mischaracterized the random match probability and misstated the probability of a DNA match among his brothers. Absent that testimony, he contended,

there was insufficient evidence to convict him.

In support of his claim regarding the accuracy of Romero's testimony, respondent submitted a report prepared by Laurence Mueller, a professor in ecology and evolutionary biology (Mueller Report). The District Court supplemented the record with the Mueller Report, even though it was not presented to any state court, because "the thesis of the report was argued during post-conviction."

Relying upon the Mueller Report, the District Court set aside the "unreliable DNA testimony" and held that without the DNA evidence "a reasonable doubt would exist in the mind of any rational trier of fact." The court granted respondent habeas relief on his *Jackson* claim.

The Ninth Circuit affirmed. The court held the Nevada Supreme Court had unreasonably applied *Jackson*. See 28 U.S.C. § 2254(d)(1). The Court of Appeals first reasoned "the admission of Romero's unreliable and misleading testimony violated Troy's due process rights," so the District Court was correct to exclude it. It then "weighed the sufficiency of the remaining evidence," including the District Court's "catalogu[e] [of] the numerous inconsistencies that would raise a reasonable doubt as to Troy's guilt in the mind of any rational juror." In light of the "stark" conflicts in the evidence and the State's concession that there was insufficient evidence absent the DNA evidence, the court held it was objectively unreasonable for the Nevada Supreme Court to reject respondent's insufficiency-of-the-evidence claim.

We granted certiorari to consider two questions: the proper standard of review for a *Jackson* claim on federal habeas, and whether such a claim may rely upon evidence outside the trial record that goes to the reliability of trial evidence.

II

Respondent's claim has now crystallized into a claim about the import of two specific inaccuracies in the testimony related to the DNA evidence, as indicated by the Mueller Report. The Mueller Report does not challenge Romero's qualifications as an expert or the validity of any of the tests that she performed. Mueller instead contends that Romero committed the so-called "prosecutor's fallacy" and that she underestimated the probability of a DNA match between respondent and one of his brothers.

The prosecutor's fallacy is the assumption that the random match probability is the same as the probability that the defendant was not the source of the DNA sample. In other words, if a juror is told the probability a member of the general population would share the same DNA is 1 in 10,000 (random match probability), and he takes that to mean there is only a 1 in 10,000 chance that someone other than the defendant is the source of the DNA found at the crime scene (source probability), then he has succumbed to the prosecutor's fallacy. It is further error to equate source probability with probability of guilt, unless there is no explanation other than guilt for a person to be the source of crime-scene DNA. This faulty reasoning may result in an erroneous statement that, based on a random match probability of 1 in 10,000, there is a .01% chance the defendant is innocent or a 99.99% chance the defendant is guilty.

The Mueller Report does not dispute Romero's opinion that only 1 in 3,000,000 people would have the same DNA profile as the rapist. Mueller correctly points out, however, that some of Romero's testimony-as well as the prosecutor's argument-suggested that the evidence also established that there was only a .000033% chance that respondent was innocent. The State concedes as much. For example, the prosecutor argued at closing the jury could be "99.999967 percent sure" in this case. And when the prosecutor asked Romero, in a classic example of erroneously equating source probability with random match probability, whether "it [would] be fair to say . . . that the chances that the DNA found in the panties-the semen in the panties-and the blood sample, the likelihood that it is not Troy Brown would be .000033," id., at 460, Romero ultimately agreed that it was "not inaccurate" to state it that way.

Looking at Romero's testimony as a whole, though, she also indicated that she was merely accepting the mathematical equivalence between 1 in 3,000,000 and the percentage figure. At the end of the colloquy about percentages, she answered affirmatively the court's question whether the percentage was "the same math just expressed differently." She pointed out that the probability a brother would match was greater than the random match probability, which also indicated to the jury that the random match probability is not the same as the likelihood that someone other than Troy was the source of the DNA.

The Mueller Report identifies a second error in Romero's testimony: her estimate of the probability that one or more of Troy's brothers' DNA would match. Romero testified there was a 1 in 6,500 (or .02%) probability that one brother would share the same DNA with another. When asked whether "that change[s] at all with two brothers," she answered no. According to Mueller, Romero's analysis was misleading in two respects. First, she used an assumption regarding the parents under which siblings have the lowest chance of matching that is biologically possible, but even under this stingy assumption she reported the chance of two brothers matching (1 in 6,500) as much lower than it is (1 in 1,024 under her assumption). Second, using the assumptions Mueller finds more appropriate, the probability of a single sibling matching respondent is 1 in 263, the probability that among two brothers one or more would match is 1 in 132, and among four brothers it is 1 in 66.

In sum, the two inaccuracies upon which this case turns are testimony equating random match probability with source probability, and an underestimate of the likelihood that one of Troy's brothers would also match the DNA left at the scene.

III

Although we granted certiorari to review respondent's *Jackson* claim, the parties now agree that the Court of Appeals' resolution of his claim under *Jackson* was in error. Indeed, respondent argues the Court of Appeals did not decide his case under *Jackson* at all, but instead resolved the question whether admission of Romero's inaccurate testimony rendered his trial fundamentally unfair and then applied *Jackson* to determine whether that error was harmless.

Although both petitioners and respondent are now aligned on the same side of the questions presented for our review, the case is not moot because "the parties continue to seek different relief" from this Court.
* * *

Respondent no longer argues it was proper for the District Court to admit the Mueller Report for the purpose of evaluating his *Jackson* claim, and concedes the "purpose of a *Jackson* analysis is to determine whether the jury acted in a rational manner in returning a guilty verdict based on the evidence before it, not whether improper evidence violated due process." There has been no suggestion that the evidence adduced at trial was insufficient to convict unless some of it was excluded. Respondent's concession thus disposes of his *Jackson* claim. The concession is also clearly correct. An appellate court's reversal for insufficiency of the evidence is in effect a determination that the government's case against the defendant was so lacking that the trial court should have entered a judgment of acquittal. Because reversal for insufficiency of the evidence is equivalent to a judgment of acquittal, such a reversal bars a retrial. See Burks v. United States, 437 U.S. 1 (1978). To make the analogy complete between a reversal for insufficiency of the evidence and the trial court's granting a judgment of acquittal, a reviewing court must consider all of the evidence admitted by the trial court, regardless whether that evidence was admitted erroneously.

Respondent therefore correctly concedes that a reviewing court must consider all of the evidence admitted at trial when considering a *Jackson* claim. Even if we set that concession aside, however, and assume that the Court of Appeals could have considered the Mueller Report in the context of a *Jackson* claim, the court made an egregious error in concluding the Nevada Supreme Court's rejection of respondent's insufficiency-of-the-evidence claim "involved an unreasonable application of . . . clearly established Federal law," 28 U.S.C. § 2254(d)(1).

Even if the Court of Appeals could have considered it, the Mueller Report provided no warrant for entirely excluding the DNA evidence or Romero's testimony from that court's consideration. The Report did not contest that the DNA evidence matched Troy. That DNA evidence remains powerful inculpatory evidence even though the State concedes Romero overstated its probative value by failing to dispel the prosecutor's fallacy. And Mueller's claim that Romero used faulty assumptions and underestimated the probability of a DNA match between brothers indicates that two experts do not agree with one another, not that Romero's estimates were unreliable.

Mueller's opinion that "the chance that among four brothers one or more would match is 1 in 66" is substantially different from Romero's estimate of a 1 in 6,500 chance that one brother would match. But even if Romero's estimate is wrong, our confidence in the jury verdict is not undermined. First, the estimate that is more pertinent to this case is 1 in 132—the probability of a match among two brothers—because two of Troy's four brothers lived in Utah. Second, although Jane Doe mentioned Trent as her assailant, and Travis lived in a nearby trailer, the evidence indicates that both (unlike Troy) were sober and went to bed early on the night of the crime. Even under Mueller's odds, a rational jury could consider the DNA evidence to be powerful evidence of guilt.

Furthermore, the Court of Appeals' discussion of the non-DNA evidence

departed from the deferential review that *Jackson* and § 2254(d)(1) demand. A federal habeas court can only set aside a state-court decision as "an unreasonable application of . . . clearly established Federal law," § 2254(d)(1), if the state court's application of that law is "objectively unreasonable," Williams v. Taylor, 529 U.S. 362, 409 (2000). And *Jackson* requires a reviewing court to review the evidence "in the light most favorable to the prosecution.". Expressed more fully, this means a reviewing court "faced with a record of historical facts that supports conflicting inferences must presume—even if it does not affirmatively appear in the record—that the trier of fact resolved any such conflicts in favor of the prosecution, and must defer to that resolution." See also Schlup v. Delo, 513 U.S. 298, 330 (1995) ("The *Jackson* standard . . . looks to whether there is sufficient evidence which, if credited, could support the conviction"). The Court of Appeals acknowledged that it must review the evidence in the light most favorable to the prosecution, but the court's recitation of inconsistencies in the testimony shows it failed to do that.

For example, the court highlights conflicting testimony regarding when Troy left the Peacock. It is true that if a juror were to accept the testimony of one bartender that Troy left the bar at 1:30 a.m., then Troy would have left the bar after the attack occurred. Yet the jury could have credited a different bartender's testimony that Troy left the Peacock at around 12:15 a.m. Resolving the conflict in favor of the prosecution, the jury must have found that Troy left the bar in time to be the assailant. It is undisputed that Troy washed his clothes immediately upon returning home. The court notes this is "plausibly consistent with him being the assailant" but also that he provided an alternative reason for washing his clothes. Viewed in the light most favorable to the prosecution, the evidence supports an inference that Troy washed the clothes immediately to clean blood from them.

* * * In sum, the Court of Appeals' analysis failed to preserve "the factfinder's role as weigher of the evidence" by reviewing "all of the evidence . . . in the light most favorable to the prosecution," *Jackson*, and it further erred in finding that the Nevada Supreme Court's resolution of the *Jackson* claim was objectively unreasonable.

IV

* * *

We have stated before that "DNA testing can provide powerful new evidence unlike anything known before." District Attorney's Office for Third Judicial Dist. v. Osborne, 129 S.Ct. 2308, 2316 (2009). Given the persuasiveness of such evidence in the eyes of the jury, it is important that it be presented in a fair and reliable manner. The State acknowledges that Romero committed the prosecutor's fallacy, and the Mueller Report suggests that Romero's testimony may have been inaccurate regarding the likelihood of a match with one of respondent's brothers. Regardless, ample DNA and non-DNA evidence in the record adduced at trial supported the jury's guilty verdict under *Jackson* * * * . * * * Accordingly, the judgment of the Court of Appeals is reversed, and the case is remanded for further proceedings consistent with this opinion.

[The concurring opinion by JUSTICE THOMAS, joined by JUSTICE SCALIA, is omitted.]

D. THE EFFECT OF AN ERROR ON THE VERDICT

2. Plain Error

Page 1608. Add after the section on Puckett v. United States

"Any Possibility" Test Is Too Permissive For Plain Error Review: United States v. Marcus

UNITED STATES v. MARCUS
Supreme Court of the United States, 2010
130 S.Ct. 2159

JUSTICE BREYER **delivered the opinion of the Court**

The question before us concerns an appellate court's "plain error" review of a claim not raised at trial. See Fed. Rule Crim. Proc. 52(b). The Second Circuit has said that it must recognize a "plain error" if there is "any possibility," however remote, that a jury convicted a defendant exclusively on the basis of actions taken before enactment of the statute that made those actions criminal. In our view, the Second Circuit's standard is inconsistent with this Court's "plain error" cases. We therefore reverse.

I

A federal grand jury indicted respondent Glenn Marcus on charges that he engaged in unlawful forced labor and sex trafficking between January 1999 and October 2001. At trial, the Government presented evidence of his conduct during that entire period. And a jury found him guilty of both charges.

On appeal, Marcus pointed out for the first time that the statutes he violated were enacted as part of the Trafficking Victims Protection Act of 2000 (TVPA), which did not become law until October 28, 2000. Marcus noted that the indictment and the evidence presented at trial permitted a jury to convict him exclusively upon the basis of actions that he took before October 28, 2000. And for that reason, Marcus argued that his conviction violated the Constitution—in Marcus' view, the Ex Post Facto Clause, Art. I, § 9, cl. 3. Marcus conceded that he had not objected on these grounds in the District Court. But, he said, the constitutional error is "plain," and his conviction therefore must be set aside.

The Government replied by arguing that Marcus' conviction was for a single course of conduct, some of which took place before, and some of which took place after, the statute's enactment date. The Constitution, it said, does not forbid the application of a new statute to such a course of conduct so long as the course of conduct continued after the enactment of the statute. The Government conceded that the conviction could not rest exclusively upon conduct which took place before the TVPA's enactment, but it argued that the possibility that the jury here had convicted on that basis was "remote." Hence, the Government claimed, it was highly unlikely that the judge's failure to make this aspect of the law clear (say, by explaining to the jury that it could not con-

vict based on preenactment conduct alone) affected Marcus' "substantial rights." And the Government thus argued that the court should not recognize a "plain error."

The Second Circuit * * * recognized that, under Circuit precedent, the Constitution did not prohibit conviction for a "continuing offense" so long as the conviction rested, at least in part, upon postenactment conduct. But, the court held, "even in the case of a continuing offense, if it was possible for the jury—wh[ich] had not been given instructions regarding the date of enactment—to convict exclusively on [the basis of] pre-enactment conduct, then the conviction constitutes a violation" of the Ex Post Facto Clause. The court noted that this was "true even under plain error review." In short, under the Second Circuit's approach, "a retrial is necessary whenever there is any possibility, no matter how unlikely, that the jury could have convicted based exclusively on pre-enactment conduct."

* * *

II

Rule 52(b) permits an appellate court to recognize a "plain error that affects substantial rights," even if the claim of error was "not brought" to the district court's "attention." * * * [T]he cases that set forth our interpretation hold that an appellate court may, in its discretion, correct an error not raised at trial only where the appellant demonstrates that (1) there is an "error"; (2) the error is "clear or obvious, rather than subject to reasonable dispute"; (3) the error "affected the appellant's substantial rights, which in the ordinary case means" it "affected the outcome of the district court proceedings"; and (4) "the error seriously affect[s] the fairness, integrity or public reputation of judicial proceedings." Puckett v. United States [Casebook page 1607]. *See also* United States v. Olano [Casebook page 1602]; Johnson v. United States [Casebook page 1604]; United States v. Cotton [Casebook page 1605].

In our view, the Second Circuit's standard is inconsistent with the third and the fourth criteria set forth in these cases. The third criterion specifies that a "plain error" must "affec[t]" the appellant's "substantial rights." In the ordinary case, to meet this standard an error must be "prejudicial," which means that there must be a reasonable probability that the error affected the outcome of the trial. The Court of Appeals, however, would notice a "plain error" and set aside a conviction whenever there exists "any possibility, no matter how unlikely, that the jury could have convicted based exclusively on preenactment conduct." This standard is irreconcilable with our "plain error" precedent.

We recognize that our cases speak of a need for a showing that the error affected the "outcome of the district court proceedings" in the "ordinary case." *Puckett.* And we have noted the possibility that certain errors, termed "structural errors," might "affect substantial rights" regardless of their actual impact on an appellant's trial. Id. (reserving the question whether "structural errors" automatically satisfy the third "plain error" criterion). But "structural errors" are "a very limited class" of errors that affect the "framework within which the trial proceeds,"such that it is often difficult to assess the effect of the error. We cannot conclude that the error here falls within that category.

The error at issue in this case created a risk that the jury would con-

vict respondent solely on the basis of conduct that was not criminal when the defendant engaged in that conduct. A judge might have minimized, if not eliminated, this risk by giving the jury a proper instruction. We see no reason why, when a judge fails to give such an instruction, a reviewing court would find it any more difficult to assess the likely consequences of that failure than with numerous other kinds of instructional errors that we have previously held to be non-"structural"—for example, instructing a jury as to an invalid alternative theory of guilt, omitting mention of an element of an offense, or erroneously instructing the jury on an element.

Marcus argues that, like the Second Circuit, we should apply the label "Ex Post Facto Clause violation" to the error in this case, and that we should then treat all errors so labeled as special, "structural," errors that warrant reversal without a showing of prejudice. But we cannot accept this argument. As an initial matter, we note that the Government has never claimed that the TVPA retroactively criminalizes preenactment conduct, and that Marcus and the Second Circuit were thus incorrect to classify the error at issue here as an Ex Post Facto Clause violation, see Marks v. United States, 430 U.S. 188, 191 (1977) ("The Ex Post Facto Clause is a limitation upon the powers of the Legislature, and does not of its own force apply to the Judicial Branch of government" (citation omitted)). Rather, if the jury, which was not instructed about the TVPA's enactment date, erroneously convicted Marcus based exclusively on noncriminal, preenactment conduct, Marcus would have a valid due process claim. Cf. Bouie v. City of Columbia,

378 U.S. 347, 353–354 (1964) (applying Due Process Clause to ex post facto judicial decisions). In any event, however Marcus' claim is labeled, we see no reason why this kind of error would automatically "affect substantial rights" without a showing of individual prejudice.

That is because errors similar to the one at issue in this case—i.e., errors that create a risk that a defendant will be convicted based exclusively on noncriminal conduct—come in various shapes and sizes. The kind and degree of harm that such errors create can consequently vary. Sometimes a proper jury instruction might well avoid harm; other times, preventing the harm might only require striking or limiting the testimony of a particular witness. And sometimes the error might infect an entire trial, such that a jury instruction would mean little. There is thus no reason to believe that all or almost all such errors always affect the framework within which the trial proceeds, or necessarily render a criminal trial fundamentally unfair or an unreliable vehicle for determining guilt or innocence.

Moreover, while the rights at issue in this case are important, they do not differ significantly in importance from the constitutional rights at issue in other cases where we have insisted upon a showing of individual prejudice. See Arizona v. Fulminante [Casebook page 1595] (collecting cases). Indeed, we have said that "if the defendant had counsel and was tried by an impartial adjudicator, there is a strong presumption that any other errors that may have occurred" are not "structural errors." No one here denies that defendant had counsel and was tried by an impartial adjudicator.

In any event, the Second Circuit's approach also cannot be reconciled with this Court's fourth "plain error" criterion, which permits an appeals court to recognize "plain error" only if the error "seriously affect[s] the fairness, integrity, or public reputation of judicial proceedings." *Johnson*. In cases applying this fourth criterion, we have suggested that, in most circumstances, an error that does not affect the jury's verdict does not significantly impugn the "fairness," "integrity," or "public reputation" of the judicial process. The Second Circuit's "any possibility, no matter how unlikely" standard, however, would require finding a "plain error" in a case where the evidence supporting a conviction consisted of, say, a few days of preenactment conduct along with several continuous years of identical postenactment conduct. Given the tiny risk that the jury would have based its conviction upon those few preenactment days alone, a refusal to recognize such an error as a "plain error" (and to set aside the verdict) is most unlikely to cast serious doubt on the "fairness," "integrity," or "public reputation" of the judicial system.

We do not intend to trivialize the claim that respondent here raises. Nor do we imply that the kind of error at issue here is unimportant. But the rule that permits courts to recognize a "plain error" does not "remove" "seriou[s]" errors "from the ambit of the Federal Rules of Criminal Procedure." Rather, the "plain error" rule, as interpreted by this Court, sets forth criteria that a claim of error not raised at trial must satisfy. The Second Circuit's rule would require reversal under the "plain error" standard for errors that do not meet those criteria. * * * .

Hence we must reject the Second Circuit's rule.

For these reasons, the judgment of the Court of Appeals is reversed. As the Court of Appeals has not yet considered whether the error at issue in this case satisfies this Court's "plain error" standard—i.e., whether the error affects "substantial rights" and "the fairness, integrity, or public reputation of judicial proceedings"—we remand the case to that court so that it may do so.

Justice Sotomayor took no part in the consideration or decision of this case.

Justice Stevens, dissenting.

The Court's opinion fairly summarizes our "plain error" cases and shows how the Court of Appeals applied a novel standard of review. Yet while it may have taken an unusual route to get there, I find nothing wrong with the Court of Appeals' judgment. I am more concerned with this Court's approach to, and policing of, Federal Rule of Criminal Procedure 52(b).

* * *

In our attempt to clarify Rule 52(b), we have, I fear, both muddied the waters and lost sight of the wisdom embodied in the Rule's spare text. Errors come in an endless variety of shapes and sizes. Because error-free trials are so rare, appellate courts must repeatedly confront the question whether a trial judge's mistake was harmless or warrants reversal. * * * This Court's ever more intensive efforts to rationalize plain-error review may have been born of a worthy instinct. But they have trapped the appellate courts in an analytic maze that, I have increasingly come to believe, is more liable to frustrate than to facilitate sound decisionmaking.

The trial error at issue in this case undermined the defendant's substantial rights by allowing the jury to convict him on the basis of an incorrect belief that lawful conduct was unlawful, and it does not take an elaborate formula to see that. Because, in my view, the Court of Appeals properly exercised its discretion to remedy the error and to order a retrial, I respectfully dissent.

[Justice Sotomayor took no part in the decision in this case.]

III. COLLATERAL ATTACK

B. FEDERAL HABEAS CORPUS: THE PROCEDURAL FRAMEWORK

2. General Principles Concerning Habeas Relief After AEDPA

Page 1623. Add after the section "Statute of Limitations"

Equitable Tolling: Holland v. Florida

HOLLAND v. FLORIDA

Supreme Court of the United States, 2010
130 S.Ct. 2549

JUSTICE BREYER **delivered the opinion of the Court.**

We here decide that the timeliness provision in the federal habeas corpus statute is subject to equitable tolling. See Antiterrorism and Effective Death Penalty Act of 1996 (AEDPA), 28 U.S.C. § 2244(d). We also consider its application in this case. In the Court of Appeals' view, when a petitioner seeks to excuse a late filing on the basis of his attorney's unprofessional conduct, that conduct, even if it is "negligent" or "grossly negligent," cannot "rise to the level of egregious attorney misconduct" that would warrant equitable tolling unless the petitioner offers "proof of bad faith, dishonesty, divided loyalty, mental impairment or so forth." In our view, this standard is too rigid. We therefore reverse the judgment of the Court of Appeals and remand for further proceedings.

I

AEDPA states that "[a] 1-year period of limitation shall apply to an application for a writ of habeas corpus by a person in custody pursuant to the judgment of a State court." § 2244(d)(1). It also says that "[t]he time during which a properly filed application for State post-conviction . . . review" is "pending shall not be counted" against the 1-year period. § 2244(d)(2).

On January 19, 2006, Albert Holland filed a pro se habeas corpus petition in the Federal District Court for the Southern District of Florida. Both Holland (the petitioner) and the State of Florida (the respondent) agree that, unless equitably tolled, the statutory limitations period applicable to Holland's petition expired approximately five weeks before the petition was filed. Holland asked the District Court to toll the limitations period for equitable reasons. We shall set forth in some detail the record facts that underlie Holland's claim.

A

In 1997, Holland was convicted of first-degree murder and sentenced to death. The Florida Supreme Court affirmed that judgment. On October 1, 2001, this Court denied Holland's petition for certiorari. And on that date—the date that our denial of the petition ended further direct review of Holland's conviction—the 1-year AEDPA limitations clock began to run. See 28 U.S.C. § 2244(d)(1)(A).

Thirty-seven days later, on November 7, 2001, Florida appointed attorney Bradley Collins to represent Holland in all state and federal post-conviction proceedings. By September 19, 2002—316 days after his appointment and 12 days before the 1–year AEDPA limitations period expired—Collins, acting on Holland's behalf, filed a motion for postconviction relief in the state trial court. That filing automatically stopped the running of the AEDPA limitations period, § 2244(d)(2), with, as we have said, 12 days left on the clock.

For the next three years, Holland's petition remained pending in the state courts. During that time, Holland wrote Collins letters asking him to make certain that all of his claims would be preserved for any subsequent federal habeas corpus review. Collins wrote back, stating, "I would like to reassure you that we are aware of state-time limitations and federal exhaustion requirements." He also said that he would "presen[t] . . . to the . . . federal courts" any of Holland's claims that the state courts denied. In a second letter Collins added, "should your Motion for Post–Conviction Relief be denied" by the state courts, "your state habeas corpus claims will then be ripe for presentation in a petition for writ of habeas corpus in federal court."

In mid-May 2003 the state trial court denied Holland relief, and Collins appealed that denial to the Florida Supreme Court. Almost two years later, in February 2005, the Florida Supreme Court heard oral argument in the case. But during that 2–year period, relations between Collins and Holland began to break down. Indeed, between April 2003 and January 2006, Collins communicated with Holland only three times—each time by letter.

Holland, unhappy with this lack of communication, twice wrote to the Florida Supreme Court, asking it to remove Collins from his case. In the second letter, filed on June 17, 2004, he said that he and Collins had experienced "a complete breakdown in communication." Holland informed the court that Collins had "not kept [him] updated on the status of [his] capital case" and that Holland had "not seen or spoken to" Collins "since April 2003." He wrote, "Mr. Collins has abandoned [me]" and said, "[I have] no idea what is going on with [my] capital case on appeal." He added that "Collins has never made any reasonable effort to establish any relationship of trust or confidence with [me]." * * * Holland concluded by asking that Collins be "dismissed (removed) off his capital case" or that he be given a hearing in order to demonstrate Collins' deficiencies. The State responded that Holland could not file any pro se papers with the court while he was represented by counsel, including papers seeking new counsel. The Florida Supreme Court agreed and denied Holland's requests.

During this same period Holland wrote various letters to the Clerk of the Florida Supreme Court. In the last of these he wrote, "[I]f I had a competent, conflict-free, postconviction, appellate attorney representing me, I would not have to write you this letter. I'm not trying to get on your nerves. I just would like to know exactly what is happening with my case on appeal to the Supreme Court of Florida." During that same time period, Holland also filed a complaint against Collins with the Florida Bar Association, but the complaint was denied.

Collins argued Holland's appeal before the Florida Supreme Court on February 10, 2005. Shortly thereafter,

Holland wrote to Collins emphasizing the importance of filing a timely petition for habeas corpus in federal court once the Florida Supreme Court issued its ruling. * * * Collins did not answer this letter.

On June 15, 2005, Holland wrote again:

"Dear Mr. Collins:

"How are you? Fine I hope.

"On March 3, 2005 I wrote you a letter, asking that you let me know the status of my case on appeal to the Supreme Court of Florida.

"Also, have you begun preparing my 28 U.S.C. § 2254 writ of Habeas Corpus petition? Please let me know, as soon as possible.

"Thank you."

But again, Collins did not reply.

Five months later, in November 2005, the Florida Supreme Court affirmed the lower court decision denying Holland relief. Three weeks after that, on December 1, 2005, the court issued its mandate, making its decision final. At that point, the AEDPA federal habeas clock again began to tick—with 12 days left on the 1–year meter. See Coates v. Byrd, 211 F.3d 1225 (C.A.11 2000) (AEDPA clock restarts when state court completes postconviction review). Twelve days later, on December 13, 2005, Holland's AEDPA time limit expired.

B

Four weeks after the AEDPA time limit expired, on January 9, 2006, Holland, still unaware of the Florida Supreme Court ruling issued in his case two months earlier, wrote Collins a third letter:

"Dear Mr. Bradley M. Collins:

"How are you? Fine I hope.

"I write this letter to ask that you please let me know the status of my appeals before the Supreme Court of Florida. Have my appeals been decided yet?

"Please send me the [necessary information] . . . so that I can determine when the deadline will be to file my 28 U.S.C. Rule 2254 Federal Habeas Corpus Petition, in accordance with all United States Supreme Court and Eleventh Circuit case law and applicable 'Antiterrorism and Effective Death Penalty Act,' if my appeals before the Supreme Court of Florida are denied.

"Please be advised that I want to preserve my privilege to federal review of all of my state convictions and sentences.

"Mr. Collins, would you please also inform me as to which United States District Court my 28 U.S.C. Rule 2254 Federal Habeas Corpus Petition will have to be timely filed in and that court's address?

"Thank you very much."

Collins did not answer.

Nine days later, on January 18, 2006, Holland, working in the prison library, learned for the first time that the Florida Supreme Court had issued a final determination in his case and that its mandate had issued—five weeks prior. He immediately wrote out his own pro se federal habeas petition and mailed it to the Federal District Court for the Southern District of Florida the next day. The petition begins by stating,

"Comes now Albert R. Holland, Jr., a Florida death row inmate and states that court appointed counsel has failed to undertake timely action to seek Federal Review in my case by filing a 28 U.S.C. Rule 2254 Petition for Writ of Habeas Corpus on my behalf."

It then describes the various constitutional claims that Holland hoped to assert in federal court.

The same day that he mailed that petition, Holland received a letter from Collins telling him that Collins intended to file a petition for certiorari in this Court from the State Supreme Court's most recent ruling. Holland answered immediately:

"Dear Mr. Bradley M. Collins:

* * *

"Since recently, the Supreme Court of Florida has denied my [postconviction] and state writ of Habeas Corpus Petition. I am left to understand that you are planning to seek certiorari on these matters.

"It's my understanding that the AEDPA time limitations is not tolled during discretionary appellate reviews, such as certiorari applications resulting from denial of state post conviction proceedings.

"Therefore, I advise you not to file certiorari if doing so affects or jeopardizes my one year grace period as prescribed by the AEDPA.

"Thank you very much."

Holland was right about the law. See *Coates,* supra, at 1226–1227 (AEDPA not tolled during pendency of petition for certiorari from judgment denying state postconviction review).

On January 26, 2006, Holland tried to call Collins from prison. But he called collect and Collins' office would not accept the call. Five days later, Collins wrote to Holland and told him for the very first time that, as Collins understood AEDPA law, the limitations period applicable to Holland's federal habeas application

had in fact expired in 2000—before Collins had begun to represent Holland. * * * Collins was wrong about the law. As we have said, Holland's 1–year limitations period did not begin to run until this Court denied Holland's petition for certiorari from the state courts' denial of relief on direct review, which occurred on October 1, 2001. And when Collins was appointed (on November 7, 2001) the AEDPA clock therefore had 328 days left to go. Holland immediately wrote back to Collins, pointing this out.

"Dear Mr. Collins:

"I received your letter dated January 31, 2006. You are incorrect in stating that 'the one-year statutory time frame for filing my 2254 petition began to run after my case was affirmed on October 5, 2000, by the Florida Supreme Court.' As stated on page three of [the recently filed] Petition for a writ of certiorari, October 1, 2001 is when the United States Supreme Court denied my initial petition for writ of certiorari and that is when my case became final. That meant that the time would be tolled once I filed my [postconviction] motion in the trial court.

"Also, Mr. Collins you never told me that my time ran out (expired). I told you to timely file my 28 U.S.C. 2254 Habeas Corpus Petition before the deadline, so that I would not be time-barred.

"You never informed me of oral arguments or of the Supreme Court of Florida's November 10, 2005 decision denying my postconviction appeals. You never kept me informed about the status of my case, although you told me that you would immediately inform me of the court's decision as soon as you heard anything.

"Mr. Collins, I filed a motion on January 19, 2006 [in federal court] to preserve my rights, because I did not want to be time-barred. Have you heard anything about the aforesaid motion? Do you know what the status of aforesaid motion is?

"Mr. Collins, please file my 2254 Habeas Petition immediately. Please do not wait any longer, even though it will be untimely filed at least it will be filed without wasting anymore time. (valuable time).

"Again, please file my 2254 Petition at once.

"Your letter is the first time that you have ever mentioned anything to me about my time had run out, before you were appointed to represent me, and that my one-year started to run on October 5, 2000.

"Please find out the status of my motion that I filed on January 19, 2006 and let me know.

"Thank you very much."

Collins did not answer this letter. Nor did he file a federal habeas petition as Holland requested.

On March 1, 2006, Holland filed another complaint against Collins with the Florida Bar Association. This time the bar asked Collins to respond, which he did, through his own attorney * * *. [O]ver three months after Holland's AEDPA statute of limitations had expired, Collins mailed a proposed federal habeas petition to Holland, asking him to review it.

But by that point Holland had already filed a pro se motion in the District Court asking that Collins be dismissed as his attorney. The State responded to that request by arguing once again that Holland could not file a pro se motion seeking to have Collins removed while he was represented by counsel, i.e., represented by Collins. But this time the court considered Holland's motion, permitted Collins to withdraw from the case, and appointed a new lawyer for Holland. And it also received briefing on whether the circumstances of the case justified the equitable tolling of the AEDPA limitations period for a sufficient period of time (approximately five weeks) to make Holland's petition timely.

C

After considering the briefs, the Federal District Court held that the facts did not warrant equitable tolling and that consequently Holland's petition was untimely. The court, noting that Collins had prepared numerous filings on Holland's behalf in the state courts, and suggesting that Holland was a difficult client, intimated, but did not hold, that Collins' professional conduct in the case was at worst merely "negligent." But the court rested its holding on an alternative rationale: It wrote that, even if Collins' "behavior could be characterized as an 'extraordinary circumstance,'" Holland "did not seek any help from the court system to find out the date [the] mandate issued denying his state habeas petition, nor did he seek aid from 'outside supporters.'" Hence, the court held, Holland did not "demonstrate" the "due diligence" necessary to invoke "equitable tolling."

On appeal, the Eleventh Circuit agreed with the District Court that Holland's habeas petition was untimely. * * * The court wrote:

"We will assume that Collins's alleged conduct is negligent, even grossly negligent. But in our view, no allegation of lawyer negligence or of failure to meet a lawyer's standard of care—in the absence of an allegation and proof of bad faith, dishonesty, divided loyalty, mental impairment or so forth on the lawyer's part—can rise to the level of egregious attorney misconduct that would entitle Petitioner to equitable tolling."

Holland made "no allegation" that Collins had made a "knowing or reckless factual misrepresentation," or that he exhibited "dishonesty," "divided loyalty," or "mental impairment." Hence, the court held, equitable tolling was per se inapplicable to Holland's habeas petition. * * *

Holland petitioned for certiorari. Because the Court of Appeals' application of the equitable tolling doctrine to instances of professional misconduct conflicts with the approach taken by other Circuits, we granted the petition.

II

We have not decided whether AEDPA's statutory limitations period may be tolled for equitable reasons. Now, like all 11 Courts of Appeals that have considered the question, we hold that § 2244(d) is subject to equitable tolling in appropriate cases.

We base our conclusion on the following considerations. First, the AEDPA statute of limitations defense is not jurisdictional. It does not set forth an inflexible rule requiring dismissal whenever its clock has run.

We have previously made clear that a nonjurisdictional federal statute of limitations is normally subject to a rebuttable presumption in favor of equitable tolling. In the case of AEDPA, the presumption's strength is reinforced by the fact that equitable principles have traditionally governed the substantive law of habeas corpus * * *.

* * *

[F]inally, we disagree with respondent that equitable tolling undermines AEDPA's basic purposes. We recognize that AEDPA seeks to eliminate delays in the federal habeas review process. But AEDPA seeks to do so without undermining basic habeas corpus principles and while seeking to harmonize the new statute with prior law, under which a petition's timeliness was always determined under equitable principles. When Congress codified new rules governing this previously judicially managed area of law, it did so without losing sight of the fact that the writ of habeas corpus plays a vital role in protecting constitutional rights. The importance of the Great Writ, the only writ explicitly protected by the Constitution, Art. I, § 9, cl. 2, along with congressional efforts to harmonize the new statute with prior law, counsels hesitancy before interpreting AEDPA's statutory silence as indicating a congressional intent to close courthouse doors that a strong equitable claim would ordinarily keep open.

* * * [W]e therefore join the Courts of Appeals in holding that § 2244(d) is subject to equitable tolling.

III

We have previously made clear that a "petitioner" is "entitled to equitable tolling" only if he shows "(1) that he has been pursuing his rights diligently, and (2) that some extraordinary circumstance stood in his way" and prevented timely filing. In this case, the "extraordinary circumstances" at issue involve an attorney's failure to satisfy professional standards of care. The Court of Appeals held that, where that is so, even attorney conduct that is "grossly negligent" can never warrant tolling absent "bad faith, dishonesty, divided loyalty, mental impairment or so forth on the lawyer's part." But in our view, the Court of Appeals' standard is too rigid.

* * *

We recognize that, in the context of procedural default, we have previously stated, without qualification, that a petitioner "must bear the risk of attorney error. "Coleman v. Thompson [Casebook page 1653]. But *Coleman* was a case about federalism, in that it asked whether federal courts may excuse a petitioner's failure to comply with a state court's procedural rules, notwithstanding the state court's determination that its own rules had been violated. Equitable tolling, by contrast, asks whether federal courts may excuse a petitioner's failure to comply with federal timing rules, an inquiry that does not implicate a state court's interpretation of state law. Holland does not argue that his attorney's misconduct provides a substantive ground for relief, nor is this a case that asks whether AEDPA's statute of limitations should be recognized at all. Rather, this case asks how equity should be applied once the statute is recognized. And given equity's resistance to rigid rules, we cannot read *Coleman* as requiring a per se approach in this context.

* * * [N]o pre-existing rule of law or precedent demands a rule like the one set forth by the Eleventh Circuit in this case. That rule is difficult to reconcile with more general equitable principles in that it fails to recognize that, at least sometimes, professional misconduct that fails to meet the Eleventh Circuit's standard could nonetheless amount to egregious behavior and create an extraordinary circumstance that warrants equitable tolling. And, given the long history of judicial application of equitable tolling, courts can easily find precedents that can guide their judgments. Several lower courts have specifically held that unprofessional attorney conduct may, in certain circumstances, prove "egregious" and can be "extraordinary" even though the conduct in question may not satisfy the Eleventh Circuit's rule.

We have previously held that a garden variety claim of excusable neglect such as a simple miscalculation that leads a lawyer to miss a filing deadline does not warrant equitable tolling. But the case before us does not involve, and we are not considering, a "garden variety claim" of attorney negligence. Rather, the facts of this case present far more serious instances of attorney misconduct. And, as we have said, although the circumstances of a case must be "extraordinary" before equitable tolling can be applied, we hold that such circumstances are not limited to those that satisfy the test that the Court of Appeals used in this case.

IV

The record facts that we have set forth in Part I of this opinion suggest that this case may well be an "extraordinary" instance in which petitioner's attorney's conduct constituted far more than "garden variety" or "excusable neglect." To be sure, Collins failed to file Holland's petition on time and appears to have been unaware of the date on which the limitations period expired-two facts that, alone, might suggest simple negligence. But, in these circumstances, the record facts we have elucidated suggest that the failure amounted to more: Here, Collins failed to file Holland's federal petition on time despite Holland's many letters that repeatedly emphasized the importance of his doing so. Collins apparently did not do the research necessary to find out the proper filing date, despite Holland's letters that went so far as to identify the applicable legal rules. Collins failed to inform Holland in a timely manner about the crucial fact that the Florida Supreme Court had decided his case, again despite Holland's many pleas for that information. And Collins failed to communicate with his client over a period of years, despite various pleas from Holland that Collins respond to his letters.

A group of teachers of legal ethics tells us that these various failures violated fundamental canons of professional responsibility, which require attorneys to perform reasonably competent legal work, to communicate with their clients, to implement clients' reasonable requests, to keep their clients informed of key developments in their cases, and never to abandon a client. And in this case, the failures seriously prejudiced a client who thereby lost what was likely his single opportunity for federal habeas review of the lawfulness of his imprisonment and of his death sentence.

We do not state our conclusion in absolute form, however, because more proceedings may be necessary. The District Court rested its ruling not on a lack of extraordinary circumstances, but rather on a lack of diligence—a ruling that respondent does not defend. We think that the District Court's conclusion was incorrect. The diligence required for equitable tolling purposes is reasonable diligence, not "maximum feasible diligence." Here, Holland not only wrote his attorney numerous letters seeking crucial information and providing direction; he also repeatedly

contacted the state courts, their clerks, and the Florida State Bar Association in an effort to have Collins—the central impediment to the pursuit of his legal remedy—removed from his case. And, the very day that Holland discovered that his AEDPA clock had expired due to Collins' failings, Holland prepared his own habeas petition pro se and promptly filed it with the District Court.

Because the District Court erroneously relied on a lack of diligence, and because the Court of Appeals erroneously relied on an overly rigid per se approach, no lower court has yet considered in detail the facts of this case to determine whether they indeed constitute extraordinary circumstances sufficient to warrant equitable relief. * * * [B]ecause we conclude that the District Court's determination must be set aside, we leave it to the Court of Appeals to determine whether the facts in this record entitle Holland to equitable tolling, or whether further proceedings, including an evidentiary hearing, might indicate that respondent should prevail.

Justice Alito, concurring in part and concurring in the judgment.

This case raises two broad questions: first, whether the statute of limitations set out in the Antiterrorism and Effective Death Penalty Act of 1996 (AEDPA), is subject to equitable tolling; and second, assuming an affirmative answer to the first question, whether petitioner in this particular case has alleged facts that are sufficient to satisfy the "extraordinary circumstances" prong of the equitable tolling test. I agree with the Court's conclusion that equitable tolling is available under AEDPA. I also agree with much of the Court's discussion concerning whether equitable tolling is available on the facts of this particular case. In particular, I agree that the Court of Appeals erred by essentially limiting the relevant inquiry to the question whether "gross negligence" of counsel may be an extraordinary circumstance warranting equitable tolling. As the Court makes clear, petitioner in this case has alleged certain facts that go well beyond any form of attorney negligence, and the Court of Appeals does not appear to have asked whether those particular facts provide an independent basis for tolling. Accordingly, I concur in the Court's decision to reverse the judgment below and remand so that the lower courts may properly apply the correct legal standard.

Although I agree that the Court of Appeals applied the wrong standard, I think that the majority does not do enough to explain the right standard. It is of course true that equitable tolling requires "extraordinary circumstances," but that conclusory formulation does not provide much guidance to lower courts charged with reviewing the many habeas petitions filed every year. I therefore write separately to set forth my understanding of the principles governing the availability of equitable tolling in cases involving attorney misconduct.

I

Generally, a litigant seeking equitable tolling bears the burden of establishing two elements: (1) that he has been pursuing his rights diligently, and (2) that some extraordinary circumstance stood in his way. The dispute in this case concerns whether and when attorney misconduct amounts to an "extraordinary circumstance" that stands in a petitioner's way and prevents the petitioner from filing a timely petition. I agree

with the majority that it is not practical to attempt to provide an exhaustive compilation of the kinds of situations in which attorney misconduct may provide a basis for equitable tolling. In my view, however, it is useful to note that several broad principles may be distilled from this Court's precedents.

First, our prior cases make it abundantly clear that attorney negligence is not an extraordinary circumstance warranting equitable tolling. * * *

Second, the mere fact that a missed deadline involves "gross negligence" on the part of counsel does not by itself establish an extraordinary circumstance. * * * [T]he principal rationale for disallowing equitable tolling based on ordinary attorney miscalculation is that the error of an attorney is constructively attributable to the client and thus is not a circumstance beyond the litigant's control. That rationale plainly applies regardless whether the attorney error in question involves ordinary or gross negligence. * * *

Allowing equitable tolling in cases involving gross rather than ordinary attorney negligence would * * * be impractical in the extreme. Missing the statute of limitations will generally, if not always, amount to negligence, and it has been aptly said that gross negligence is ordinary negligence with a vituperative epithet added. Therefore, if gross negligence may be enough for equitable tolling, there will be a basis for arguing that tolling is appropriate in almost every counseled case involving a missed deadline. This would not just impose a severe burden on the district courts; it would also make the availability of tolling turn on the highly artificial distinction between gross and ordinary negligence. That line would be hard to administer, would needlessly consume scarce judicial resources, and would almost certainly yield inconsistent and often unsatisfying results.

* * *

II

Although attorney negligence, however styled, does not provide a basis for equitable tolling, the AEDPA statute of limitations may be tolled if the missed deadline results from attorney misconduct that is not constructively attributable to the petitioner. In this case, petitioner alleges facts that amount to such misconduct. In particular, he alleges that his attorney essentially "abandoned" him, as evidenced by counsel's near-total failure to communicate with petitioner or to respond to petitioner's many inquiries and requests over a period of several years. Petitioner also appears to allege that he made reasonable efforts to terminate counsel due to his inadequate representation and to proceed pro se, and that such efforts were successfully opposed by the State on the perverse ground that petitioner failed to act through appointed counsel.

If true, petitioner's allegations would suffice to establish extraordinary circumstances beyond his control. Common sense dictates that a litigant cannot be held constructively responsible for the conduct of an attorney who is not operating as his agent in any meaningful sense of that word. That is particularly so if the litigant's reasonable efforts to terminate the attorney's representation have been thwarted by forces wholly beyond the petitioner's control. The Court of Appeals apparently did not consider petitioner's abandonment argument or assess whether the State

improperly prevented petitioner from either obtaining new representation or assuming the responsibility of representing himself. Accordingly, I agree with the majority that the appropriate disposition is to reverse and remand so that the lower courts may apply the correct standard to the facts alleged here.

JUSTICE SCALIA, with whom JUSTICE THOMAS **joins as to all but Part I, dissenting.**

* * * In my view § 2244(d) leaves no room for equitable exceptions, and Holland could not qualify even if it did.

I

[JUSTICE SCALIA reads the AEDPA to set forth particularized timing requirements that do not support a defense of equitable tolling.]

II

A

Even if § 2244(d) left room for equitable tolling in some situations, tolling surely should not excuse the delay here. * * * Because the attorney is the litigant's agent, the attorney's acts (or failures to act) within the scope of the representation are treated as those of his client, and thus such acts (or failures to act) are necessarily not extraordinary circumstances.

* * *

B

* * * [T]he Court does not actually hold that Holland is entitled to equitable tolling. It concludes only that the Eleventh Circuit applied the wrong rule and remands the case for a re-do. That would be appropriate if the Court identified a legal error in the Eleventh Circuit's analysis and set forth the proper standard it should have applied.

The Court does neither. It rejects as "too rigid" the Eleventh Circuit's test—which requires, beyond ordinary attorney negligence, "an allegation and proof of bad faith, dishonesty, divided loyalty, mental impairment or so forth on the lawyer's part." But the Court never explains why that "or so forth" test, which explicitly leaves room for other kinds of egregious attorney error, is insufficiently elastic.

* * *

Consistent with its failure to explain the error in the Eleventh Circuit's test, the Court offers almost no clue about what test that court should have applied. The Court unhelpfully advises the Court of Appeals that its test is too narrow, with no explanation besides the assertion that its test left out cases where tolling might be warranted, and no precise indication of what those cases might be. The only thing the Court offers that approaches substantive instruction is its implicit approval of "fundamental canons of professional responsibility," articulated by an ad hoc group of legal-ethicist amici consisting mainly of professors of that least analytically rigorous and hence most subjective of law-school subjects, legal ethics. The Court does not even try to justify importing into eq-uity the "prevailing professional norms" we have held implicit in the right to counsel. In his habeas action Holland has no right to counsel. I object to this transparent attempt to smuggle *Strickland* into a realm the Sixth Amendment does not reach.

C

* * *

The Court's impulse to intervene when a litigant's lawyer has made mistakes is understandable; the temptation to tinker with technical rules to achieve what appears a just result is often strong, especially when the client faces a capital sentence. But the Constitution does not empower federal courts to rewrite, in the name of equity, rules that Congress has made. Endowing unelected judges with that power is irreconcilable with our system, for it "would literally place the whole rights and property of the community under the arbitrary will of the judge," arming him with "a despotic and sovereign authority," 1 J. Story, Commentaries on Equity Jurisprudence § 19, p. 19 (14th ed.1918). The danger is doubled when we disregard our own precedent, leaving only our own consciences to constrain our discretion. * * * I respectfully dissent.

3. Factual Findings and Mixed Questions of Law and Fact.

Page 1630. Add at the end of the section.

Recent Applications of Section 2254(d)

In the 2010–11 Term, the Supreme Court decided three cases involving habeas claims of ineffective counsel. In each case the Court applied the deferential standards of review mandated by section 2254(d). The Court provides extensive analysis of the proper standards of review under this section, and also determines that review of a state court's determinations under section 2254(d) is limited to the information available to the state court. Those three decisions—*Premo v. Moore, Harrington v. Richter, and Cullen v. Pinholster*—are set forth in full case form in Chapter Ten of this Supplement.

D. LIMITATIONS ON OBTAINING HABEAS RELIEF

4. Adequate and Independent State Grounds

Page 1675. Add the following two notes after the section "State Ground That Is Not Adequate"

Discretionary Rules as Adequate State Grounds: Beard v. Kindler

In Beard v. Kindler, 130 S.Ct. 612 (2009), the Court considered whether a discretionary state rule could ever be an adequate state ground, the violation of which would preclude federal habeas review of a state conviction. Kindler challenged his Pennsylvania state court conviction, but the state court exercised its discretion under the state's "fugitive dismissal rule" to dismiss the challenge because he had fled to Canada. Chief Justice Roberts, writing for the Court, set forth the issue:

> A federal habeas court will not review a claim rejected by a state court "if the decision of [the state] court rests on a state law ground that is independent of the federal question and adequate to support the judgment." Coleman v. Thompson. We granted certiorari to decide the following question: "Is a state procedural rule automatically 'inadequate' under the adequate-state-grounds doctrine-and therefore unenforceable on federal habeas corpus review-because the state rule is discretionary rather than mandatory?"

The Court answered that question in the negative. The Chief Justice explained the result as follows:

> We have framed the adequacy inquiry by asking whether the state rule in question was "firmly established and regularly followed." We hold that a discretionary state procedural rule can serve as an adequate ground to bar federal habeas review. Nothing inherent in such a rule renders it inadequate for purposes of the adequate state ground doctrine. To the contrary, a discretionary rule can be "firmly established" and "regularly followed"—even if the appropriate exercise of discretion may permit consideration of a federal claim in some cases but not others.

> A contrary holding would pose an unnecessary dilemma for the States: States could preserve flexibility by granting courts discretion to excuse procedural errors, but only at the cost of undermining the finality of state court judgments. Or States could preserve the finality of their judgments by withholding such discretion, but only at the cost of precluding any flexibility in applying the rules.

> We are told that, if forced to choose, many States would opt for mandatory rules to avoid the high costs that come with plenary federal review. That would be unfortunate in many cases, as discre-

tionary rules are often desirable. * * * The result would be particularly unfortunate for criminal defendants, who would lose the opportunity to argue that a procedural default should be excused through the exercise of judicial discretion.

* * * In light of the federalism and comity concerns that motivate the adequate state ground doctrine in the habeas context, it would seem particularly strange to disregard state procedural rules that are substantially similar to those to which we give full force in our own courts. Even stranger to do so with respect to rules in place in nearly every State, and all at one fell swoop.

The Court rejected a request from the Commonwealth to "state a standard for inadequacy." But the Court declined the invitation, noting that "[t]he procedural default at issue here—escape from prison—is hardly a typical procedural default, making this case an unsuitable vehicle for providing broad guidance on the adequate state ground doctrine."

Justice Alito took no part in the consideration of the case. Justice Kennedy, joined by Justice Thomas, wrote a concurring opinion.

Flexible Rules as Adequate State Grounds: Walker v. Martin

Most states set determinate time limits for collateral relief applications. But California courts apply a general "reasonableness standard" to judge whether a habeas petition is timely filed. Under that standard, a habeas petition should be filed "as promptly as the circumstances allow" and a prisoner must seek habeas relief without "substantial delay" as measured from the time the petitioner or counsel knew, or reasonably should have known, of the information offered in support of the claim and the legal basis of the claim. California courts have discretion to bypass a timeliness issue and, instead, summarily reject the petition for want of merit.

In Walker v. Martin, 131 S.Ct. 1120 (2011), Martin was convicted of murder and robbery, and was sentenced to life in prison without parole. After the California Supreme Court denied Martin's first state habeas petition, he filed a federal habeas petition. The district court ordered a stay to permit Martin to return to state court to raise ineffective-assistance-of-counsel claims he had not previously aired. Martin raised those claims in his second habeas petition in the California Supreme Court, but gave no reason for his failure to assert the additional claims until nearly five years after his sentence and conviction became final. The California Supreme Court denied the petition, citing its case law on timeliness. Having exhausted his state-court remedies, Martin filed an amended federal habeas petition. The district court dismissed his belatedly asserted claims as untimely under California law. The Ninth Circuit vacated that order and directed the District Court to determine the "adequacy" of the State's time bar. Again rejecting Martin's petition, the district court found California's bar an adequate state ground for denying Martin's new pleas. But the Ninth Circuit disagreed. It concluded that

that the California time bar was too flexible to be firmly defined or consistently applied; and it remanded for a determination of the merits of Martin's claims.

The Supreme Court, in a unanimous opinion by Justice Ginsburg, held that the Ninth Circuit was in error and that California's timeliness requirement qualified as an independent state ground adequate to bar habeas corpus relief in federal court. Justice Ginsburg noted that under Beard v. Kindler [immediately above in this Supplement] a state rule can be "firmly established" and "regularly followed"—and therefore adequate—"even if the appropriate exercise of discretion may permit consideration of a federal claim in some cases but not others." The Court found that California's time rule, although discretionary flexible, met the Beard v. Kindler "firmly established" criterion. The California Supreme Court framed the requirement in a trilogy of cases, instructing habeas petitioners to allege with specificity the absence of substantial delay, good cause for delay, or eligibility for one of four exceptions to the time bar. And California's case law made it plain that Martin's nearly five-year delay was "substantial."

Justice Ginsburg was not persuaded by Martin's argument that the terms "reasonable time" period and "substantial delay" made California's rule too vague to be regarded as "firmly established." While indeterminate language is typical of discretionary rules, application of those rules in particular circumstances can supply the requisite clarity. Congressional statutes and the Court's own decisions have employed time limitations that are not stated in precise, numerical terms. Nor was California's time rule vulnerable on the ground that it is not regularly followed. Each year, the California State Supreme Court summarily denies hundreds of habeas petitions by citing its cases on timeliness. Nor should a discretionary rule be disregarded automatically upon a showing that outcomes under the rule vary from case to case. Discretion enables a court to home in on case-specific considerations and to avoid the harsh results that may attend consistent application of an unyielding rule. Justice Ginsburg observed that state ground may be found inadequate when a court has exercised its discretion in a surprising or unfair manner, but Martin made no such contention here.

Justice Ginsburg concluded as follows:

> Sound procedure often requires discretion to exact or excuse compliance with strict rules, and we have no cause to discourage standards allowing courts to exercise such discretion. As this Court observed in *Kindler*, if forced to choose between mandatory rules certain to be found "adequate," or more supple prescriptions that federal courts may disregard as "inadequate," "many States [might] opt for mandatory rules to avoid the high costs that come with plenary federal review." 130 S.Ct., at 618. "Th[at] result would be particularly unfortunate for [habeas petitioners], who would lose the

opportunity to argue that a procedural default should be excused through the exercise of judicial discretion." Id., at 130 S.Ct., at 618.

* * *

Today's decision, trained on California's timeliness rule for habeas petitions, leaves unaltered this Court's repeated recognition that federal courts must carefully examine state procedural requirements to ensure that they do not operate to discriminate against claims of federal rights. On the record before us, however, there is no basis for concluding that California's timeliness rule operates to the particular disadvantage of petitioners asserting federal rights.

5. Abuse of the Writ

Page 1680. Add at the end of the section.

Is a Claim "Successive" When Brought In a Challenge to a Resentencing, When It Could Have Been Brought to Challenge the Initial Sentencing? Magwood v. Patterson

In Magwood v. Patterson, 130 S.Ct. 2788 (2010), Magwood was sentenced to death for murder. After the Alabama courts denied relief on direct appeal and in postconviction proceedings, he sought federal habeas relief. The District Court conditionally granted the writ as to his sentence, mandating that he be released or resentenced. The state trial court sentenced him to death a second time. He filed another federal habeas application, challenging this new sentence on a new ground: that he did not have fair warning at the time of his offense that his conduct would permit a death sentence under Alabama law. This fair warning argument could have been used to attack his initial death sentence but was not. The Court of Appeals held that Magwood's challenge to his new death sentence was an unreviewable "second or successive" challenge under 28 U.S.C. § 2244(b) because he could have raised his fair-warning claim in his earlier habeas application challenging the initial sentence.

The Supreme Court, in an opinion by Justice Thomas, held that the bar on successive applications did not apply, because Magwood was bringing a challenge to a new judgment—the resentencing—for the first time. Justice Thomas rejected the government's argument that the bar of section 2244(b) applied to claims and not to applications. He analyzed the arguments of the parties as follows:

> The State contends that although § 2244(b), as amended by AEDPA, applies the phrase "second or successive" to "application[s]," it "is a claim-focused statute," and "[c]laims, not applications, are barred by § 2244(b)." According to the State, the phrase should be read to reflect a principle that "a prisoner is entitled to one, but only one, full and fair opportunity to wage a collateral attack." The State asserts that under this "one opportunity" rule, Magwood's

fair-warning claim was successive because he had an opportunity to raise it in his first application, but did not do so.

Magwood, in contrast, reads § 2244(b) to apply only to a "second or successive" application challenging the same state-court judgment. According to Magwood, his 1986 resentencing led to a new judgment, and his first application challenging that new judgment cannot be "second or successive" such that § 2244(b) would apply. We agree.

* * *

We have described the phrase "second or successive" as a "term of art." To determine its meaning, we look first to the statutory context. The limitations imposed by § 2244(b) apply only to a "habeas corpus application under § 2254," that is, an "application for a writ of habeas corpus on behalf of a person in custody pursuant to the judgment of a State court," § 2254(b)(1) (emphasis added). The reference to a state-court judgment in § 2254(b) is significant because the term "application" cannot be defined in a vacuum. A § 2254 petitioner is applying for something: His petition seeks invalidation (in whole or in part) of the judgment authorizing the prisoner's confinement. If his petition results in a district court's granting of the writ, the State may seek a new judgment (through a new trial or a new sentencing proceeding). Thus, both § 2254(b)'s text and the relief it provides indicate that the phrase "second or successive" must be interpreted with respect to the judgment challenged.

* * *

Appearing to recognize that Magwood has the stronger textual argument, the State argues that we should rule based on the statutory purpose. According to the State, a "one opportunity" rule is consistent with the statutory text, and better reflects AEDPA's purpose of preventing piecemeal litigation and gamesmanship.

We are not persuaded. AEDPA uses the phrase "second or successive" to modify "application." See §§ 2244(b)(1), (2). The State reads the phrase to modify "claims." We cannot replace the actual text with speculation as to Congress' intent. * * * . Therefore, although we agree with the State that many of the rules under § 2244(b) focus on claims, that does not entitle us to rewrite the statute to make the phrase "second or successive" modify claims as well.

Justice Thomas noted a negative consequence of the government's reading of § 2244(b) to prohibit successive claims as opposed to successive applications:

The State's reading leads to a second, more fundamental error. Under the State's "one opportunity" rule, the phrase "second or successive" would apply to any claim that the petitioner had a full and fair opportunity to raise in a prior application. And the phrase "second or successive" would not apply to a claim that the petitioner did not have a full and fair opportunity to raise previously.

This reading of § 2244(b) would considerably undermine—if not render superfluous—the exceptions to dismissal set forth in § 2244(b)(2). That section describes circumstances when a claim not presented earlier may be considered: intervening and retroactive case law, or newly discovered facts suggesting "that ... no reasonable factfinder would have found the applicant guilty of the underlying offense." § 2244(b)(2)(B)(ii). In either circumstance, a petitioner cannot be said to have had a prior opportunity to raise the claim, so under the State's rule the claim would not be successive and § 2244(b)(2) would not apply to it at all. This would be true even if the claim were raised in a second application challenging the same judgment.

Accordingly, the Court held that Magwood's claim that his resentencing to death was invalid for lack of fair-warning was not barred by § 2244. The Court noted that the government was free to argue on remand that the claim had been procedurally defaulted.

Justice Breyer issued a short opinion concurring in part and concurring the judgment, which was joined by Justices Stevens and Sotomayor.

Justice Kennedy dissented in an opinion joined by Chief Justice Roberts, Justice Ginsburg and Justice Alito. Justice Kennedy stated as follows:

The Court today decides that a state prisoner who succeeds in his first federal habeas petition on a discrete sentencing claim may later file a second petition raising numerous previously unraised claims, even if that petition is an abuse of the writ of habeas corpus. * * * The design and purpose of AEDPA is to avoid abuses of the writ of habeas corpus, in recognition of the potential for the writ's intrusive effect on state criminal justice systems. But today's opinion, with considerable irony, is not only a step back from AEDPA protection for States but also a step back even from abuse-of-the-writ principles that were in place before AEDPA. So this respectful dissent becomes necessary.

* * *

In the present case the Court should conclude that Magwood has filed a "second or successive habeas corpus application." In 1983, he filed a first federal habeas petition raising nine claims, including that the trial court improperly failed to consider two mitigating factors when it imposed Magwood's death sentence. The District Court granted Magwood's petition and ordered relief only on the mitigating factor claim. The state trial court then held a new sentencing proceeding, in which it considered all of the mitigating factors and reimposed the death penalty. In 1997, Magwood brought a second habeas petition, this time raising an argument that could have been, but was not, raised in his first petition. The argument was that he was not eligible for the death penalty because he did not have fair notice that his crime rendered him death eligible. There is no reason that Magwood could not have raised the identical argument in his first habeas petition. Because Magwood had a full and fair opportunity to adjudicate his death-eligibility claim in his first petition in 1983, his 1997 petition raising this claim is barred as "second or successive."

* * *

Had Magwood been unsuccessful in his first petition, all agree that claims then available, but not raised, would be barred. But because he prevailed in his attack on one part of his sentencing proceeding the first time around, the Court rules that he is free, postsentencing, to pursue claims on federal habeas review that might have been raised earlier. The Court is mistaken in concluding that Congress, in enacting a statute aimed at placing new restrictions on successive petitions, would have intended this irrational result.

* * *

THE FEDERAL RULES OF CRIMINAL PROCEDURE

TITLE I. APPLICABILITY

Rule 1. Scope; Definitions

(a) Scope.

(1) *In General.* These rules govern the procedure in all criminal proceedings in the United States district courts, the United States courts of appeals, and the Supreme Court of the United States.

(2) *State or Local Judicial Officer.* When a rule so states, it applies to a proceeding before a state or local judicial officer.

(3) *Territorial Courts.* These rules also govern the procedure in all criminal proceedings in the following courts:

(A) the district court of Guam;

(B) the district court for the Northern Mariana Islands, except as otherwise provided by law; and

(C) the district court of the Virgin Islands, except that the prosecution of offenses in that court must be by indictment or information as otherwise provided by law.

(4) *Removed Proceedings.* Although these rules govern all proceedings after removal from a state court, state law governs a dismissal by the prosecution.

(5) *Excluded Proceedings.* Proceedings not governed by these rules include:

(A) the extradition and rendition of a fugitive;

(B) a civil property forfeiture for violating a federal statute;

(C) the collection of a fine or penalty;

(D) a proceeding under a statute governing juvenile delinquency to the extent the procedure is inconsistent with the statute, unless Rule 20(d) provides otherwise;

(E) a dispute between seamen under 22 U.S.C. §§ 256–258; and

(F) a proceeding against a witness in a foreign country under 28 U.S.C. § 1784.

(b) Definitions. The following definitions apply to these rules:

(1) "Attorney for the government" means:

(A) the Attorney General or an authorized assistant;

(B) a United States attorney or an authorized assistant;

(C) when applicable to cases arising under Guam law, the Guam Attorney General or other person whom Guam law authorizes to act in the matter; and

(D) any other attorney authorized by law to conduct proceedings under these rules as a prosecutor.

(2) "Court" means a federal judge performing functions authorized by law.

(3) "Federal judge" means:

(A) a justice or judge of the United States as these terms are defined in 28 U.S.C. § 451;

(B) a magistrate judge; and

(C) a judge confirmed by the United States Senate and empowered by statute in any commonwealth, territory, or possession to perform a function to which a particular rule relates.

(4) "Judge" means a federal judge or a state or local judicial officer.

(5) "Magistrate judge" means a United States magistrate judge as defined in 28 U.S.C. §§ 631–639.

(6) "Oath" includes an affirmation.

(7) "Organization" is defined in 18 U.S.C. § 18.

(8) "Petty offense" is defined in 18 U.S.C. § 19.

(9) "State" includes the District of Columbia, and any commonwealth, territory, or possession of the United States.

(10) "State or local judicial officer" means:

(A) a state or local officer authorized to act under 18 U.S.C. § 3041; and

(B) a judicial officer empowered by statute in the District of Columbia or in any commonwealth, territory, or possession to perform a function to which a particular rule relates.

(11) "Victim" means a "crime victim" as defined in 18 U.S.C. § 3771(e).

(c) Authority of a Justice or Judge of the United States. When these rules authorize a magistrate judge to act, any other federal judge may also act.

Rule 2. Interpretation

These rules are to be interpreted to provide for the just determination of every criminal proceeding, to secure simplicity in procedure and fairness in administration, and to eliminate unjustifiable expense and delay.

TITLE II. PRELIMINARY PROCEEDINGS

Rule 3. The Complaint

The complaint is a written statement of the essential facts constituting the offense charged. It must be made under oath before a magistrate judge or, if none is reasonably available, before a state or local judicial officer.

Rule 4. Arrest Warrant or Summons on a Complaint

(a) Issuance. If the complaint or one or more affidavits filed with the complaint establish probable cause to believe that an offense has been committed and that the defendant committed it, the judge must issue an arrest warrant to an officer authorized to execute it. At the request of an attorney for the government, the judge must issue a summons, instead of a warrant, to a person authorized to serve it. A judge may issue more than one warrant or summons on the same complaint. If a defendant fails to appear in response to a summons, a judge may, and upon request of an attorney for the government must, issue a warrant.

(b) Form.

(1) *Warrant.* A warrant must:

(A) contain the defendant's name or, if it is unknown, a name or description by which the defendant can be identified with reasonable certainty;

(B) describe the offense charged in the complaint;

(C) command that the defendant be arrested and brought without unnecessary delay before a magistrate judge or, if none is reasonably available, before a state or local judicial officer; and

(D) be signed by a judge.

(2) *Summons.* A summons must be in the same form as a warrant except that it must require the defendant to appear before a magistrate judge at a stated time and place.

(c) Execution or Service, and Return.

(1) *By Whom.* Only a marshal or other authorized officer may execute a warrant. Any person authorized to serve a summons in a federal civil action may serve a summons.

(2) *Location.* A warrant may be executed, or a summons served, within the jurisdiction of the United States or anywhere else a federal statute authorizes an arrest.

(3) *Manner.*

(A) A warrant is executed by arresting the defendant. Upon arrest, an officer possessing the warrant must show it to the defendant. If the officer does not possess the warrant, the officer must inform the defendant of the warrant's existence and of the offense charged and, at the defendant's request, must show the warrant to the defendant as soon as possible.

(B) A summons is served on an individual defendant:

(i) by delivering a copy to the defendant personally; or

(ii) by leaving a copy at the defendant's residence or usual place of abode with a person of suitable age and discretion residing at that location and by mailing a copy to the defendant's last known address.

(C) A summons is served on an organization by delivering a copy to an officer, to a managing or general agent, or to another agent appointed or legally authorized to receive service of process. A copy must also be mailed to the organization's last known address within the district or to its principal place of business elsewhere in the United States.

(4) *Return*.

(A) After executing a warrant, the officer must return it to the judge before whom the defendant is brought in accordance with Rule 5. At the request of an attorney for the government, an unexecuted warrant must be brought back to and canceled by a magistrate judge or, if none is reasonably available, by a state or local judicial officer.

(B) The person to whom a summons was delivered for service must return it on or before the return day.

(C) At the request of an attorney for the government, a judge may deliver an unexecuted warrant, an unserved summons, or a copy of the warrant or summons to the marshal or other authorized person for execution or service.

Rule 5. Initial Appearance

(a) In General.

(1) *Appearance Upon an Arrest*.

(A) A person making an arrest within the United States must take the defendant without unnecessary delay before a magistrate judge, or before a state or local judicial officer as Rule 5(c) provides, unless a statute provides otherwise.

(B) A person making an arrest outside the United States must take the defendant without unnecessary delay before a magistrate judge, unless a statute provides otherwise.

(2) *Exceptions*.

(A) An officer making an arrest under a warrant issued upon a complaint charging solely a violation of 18 U.S.C. § 1073 need not comply with this rule if:

(i) the person arrested is transferred without unnecessary delay to the custody of appropriate state or local authorities in the district of arrest; and

(ii) an attorney for the government moves promptly, in the district where the warrant was issued, to dismiss the complaint.

(B) If a defendant is arrested for violating probation or supervised release, Rule 32.1 applies.

(C) If a defendant is arrested for failing to appear in another district, Rule 40 applies.

(3) *Appearance Upon a Summons.* When a defendant appears in response to a summons under Rule 4, a magistrate judge must proceed under Rule 5(d) or (e), as applicable.

(b) Arrest Without a Warrant. If a defendant is arrested without a warrant, a complaint meeting Rule 4(a)'s requirement of probable cause must be promptly filed in the district where the offense was allegedly committed.

(c) Place of Initial Appearance; Transfer to Another District.

(1) *Arrest in the District Where the Offense Was Allegedly Committed.* If the defendant is arrested in the district where the offense was allegedly committed:

(A) the initial appearance must be in that district; and

(B) if a magistrate judge is not reasonably available, the initial appearance may be before a state or local judicial officer.

(2) *Arrest in a District Other Than Where the Offense Was Allegedly Committed.* If the defendant was arrested in a district other than where the offense was allegedly committed, the initial appearance must be:

(A) in the district of arrest; or

(B) in an adjacent district if:

(i) the appearance can occur more promptly there; or

(ii) the offense was allegedly committed there and the initial appearance will occur on the day of arrest.

(3) *Procedures in a District Other Than Where the Offense Was Allegedly Committed.* If the initial appearance occurs in a district other than where the offense was allegedly committed, the following procedures apply:

(A) the magistrate judge must inform the defendant about the provisions of Rule 20;

(B) if the defendant was arrested without a warrant, the district court where the offense was allegedly committed must first issue a warrant before the magistrate judge transfers the defendant to that district;

(C) the magistrate judge must conduct a preliminary hearing if required by Rule 5.1;

(D) the magistrate judge must transfer the defendant to the district where the offense was allegedly committed if:

(i) the government produces the warrant, a certified copy of the warrant, or a reliable electronic form of either; and

(ii) the judge finds that the defendant is the same person named in the indictment, information, or warrant; and

(E) when a defendant is transferred and discharged, the clerk must promptly transmit the papers and any bail to the clerk in the district where the offense was allegedly committed.

(d) Procedure in a Felony Case.

(1) *Advice.* If the defendant is charged with a felony, the judge must inform the defendant of the following:

(A) the complaint against the defendant, and any affidavit filed with it;

(B) the defendant's right to retain counsel or to request that counsel be appointed if the defendant cannot obtain counsel;

(C) the circumstances, if any, under which the defendant may secure pretrial release;

(D) any right to a preliminary hearing; and

(E) the defendant's right not to make a statement, and that any statement made may be used against the defendant.

(2) *Consulting with Counsel.* The judge must allow the defendant reasonable opportunity to consult with counsel.

(3) *Detention or Release.* The judge must detain or release the defendant as provided by statute or these rules.

(4) *Plea.* A defendant may be asked to plead only under Rule 10.

(e) Procedure in a Misdemeanor Case. If the defendant is charged with a misdemeanor only, the judge must inform the defendant in accordance with Rule 58(b)(2).

(f) Video Teleconferencing. Video teleconferencing may be used to conduct an appearance under this rule if the defendant consents.

Rule 5.1 Preliminary Hearing

(a) In General. If a defendant is charged with an offense other than a petty offense, a magistrate judge must conduct a preliminary hearing unless:

(1) the defendant waives the hearing;

(2) the defendant is indicted;

(3) the government files an information under Rule 7(b) charging the defendant with a felony;

(4) the government files an information charging the defendant with a misdemeanor; or

(5) the defendant is charged with a misdemeanor and consents to trial before a magistrate judge.

(b) Selecting a District. A defendant arrested in a district other than where the offense was allegedly committed may elect to have the preliminary hearing conducted in the district where the prosecution is pending.

(c) Scheduling. The magistrate judge must hold the preliminary hearing within a reasonable time, but no later than 14 days after the initial appearance if the defendant is in custody and no later than 21 days if not in custody.

(d) Extending the Time. With the defendant's consent and upon a showing of good cause—taking into account the public interest in the prompt disposition of criminal cases—a magistrate judge may extend the time limits in Rule 5.1(c) one or more times. If the defendant does not consent, the magistrate judge may extend the time limits only on a showing that extraordinary circumstances exist and justice requires the delay.

(e) Hearing and Finding. At the preliminary hearing, the defendant may cross-examine adverse witnesses and may introduce evidence but may not object to evidence on the ground that it was unlawfully acquired. If the magistrate judge finds probable cause to believe an offense has been committed and the defendant committed it, the magistrate judge must promptly require the defendant to appear for further proceedings.

(f) Discharging the Defendant. If the magistrate judge finds no probable cause to believe an offense has been committed or the defendant committed it, the magistrate judge must dismiss the complaint and discharge the defendant. A discharge does not preclude the government from later prosecuting the defendant for the same offense.

(g) Recording the Proceedings. The preliminary hearing must be recorded by a court reporter or by a suitable recording device. A recording of the proceeding may be made available to any party upon request. A copy of the recording and a transcript may be provided to any party upon request and upon any payment required by applicable Judicial Conference regulations.

(h) Producing a Statement.

(1) *In General.* Rule 26.2(a)-(d) and (f) applies at any hearing under this rule, unless the magistrate judge for good cause rules otherwise in a particular case.

(2) *Sanctions for Not Producing a Statement*. If a party disobeys a Rule 26.2 order to deliver a statement to the moving party, the magistrate judge must not consider the testimony of a witness whose statement is withheld.

TITLE III. THE GRAND JURY, THE INDICTMENT, AND THE INFORMATION

Rule 6. The Grand Jury

(a) Summoning a Grand Jury.

(1) *In General.* When the public interest so requires, the court must order that one or more grand juries be summoned. A grand jury must have 16 to 23 members, and the court must order that enough legally qualified persons be summoned to meet this requirement.

(2) *Alternate Jurors.* When a grand jury is selected, the court may also select alternate jurors. Alternate jurors must have the same qualifications and be selected in the same manner as any other juror. Alternate jurors replace jurors in the same sequence in which the alternates were selected. An alternate juror who replaces a juror is subject to the same challenges, takes the same oath, and has the same authority as the other jurors.

(b) Objection to the Grand Jury or to a Grand Juror.

(1) *Challenges.* Either the government or a defendant may challenge the grand jury on the ground that it was not lawfully drawn, summoned, or selected, and may challenge an individual juror on the ground that the juror is not legally qualified.

(2) *Motion to Dismiss an Indictment.* A party may move to dismiss the indictment based on an objection to the grand jury or on an individual juror's lack of legal qualification, unless the court has previously ruled on the same objection under Rule 6(b)(1). The motion to dismiss is governed by 28 U.S.C. § 1867(e). The court must not dismiss the indictment on the ground that a grand juror was not legally qualified if the record shows that at least 12 qualified jurors concurred in the indictment.

(c) Foreperson and Deputy Foreperson. The court will appoint one juror as the foreperson and another as the deputy foreperson. In the foreperson's absence, the deputy foreperson will act as the foreperson. The foreperson may administer oaths and affirmations and will sign all indictments. The foreperson—or another juror designated by the foreperson— will record the number of jurors concurring in every indictment and will file the record with the clerk, but the record may not be made public unless the court so orders.

(d) Who May Be Present.

(1) *While the Grand Jury Is in Session.* The following persons may be present while the grand jury is in session: attorneys for the government, the witness being questioned, interpreters when needed, and a court reporter or an operator of a recording device.

(2) *During Deliberations and Voting.* No person other than the jurors, and any interpreter needed to assist a hearing-impaired or speech-impaired juror, may be present while the grand jury is deliberating or voting.

(e) Recording and Disclosing the Proceedings.

(1) *Recording the Proceedings.* Except while the grand jury is deliberating or voting, all proceedings must be recorded by a court reporter or by a suitable recording device. But the validity of a prosecution is not affected by the unintentional failure to make a recording. Unless the court orders otherwise, an attorney for the government will retain control of the recording, the reporter's notes, and any transcript prepared from those notes.

(2) *Secrecy.*

(A) No obligation of secrecy may be imposed on any person except in accordance with Rule 6(e)(2)(B).

(B) Unless these rules provide otherwise, the following persons must not disclose a matter occurring before the grand jury:

> (i) a grand juror;

> (ii) an interpreter;

> (iii) a court reporter;

> (iv) an operator of a recording device;

> (v) a person who transcribes recorded testimony;

> (vi) an attorney for the government; or

> (vii) a person to whom disclosure is made under Rule 6(e)(3)(A)(ii)or (iii).

(3) *Exceptions.*

(A) Disclosure of a grand-jury matter—other than the grand jury's deliberations or any grand juror's vote—may be made to:

> (i) an attorney for the government for use in performing that attorney's duty;

> (ii) any government personnel—including those of a state, state subdivision, Indian tribe, or foreign government—that an attorney for the government considers necessary to assist in performing that attorney's duty to enforce federal criminal law; or

> (iii) a person authorized by 18 U.S.C. § 3322.

(B) A person to whom information is disclosed under Rule 6(e)(3)(A)(ii) may use that information only to assist an attorney for the government in performing that attorney's duty to enforce federal criminal law. An attorney for the government must promptly provide the court that impaneled the grand jury with the names of all persons to whom a disclosure has been made, and must certify that the attorney has advised those persons of their obligation of secrecy under this rule.

(C) An attorney for the government may disclose any grand-jury matter to another federal grand jury.

(D) An attorney for the government may disclose any grand-jury matter involving foreign intelligence, counterintelligence (as defined in 50 U.S.C. § 401a), or foreign intelligence information (as defined in Rule 6(e)(3)(D)(iii)) to any federal law enforcement, intelligence, protective, immigration, national defense, or national security official to assist the official receiving the information in the performance of that official's duties. An attorney for the government may also disclose any grand-jury matter involving, within the United States or elsewhere, a threat of attack or other grave hostile acts of a foreign power or its agent, a threat of domestic or international sabotage or terrorism, or clandestine intelligence gathering activities by an intelligence service or network of a foreign power or by its agent, to any appropriate federal, state, state subdivision, Indian Tribal, or foreign government official, for the purpose of preventing or responding to such threat or activities.

(i) Any official who receives information under Rule 6(e)(3)(D) may use the information only as necessary in the conduct of that person's official duties subject to any limitations on the unauthorized disclosure of such information. Any state, state subdivision, Indian Tribal, or foreign government official who receives information under Rule 6(e)(3)(D) may use the information only in a manner consistent with any guidelines issued by the Attorney General and the Director of National Intelligence.

(ii) Within a reasonable time after disclosure is made under Rule 6(e)(3)(D), an attorney for the government must file, under seal, a notice with the court in the district where the grand jury convened stating that such information was disclosed and the departments, agencies, or entities to which the disclosure was made.

(iii) As used in Rule 6(e)(3)(D), the term "foreign intelligence information" means:

(a) information, whether or not it concerns a United States person, that relates to the ability of the United States to protect against—

actual or potential attack or other grave hostile acts of a foreign power or its agent;

sabotage or international terrorism by a foreign power or its agent; or clandestine intelligence activities by an intelligence service or network of a foreign power or by its agent; or

(b) information, whether or not it concerns a United States person, with respect to a foreign power or foreign territory that relates to the national defense or the security of the United States; or the conduct of the foreign affairs of the United States.

(E) The court may authorize disclosure—at a time, in a manner, and subject to any other conditions that it directs—of a grand-jury matter:

(i) preliminarily to or in connection with a judicial proceeding;

(ii) at the request of a defendant who shows that a ground may exist to dismiss the indictment because of a matter that occurred before the grand jury;

(iii) at the request of the government, when sought by a foreign court or prosecutor for use in an official criminal investigation;

(iv) at the request of the government if it shows that the matter may disclose a violation of State, Indian tribal or foreign criminal law, as long as the disclosure is to an appropriate state, state-subdivision, Indian tribal, or foreign government official for the purpose of enforcing that law; or

(v) at the request of the government if it shows that the matter may disclose a violation of military criminal law under the Uniform Code of Military Justice, as long as the disclosure is to an appropriate military official for the purpose of enforcing that law.

(F) A petition to disclose a grand-jury matter under Rule 6(e)(3)(E)(i) must be filed in the district where the grand jury convened. Unless the hearing is ex parte—as it may be when the government is the petitioner—the petitioner must serve the petition on, and the court must afford a reasonable opportunity to appear and be heard to:

(i) an attorney for the government;

(ii) the parties to the judicial proceeding; and

(iii) any other person whom the court may designate.

(G) If the petition to disclose arises out of a judicial proceeding in another district, the petitioned court must transfer the petition to the other court unless the petitioned court can reasonably determine whether disclosure is proper. If the petitioned court decides to transfer, it must send to the transferee court the material sought to be disclosed, if feasible, and a written evaluation of the need for continued grand-jury secrecy. The transferee court must afford those persons identified in Rule 6(e)(3)(F) a reasonable opportunity to appear and be heard.

(4) *Sealed Indictment.* The magistrate judge to whom an indictment is returned may direct that the indictment be kept secret until the defendant is in custody or has been released pending trial. The clerk must then seal the indictment, and no person may disclose the indictment's existence except as necessary to issue or execute a warrant or summons.

(5) *Closed Hearing.* Subject to any right to an open hearing in a contempt proceeding, the court must close any hearing to the extent necessary to prevent disclosure of a matter occurring before a grand jury.

(6) *Sealed Records.* Records, orders, and subpoenas relating to grand-jury proceedings must be kept under seal to the extent and as long as necessary to prevent the unauthorized disclosure of a matter occurring before a grand jury.

(7) *Contempt.* A knowing violation of Rule 6, or of any guidelines jointly issued by the Attorney General and the Director of National Intelligence under Rule 6, may be punished as a contempt of court.

(f) Indictment and Return. A grand jury may indict only if at least 12 jurors concur. The grand jury—or its foreperson or deputy foreperson—must return the indictment to a magistrate judge in open court. If a complaint or information is pending against the defendant and 12 jurors do not concur in the indictment, the foreperson must promptly and in writing report the lack of concurrence to the magistrate judge.

(g) Discharging the Grand Jury. A grand jury must serve until the court discharges it, but it may serve more than 18 months only if the court, having determined that an extension is in the public interest, extends the grand jury's service. An extension may be granted for no more than 6 months, except as otherwise provided by statute.

(h) Excusing a Juror. At any time, for good cause, the court may excuse a juror either temporarily or permanently, and if permanently, the court may impanel an alternate juror in place of the excused juror.

(i) "Indian Tribe" Defined. "Indian tribe" means an Indian tribe recognized by the Secretary of the Interior on a list published in the Federal Register under 25 U.S.C. § 479a–1.

Rule 7. The Indictment and the Information

(a) When Used.

(1) *Felony.* An offense (other than criminal contempt) must be prosecuted by an indictment if it is punishable:

    (A) by death; or

    (B) by imprisonment for more than one year.

(2) *Misdemeanor.* An offense punishable by imprisonment for one year or less may be prosecuted in accordance with Rule 58(b)(1).

(b) Waiving Indictment. An offense punishable by imprisonment for more than one year may be prosecuted by information if the defendant—in open court and after being advised of the nature of the charge and of the defendant's rights—waives prosecution by indictment.

(c) Nature and Contents.

(1) *In General.* The indictment or information must be a plain, concise, and definite written statement of the essential facts constituting the offense charged and must be signed by an attorney for the government. It need not contain a formal introduction or conclusion. A count may incorporate by reference an allegation made in another count. A count may allege that the means by which the defendant committed the offense are unknown or that the defendant committed it by one or more specified means. For each count, the indictment or information must give the official or customary citation of the statute, rule, regulation, or other provision of law that the defendant is alleged to have violated. For purposes of an indictment referred to in section 3282 of title 18, United States Code, for which the identity of the defendant is unknown, it shall be sufficient for the indictment to describe the defendant as an individual whose name is unknown, but who has a particular DNA profile, as that term is defined in that section 3282.

(2) *Citation Error.* Unless the defendant was misled and thereby prejudiced, neither an error in a citation nor a citation's omission is a ground to dismiss the indictment or information or to reverse a conviction.

(d) Surplusage. Upon the defendant's motion, the court may strike surplusage from the indictment or information.

(e) Amending an Information. Unless an additional or different offense is charged or a substantial right of the defendant is prejudiced, the court may permit an information to be amended at any time before the verdict or finding.

(f) Bill of Particulars. The court may direct the government to file a bill of particulars. The defendant may move for a bill of particulars before or within 14 days after arraignment or at a later time if the court permits. The government may amend a bill of particulars subject to such conditions as justice requires.

Rule 8. Joinder of Offenses or Defendants

(a) Joinder of Offenses. The indictment or information may charge a defendant in separate counts with 2 or more offenses if the offenses charged—whether felonies or misdemeanors or both—are of the same or similar character, or are based on the same act or transaction, or are connected with or constitute parts of a common scheme or plan.

(b) Joinder of Defendants. The indictment or information may charge 2 or more defendants if they are alleged to have participated in the same act or transaction, or in the same series of acts or transactions, constituting an offense or offenses. The defendants may be charged in one or more counts together or separately. All defendants need not be charged in each count.

Rule 9. Arrest Warrant or Summons on an Indictment or Information

(a) Issuance. The court must issue a warrant—or at the government's request, a summons—for each defendant named in an indictment or named in an information if one or more affidavits accompanying the information establish probable cause to believe that an offense has been committed and that the defendant committed it. The court may issue more than one warrant or summons for the same defendant. If a defendant fails to appear in response to a summons, the court may, and upon request of an attorney for the government must, issue a warrant. The court must issue the arrest warrant to an officer authorized to execute it or the summons to a person authorized to serve it.

(b) Form.

(1) *Warrant.* The warrant must conform to Rule 4(b)(1) except that it must be signed by the clerk and must describe the offense charged in the indictment or information.

(2) *Summons.* The summons must be in the same form as a warrant except that it must require the defendant to appear before the court at a stated time and place.

(c) Execution or Service; Return; Initial Appearance.

(1) *Execution or Service.*

(A) The warrant must be executed or the summons served as provided in Rule 4(c)(1), (2), and (3).

(B) The officer executing the warrant must proceed in accordance with Rule 5(a)(1).

(2) *Return.* A warrant or summons must be returned in accordance with Rule 4(c)(4).

(3) *Initial Appearance.* When an arrested or summoned defendant first appears before the court, the judge must proceed under Rule 5.

TITLE IV. ARRAIGNMENT AND PREPARATION FOR TRIAL

Rule 10. Arraignment

(a) In General. An arraignment must be conducted in open court and must consist of:

(1) ensuring that the defendant has a copy of the indictment or information;

(2) reading the indictment or information to the defendant or stating to the defendant the substance of the charge; and then

(3) asking the defendant to plead to the indictment or information.

(b) Waiving Appearance. A defendant need not be present for the arraignment if:

(1) the defendant has been charged by indictment or misdemeanor information;

(2) the defendant, in a written waiver signed by both the defendant and defense counsel, has waived appearance and has affirmed that the defendant received a copy of the indictment or information and that the plea is not guilty; and

(3) the court accepts the waiver.

(c) Video Teleconferencing. Video teleconferencing may be used to arraign a defendant if the defendant consents.

Rule 11. Pleas

(a) Entering a Plea.

(1) *In General.* A defendant may plead not guilty, guilty, or (with the court's consent) nolo contendere.

(2) *Conditional Plea.* With the consent of the court and the government, a defendant may enter a conditional plea of guilty or nolo contendere, reserving in writing the right to have an appellate court review an adverse determination of a specified pretrial motion. A defendant who prevails on appeal may then withdraw the plea.

(3) *Nolo Contendere Plea.* Before accepting a plea of nolo contendere, the court must consider the parties' views and the public interest in the effective administration of justice.

(4) *Failure to Enter a Plea.* If a defendant refuses to enter a plea or if a defendant organization fails to appear, the court must enter a plea of not guilty.

(b) Considering and Accepting a Guilty or Nolo Contendere Plea.

(1) *Advising and Questioning the Defendant.* Before the court accepts a plea of guilty or nolo contendere, the defendant may be placed under oath, and the court must address the defendant personally in open court. During this address, the court must inform the defendant of, and determine that the defendant understands, the following:

(A) the government's right, in a prosecution for perjury or false statement, to use against the defendant any statement that the defendant gives under oath;

(B) the right to plead not guilty, or having already so pleaded, to persist in that plea;

(C) the right to a jury trial;

(D) the right to be represented by counsel—and if necessary have the court appoint counsel—at trial and at every other stage of the proceeding;

(E) the right at trial to confront and cross-examine adverse witnesses, to be protected from compelled self-incrimination, to testify and present evidence, and to compel the attendance of witnesses;

(F) the defendant's waiver of these trial rights if the court accepts a plea of guilty or nolo contendere;

(G) the nature of each charge to which the defendant is pleading;

(H) any maximum possible penalty, including imprisonment, fine, and term of supervised release;

(I) any mandatory minimum penalty;

(J) any applicable forfeiture;

(K) the court's authority to order restitution;

(L) the court's obligation to impose a special assessment;

(M) in determining a sentence, the court's obligation to calculate the applicable sentencing-guideline range and to consider that range, possible departures under the Sentencing Guidelines, and other sentencing factors under 18 U.S.C. § 3553(a); and

(N) the terms of any plea-agreement provision waiving the right to appeal or to collaterally attack the sentence.

(2) *Ensuring That a Plea Is Voluntary.* Before accepting a plea of guilty or nolo contendere, the court must address the defendant personally in open court and determine that the plea is voluntary and did not result from force, threats, or promises (other than promises in a plea agreement).

(3) *Determining the Factual Basis for a Plea.* Before entering judgment on a guilty plea, the court must determine that there is a factual basis for the plea.

(c) Plea Agreement Procedure.

(1) *In General.* An attorney for the government and the defendant's attorney, or the defendant when proceeding pro se, may discuss and reach a plea agreement. The court must not participate in these discussions. If the defendant pleads guilty or nolo contendere to either a charged offense or a lesser or related offense, the plea agreement may specify that an attorney for the government will:

(A) not bring, or will move to dismiss, other charges;

(B) recommend, or agree not to oppose the defendant's request, that a particular sentence or sentencing range is appropriate or that a particular provision of the Sentencing Guidelines, or policy statement, or sentencing factor does or does not apply (such a recommendation or request does not bind the court); or

(C) agree that a specific sentence or sentencing range is the appropriate disposition of the case, or that a particular provision of the Sentencing Guidelines, or policy statement, or sentencing factor does or does not apply (such a recommendation or request binds the court once the court accepts the plea agreement).

(2) *Disclosing a Plea Agreement.* The parties must disclose the plea agreement in open court when the plea is offered, unless the court for good cause allows the parties to disclose the plea agreement in camera.

(3) *Judicial Consideration of a Plea Agreement.*

(A) To the extent the plea agreement is of the type specified in Rule 11(c)(1)(A) or (C), the court may accept the agreement, reject it, or defer a decision until the court has reviewed the presentence report.

(B) To the extent the plea agreement is of the type specified in Rule 11(c)(1)(B), the court must advise the defendant that the defendant has no right to withdraw the plea if the court does not follow the recommendation or request.

(4) *Accepting a Plea Agreement.* If the court accepts the plea agreement, it must inform the defendant that to the extent the plea agreement is of the type specified in Rule 11(c)(1)(A) or (C), the agreed disposition will be included in the judgment.

(5) *Rejecting a Plea Agreement.* If the court rejects a plea agreement containing provisions of the type specified in Rule 11(c)(1)(A) or (C), the court must do the following on the record and in open court (or, for good cause, in camera):

(A) inform the parties that the court rejects the plea agreement;

(B) advise the defendant personally that the court is not required to follow the plea agreement and give the defendant an opportunity to withdraw the plea; and

(C) advise the defendant personally that if the plea is not withdrawn, the court may dispose of the case less favorably toward the defendant than the plea agreement contemplated.

(d) Withdrawing a Guilty or Nolo Contendere Plea. A defendant may withdraw a plea of guilty or nolo contendere:

(1) before the court accepts the plea, for any reason or no reason; or

(2) after the court accepts the plea, but before it imposes sentence if:

(A) the court rejects a plea agreement under Rule 11(c)(5); or

(B) the defendant can show a fair and just reason for requesting the withdrawal.

(e) Finality of a Guilty or Nolo Contendere Plea. After the court imposes sentence, the defendant may not withdraw a plea of guilty or nolo contendere, and the plea may be set aside only on direct appeal or collateral attack.

(f) Admissibility or Inadmissibility of a Plea, Plea Discussions, and Related Statements. The admissibility or inadmissibility of a plea, a plea discussion, and any related statement is governed by Federal Rule of Evidence 410.

(g) Recording the Proceedings. The proceedings during which the defendant enters a plea must be recorded by a court reporter or by a suitable recording device. If there is a guilty plea or a nolo contendere plea, the record must include the inquiries and advice to the defendant required under Rule 11(b) and (c).

(h) Harmless Error. A variance from the requirements of this rule is harmless error if it does not affect substantial rights.

Rule 12. Pleadings and Pretrial Motions

(a) Pleadings. The pleadings in a criminal proceeding are the indictment, the information, and the pleas of not guilty, guilty, and nolo contendere.

(b) Pretrial Motions.

(1) *In General.* Rule 47 applies to a pretrial motion.

(2) *Motions That May Be Made Before Trial.* A party may raise by pretrial motion any defense, objection, or request that the court can determine without a trial of the general issue.

(3) *Motions That Must Be Made Before Trial*. The following must be raised before trial:

(A) a motion alleging a defect in instituting the prosecution;

(B) a motion alleging a defect in the indictment or information—but at any time while the case is pending, the court may hear a claim that the indictment or information fails to invoke the court's jurisdiction or to state an offense;

(C) a motion to suppress evidence;

(D) a Rule 14 motion to sever charges or defendants; and

(E) a Rule 16 motion for discovery.

(4) *Notice of the Government's Intent to Use Evidence.*

(A) *At the Government's Discretion.* At the arraignment or as soon afterward as practicable, the government may notify the defendant of its intent to use specified evidence at trial in order to afford the defendant an opportunity to object before trial under Rule 12(b)(3)(C).

(B) *At the Defendant's Request.* At the arraignment or as soon afterward as practicable, the defendant may, in order to have an opportunity to move to suppress evidence under Rule 12(b)(3)(C), request notice of the government's intent to use (in its evidence-in-chief at trial) any evidence that the defendant may be entitled to discover under Rule 16.

(c) Motion Deadline. The court may, at the arraignment or as soon afterward as practicable, set a deadline for the parties to make pretrial motions and may also schedule a motion hearing.

(d) Ruling on a Motion. The court must decide every pretrial motion before trial unless it finds good cause to defer a ruling. The court must not defer ruling on a pretrial motion if the deferral will adversely affect a party's right to appeal. When factual issues are involved in deciding a motion, the court must state its essential findings on the record.

(e) Waiver of a Defense, Objection, or Request. A party waives any Rule 12(b)(3) defense, objection, or request not raised by the deadline the court sets under Rule 12(c) or by any extension the court provides. For good cause, the court may grant relief from the waiver.

(f) Recording the Proceedings. All proceedings at a motion hearing, including any findings of fact and conclusions of law made orally by the court, must be recorded by a court reporter or a suitable recording device.

(g) Defendant's Continued Custody or Release Status. If the court grants a motion to dismiss based on a defect in instituting the prosecution, in the indictment, or in the information, it may order the defendant to be released or detained under 18 U.S.C. § 3142 for a specified time until a new indictment or information is filed. This rule does not affect any federal statutory period of limitations.

(h) Producing Statements at a Suppression Hearing. Rule 26.2 applies at a suppression hearing under Rule 12(b)(3)(C). At a suppression hearing, a law enforcement officer is considered a government witness.

Rule 12.1. Notice of an Alibi Defense

(a) Government's Request for Notice and Defendant's Response.

(1) *Government's Request.* An attorney for the government may request in writing that the defendant notify an attorney for the government of any intended alibi defense. The request must state the time, date, and place of the alleged offense.

(2) *Defendant's Response.* Within 14 days after the request, or at some other time the court sets, the defendant must serve written notice on an attorney for the government of any intended alibi defense. The defendant's notice must state:

(A) each specific place where the defendant claims to have been at the time of the alleged offense; and

(B) the name, address, and telephone number of each alibi witness on whom the defendant intends to rely.

(b) Disclosing Government Witnesses.

(1) *Disclosure.*

(A) *In General.* If the defendant serves a Rule 12.1(a)(2) notice, an attorney for the government must disclose in writing to the defendant or the defendant's attorney:

(i) the name of each witness—and the address and telephone number of each witness other than a victim—that the government intends to rely on to establish that the defendant was present at the scene of the alleged offense; and

(ii) each government rebuttal witness to the defendant's alibi defense.

(B) *Victim's Address and Telephone Number.* If the government intends to rely on a victim's testimony to establish that the defendant was present at the scene of the alleged offense and the defendant establishes a need for the victim's address and telephone number, the court may:

(i) order the government to provide the information in writing to the defendant or the defendant's attorney; or

(ii) fashion a reasonable procedure that allows preparation of the defense and also protects the victim's interests.

(2) *Time to Disclose.* Unless the court directs otherwise, an attorney for the government must give its Rule 12.1(b)(1) disclosure within 14 days after the defendant serves notice of an intended alibi defense under Rule 12.1(a)(2), but no later than 14 days before trial.

(c) Continuing Duty to Disclose.

(1) *In General.* Both an attorney for the government and the defendant must promptly disclose in writing to the other party the name of each additional witness—and the address and telephone number of each additional witness other than a victim—if:

(A) the disclosing party learns of the witness before or during trial; and

(B) the witness should have been disclosed under Rule 12.1(a) or (b) if the disclosing party had known of the witness earlier.

(2) *Address and Telephone Number of an Additional Victim Witness.* The address and telephone number of an additional victim witness must not be disclosed except as provided in Rule 12.1(b)(1)(B).

(d) Exceptions. For good cause, the court may grant an exception to any requirement of Rule 12.1(a)-(c).

(e) Failure to Comply. If a party fails to comply with this rule, the court may exclude the testimony of any undisclosed witness regarding the defendant's alibi. This rule does not limit the defendant's right to testify.

(f) Inadmissibility of Withdrawn Intention. Evidence of an intention to rely on an alibi defense, later withdrawn, or of a statement made in connection with that intention, is not, in any civil or criminal proceeding, admissible against the person who gave notice of the intention.

Rule 12.2. Notice of an Insanity Defense; Mental Examination

(a) Notice of an Insanity Defense. A defendant who intends to assert a defense of insanity at the time of the alleged offense must so notify an attorney for the government in writing within the time provided for filing a pretrial motion, or at any later time the court sets, and file a copy of the notice with the clerk. A defendant who fails to do so cannot rely on an insanity defense. The court may, for good cause, allow the defendant to file the notice late, grant additional trial-preparation time, or make other appropriate orders.

(b) Notice of Expert Evidence of a Mental Condition. If a defendant intends to introduce expert evidence relating to a mental disease or defect or any other mental condition of the defendant bearing on either (1) the issue of guilt or (2) the issue of punishment in a capital case, the defendant must—within the time provided for filing a pretrial motion or at any later time the court sets—notify an attorney for the government in writing of this intention and file a copy of the notice with the clerk. The court may, for good cause, allow the defendant to file the notice late, grant the parties additional trial-preparation time, or make other appropriate orders.

(c) Mental Examination.

(1) *Authority to Order an Examination; Procedures.*

(A) The court may order the defendant to submit to a competency examination under 18 U.S.C. § 4241.

(B) If the defendant provides notice under Rule 12.2(a), the court must, upon the government's motion, order the defendant to be examined under 18 U.S.C. § 4242. If the defendant provides notice under Rule 12.2(b) the court may, upon the government's motion, order the defendant to be examined under procedures ordered by the court.

(2) *Disclosing Results and Reports of Capital Sentencing Examination.* The results and reports of any examination conducted solely under Rule 12.2(c)(1) after notice under Rule 12.2(b)(2) must be sealed and must not be disclosed to any attorney for the government or the defendant unless the defendant is found guilty of one or more capital crimes and the defendant confirms an intent to offer during sentencing proceedings expert evidence on mental condition.

(3) *Disclosing Results and Reports of the Defendant's Expert Examination.* After disclosure under Rule 12.2(c)(2) of the results and reports of the government's examination, the defendant must disclose to the government the results and reports of any examination on mental condition conducted by the defendant's expert about which the defendant intends to introduce expert evidence.

(4) *Inadmissibility of a Defendant's Statements.* No statement made by a defendant in the course of any examination conducted under this rule (whether conducted with or without the defendant's consent), no testimony by the expert based on the statement, and no other fruits of the statement may be admitted into evidence against the defendant in any criminal proceeding except on an issue regarding mental condition on which the defendant:

(A) has introduced evidence of incompetency or evidence requiring notice under Rule 12.2(a) or (b)(1), or

(B) has introduced expert evidence in a capital sentencing proceeding requiring notice under Rule 12.2(b)(2).

(d) Failure to Comply.

(1) *Failure to Give Notice or to Submit to Examination.* The court may exclude any expert evidence from the defendant on the issue of the defendant's mental disease, mental defect, or any other mental condition bearing on the defendant's guilt or the issue of punishment in a capital case if the defendant fails to:

(A) give notice under Rule 12.2(b); or

(B) submit to an examination when ordered under Rule 12.2(c)

(2) *Failure to Disclose.* The court may exclude any expert evidence for which the defendant has failed to comply with the disclosure requirement of Rule 12.2(c)(3).

(e) Inadmissibility of Withdrawn Intention. Evidence of an intention as to which notice was given under Rule 12.2(a) or (b), later withdrawn, is not, in any civil or criminal proceeding, admissible against the person who gave notice of the intention.

Rule 12.3. Notice of a Public–Authority Defense

(a) Notice of the Defense and Disclosure of Witnesses.

(1) *Notice in General.* If a defendant intends to assert a defense of actual or believed exercise of public authority on behalf of a law enforcement agency or federal intelligence agency at the time of the alleged offense, the defendant must so notify an attorney for the government in writing and must file a copy of the notice with the clerk within the time provided for filing a pretrial motion, or at any later time the court sets. The notice filed with the clerk must be under seal if the notice identifies a federal intelligence agency as the source of public authority.

(2) *Contents of Notice.* The notice must contain the following information:

(A) the law enforcement agency or federal intelligence agency involved;

(B) the agency member on whose behalf the defendant claims to have acted; and

(C) the time during which the defendant claims to have acted with public authority.

(3) *Response to the Notice.* An attorney for the government must serve a written response on the defendant or the defendant's attorney within 14 days after receiving the defendant's notice, but no later than 21 days before trial. The response must admit or deny that the defendant exercised the public authority identified in the defendant's notice.

(4) *Disclosing Witnesses.*

(A) *Government's Request.* An attorney for the government may request in writing that the defendant disclose the name, address, and telephone number of each witness the defendant intends to rely on to establish a public-authority defense. An attorney for the government may serve the request when the government serves its response to the defendant's notice under Rule 12.3(a)(3), or later, but must serve the request no later than 21 days before trial.

(B) *Defendant's Response.* Within 14 days after receiving the government's request, the defendant must serve on an attorney for the government a written statement of the name, address, and telephone number of each witness.

(C) *Government's Reply.* Within 14 days after receiving the defendant's statement, an attorney for the government must serve on the defendant or the defendant's attorney a written statement of the name of each witness—and the address and telephone number of each witness other than a victim—the government intends to rely on to oppose the defendant's public-authority defense.

(D) *Victim's Address and Telephone Number.* If the government intends to rely on a victim's testimony to oppose the defendant's public-authority defense and the defendant establishes a need for the victim's address and telephone number, the court may:

(i) order the government to provide the information in writing to the defendant or the defendant's attorney; or

(ii) fashion a reasonable procedure that allows for preparing the defense and also protects the victim's interests.

(5) *Additional Time.* The court may, for good cause, allow a party additional time to comply with this rule.

(b) Continuing Duty to Disclose.

(1) *In General.* Both an attorney for the government and the defendant must promptly disclose in writing to the other party the name of any additional witness—and the address, and telephone number of any additional witness other than a victim—if:

(A) the disclosing party learns of the witness before or during trial; and

(B) the witness should have been disclosed under Rule 12.3(a)(4) if the disclosing party had known of the witness earlier.

(2) *Address and Telephone Number of an Additional Victim–Witness.* The address and telephone number of an additional victim-witness must not be disclosed except as provided in Rule 12.3(a)(4)(D).

(c) Failure to Comply. If a party fails to comply with this rule, the court may exclude the testimony of any undisclosed witness regarding the public-authority defense. This rule does not limit the defendant's right to testify.

(d) Protective Procedures Unaffected. This rule does not limit the court's authority to issue appropriate protective orders or to order that any filings be under seal.

(e) Inadmissibility of Withdrawn Intention. Evidence of an intention as to which notice was given under Rule 12.3(a), later withdrawn, is not, in any civil or criminal proceeding, admissible against the person who gave notice of the intention.

Rule 12.4. Disclosure Statement

(a) Who Must File.

(1) *Nongovernmental Corporate Party.* Any nongovernmental corporate party to a proceeding in a district court must file a statement that identifies any parent corporation and any publicly held corporation that owns 10% or more of its stock or states that there is no such corporation.

(2) *Organizational Victim.* If an organization is a victim of the alleged criminal activity, the government must file a statement identifying the victim. If the organizational victim is a corporation, the statement must also disclose the information required by Rule 12.4(a)(1) to the extent it can be obtained through due diligence.

(b) Time for Filing; Supplemental Filing. A party must:

(1) file the Rule 12.4(a) statement upon the defendant's initial appearance; and

(2) promptly file a supplemental statement upon any change in the information that the statement requires.

Rule 13. Joint Trial of Separate Cases

The court may order that separate cases be tried together as though brought in a single indictment or information if all offenses and all defendants could have been joined in a single indictment or information.

Rule 14. Relief from Prejudicial Joinder

(a) Relief. If the joinder of offenses or defendants in an indictment, an information, or a consolidation for trial appears to prejudice a defendant or the government, the court may order separate trials of counts, sever the defendants' trials, or provide any other relief that justice requires.

(b) Defendant's Statements. Before ruling on a defendant's motion to sever, the court may order an attorney for the government to deliver to the court for in camera inspection any defendant's statement that the government intends to use as evidence.

Rule 15. Depositions

(a) When Taken.

(1) *In General.* A party may move that a prospective witness be deposed in order to preserve testimony for trial. The court may grant the motion because of exceptional circumstances and in the interest of justice. If the court orders the deposition to be taken, it may also require the deponent to produce at the deposition any designated material that is not privileged, including any book, paper, document, record, recording, or data.

(2) *Detained Material Witness.* A witness who is detained under 18 U.S.C. § 3144 may request to be deposed by filing a written motion and giving notice to the parties. The court may then order that the deposition be taken and may discharge the witness after the witness has signed under oath the deposition transcript.

(b) Notice.

(1) *In General.* A party seeking to take a deposition must give every other party reasonable written notice of the deposition's date and location. The notice must state the name and address of each deponent. If requested by a party receiving the notice, the court may, for good cause, change the deposition's date or location.

(2) *To the Custodial Officer.* A party seeking to take the deposition must also notify the officer who has custody of the defendant of the scheduled date and location.

(c) Defendant's Presence.

(1) *Defendant in Custody.* The officer who has custody of the defendant must produce the defendant at the deposition and keep the defendant in the witness's presence during the examination, unless the defendant:

    (A) waives in writing the right to be present; or

    (B) persists in disruptive conduct justifying exclusion after being warned by the court that disruptive conduct will result in the defendant's exclusion.

(2) *Defendant Not in Custody.* A defendant who is not in custody has the right upon request to be present at the deposition, subject to any conditions imposed by the court. If the government tenders the defendant's expenses as provided in Rule 15(d) but the defendant still fails to appear, the defendant—absent good cause—waives both the right to appear and any objection to the taking and use of the deposition based on that right.

(d) Expenses. If the deposition was requested by the government, the court may—or if the defendant is unable to bear the deposition expenses, the court must—order the government to pay:

(1) any reasonable travel and subsistence expenses of the defendant and the defendant's attorney to attend the deposition; and

(2) the costs of the deposition transcript.

(e) Manner of Taking. Unless these rules or a court order provides otherwise, a deposition must be taken and filed in the same manner as a deposition in a civil action, except that:

(1) A defendant may not be deposed without that defendant's consent.

(2) The scope and manner of the deposition examination and cross-examination must be the same as would be allowed during trial.

(3) The government must provide to the defendant or the defendant's attorney, for use at the deposition, any statement of the deponent in the government's possession to which the defendant would be entitled at trial.

(f) Use as Evidence. A party may use all or part of a deposition as provided by the Federal Rules of Evidence.

(g) Objections. A party objecting to deposition testimony or evidence must state the grounds for the objection during the deposition.

(h) Depositions by Agreement Permitted. The parties may by agreement take and use a deposition with the court's consent.

Rule 16. Discovery and Inspection

(a) Government's Disclosure.

(1) *Information Subject to Disclosure.*

(A) *Defendant's Oral Statement.* Upon a defendant's request, the government must disclose to the defendant the substance of any relevant oral statement made by the defendant, before or after arrest, in response to interrogation by a person the defendant knew was a government agent if the government intends to use the statement at trial.

(B) *Defendant's Written or Recorded Statement.* Upon a defendant's request, the government must disclose to the defendant, and make available for inspection, copying, or photographing, all of the following:

(i) any relevant written or recorded statement by the defendant if: the statement is within the government's possession, custody, or control; and the attorney for the government knows—or through due diligence could know—that the statement exists;

(ii) the portion of any written record containing the substance of any relevant oral statement made before or after arrest if the defendant made the statement in response to interrogation by a person the defendant knew was a government agent; and

(iii) the defendant's recorded testimony before a grand jury relating to the charged offense.

(C) *Organizational Defendant.* Upon a defendant's request, if the defendant is an organization, the government must disclose to the defendant any statement described in Rule 16(a)(1)(A) and (B) if the government contends that the person making the statement:

(i) was legally able to bind the defendant regarding the subject of the statement because of that person's position as the defendant's director, officer, employee, or agent; or

(ii) was personally involved in the alleged conduct constituting the offense and was legally able to bind the defendant regarding that conduct because of that person's position as the defendant's director, officer, employee, or agent.

(D) *Defendant's Prior Record.* Upon a defendant's request, the government must furnish the defendant with a copy of the defendant's prior criminal record that is within the government's possession, custody, or control if the attorney for the government knows—or through due diligence could know—that the record exists.

(E) *Documents and Objects.* Upon a defendant's request, the government must permit the defendant to inspect and to copy or photograph books, papers, documents, data, photographs, tangible objects, buildings or places, or copies or portions of any of these items, if the item is within the government's possession, custody, or control and:

(i) the item is material to preparing the defense;

(ii) the government intends to use the item in its case-in-chief at trial; or

(iii) the item was obtained from or belongs to the defendant.

(F) *Reports of Examinations and Tests.* Upon a defendant's request, the government must permit a defendant to inspect and to copy or photograph the results or reports of any physical or mental examination and of any scientific test or experiment if:

(i) the item is within the government's possession, custody, or control;

(ii) the attorney for the government knows—or through due diligence could know—that the item exists; and

(iii) the item is material to preparing the defense or the government intends to use the item in its case-in-chief at trial.

(G) *Expert Witnesses.* At the defendant's request, the government must give the defendant a written summary of any testimony that the government intends to use under Rules 702, 703, or 705 of the

Federal Rules of Evidence during its case-in-chief at trial. If the government requests discovery under subdivision (b)(i)(C)(ii) and the defendant complies, the government must, at the defendant's request, give to the defendant a written summary of testimony that the government intends to use under Rules 702, 703, or 705 of the Federal Rules of Evidence as evidence at trial on the issue of the defendant's mental condition. The summary provided under this subparagraph must describe the witness's opinions, the bases and reasons for those opinions, and the witness's qualifications.

(2) *Information Not Subject to Disclosure.* Except as Rule 16(a)(1) provides otherwise, this rule does not authorize the discovery or inspection of reports, memoranda, or other internal government documents made by an attorney for the government or other government agent in connection with investigating or prosecuting the case. Nor does this rule authorize the discovery or inspection of statements made by prospective government witnesses except as provided in 18 U.S.C. § 3500.

(3) *Grand Jury Transcripts.* This rule does not apply to the discovery or inspection of a grand jury's recorded proceedings, except as provided in Rules 6, 12(h), 16(a)(1), and 26.2.

(b) Defendant's Disclosure.

(1) *Information Subject to Disclosure.*

(A) *Documents and Objects.* If a defendant requests disclosure under Rule 16(a)(1)(E) and the government complies, then the defendant must permit the government, upon request, to inspect and to copy or photograph books, papers, documents, data, photographs, tangible objects, buildings or places, or copies or portions of any of these items if:

(i) the item is within the defendant's possession, custody, or control; and

(ii) the defendant intends to use the item in the defendant's case-in-chief at trial.

(B) *Reports of Examinations and Tests.* If a defendant requests disclosure under Rule 16(a)(1)(F) and the government complies, the defendant must permit the government, upon request, to inspect and to copy or photograph the results or reports of any physical or mental examination and of any scientific test or experiment if:

(i) the item is within the defendant's possession, custody, or control; and

(ii) the defendant intends to use the item in the defendant's case-in-chief at trial, or intends to call the witness who prepared the report and the report relates to the witness's testimony.

(C) *Expert Witnesses.* The defendant must, at the government's request, give to the government a written summary of any testimony that the defendant intends to use under Rules 702, 703, or 705 of the Federal Rules of Evidence as evidence at trial, if—

    (i) the defendant requests disclosure under subdivision (a)(1)(G) and the government complies; or

    (ii) the defendant has given notice under Rule 12.2(b) of an intent to present expert testimony on the defendant's mental condition.

This summary must describe the witness's opinions, the bases and reasons for those opinions, and the witness's qualifications.

(2) *Information Not Subject to Disclosure.* Except for scientific or medical reports, Rule 16(b)(1) does not authorize discovery or inspection of:

    (A) reports, memoranda, or other documents made by the defendant, or the defendant's attorney or agent, during the case's investigation or defense; or

    (B) a statement made to the defendant, or the defendant's attorney or agent, by:

        (i) the defendant;

        (ii) a government or defense witness; or

        (iii) a prospective government or defense witness.

(c) Continuing Duty to Disclose. A party who discovers additional evidence or material before or during trial must promptly disclose its existence to the other party or the court if:

    (1) the evidence or material is subject to discovery or inspection under this rule; and

    (2) the other party previously requested, or the court ordered, its production.

(d) Regulating Discovery.

(1) *Protective and Modifying Orders.* At any time the court may, for good cause, deny, restrict, or defer discovery or inspection, or grant other appropriate relief. The court may permit a party to show good cause by a written statement that the court will inspect ex parte. If relief is granted, the court must preserve the entire text of the party's statement under seal.

(2) *Failure to Comply.* If a party fails to comply with this rule, the court may:

    (A) order that party to permit the discovery or inspection; specify its time, place, and manner; and prescribe other just terms and conditions;

    (B) grant a continuance;

    (C) prohibit that party from introducing the undisclosed evidence; or

(D) enter any other order that is just under the circumstances.

Rule 17. Subpoena

(a) Content. A subpoena must state the court's name and the title of the proceeding, include the seal of the court, and command the witness to attend and testify at the time and place the subpoena specifies. The clerk must issue a blank subpoena—signed and sealed—to the party requesting it, and that party must fill in the blanks before the subpoena is served.

(b) Defendant Unable to Pay. Upon a defendant's ex parte application, the court must order that a subpoena be issued for a named witness if the defendant shows an inability to pay the witness's fees and the necessity of the witness's presence for an adequate defense. If the court orders a subpoena to be issued, the process costs and witness fees will be paid in the same manner as those paid for witnesses the government subpoenas.

(c) Producing Documents and Objects.

(1) *In General.* A subpoena may order the witness to produce any books, papers, documents, data, or other objects the subpoena designates. The court may direct the witness to produce the designated items in court before trial or before they are to be offered in evidence. When the items arrive, the court may permit the parties and their attorneys to inspect all or part of them.

(2) *Quashing or Modifying the Subpoena.* On motion made promptly, the court may quash or modify the subpoena if compliance would be unreasonable or oppressive.

(3) *Subpoena for Personal or Confidential Information About a Victim.* After a complaint, indictment, or information is filed, a subpoena requiring the production of personal or confidential information about a victim may be served on a third party only by court order. Before entering the order and unless there are exceptional circumstances, the court must require giving notice to the victim so that the victim can move to quash or modify the subpoena or otherwise object.

(d) Service. A marshal, a deputy marshal, or any nonparty who is at least 18 years old may serve a subpoena. The server must deliver a copy of the subpoena to the witness and must tender to the witness one day's witness-attendance fee and the legal mileage allowance. The server need not tender the attendance fee or mileage allowance when the United States, a federal officer, or a federal agency has requested the subpoena.

(e) Place of Service.

(1) *In the United States.* A subpoena requiring a witness to attend a hearing or trial may be served at any place within the United States.

(2) *In a Foreign Country.* If the witness is in a foreign country, 28 U.S.C. § 1783 governs the subpoena's service.

(f) Issuing a Deposition Subpoena.

(1) *Issuance.* A court order to take a deposition authorizes the clerk in the district where the deposition is to be taken to issue a subpoena for any witness named or described in the order.

(2) *Place.* After considering the convenience of the witness and the parties, the court may order—and the subpoena may require—the witness to appear anywhere the court designates.

(g) Contempt. The court (other than a magistrate judge) may hold in contempt a witness who, without adequate excuse, disobeys a subpoena issued by a federal court in that district. A magistrate judge may hold in contempt a witness who, without adequate excuse, disobeys a subpoena issued by that magistrate judge as provided in 28 U.S.C. § 636(e).

(h) Information Not Subject to a Subpoena. No party may subpoena a statement of a witness or of a prospective witness under this rule. Rule 26.2 governs the production of the statement.

Rule 17.1. Pretrial Conference

On its own, or on a party's motion, the court may hold one or more pretrial conferences to promote a fair and expeditious trial. When a conference ends, the court must prepare and file a memorandum of any matters agreed to during the conference. The government may not use any statement made during the conference by the defendant or the defendant's attorney unless it is in writing and is signed by the defendant and the defendant's attorney.

TITLE V. VENUE

Rule 18. Place of Prosecution and Trial

Unless a statute or these rules permit otherwise, the government must prosecute an offense in a district where the offense was committed. The court must set the place of trial within the district with due regard for the convenience of the defendant, any victim, and the witnesses, and the prompt administration of justice.

Rule 19. [Reserved]

Rule 20. Transfer for Plea and Sentence

(a) Consent to Transfer. A prosecution may be transferred from the district where the indictment or information is pending, or from which a warrant on a complaint has been issued, to the district where the defendant is arrested, held, or present if:

(1) the defendant states in writing a wish to plead guilty or nolo contendere and to waive trial in the district where the indictment, information, or complaint is pending, consents in writing to the court's disposing of the case in the transferee district, and files the statement in the transferee district; and

(2) the United States attorneys in both districts approve the transfer in writing.

(b) Clerk's Duties. After receiving the defendant's statement and the required approvals, the clerk where the indictment, information, or complaint is pending must send the file, or a certified copy, to the clerk in the transferee district.

(c) Effect of a Not Guilty Plea. If the defendant pleads not guilty after the case has been transferred under Rule 20(a), the clerk must return the papers to the court where the prosecution began, and that court must restore the proceeding to its docket. The defendant's statement that the defendant wished to plead guilty or nolo contendere is not, in any civil or criminal proceeding, admissible against the defendant.

(d) Juveniles.

(1) *Consent to Transfer.* A juvenile, as defined in 18 U.S.C. § 5031, may be proceeded against as a juvenile delinquent in the district where the juvenile is arrested, held, or present if:

(A) the alleged offense that occurred in the other district is not punishable by death or life imprisonment;

(B) an attorney has advised the juvenile;

(C) the court has informed the juvenile of the juvenile's rights—including the right to be returned to the district where the offense allegedly occurred—and the consequences of waiving those rights;

(D) the juvenile, after receiving the court's information about rights, consents in writing to be proceeded against in the transferee district, and files the consent in the transferee district;

(E) the United States attorneys for both districts approve the transfer in writing; and

(F) the transferee court approves the transfer.

(2) *Clerk's Duties.* After receiving the juvenile's written consent and the required approvals, the clerk where the indictment, information, or complaint is pending or where the alleged offense occurred must send the file, or a certified copy, to the clerk in the transferee district.

Rule 21. Transfer for Trial

(a) For Prejudice. Upon the defendant's motion, the court must transfer the proceeding against that defendant to another district if the court is satisfied that so great a prejudice against the defendant exists in the transferring district that the defendant cannot obtain a fair and impartial trial there.

(b) For Convenience. Upon the defendant's motion, the court may transfer the proceeding, or one or more counts, against that defendant to another district for the convenience of the parties, any victim, and the witnesses, and in the interest of justice.

(c) Proceedings on Transfer. When the court orders a transfer, the clerk must send to the transferee district the file, or a certified copy, and any bail taken. The prosecution will then continue in the transferee district.

(d) Time to File a Motion to Transfer. A motion to transfer may be made at or before arraignment or at any other time the court or these rules prescribe.

Rule 22. [Transferred]

TITLE VI. TRIAL

Rule 23. Jury or Nonjury Trial

(a) Jury Trial. If the defendant is entitled to a jury trial, the trial must be by jury unless:

(1) the defendant waives a jury trial in writing;

(2) the government consents; and

(3) the court approves.

(b) Jury Size.

(1) *In General.* A jury consists of 12 persons unless this rule provides otherwise.

(2) *Stipulation for a Smaller Jury.* At any time before the verdict, the parties may, with the court's approval, stipulate in writing that:

(A) the jury may consist of fewer than 12 persons; or

(B) a jury of fewer than 12 persons may return a verdict if the court finds it necessary to excuse a juror for good cause after the trial begins.

(3) *Court Order for a Jury of 11.* After the jury has retired to deliberate, the court may permit a jury of 11 persons to return a verdict, even without a stipulation by the parties, if the court finds good cause to excuse a juror.

(c) Nonjury Trial. In a case tried without a jury, the court must find the defendant guilty or not guilty. If a party requests before the finding of guilty or not guilty, the court must state its specific findings of fact in open court or in a written decision or opinion.

Rule 24. Trial Jurors

(a) Examination.

(1) *In General.* The court may examine prospective jurors or may permit the attorneys for the parties to do so.

(2) *Court Examination.* If the court examines the jurors, it must permit the attorneys for the parties to:

(A) ask further questions that the court considers proper; or

(B) submit further questions that the court may ask if it considers them proper.

(b) Peremptory Challenges. Each side is entitled to the number of peremptory challenges to prospective jurors specified below. The court may allow additional peremptory challenges to multiple defendants, and may allow the defendants to exercise those challenges separately or jointly.

(1) *Capital Case.* Each side has 20 peremptory challenges when the government seeks the death penalty.

(2) *Other Felony Case.* The government has 6 peremptory challenges and the defendant or defendants jointly have 10 peremptory challenges when the defendant is charged with a crime punishable by imprisonment of more than one year.

(3) *Misdemeanor Case.* Each side has 3 peremptory challenges when the defendant is charged with a crime punishable by fine, imprisonment of one year or less, or both.

(c) Alternate Jurors.

(1) *In General.* The court may impanel up to 6 alternate jurors to replace any jurors who are unable to perform or who are disqualified from performing their duties.

(2) *Procedure.*

(A) Alternate jurors must have the same qualifications and be selected and sworn in the same manner as any other juror.

(B) Alternate jurors replace jurors in the same sequence in which the alternates were selected. An alternate juror who replaces a juror has the same authority as the other jurors.

(3) *Retaining Alternate Jurors.* The court may retain alternate jurors after the jury retires to deliberate. The court must ensure that a retained alternate does not discuss the case with anyone until that alternate replaces a juror or is discharged. If an alternate replaces a juror after deliberations have begun, the court must instruct the jury to begin its deliberations anew.

(4) *Peremptory Challenges.* Each side is entitled to the number of additional peremptory challenges to prospective alternate jurors specified below. These additional challenges may be used only to remove alternate jurors.

(A) *One or Two Alternates.* One additional peremptory challenge is permitted when one or two alternates are impaneled.

(B) *Three or Four Alternates.* Two additional peremptory challenges are permitted when three or four alternates are impaneled.

(C) *Five or Six Alternates.* Three additional peremptory challenges are permitted when five or six alternates are impaneled.

Rule 25. Judge's Disability

(a) During Trial. Any judge regularly sitting in or assigned to the court may complete a jury trial if:

(1) the judge before whom the trial began cannot proceed because of death, sickness, or other disability; and

(2) the judge completing the trial certifies familiarity with the trial record.

(b) After a Verdict or Finding of Guilty.

(1) *In General.* After a verdict or finding of guilty, any judge regularly sitting in or assigned to a court may complete the court's duties if the judge who presided at trial cannot perform those duties because of absence, death, sickness, or other disability.

(2) *Granting a New Trial.* The successor judge may grant a new trial if satisfied that:

(A) a judge other than the one who presided at the trial cannot perform the post-trial duties; or

(B) a new trial is necessary for some other reason.

Rule 26. Taking Testimony

In every trial the testimony of witnesses must be taken in open court, unless otherwise provided by a statute or by rules adopted under 28 U.S.C. §§ 2072–2077.

Rule 26.1. Foreign Law Determination

A party intending to raise an issue of foreign law must provide the court and all parties with reasonable written notice. Issues of foreign law are questions of law, but in deciding such issues a court may consider any relevant material or source—including testimony—without regard to the Federal Rules of Evidence.

Rule 26.2. Producing a Witness's Statement

(a) Motion to Produce. After a witness other than the defendant has testified on direct examination, the court, on motion of a party who did not call the witness, must order an attorney for the government or the defendant and the defendant's attorney to produce, for the examination and use of the moving party, any statement of the witness that is in their possession and that relates to the subject matter of the witness's testimony.

(b) Producing the Entire Statement. If the entire statement relates to the subject matter of the witness's testimony, the court must order that the statement be delivered to the moving party.

(c) Producing a Redacted Statement. If the party who called the witness claims that the statement contains information that is privileged or does not relate to the subject matter of the witness's testimony, the court must inspect the statement in camera. After excising any privileged or unrelated portions, the court must order delivery of the redacted statement to the moving party. If the defendant objects to an excision, the court must preserve the entire statement with the excised portion indicated, under seal, as part of the record.

(d) Recess to Examine a Statement. The court may recess the proceedings to allow time for a party to examine the statement and prepare for its use.

(e) Sanction for Failure to Produce or Deliver a Statement. If the party who called the witness disobeys an order to produce or deliver a statement, the court must strike the witness's testimony from the record. If an attorney for the government disobeys the order, the court must declare a mistrial if justice so requires.

(f) "Statement" Defined. As used in this rule, a witness's "statement" means:

(1) a written statement that the witness makes and signs, or otherwise adopts or approves;

(2) a substantially verbatim, contemporaneously recorded recital of the witness's oral statement that is contained in any recording or any transcription of a recording; or

(3) the witness's statement to a grand jury, however taken or recorded, or a transcription of such a statement.

(g) Scope. This rule applies at trial, at a suppression hearing under Rule 12, and to the extent specified in the following rules:

(1) Rule 5.1(h) (preliminary hearing);

(2) Rule 32(i)(2) (sentencing);

(3) Rule 32.1(e) (hearing to revoke or modify probation or supervised release);

(4) Rule 46(j) (detention hearing); and

(5) Rule 8 of the Rules Governing Proceedings under 28 U.S.C. § 2255.

Rule 26.3. Mistrial

Before ordering a mistrial, the court must give each defendant and the government an opportunity to comment on the propriety of the order, to state whether that party consents or objects, and to suggest alternatives.

Rule 27. Proving an Official Record

A party may prove an official record, an entry in such a record, or the lack of a record or entry in the same manner as in a civil action.

Rule 28. Interpreters

The court may select, appoint, and set the reasonable compensation for an interpreter. The compensation must be paid from funds provided by law or by the government, as the court may direct.

Rule 29. Motion for a Judgment of Acquittal

(a) Before Submission to the Jury. After the government closes its evidence or after the close of all the evidence, the court on the defendant's motion must enter a judgment of acquittal of any offense for which the evidence is insufficient to sustain a conviction. The court may on its own consider whether the evidence is insufficient to sustain a conviction. If the court denies a motion for a judgment of acquittal at the close of the government's evidence, the defendant may offer evidence without having reserved the right to do so.

(b) Reserving Decision. The court may reserve decision on the motion, proceed with the trial (where the motion is made before the close of all the evidence), submit the case to the jury, and decide the motion either before the jury returns a verdict or after it returns a verdict of guilty or is discharged without having returned a verdict. If the court reserves decision, it must decide the motion on the basis of the evidence at the time the ruling was reserved.

(c) After Jury Verdict or Discharge.

(1) *Time for a Motion.* A defendant may move for a judgment of acquittal, or renew such a motion, within 14 days after a guilty verdict or after the court discharges the jury, whichever is later.

(2) *Ruling on the Motion.* If the jury has returned a guilty verdict, the court may set aside the verdict and enter an acquittal. If the jury has failed to return a verdict, the court may enter a judgment of acquittal.

(3) *No Prior Motion Required.* A defendant is not required to move for a judgment of acquittal before the court submits the case to the jury as a prerequisite for making such a motion after jury discharge.

(d) Conditional Ruling on a Motion for a New Trial.

(1) *Motion for a New Trial.* If the court enters a judgment of acquittal after a guilty verdict, the court must also conditionally determine whether any motion for a new trial should be granted if the judgment of acquittal is later vacated or reversed. The court must specify the reasons for that determination.

(2) *Finality.* The court's order conditionally granting a motion for a new trial does not affect the finality of the judgment of acquittal.

(3) *Appeal.*

(A) *Grant of a Motion for a New Trial.* If the court conditionally grants a motion for a new trial and an appellate court later reverses the judgment of acquittal, the trial court must proceed with the new trial unless the appellate court orders otherwise.

(B) *Denial of a Motion for a New Trial.* If the court conditionally denies a motion for a new trial, an appellee may assert that the denial was erroneous. If the appellate court later reverses the judgment of acquittal, the trial court must proceed as the appellate court directs.

Rule 29.1. Closing Argument

Closing arguments proceed in the following order:

(a) the government argues;

(b) the defense argues; and

(c) the government rebuts.

Rule 30. Jury Instructions

(a) In General. Any party may request in writing that the court instruct the jury on the law as specified in the request. The request must be made at the close of the evidence or at any earlier time that the court reasonably sets. When the request is made, the requesting party must furnish a copy to every other party.

(b) Ruling on a Request. The court must inform the parties before closing arguments how it intends to rule on the requested instructions.

(c) Time for Giving Instructions. The court may instruct the jury before or after the arguments are completed, or at both times.

(d) Objections to Instructions. A party who objects to any portion of the instructions or to a failure to give a requested instruction must inform the court of the specific objection and the grounds for the objection before the jury retires to deliberate. An opportunity must be given to object out of the jury's hearing and, on request, out of the jury's presence. Failure to object in accordance with this rule precludes appellate review, except as permitted under Rule 52(b).

Rule 31. Jury Verdict

(a) Return. The jury must return its verdict to a judge in open court. The verdict must be unanimous.

(b) Partial Verdicts, Mistrial, and Retrial.

(1) *Multiple Defendants.* If there are multiple defendants, the jury may return a verdict at any time during its deliberations as to any defendant about whom it has agreed.

(2) *Multiple Counts.* If the jury cannot agree on all counts as to any defendant, the jury may return a verdict on those counts on which it has agreed.

(3) *Mistrial and Retrial.* If the jury cannot agree on a verdict on one or more counts, the court may declare a mistrial on those counts. The government may retry any defendant on any count on which the jury could not agree.

(c) Lesser Offense or Attempt. A defendant may be found guilty of any of the following:

(1) an offense necessarily included in the offense charged;

(2) an attempt to commit the offense charged; or

(3) an attempt to commit an offense necessarily included in the offense charged, if the attempt is an offense in its own right.

(d) Jury Poll. After a verdict is returned but before the jury is discharged, the court must on a party's request, or may on its own, poll the jurors individually. If the poll reveals a lack of unanimity, the court may direct the jury to deliberate further or may declare a mistrial and discharge the jury.

TITLE VII. POST–CONVICTION PROCEDURES

Rule 32. Sentencing and Judgment

(a) [Reserved.]

(b) Time of Sentencing.

(1) *In General.* The court must impose sentence without unnecessary delay.

(2) *Changing Time Limits.* The court may, for good cause, change any time limits prescribed in this rule.

(c) Presentence Investigation.

(1) *Required Investigation.*

(A) *In General.* The probation officer must conduct a presentence investigation and submit a report to the court before it imposes sentence unless:

(i) 18 U.S.C. § 3593(c) or another statute requires otherwise; or

(ii) the court finds that the information in the record enables it to meaningfully exercise its sentencing authority under 18 U.S.C. § 3553, and the court explains its finding on the record.

(B) *Restitution.* If the law permits restitution, the probation officer must conduct an investigation and submit a report that contains sufficient information for the court to order restitution.

(2) *Interviewing the Defendant.* The probation officer who interviews a defendant as part of a presentence investigation must, on request, give the defendant's attorney notice and a reasonable opportunity to attend the interview.

(d) Presentence Report.

(1) *Applying the Advisory Sentencing Guidelines.* The presentence report must:

(A) identify all applicable guidelines and policy statements of the Sentencing Commission;

(B) calculate the defendant's offense level and criminal history category;

(C) state the resulting sentencing range and kinds of sentences available;

(D) identify any factor relevant to:

(i) the appropriate kind of sentence, or

(ii) the appropriate sentence within the applicable sentencing range; and

(E) identify any basis for departing from the applicable sentencing range.

(2) *Additional Information.* The presentence report must also contain the following:

(A) the defendant's history and characteristics, including:

(i) any prior criminal record;

(ii) the defendant's financial condition; and

(iii) any circumstances affecting the defendant's behavior that may be helpful in imposing sentence or in correctional treatment;

(B) information that assesses any financial, social, psychological, and medical impact on any victim;

(C) when appropriate, the nature and extent of nonprison programs and resources available to the defendant;

(D) when the law provides for restitution, information sufficient for a restitution order;

(E) if the court orders a study under 18 U.S.C. § 3552(b), any resulting report and recommendation; and

(F) any other information that the court requires, including information relevant to the factors under 18 U.S.C. § 3553(a); and

(G) specify whether the government seeks forfeiture under Rule 32.2 and any other provision of law.

(3) *Exclusions.* The presentence report must exclude the following:

(A) any diagnoses that, if disclosed, might seriously disrupt a rehabilitation program;

(B) any sources of information obtained upon a promise of confidentiality; and

(C) any other information that, if disclosed, might result in physical or other harm to the defendant or others.

(e) Disclosing the Report and Recommendation.

(1) *Time to Disclose.* Unless the defendant has consented in writing, the probation officer must not submit a presentence report to the court or disclose its contents to anyone until the defendant has pleaded guilty or nolo contendere, or has been found guilty.

(2) *Minimum Required Notice.* The probation officer must give the presentence report to the defendant, the defendant's attorney, and an attorney for the government at least 35 days before sentencing unless the defendant waives this minimum period.

(3) *Sentence Recommendation.* By local rule or by order in a case, the court may direct the probation officer not to disclose to anyone other than the court the officer's recommendation on the sentence.

(f) Objecting to the Report.

(1) *Time to Object.* Within 14 days after receiving the presentence report, the parties must state in writing any objections, including objections to material information, sentencing guideline ranges, and policy statements contained in or omitted from the report.

(2) *Serving Objections.* An objecting party must provide a copy of its objections to the opposing party and to the probation officer.

(3) *Action on Objections*. After receiving objections, the probation officer may meet with the parties to discuss the objections. The probation officer may then investigate further and revise the presentence report as appropriate.

(g) Submitting the Report. At least 7 days before sentencing, the probation officer must submit to the court and to the parties the presentence report and an addendum containing any unresolved objections, the grounds for those objections, and the probation officer's comments on them.

(h) Notice of Possible Departure from Sentencing Guidelines. Before the court may depart from the applicable sentencing range on a ground not identified for departure either in the presentence report or in a party's prehearing submission, the court must give the parties reasonable notice that it is contemplating such a departure. The notice must specify any ground on which the court is contemplating a departure.

(i) Sentencing.

(1) *In General.* At sentencing, the court:

(A) must verify that the defendant and the defendant's attorney have read and discussed the presentence report and any addendum to the report;

(B) must give to the defendant and an attorney for the government a written summary of—or summarize in camera—any information excluded from the presentence report under Rule 32(d)(3) on which the court will rely in sentencing, and give them a reasonable opportunity to comment on that information;

(C) must allow the parties' attorneys to comment on the probation officer's determinations and other matters relating to an appropriate sentence; and

(D) may, for good cause, allow a party to make a new objection at any time before sentence is imposed.

(2) *Introducing Evidence; Producing a Statement.* The court may permit the parties to introduce evidence on the objections. If a witness testifies at sentencing, Rule 26.2(a)-(d) and (f) applies. If a party fails to comply with a Rule 26.2 order to produce a witness's statement, the court must not consider that witness's testimony.

(3) *Court Determinations.* At sentencing, the court:

(A) may accept any undisputed portion of the presentence report as a finding of fact;

(B) must—for any disputed portion of the presentence report or other controverted matter—rule on the dispute or determine that a ruling is unnecessary either because the matter will not affect sentencing, or because the court will not consider the matter in sentencing; and

(C) must append a copy of the court's determinations under this rule to any copy of the presentence report made available to the Bureau of Prisons.

(4) *Opportunity to Speak.*

(A) *By a Party.* Before imposing sentence, the court must:

(i) provide the defendant's attorney an opportunity to speak on the defendant's behalf;

(ii) address the defendant personally in order to permit the defendant to speak or present any information to mitigate the sentence; and

(iii) provide an attorney for the government an opportunity to speak equivalent to that of the defendant's attorney.

(B) *By a Victim.* Before imposing sentence, the court must address any victim of the crime who is present at sentencing and must permit the victim to be reasonably heard.

(C) *In Camera Proceedings.* Upon a party's motion and for good cause, the court may hear in camera any statement made under Rule 32(i)(4).

(j) Defendant's Right to Appeal.

(1) *Advice of a Right to Appeal.*

(A) *Appealing a Conviction.* If the defendant pleaded not guilty and was convicted, after sentencing the court must advise the defendant of the right to appeal the conviction.

(B) *Appealing a Sentence.* After sentencing—regardless of the defendant's plea—the court must advise the defendant of any right to appeal the sentence.

(C) *Appeal Costs.* The court must advise a defendant who is unable to pay appeal costs of the right to ask for permission to appeal in forma pauperis.

(2) *Clerk's Filing of Notice.* If the defendant so requests, the clerk must immediately prepare and file a notice of appeal on the defendant's behalf.

(k) Judgment.

(1) *In General.* In the judgment of conviction, the court must set forth the plea, the jury verdict or the court's findings, the adjudication, and the sentence. If the defendant is found not guilty or is otherwise entitled to be discharged, the court must so order. The judge must sign the judgment, and the clerk must enter it.

(2) *Criminal Forfeiture.* Forfeiture procedures are governed by Rule 32.2.

Rule 32.1. Revoking or Modifying Probation or Supervised Release

(a) Initial Appearance.

(1) *Person In Custody.* A person held in custody for violating probation or supervised release must be taken without unnecessary delay before a magistrate judge.

(A) If the person is held in custody in the district where an alleged violation occurred, the initial appearance must be in that district.

(B) If the person is held in custody in a district other than where an alleged violation occurred, the initial appearance must be in that district, or in an adjacent district if the appearance can occur more promptly there.

(2) *Upon a Summons.* When a person appears in response to a summons for violating probation or supervised release, a magistrate judge must proceed under this rule.

(3) *Advice.* The judge must inform the person of the following:

(A) the alleged violation of probation or supervised release;

(B) the person's right to retain counsel or to request that counsel be appointed if the person cannot obtain counsel; and

(C) the person's right, if held in custody, to a preliminary hearing under Rule 32.1(b)(1).

(4) *Appearance in the District With Jurisdiction.* If the person is arrested or appears in the district that has jurisdiction to conduct a revocation hearing—either originally or by transfer of jurisdiction—the court must proceed under Rule 32.1(b)–(e).

(5) *Appearance in a District Lacking Jurisdiction.* If the person is arrested or appears in a district that does not have jurisdiction to conduct a revocation hearing, the magistrate judge must:

(A) if the alleged violation occurred in the district of arrest, conduct a preliminary hearing under Rule 32.1(b) and either:

(i) transfer the person to the district that has jurisdiction, if the judge finds probable cause to believe that a violation occurred; or

(ii) dismiss the proceedings and so notify the court that has jurisdiction, if the judge finds no probable cause to believe that a violation occurred; or

(B) if the alleged violation did not occur in the district of arrest, transfer the person to the district that has jurisdiction if:

(i) the government produces certified copies of the judgment, warrant, and warrant application, or produces copies of those certified documents by reliable electronic means; and

(ii) the judge finds that the person is the same person named in the warrant.

(6) *Release or Detention.* The magistrate judge may release or detain the person under 18 U.S.C. § 3143(a)(1) pending further proceedings. The burden of establishing by clear and convincing evidence that the person will not flee or pose a danger to any other person or to the community rests with the person.

(b) Revocation.

(1) *Preliminary Hearing.*

(A) *In General.* If a person is in custody for violating a condition of probation or supervised release, a magistrate judge must promptly conduct a hearing to determine whether there is probable cause to believe that a violation occurred. The person may waive the hearing.

(B) *Requirements.* The hearing must be recorded by a court reporter or by a suitable recording device. The judge must give the person:

(i) notice of the hearing and its purpose, the alleged violation, and the person's right to retain counsel or to request that counsel be appointed if the person cannot obtain counsel;

(ii) an opportunity to appear at the hearing and present evidence; and

(iii) upon request, an opportunity to question any adverse witness, unless the judge determines that the interest of justice does not require the witness to appear.

(C) *Referral.* If the judge finds probable cause, the judge must conduct a revocation hearing. If the judge does not find probable cause, the judge must dismiss the proceeding.

(2) *Revocation Hearing.* Unless waived by the person, the court must hold the revocation hearing within a reasonable time in the district having jurisdiction. The person is entitled to:

(A) written notice of the alleged violation;

(B) disclosure of the evidence against the person;

(C) an opportunity to appear, present evidence, and question any adverse witness unless the court determines that the interest of justice does not require the witness to appear;

(D) notice of the person's right to retain counsel or to request that counsel be appointed if the person cannot obtain counsel; and

(E) an opportunity to make a statement and present any information in mitigation.

(c) Modification.

(1) *In General.* Before modifying the conditions of probation or supervised release, the court must hold a hearing, at which the person has the right to counsel and an opportunity to make a statement and present any information in mitigation.

(2) *Exceptions.* A hearing is not required if:

(A) the person waives the hearing; or

(B) the relief sought is favorable to the person and does not extend the term of probation or of supervised release; and

(C) an attorney for the government has received notice of the relief sought, has had a reasonable opportunity to object, and has not done so.

(d) Disposition of the Case. The court's disposition of the case is governed by 18 U.S.C. § 3563 and § 3565 (probation) and § 3583 (supervised release).

(e) Producing a Statement. Rule 26.2(a)–(d) and (f) applies at a hearing under this rule. If a party fails to comply with a Rule 26.2 order to produce a witness's statement, the court must not consider that witness's testimony.

Rule 32.2. Criminal Forfeiture

(a) Notice to the Defendant. A court must not enter a judgment of forfeiture in a criminal proceeding unless the indictment or information contains notice to the defendant that the government will seek the forfeiture of property as part of any sentence in accordance with the applicable statute. The notice should not be designated as a count of the indictment or information. The indictment or information need not identify the property subject to forfeiture or specify the amount of any forfeiture money judgment that the government seeks.

(b) Entering a Preliminary Order of Forfeiture.

(1) *Forfeiture Phase of the Trial.*

(A) Forfeiture Determinations. As soon as practical after a verdict or finding of guilty, or after a plea of guilty or nolo contendere is accepted, on any count in an indictment or information regarding which criminal forfeiture is sought, the court must determine what property is subject to forfeiture under the applicable statute. If the government seeks forfeiture of specific property, the court must determine whether the government has established the requisite nexus between the property and the offense. If the government seeks a personal money judgment, the court must determine the amount of money that the defendant will be ordered to pay.

(B) Evidence and Hearing. The court's determination may be based on evidence already in the record, including any written plea agreement, and on any additional evidence or information submitted by the parties and accepted by the court as relevant and reliable. If the forfeiture is contested, on either party's request the court must conduct a hearing after the verdict or finding of guilty.

(2) *Preliminary Order.*

(A) Contents of a Specific Order. If the court finds that property is subject to forfeiture, it must promptly enter a preliminary order of forfeiture setting forth the amount of any money judgment, directing the forfeiture of specific property, and directing the forfeiture of any substitute property if the government has met the statutory criteria. The court must enter the order without regard to any third party's interest in the property. Determining whether a third party has such an interest must be deferred until any third party files a claim in an ancillary proceeding under Rule 32.2(c).

(B) Timing. Unless doing so is impractical, the court must enter the preliminary order sufficiently in advance of sentencing to allow the parties to suggest revisions or modifications before the order becomes final as to the defendant under Rule 32.2(b)(4).

(C) General Order. If, before sentencing, the court cannot identify all the specific property subject to forfeiture or calculate the total amount of the money judgment, the court may enter a forfeiture order that:

> **(i)** lists any identified property;

> **(ii)** describes other property in general terms; and

> **(iii)** states that the order will be amended under Rule 32.2(e)(1) when additional specific property is identified or the amount of the money judgment has been calculated.

(3) *Seizing Property.* The entry of a preliminary order of forfeiture authorizes the Attorney General (or a designee) to seize the specific property subject to forfeiture; to conduct any discovery the court considers proper in identifying, locating, or disposing of the property; and to commence proceedings that comply with any statutes governing third-party rights. The court may include in the order of forfeiture conditions reasonably necessary to preserve the property's value pending any appeal.

(4) *Sentence and Judgment.*

(A) When Final. At sentencing—or at any time before sentencing if the defendant consents—the preliminary forfeiture order becomes final as to the defendant. If the order directs the defendant to forfeit specific property, it remains preliminary as to third parties until the ancillary proceeding is concluded under Rule 32.2(c).

(B) Notice and Inclusion in the Judgment. The court must include the forfeiture when orally announcing the sentence or must otherwise ensure that the defendant knows of the forfeiture at sentencing. The court must also include the forfeiture order, directly or by reference, in the judgment, but the court's failure to do so may be corrected at any time under Rule 36.

(C) Time to Appeal. The time for the defendant or the government to file an appeal from the forfeiture order, or from the court's failure to enter an order, begins to run when judgment is entered. If the court later amends or declines to amend a forfeiture order to include additional property under Rule 32.2(e), the defendant or the government may file an appeal regarding that property under Federal Rule of Appellate Procedure 4(b). The time for that appeal runs from the date when the order granting or denying the amendment becomes final.

(5) *Jury Determination.*

(A) Retaining the Jury. In any case tried before a jury, if the indictment or information states that the government is seeking forfeiture, the court must determine before the jury begins deliberating whether either party requests that the jury be retained to determine the forfeitability of specific property if it returns a guilty verdict.

(B) Special Verdict Form. If a party timely requests to have the jury determine forfeiture, the government must submit a proposed Special Verdict Form listing each property subject to forfeiture and asking the jury to determine whether the government has established the requisite nexus between the property and the offense committed by the defendant.

(6) *Notice of the Forfeiture Order.*

(A) Publishing and Sending Notice. If the court orders the forfeiture of specific property, the government must publish notice of the order and send notice to any person who reasonably appears to be a potential claimant with standing to contest the forfeiture in the ancillary proceeding.

(B) Content of the Notice. The notice must describe the forfeited property, state the times under the applicable statute when a petition contesting the forfeiture must be filed, and state the name and contact information for the government attorney to be served with the petition.

(C) Means of Publication; Exceptions to Publication Requirement. Publication must take place as described in Supplemental Rule G(4)(a)(iii) of the Federal Rules of Civil Procedure, and may be by any means described in Supplemental Rule G(4)(a)(iv). Publication is unnecessary if any exception in Supplemental Rule G(4)(a)(i) applies.

(D) Means of Sending the Notice. The notice may be sent in accordance with Supplemental Rules G(4)(b)(iii)-(v) of the Federal Rules of Civil Procedure.

(7) *Interlocutory Sale.* At any time before entry of a final forfeiture order, the court, in accordance with Supplemental Rule G(7) of the Federal Rules of Civil Procedure, may order the interlocutory sale of property alleged to be forfeitable.

(c) Ancillary Proceeding; Entering a Final Order of Forfeiture.

(1) *In General.* If, as prescribed by statute, a third party files a petition asserting an interest in the property to be forfeited, the court must conduct an ancillary proceeding, but no ancillary proceeding is required to the extent that the forfeiture consists of a money judgment.

(A) In the ancillary proceeding, the court may, on motion, dismiss the petition for lack of standing, for failure to state a claim, or for any other lawful reason. For purposes of the motion, the facts set forth in the petition are assumed to be true.

(B) After disposing of any motion filed under Rule 32.2(c)(1)(A) and before conducting a hearing on the petition, the court may permit the parties to conduct discovery in accordance with the Federal Rules of Civil Procedure if the court determines that discovery is necessary or desirable to resolve factual issues. When discovery ends, a party may move for summary judgment under Federal Rule of Civil Procedure 56.

(2) *Entering a Final Order.* When the ancillary proceeding ends, the court must enter a final order of forfeiture by amending the preliminary order as necessary to account for any third-party rights. If no third party files a timely petition, the preliminary order becomes the final order of forfeiture if the court finds that the defendant (or any combination of defendants convicted in the case) had an interest in the property that is forfeitable under the applicable statute. The defendant may not object to the entry of the final order on the ground that the property belongs, in whole or in part, to a codefendant or third party; nor may a third party object to the final order on the ground that the third party had an interest in the property.

(3) *Multiple Petitions.* If multiple third-party petitions are filed in the same case, an order dismissing or granting one petition is not appealable until rulings are made on all the petitions, unless the court determines that there is no just reason for delay.

(4) *Ancillary Proceeding Not Part of Sentencing.* An ancillary proceeding is not part of sentencing.

(d) Stay Pending Appeal. If a defendant appeals from a conviction or an order of forfeiture, the court may stay the order of forfeiture on terms appropriate to ensure that the property remains available pending appellate review. A stay does not delay the ancillary proceeding or the determination of a third party's rights or interests. If the court rules in favor of any third party while an appeal is pending, the court may amend the order of forfeiture but must not transfer any property interest to a third party until the decision on appeal becomes final, unless the defendant consents in writing or on the record.

(e) Subsequently Located Property; Substitute Property.

(1) *In General.* On the government's motion, the court may at any time enter an order of forfeiture or amend an existing order of forfeiture to include property that:

(A) is subject to forfeiture under an existing order of forfeiture but was located and identified after that order was entered; or

(B) is substitute property that qualifies for forfeiture under an applicable statute.

(2) *Procedure.* If the government shows that the property is subject to forfeiture under Rule 32.2(e)(1), the court must:

(A) enter an order forfeiting that property, or amend an existing preliminary or final order to include it; and

(B) if a third party files a petition claiming an interest in the property, conduct an ancillary proceeding under Rule 32.2(c).

(3) *Jury Trial Limited.* There is no right to a jury trial under Rule 32.2(e).

Rule 33. New Trial

(a) Defendant's Motion. Upon the defendant's motion, the court may vacate any judgment and grant a new trial if the interest of justice so requires. If the case was tried without a jury, the court may take additional testimony and enter a new judgment.

(b) Time to File.

(1) *Newly Discovered Evidence.* Any motion for a new trial grounded on newly discovered evidence must be filed within 3 years after the verdict or finding of guilty. If an appeal is pending, the court may not grant a motion for a new trial until the appellate court remands the case.

(2) *Other Grounds.* Any motion for a new trial grounded on any reason other than newly discovered evidence must be filed within 14 days after the verdict or finding of guilty.

Rule 34. Arresting Judgment

(a) In General. Upon the defendant's motion or on its own, the court must arrest judgment if:

(1) the indictment or information does not charge an offense; or

(2) the court does not have jurisdiction of the charged offense.

(b) Time to File. The defendant must move to arrest judgment within 14 days after the court accepts a verdict or finding of guilty, or after a plea of guilty or nolo contendere.

Rule 35. Correcting or Reducing a Sentence

(a) Correcting Clear Error. Within 14 days after sentencing, the court may correct a sentence that resulted from arithmetical, technical, or other clear error.

(b) Reducing a Sentence for Substantial Assistance.

(1) *In General.* Upon the government's motion made within one year of sentencing, the court may reduce a sentence if the defendant, after sentencing, provided substantial assistance in investigating or prosecuting another person.

(2) *Later Motion.* Upon the government's motion made more than one year after sentencing, the court may reduce a sentence if the defendant's substantial assistance involved:

(A) information not known to the defendant until one year or more after sentencing;

(B) information provided by the defendant to the government within one year of sentencing, but which did not become useful to the government until more than one year after sentencing; or

(C) information the usefulness of which could not reasonably have been anticipated by the defendant until more than one year after sentencing and which was promptly provided to the government after its usefulness was reasonably apparent to the defendant.

(3) *Evaluating Substantial Assistance.* In evaluating whether the defendant has provided substantial assistance, the court may consider the defendant's presentence assistance.

(4) *Below Statutory Minimum.* When acting under Rule 35(b), the court may reduce the sentence to a level below the minimum sentence established by statute.

(c) **"Sentencing Defined"**. As used in this rule, "Sentencing" means the oral announcement of the sentence.

Rule 36. Clerical Error

After giving any notice it considers appropriate, the court may at any time correct a clerical error in a judgment, order, or other part of the record, or correct an error in the record arising from oversight or omission.

Rule 37. [Reserved]

Rule 38. Staying a Sentence or a Disability

(a) **Death Sentence.** The court must stay a death sentence if the defendant appeals the conviction or sentence.

(b) **Imprisonment.**

(1) *Stay Granted.* If the defendant is released pending appeal, the court must stay a sentence of imprisonment.

(2) *Stay Denied; Place of Confinement.* If the defendant is not released pending appeal, the court may recommend to the Attorney General that the defendant be confined near the place of the trial or appeal for a period reasonably necessary to permit the defendant to assist in preparing the appeal.

(c) **Fine.** If the defendant appeals, the district court, or the court of appeals under Federal Rule of Appellate Procedure 8, may stay a sentence to pay a fine or a fine and costs. The court may stay the sentence on any terms considered appropriate and may require the defendant to:

(1) deposit all or part of the fine and costs into the district court's registry pending appeal;

(2) post a bond to pay the fine and costs; or

(3) submit to an examination concerning the defendant's assets and, if appropriate, order the defendant to refrain from dissipating assets.

(d) **Probation.** If the defendant appeals, the court may stay a sentence of probation. The court must set the terms of any stay.

(e) **Restitution and Notice to Victims.**

(1) *In General.* If the defendant appeals, the district court, or the court of appeals under Federal Rule of Appellate Procedure 8, may stay— on any terms considered appropriate—any sentence providing for restitution under 18 U.S.C. § 3556 or notice under 18 U.S.C. § 3555.

(2) *Ensuring Compliance.* The court may issue any order reasonably necessary to ensure compliance with a restitution order or a notice order after disposition of an appeal, including:

(A) a restraining order;

(B) an injunction;

(C) an order requiring the defendant to deposit all or part of any monetary restitution into the district court's registry; or

(D) an order requiring the defendant to post a bond.

(f) Forfeiture. A stay of a forfeiture order is governed by Rule 32.2(d).

(g) Disability. If the defendant's conviction or sentence creates a civil or employment disability under federal law, the district court, or the court of appeals under Federal Rule of Appellate Procedure 8, may stay the disability pending appeal on any terms considered appropriate. The court may issue any order reasonably necessary to protect the interest represented by the disability pending appeal, including a restraining order or an injunction.

Rule 39. [Reserved]

TITLE VIII. SUPPLEMENTARY AND SPECIAL PROCEEDINGS

Rule 40. Arrest for Failing to Appear in Another District or for Violating Conditions of Release Set in Another District

(a) In General. A person must be taken without unnecessary delay before a magistrate judge in the district of arrest if the person has been arrested under a warrant issued in another district for:

(i) failing to appear as required by the terms of that person's release under 18 U.S.C. §§ 3141–3156 or by a subpoena; or

(ii) violating conditions of release set in another district.

(b) Proceedings. The judge must proceed under Rule 5(c)(3) as applicable.

(c) Release or Detention Order. The judge may modify any previous release or detention order issued in another district, but must state in writing the reasons for doing so.

Rule 41. Search and Seizure

(a) Scope and Definitions.

(1) *Scope.* This rule does not modify any statute regulating search or seizure, or the issuance and execution of a search warrant in special circumstances.

(2) *Definitions.* The following definitions apply under this rule:

(A) "Property" includes documents, books, papers, any other tangible objects, and information.

(B) "Daytime" means the hours between 6:00 a.m. and 10:00 p.m. according to local time.

(C) "Federal law enforcement officer" means a government agent (other than an attorney for the government) who is engaged in enforcing the criminal laws and is within any category of officers authorized by the Attorney General to request a search warrant.

(D) "Domestic terrorism" and "international terrorism" have the meanings set out in 18 U.S.C. § 2331.

(E) "Tracking device" has the meaning set out in 18 U.S.C. § 3117(b).

(b) Authority to Issue a Warrant. At the request of a federal law enforcement officer or an attorney for the government:

(1) a magistrate judge with authority in the district—or if none is reasonably available, a judge of a state court of record in the district—has authority to issue a warrant to search for and seize a person or property located within the district;

(2) a magistrate judge with authority in the district has authority to issue a warrant for a person or property outside the district if the person or property is located within the district when the warrant is issued but might move or be moved outside the district before the warrant is executed;

(3) a magistrate judge—in an investigation of domestic terrorism or international terrorism—with authority in any district in which activities related to the terrorism may have occurred, has authority to issue a warrant for a person or property within or outside that district; and

(4) a magistrate judge with authority in the district has authority to issue a warrant to install within the district a tracking device; the warrant may authorize use of the device to track the movement of a person or property located within the district, outside the district, or both; and

(5) a magistrate judge having authority in any district where activities related to the crime may have occurred, or in the District of Columbia, may issue a warrant for property that is located outside the jurisdiction of any state or district, but within any of the following:

(A) a United States territory, possession, or commonwealth;

(B) the premises—no matter who owns them—of a United States diplomatic or consular mission in a foreign state, including any appurtenant building, part of a building, or land used for the mission's purposes; or

(C) a residence and any appurtenant land owned or leased by the United States and used by United States personnel assigned to a United States diplomatic or consular mission in a foreign state.

(c) Persons or Property Subject to Search or Seizure. A warrant may be issued for any of the following:

(1) evidence of a crime;

(2) contraband, fruits of crime, or other items illegally possessed;

(3) property designed for use, intended for use, or used in committing a crime; or

(4) a person to be arrested or a person who is unlawfully restrained.

(d) Obtaining a Warrant.

(1) *In General.* After receiving an affidavit or other information, a magistrate judge—or if authorized by Rule 41(b), a judge of a state court of record—must issue the warrant if there is probable cause to search for and seize a person or property or to install and use a tracking device.

(2) *Requesting a Warrant in the Presence of a Judge.*

(A) *Warrant on an Affidavit.* When a federal law enforcement officer or an attorney for the government presents an affidavit in support of a warrant, the judge may require the affiant to appear personally and may examine under oath the affiant and any witness the affiant produces.

(B) *Warrant on Sworn Testimony.* The judge may wholly or partially dispense with a written affidavit and base a warrant on sworn testimony if doing so is reasonable under the circumstances.

(C) *Recording Testimony.* Testimony taken in support of a warrant must be recorded by a court reporter or by a suitable recording device, and the judge must file the transcript or recording with the clerk, along with any affidavit.

(3) *Requesting a Warrant by Telephonic or Other Means.*

(A) *In General.* A magistrate judge may issue a warrant based on information communicated by telephone or other reliable electronic means.

(B) *Recording Testimony.* Upon learning that an applicant is requesting a warrant under Rule 41(d)(3)(A), a magistrate judge must:

> (i) place under oath the applicant and any person on whose testimony the application is based; and

> (ii) make a verbatim record of the conversation with a suitable recording device, if available, or by a court reporter, or in writing.

(C) *Certifying Testimony.* The magistrate judge must have any recording or court reporter's notes transcribed, certify the transcription's accuracy, and file a copy of the record and the transcription with the clerk. Any written verbatim record must be signed by the magistrate judge and filed with the clerk.

(D) *Suppression Limited.* Absent a finding of bad faith, evidence obtained from a warrant issued under Rule 41(d)(3)(A) is not subject to suppression on the ground that issuing the warrant in that manner was unreasonable under the circumstances.

(e) Issuing the Warrant.

(1) *In General.* The magistrate judge or a judge of a state court of record must issue the warrant to an officer authorized to execute it.

(2) *Contents of the Warrant.*

(A) *Warrant to Search for and Seize a Person or Property.* Except for a tracking-device warrant, the warrant must identify the person or property to be searched, identify any person or property to be seized, and designate the magistrate judge to whom it must be returned. The warrant must command the officer to:

(i) execute the warrant within a specified time no longer than 14 days;

(ii) execute the warrant during the daytime, unless the judge for good cause expressly authorizes execution at another time; and

(iii) return the warrant to the magistrate judge designated in the warrant.

(B) *Warrant Seeking Electronically Stored Information.* A warrant under Rule 41(e)(2)(A) may authorize the seizure of electronic storage media or the seizure or copying of electronically stored information. Unless otherwise specified, the warrant authorizes a later review of the media or information consistent with the warrant. The time for executing the warrant in Rule 41(e)(2)(A) and (f)(1)(A) refers to the seizure or on-site copying of the media or information, and not to any later off-site copying or review.

(C) *Warrant for a Tracking Device.* A tracking-device warrant must identify the person or property to be tracked, designate the magistrate judge to whom it must be returned, and specify a reasonable length of time that the device may be used. The time must not exceed 45 days from the date the warrant was issued. The court may, for good cause, grant one or more extensions for a reasonable period not to exceed 45 days each. The warrant must command the officer to:

(i) complete any installation authorized by the warrant within a specified time no longer than 10 calendar days;

(ii) perform any installation authorized by the warrant during the daytime, unless the judge for good cause expressly authorizes installation at another time; and

(iii) return the warrant to the judge designated in the warrant.

(3) *Warrant by Telephonic or Other Means.* If a magistrate judge decides to proceed under Rule 41(d)(3)(A), the following additional procedures apply:

(A) *Preparing a Proposed Duplicate Original Warrant.* The applicant must prepare a "proposed duplicate original warrant" and must read or otherwise transmit the contents of that document verbatim to the magistrate judge.

(B) *Preparing an Original Warrant.* If the applicant reads the contents of the proposed duplicate original warrant, the magistrate judge must enter the contents into an original warrant. If the applicant transmits those contents by reliable electronic means, that transmission may serve as the original warrant.

(C) *Modification.* The magistrate judge may modify the original warrant. The judge must transmit any modified warrant to the applicant by reliable electronic means under Rule 41(e)(3)(D) or direct the applicant to modify the proposed duplicate original warrant accordingly.

(D) *Signing the Warrant.* Upon determining to issue the warrant, the magistrate judge must immediately sign the original warrant, enter on its face the exact time and date it is issued, and transmit it by reliable electronic means to the applicant or direct the applicant to sign the judge's name on the duplicate original warrant.

(f) Executing and Returning the Warrant.

(1) Warrant to Search for and Seize a Person or Property.

(A) *Noting the Time.* The officer executing the warrant must enter on it the exact date and time it was executed.

(B) *Inventory.* An officer present during the execution of the warrant must prepare and verify an inventory of any property seized. The officer must do so in the presence of another officer and the person from whom, or from whose premises, the property was taken. If either one is not present, the officer must prepare and verify the inventory in the presence of at least one other credible person. In a case involving the seizure of electronic storage media or the seizure or copying of electronically stored information, the inventory may be limited to describing the physical storage media that were seized or copied. The officer may retain a copy of the electronically stored information that was seized or copied.

(C) *Receipt.* The officer executing the warrant must give a copy of the warrant and a receipt for the property taken to the person from whom, or from whose premises, the property was taken or leave a copy of the warrant and receipt at the place where the officer took the property.

(D) *Return.* The officer executing the warrant must promptly return it—together with a copy of the inventory—to the magistrate judge designated on the warrant. The judge must, on request, give a copy of the inventory to the person from whom, or from whose premises, the property was taken and to the applicant for the warrant.

(2) Warrant for a Tracking Device.

(A) *Noting the Time.* The officer executing a tracking-device warrant must enter on it the exact date and time the device was installed and the period during which it was used.

(B) *Return.* Within 10 calendar days after the use of the tracking device has ended, the officer executing the warrant must return it to the judge designated in the warrant.

(C) *Service.* Within 10 calendar days after the use of the tracking device has ended, the officer executing a tracking-device warrant must serve a copy of the warrant on the person who was tracked or whose property was tracked. Service may be accomplished by delivering a copy to the person who, or whose property, was tracked; or by leaving a copy at the person's residence or usual place of abode with an individual of suitable age and discretion who resides at that location and by mailing a copy to the person's last known address. Upon request of the government, the judge may delay notice as provided in Rule 41(f)(3).

(3) Delayed Notice. Upon the government's request, a magistrate judge—or if authorized by Rule 41(b), a judge of a state court of record—may delay any notice required by this rule if the delay is authorized by statute.

(g) Motion to Return Property. A person aggrieved by an unlawful search and seizure of property or by the deprivation of property may move for the property's return. The motion must be filed in the district where the property was seized. The court must receive evidence on any factual issue necessary to decide the motion. If it grants the motion, the court must return the property to the movant, but may impose reasonable conditions to protect access to the property and its use in later proceedings.

(h) Motion to Suppress. A defendant may move to suppress evidence in the court where the trial will occur, as Rule 12 provides.

(i) Forwarding Papers to the Clerk. The magistrate judge to whom the warrant is returned must attach to the warrant a copy of the return, of the inventory, and of all other related papers and must deliver them to the clerk in the district where the property was seized.

Rule 42. Criminal Contempt

(a) Disposition After Notice. Any person who commits criminal contempt may be punished for that contempt after prosecution on notice.

(1) *Notice.* The court must give the person notice in open court, in an order to show cause, or in an arrest order. The notice must:

(A) state the time and place of the trial;

(B) allow the defendant a reasonable time to prepare a defense; and

(C) state the essential facts constituting the charged criminal contempt and describe it as such.

(2) *Appointing a Prosecutor.* The court must request that the contempt be prosecuted by an attorney for the government, unless the interest of justice requires the appointment of another attorney. If the government declines the request, the court must appoint another attorney to prosecute the contempt.

(3) *Trial and Disposition.* A person being prosecuted for criminal contempt is entitled to a jury trial in any case in which federal law so provides and must be released or detained as Rule 46 provides. If the criminal contempt involves disrespect toward or criticism of a judge, that judge is disqualified from presiding at the contempt trial or hearing unless the defendant consents. Upon a finding or verdict of guilty, the court must impose the punishment.

(b) Summary Disposition. Notwithstanding any other provision of these rules, the court (other than a magistrate judge) may summarily punish a person who commits criminal contempt in its presence if the judge saw or heard the contemptuous conduct and so certifies; a magistrate judge may summarily punish a person as provided in 28 U.S.C. § 636(e). The contempt order must recite the facts, be signed by the judge, and be filed with the clerk.

TITLE IX. GENERAL PROVISIONS

Rule 43. Defendant's Presence

(a) When Required. Unless this rule, Rule 5, or Rule 10 provides otherwise, the defendant must be present at:

(1) the initial appearance, the initial arraignment, and the plea;

(2) every trial stage, including jury impanelment and the return of the verdict; and

(3) sentencing.

(b) When Not Required. A defendant need not be present under any of the following circumstances:

(1) *Organizational Defendant.* The defendant is an organization represented by counsel who is present.

(2) *Misdemeanor Offense.* The offense is punishable by fine or by imprisonment for not more than one year, or both, and with the defendant's written consent, the court permits arraignment, plea, trial, and sentencing to occur in the defendant's absence.

(3) *Conference or Hearing on a Legal Question.* The proceeding involves only a conference or hearing on a question of law.

(4) *Sentence Correction.* The proceeding involves the correction or reduction of sentence under Rule 35 or 18 U.S.C. § 3582(c).

(c) Waiving Continued Presence.

(1) *In General.* A defendant who was initially present at trial, or who had pleaded guilty or nolo contendere, waives the right to be present under the following circumstances:

(A) when the defendant is voluntarily absent after the trial has begun, regardless of whether the court informed the defendant of an obligation to remain during trial;

(B) in a noncapital case, when the defendant is voluntarily absent during sentencing; or

(C) when the court warns the defendant that it will remove the defendant from the courtroom for disruptive behavior, but the defendant persists in conduct that justifies removal from the courtroom.

(2) *Waiver's Effect.* If the defendant waives the right to be present, the trial may proceed to completion, including the verdict's return and sentencing, during the defendant's absence.

Rule 44. Right to and Appointment of Counsel

(a) Right to Appointed Counsel. A defendant who is unable to obtain counsel is entitled to have counsel appointed to represent the defendant at every stage of the proceeding from initial appearance through appeal, unless the defendant waives this right.

(b) Appointment Procedure. Federal law and local court rules govern the procedure for implementing the right to counsel.

(c) Inquiry Into Joint Representation.

(1) *Joint Representation.* Joint representation occurs when:

(A) two or more defendants have been charged jointly under Rule 8(b) or have been joined for trial under Rule 13; and

(B) the defendants are represented by the same counsel, or counsel who are associated in law practice.

(2) *Court's Responsibilities in Cases of Joint Representation.* The court must promptly inquire about the propriety of joint representation and must personally advise each defendant of the right to the effective assistance of counsel, including separate representation. Unless there is good cause to believe that no conflict of interest is likely to arise, the court must take appropriate measures to protect each defendant's right to counsel.

Rule 45. Computing and Extending Time

(a) Computing Time. The following rules apply in computing any time period specified in these rules, in any local rule or court order, or in any statute that does not specify a method of computing time.

(1) *Period Stated in Days or a Longer Unit.* When the period is stated in days or a longer unit of time:

(A) exclude the day of the event that triggers the period;

(B) count every day, including intermediate Saturdays, Sundays, and legal holidays; and

(C) include the last day of the period, but if the last day is a Saturday, Sunday, or legal holiday, the period continues to run until the end of the next day that is not a Saturday, Sunday, or legal holiday.

(2) *Period Stated in Hours.* When the period is stated in hours:

(A) begin counting immediately on the occurrence of the event that triggers the period;

(B) count every hour, including hours during intermediate Saturdays, Sundays, and legal holidays; and

(C) if the period would end on a Saturday, Sunday, or legal holiday, the period continues to run until the same time on the next day that is not a Saturday, Sunday, or legal holiday.

(3) *Inaccessibility of the Clerk's Office.* Unless the court orders otherwise, if the clerk's office is inaccessible:

(A) on the last day for filing under Rule 45(a)(1), then the time for filing is extended to the first accessible day that is not a Saturday, Sunday, or legal holiday; or

(B) during the last hour for filing under Rule 45(a)(2), then the time for filing is extended to the same time on the first accessible day that is not a Saturday, Sunday, or legal holiday.

(4) *"Last Day" Defined.* Unless a different time is set by a statute, local rule, or court order, the last day ends:

(A) for electronic filing, at midnight in the court's time zone; and

(B) for filing by other means, when the clerk's office is scheduled to close.

(5) *"Next Day" Defined.* The "next day" is determined by continuing to count forward when the period is measured after an event and backward when measured before an event.

(6) *"Legal Holiday" Defined.* "Legal holiday" means:

(A) the day set aside by statute for observing New Year's Day, Martin Luther King Jr.'s Birthday, Washington's Birthday, Memorial Day, Independence Day, Labor Day, Columbus Day, Veterans' Day, Thanksgiving Day, or Christmas Day;

(B) any day declared a holiday by the President or Congress; and

(C) for periods that are measured after an event, any other day declared a holiday by the state where the district court is located.

(b) Extending Time.

(1) *In General.* When an act must or may be done within a specified period, the court on its own may extend the time, or for good cause may do so on a party's motion made:

(A) before the originally prescribed or previously extended time expires; or

(B) after the time expires if the party failed to act because of excusable neglect.

(c) Additional Time After Certain Kinds of Service. Whenever a party must or may act within a specified period after service and service is made in the manner provided under Federal Rule of Civil Procedure 5(b)(2)(B), (C), or (D), 3 days are added after the period would otherwise expire under subdivision (a).

Rule 46. Release from Custody; Supervising Detention

(a) Before Trial. The provisions of 18 U.S.C. §§ 3142 and 3144 govern pretrial release.

(b) During Trial. A person released before trial continues on release during trial under the same terms and conditions. But the court may order different terms and conditions or terminate the release if necessary to ensure that the person will be present during trial or that the person's conduct will not obstruct the orderly and expeditious progress of the trial.

(c) Pending Sentencing or Appeal. The provisions of 18 U.S.C. § 3143 govern release pending sentencing or appeal. The burden of establishing that the defendant will not flee or pose a danger to any other person or to the community rests with the defendant.

(d) Pending Hearing on a Violation of Probation or Supervised Release. Rule 32.1(a)(6) governs release pending a hearing on a violation of probation or supervised release.

(e) Surety. The court must not approve a bond unless any surety appears to be qualified. Every surety, except a legally approved corporate surety, must demonstrate by affidavit that its assets are adequate. The court may require the affidavit to describe the following:

(1) the property that the surety proposes to use as security;

(2) any encumbrance on that property;

(3) the number and amount of any other undischarged bonds and bail undertakings the surety has issued; and

(4) any other liability of the surety.

(f) Bail Forfeiture.

(1) *Declaration.* The court must declare the bail forfeited if a condition of the bond is breached.

(2) *Setting Aside.* The court may set aside in whole or in part a bail forfeiture upon any condition the court may impose if:

(A) the surety later surrenders into custody the person released on the surety's appearance bond; or

(B) it appears that justice does not require bail forfeiture.

(3) *Enforcement.*

(A) *Default Judgment and Execution.* If it does not set aside a bail forfeiture, the court must, upon the government's motion, enter a default judgment.

(B) *Jurisdiction and Service.* By entering into a bond, each surety submits to the district court's jurisdiction and irrevocably appoints the district clerk as its agent to receive service of any filings affecting its liability.

(C) *Motion to Enforce.* The court may, upon the government's motion, enforce the surety's liability without an independent action. The government must serve any motion, and notice as the court prescribes, on the district clerk. If so served, the clerk must promptly mail a copy to the surety at its last known address.

(4) *Remission.* After entering a judgment under Rule 46(f)(3), the court may remit in whole or in part the judgment under the same conditions specified in Rule 46(f)(2).

(g) Exoneration. The court must exonerate the surety and release any bail when a bond condition has been satisfied or when the court has set aside or remitted the forfeiture. The court must exonerate a surety who deposits cash in the amount of the bond or timely surrenders the defendant into custody.

(h) Supervising Detention Pending Trial.

(1) *In General.* To eliminate unnecessary detention, the court must supervise the detention within the district of any defendants awaiting trial and of any persons held as material witnesses.

(2) *Reports.* An attorney for the government must report biweekly to the court, listing each material witness held in custody for more than 10 days pending indictment, arraignment, or trial. For each material witness listed in the report, an attorney for the government must state why the witness should not be released with or without a deposition being taken under Rule 15(a).

(i) Forfeiture of Property. The court may dispose of a charged offense by ordering the forfeiture of 18 U.S.C. § 3142(c)(1)(B)(xi) property under 18 U.S.C. § 3146(d), if a fine in the amount of the property's value would be an appropriate sentence for the charged offense.

(j) Producing a Statement.

(1) *In General.* Rule 26.2(a)-(d) and (f) applies at a detention hearing under 18 U.S.C. § 3142, unless the court for good cause rules otherwise.

(2) *Sanctions for Not Producing a Statement.* If a party disobeys a Rule 26.2 order to produce a witness's statement, the court must not consider that witness's testimony at the detention hearing.

Rule 47. Motions and Supporting Affidavits

(a) In General. A party applying to the court for an order must do so by motion.

(b) Form and Content of a Motion. A motion—except when made during a trial or hearing—must be in writing, unless the court permits the party to make the motion by other means. A motion must state the grounds on which it is based and the relief or order sought. A motion may be supported by affidavit.

(c) Timing of a Motion. A party must serve a written motion—other than one that the court may hear ex parte—and any hearing notice at least 7 days before the hearing date, unless a rule or court order sets a different period. For good cause, the court may set a different period upon ex parte application.

(d) Affidavit Supporting a Motion. The moving party must serve any supporting affidavit with the motion. A responding party must serve any opposing affidavit at least one day before the hearing, unless the court permits later service.

Rule 48. Dismissal

(a) By the Government. The government may, with leave of court, dismiss an indictment, information, or complaint. The government may not dismiss the prosecution during trial without the defendant's consent.

(b) By the Court. The court may dismiss an indictment, information, or complaint if unnecessary delay occurs in:

(1) presenting a charge to a grand jury;

(2) filing an information against a defendant; or

(3) bringing a defendant to trial.

Rule 49. Serving and Filing Papers

(a) When Required. A party must serve on every other party any written motion (other than one to be heard ex parte), written notice, designation of the record on appeal, or similar paper.

(b) How Made. Service must be made in the manner provided for a civil action. When these rules or a court order requires or permits service on a party represented by an attorney, service must be made on the attorney instead of the party, unless the court orders otherwise.

(c) Notice of a Court Order. When the court issues an order on any post-arraignment motion, the clerk must provide notice in a manner provided for in a civil action. Except as Federal Rule of Appellate Procedure 4(b) provides otherwise, the clerk's failure to give notice does not affect the time to appeal, or relieve—or authorize the court to relieve—a party's failure to appeal within the allowed time.

(d) Filing. A party must file with the court a copy of any paper the party is required to serve. A paper must be filed in a manner provided for in a civil action.

Rule 49.1. Privacy Protection for Filings Made with the Court

(a) Redacted Filings. Unless the court orders otherwise, in an electronic or paper filing with the court that contains an individual's social-security number, taxpayer-identification number, or birth date, the name of an individual known to be a minor, a financial-account number, or the home address of an individual, a party or nonparty making the filing may include only:

(1) the last four digits of the social-security number and taxpayer-identification number;

(2) the year of the individual's birth;

(3) the minor's initials;

(4) the last four digits of the financial-account number; and

(5) the city and state of the home address.

(b) Exemptions from the Redaction Requirement. The redaction requirement does not apply to the following:

(1) a financial-account number or real property address that identifies the property allegedly subject to forfeiture in a forfeiture proceeding;

(2) the record of an administrative or agency proceeding;

(3) the official record of a state-court proceeding;

(4) the record of a court or tribunal, if that record was not subject to the redaction requirement when originally filed;

(5) a filing covered by Rule 49.1(d);

(6) a pro se filing in an action brought under 28 U.S.C. §§ 2241, 2254, or 2255;

(7) a court filing that is related to a criminal matter or investigation and that is prepared before the filing of a criminal charge or is not filed as part of any docketed criminal case;

(8) an arrest or search warrant; and

(9) a charging document and an affidavit filed in support of any charging document.

(c) Immigration Cases. A filing in an action brought under 28 U.S.C. § 2241 that relates to the petitioner's immigration rights is governed by Federal Rule of Civil Procedure 5.2.

(d) Filings Made Under Seal. The court may order that a filing be made under seal without redaction. The court may later unseal the filing or order the person who made the filing to file a redacted version for the public record.

(e) Protective Orders. For good cause, the court may by order in a case:

(1) require redaction of additional information; or

(2) limit or prohibit a nonparty's remote electronic access to a document filed with the court.

(f) Option for Additional Unredacted Filing Under Seal. A person making a redacted filing may also file an unredacted copy under seal. The court must retain the unredacted copy as part of the record.

(g) Option for Filing a Reference List. A filing that contains redacted information may be filed together with a reference list that identifies each item of redacted information and specifies an appropriate identifier that uniquely corresponds to each item listed. The list must be filed under seal and may be amended as of right. Any reference in the case to a listed identifier will be construed to refer to the corresponding item of information.

(h) Waiver of Protection of Identifiers. A person waives the protection of Rule 49.1 (a) as to the person's own information by filing it without redaction and not under seal.

Rule 50. Prompt Disposition

Scheduling preference must be given to criminal proceedings as far as practicable.

Rule 51. Preserving Claimed Error

(a) Exceptions Unnecessary. Exceptions to rulings or orders of the court are unnecessary.

(b) Preserving a Claim of Error. A party may preserve a claim of error by informing the court—when the court ruling or order is made or sought—of the action the party wishes the court to take, or the party's objection to the court's action and the grounds for that objection. If a party does not have an opportunity to object to a ruling or order, the absence of an objection does not later prejudice that party. A ruling or order that admits or excludes evidence is governed by Federal Rule of Evidence 103.

Rule 52. Harmless and Plain Error

(a) Harmless Error. Any error, defect, irregularity, or variance that does not affect substantial rights must be disregarded.

(b) Plain Error. A plain error that affects substantial rights may be considered even though it was not brought to the court's attention.

Rule 53. Courtroom Photographing and Broadcasting Prohibited

Except as otherwise provided by a statute or these rules, the court must not permit the taking of photographs in the courtroom during judicial proceedings or the broadcasting of judicial proceedings from the courtroom.

Rule 54. [Transferred]

[Editor's Note: All of Rule 54 was moved to Rule 1]

Rule 55. Records

The clerk of the district court must keep records of criminal proceedings in the form prescribed by the Director of the Administrative Office of the United States Courts. The clerk must enter in the records every court order or judgment and the date of entry.

Rule 56. When Court Is Open

(a) In General. A district court is considered always open for any filing, and for issuing and returning process, making a motion, or entering an order.

(b) Office Hours. The clerk's office—with the clerk or a deputy in attendance—must be open during business hours on all days except Saturdays, Sundays, and legal holidays.

(c) Special Hours. A court may provide by local rule or order that its clerk's office will be open for specified hours on Saturdays or legal holidays other than those set aside by statute for observing New Year's Day, Martin Luther King, Jr.'s Birthday, Washington's Birthday, Memorial Day, Independence Day, Labor Day, Columbus Day, Veterans' Day, Thanksgiving Day, and Christmas Day.

Rule 57. District Court Rules

(a) In General.

(1) *Adopting Local Rules.* Each district court acting by a majority of its district judges may, after giving appropriate public notice and an opportunity to comment, make and amend rules governing its practice. A local rule must be consistent with—but not duplicative of—federal statutes and rules adopted under 28 U.S.C. § 2072 and must conform to any uniform numbering system prescribed by the Judicial Conference of the United States.

(2) *Limiting Enforcement.* A local rule imposing a requirement of form must not be enforced in a manner that causes a party to lose rights because of an unintentional failure to comply with the requirement.

(b) Procedure When There Is No Controlling Law. A judge may regulate practice in any manner consistent with federal law, these rules, and the local rules of the district. No sanction or other disadvantage may be imposed for noncompliance with any requirement not in federal law, federal rules, or the local district rules unless the alleged violator was furnished with actual notice of the requirement before the noncompliance.

(c) Effective Date and Notice. A local rule adopted under this rule takes effect on the date specified by the district court and remains in effect unless amended by the district court or abrogated by the judicial council of the circuit in which the district is located. Copies of local rules and their amendments, when promulgated, must be furnished to the judicial council and the Administrative Office of the United States Courts and must be made available to the public.

Rule 58. Petty Offenses and Other Misdemeanors

(a) Scope.

(1) *In General.* These rules apply in petty offense and other misdemeanor cases and on appeal to a district judge in a case tried by a magistrate judge, unless this rule provides otherwise.

(2) *Petty Offense Case Without Imprisonment.* In a case involving a petty offense for which no sentence of imprisonment will be imposed, the court may follow any provision of these rules that is not inconsistent with this rule and that the court considers appropriate.

(3) *Definition.* As used in this rule, the term "petty offense for which no sentence of imprisonment will be imposed" means a petty offense for which the court determines that, in the event of conviction, no sentence of imprisonment will be imposed.

(b) Pretrial Procedure.

(1) *Charging Document.* The trial of a misdemeanor may proceed on an indictment, information, or complaint. The trial of a petty offense may also proceed on a citation or violation notice.

(2) *Initial Appearance.* At the defendant's initial appearance on a petty offense or other misdemeanor charge, the magistrate judge must inform the defendant of the following:

(A) the charge, and the minimum and maximum penalties, including imprisonment, fines, any special assessment under 18 U.S.C. § 3013, and restitution under 18 U.S.C. § 3556;

(B) the right to retain counsel;

(C) the right to request the appointment of counsel if the defendant is unable to retain counsel—unless the charge is a petty offense for which the appointment of counsel is not required;

(D) the defendant's right not to make a statement, and that any statement made may be used against the defendant;

(E) the right to trial, judgment, and sentencing before a district judge—unless:

(i) the charge is a petty offense; or

(ii) the defendant consents to trial, judgment, and sentencing before a magistrate judge;

(F) the right to a jury trial before either a magistrate judge or a district judge—unless the charge is a petty offense; and

(G) any right to a preliminary hearing under Rule 5.1, and the general circumstances, if any, under which the defendant may secure pretrial release.

(3) *Arraignment.*

(A) *Plea Before a Magistrate Judge.* A magistrate judge may take the defendant's plea in a petty offense case. In every other misdemeanor case, a magistrate judge may take the plea only if the defendant consents either in writing or on the record to be tried before a magistrate judge and specifically waives trial before a district judge. The defendant may plead not guilty, guilty, or (with the consent of the magistrate judge) nolo contendere.

(B) *Failure to Consent.* Except in a petty offense case, the magistrate judge must order a defendant who does not consent to trial before a magistrate judge to appear before a district judge for further proceedings.

(c) Additional Procedures in Certain Petty Offense Cases. The following procedures also apply in a case involving a petty offense for which no sentence of imprisonment will be imposed:

(1) *Guilty or Nolo Contendere Plea.* The court must not accept a guilty or nolo contendere plea unless satisfied that the defendant understands the nature of the charge and the maximum possible penalty.

(2) *Waiving Venue.*

(A) *Conditions of Waiving Venue.* If a defendant is arrested, held, or present in a district different from the one where the indictment, information, complaint, citation, or violation notice is pending, the defendant may state in writing a desire to plead guilty or nolo contendere; to waive venue and trial in the district where the proceeding is pending; and to consent to the court's disposing of the case in the district where the defendant was arrested, is held, or is present.

(B) *Effect of Waiving Venue.* Unless the defendant later pleads not guilty, the prosecution will proceed in the district where the defendant was arrested, is held, or is present. The district clerk must notify the clerk in the original district of the defendant's waiver of venue. The defendant's statement of a desire to plead guilty or nolo contendere is not admissible against the defendant.

(3) *Sentencing.* The court must give the defendant an opportunity to be heard in mitigation and then proceed immediately to sentencing. The court may, however, postpone sentencing to allow the probation service to investigate or to permit either party to submit additional information.

(4) *Notice of a Right to Appeal.* After imposing sentence in a case tried on a not-guilty plea, the court must advise the defendant of a right to appeal the conviction and of any right to appeal the sentence. If the defendant was convicted on a plea of guilty or nolo contendere, the court must advise the defendant of any right to appeal the sentence.

(d) Paying a Fixed Sum in Lieu of Appearance.

(1) *In General.* If the court has a local rule governing forfeiture of collateral, the court may accept a fixed-sum payment in lieu of the defendant's appearance and end the case, but the fixed sum may not exceed the maximum fine allowed by law.

(2) *Notice to Appear.* If the defendant fails to pay a fixed sum, request a hearing, or appear in response to a citation or violation notice, the district clerk or a magistrate judge may issue a notice for the defendant to appear before the court on a date certain. The notice may give the defendant an additional opportunity to pay a fixed sum in lieu of appearance. The district clerk must serve the notice on the defendant by mailing a copy to the defendant's last known address.

(3) *Summons or Warrant.* Upon an indictment, or upon a showing by one of the other charging documents specified in Rule 58(b)(1) of probable cause to believe that an offense has been committed and that the defendant has committed it, the court may issue an arrest warrant or, if no warrant is requested by an attorney for the government, a summons. The showing of probable cause must be made under oath or under penalty of perjury, but the affiant need not appear before the court. If the defendant fails to appear before the court in response to a summons, the court may summarily issue a warrant for the defendant's arrest.

(e) Recording the Proceedings. The court must record any proceedings under this rule by using a court reporter or a suitable recording device.

(f) New Trial. Rule 33 applies to a motion for a new trial.

(g) Appeal.

(1) *From a District Judge's Order or Judgment.* The Federal Rules of Appellate Procedure govern an appeal from a district judge's order or a judgment of conviction or sentence.

(2) *From a Magistrate Judge's Order or Judgment.*

(A) *Interlocutory Appeal.* Either party may appeal an order of a magistrate judge to a district judge within 14 days of its entry if a district judge's order could similarly be appealed. The party appealing must file a notice with the clerk specifying the order being appealed and must serve a copy on the adverse party.

(B) *Appeal from a Conviction or Sentence.* A defendant may appeal a magistrate judge's judgment of conviction or sentence to a district judge within 14 days of its entry. To appeal, the defendant must file a notice with the clerk specifying the judgment being appealed and must serve a copy on an attorney for the government.

(C) *Record.* The record consists of the original papers and exhibits in the case; any transcript, tape, or other recording of the proceedings; and a certified copy of the docket entries. For purposes of the appeal, a copy of the record of the proceedings must be made available to a defendant who establishes by affidavit an inability to pay or give security for the record. The Director of the Administrative Office of the United States Courts must pay for those copies.

(D) *Scope of Appeal.* The defendant is not entitled to a trial de novo by a district judge. The scope of the appeal is the same as in an appeal to the court of appeals from a judgment entered by a district judge.

(3) *Stay of Execution and Release Pending Appeal.* Rule 38 applies to a stay of a judgment of conviction or sentence. The court may release the defendant pending appeal under the law relating to release pending appeal from a district court to a court of appeals.

Rule 59. Matters Before a Magistrate Judge

(a) Nondispositive Matters. A district judge may refer to a magistrate judge for determination any matter that does not dispose of a charge or defense. The magistrate judge must promptly conduct the required proceedings and, when appropriate, enter on the record an oral or written order stating the determination. A party may serve and file objections to the order within 14 days after being served with a copy of a written order or after the oral order is stated on the record, or at some other time the court sets. The district judge must consider timely objections and modify or set aside any part of the order that is contrary to law or clearly erroneous. Failure to object in accordance with this rule waives a party's right to review.

(b) Dispositive Matters.

(1) *Referral to Magistrate Judge.* A district judge may refer to a magistrate judge for recommendation a defendant's motion to dismiss or quash an indictment or information, a motion to suppress evidence, or any matter that may dispose of a charge or defense. The magistrate judge must promptly conduct the required proceedings. A record must be made of any evidentiary proceeding and of any other proceeding if the magistrate judge considers it necessary. The magistrate judge must enter on the record a recommendation for disposing of the matter, including any proposed findings of fact. The clerk must immediately serve copies on all parties.

(2) *Objections to Findings and Recommendations.* Within 14 days after being served with a copy of the recommended disposition, or at some other time the court sets, a party may serve and file specific written objections to the proposed findings and recommendations. Unless the district judge directs otherwise, the objecting party must promptly arrange for transcribing the record, or whatever portions of it the parties agree to or the magistrate judge considers sufficient. Failure to object in accordance with this rule waives a party's right to review.

(3) De Novo *Review of Recommendations.* The district judge must consider de novo any objection to the magistrate judge's recommendations. The district judge may accept, reject, or modify the recommendation, receive further evidence, or resubmit the matter to the magistrate judge with instructions.

Rule 60. Victim's Rights

(a) In General.

(1) *Notice of a Proceeding.* The government must use its best efforts to give the victim reasonable, accurate, and timely notice of any public court proceeding involving the crime.

(2) *Attending the Proceeding.* The court must not exclude a victim from a public court proceeding involving the crime, unless the court determines by clear and convincing evidence that the victim's testimony would be materially altered if the victim heard other testimony at that proceeding. In determining whether to exclude a victim, the court must make every effort to permit the fullest attendance possible by the victim and must consider reasonable alternatives to exclusion. The reasons for any exclusion must be clearly stated on the record.

(3) *Right to Be Heard on Release, a Plea, or Sentencing.* The court must permit a victim to be reasonably heard at any public proceeding in the district court concerning release, plea, or sentencing involving the crime.

(b) Enforcement and Limitations.

(1) *Time for Deciding a Motion.* The court must promptly decide any motion asserting a victim's rights described in these rules.

(2) *Who May Assert the Rights.* A victim's rights described in these rules may be asserted by the victim, the victim's lawful representative, the attorney for the government, or any other person authorized by 18 U.S.C. § 3771(d) and (e).

(3) *Multiple Victims.* If the court finds that the number of victims makes it impracticable to accord all of them their rights as described in these rules, the court must fashion a reasonable procedure that gives effect to these rights without unduly complicating or prolonging the proceedings.

(4) *Where Rights May Be Asserted.* A victim's rights described in these rules must be asserted in the district where the defendant is being prosecuted for the crime.

(5) *Limitations on Relief.* A victim may move to reopen a plea or sentence only if:

> (A) the victim asked to be heard before or during the proceeding at issue, and the request was denied;

(B) the victim petitions the court of appeals for a writ of mandamus within 10 days after the denial, and the writ is granted; and

(C) in the case of a plea, the accused has not pleaded to the highest offense charged.

(6) *No New Trial.* A failure to afford a victim any right described in these rules is not grounds for a new trial.

Rule 61. Title

These rules may be known and cited as the Federal Rules of Criminal Procedure.